T0323425

Developing Public Service Leaders

Developing Public Service Leaders

Elite Orchestration, Change Agency, Leaderism, and Neoliberalization

Mike Wallace
Michael Reed
Dermot O'Reilly
Michael Tomlinson
Jonathan Morris
Rosemary Deem

OXFORD
UNIVERSITY PRESS

OXFORD
UNIVERSITY PRESS

Great Clarendon Street, Oxford, OX2 6DP,
United Kingdom

Oxford University Press is a department of the University of Oxford.
It furthers the University's objective of excellence in research, scholarship,
and education by publishing worldwide. Oxford is a registered trade mark of
Oxford University Press in the UK and in certain other countries

Impression: 1

Published in the United States of America by Oxford University Press
198 Madison Avenue, New York, NY 10016, United States of America

British Library Cataloguing in Publication Data
Data available

Library of Congress Control Number: 2022913612

ISBN 978–0–19–955210–8

DOI: 10.1093/oso/9780199552108.001.0001

Printed and bound by
CPI Group (UK) Ltd, Croydon, CR0 4YY

First look

Why read this book? To inform the decision every potential reader must make about whether to invest time in reading it and, if so, in what depth, we capture here what we see as our significant contribution to knowledge—an explanatory answer to part of a topical question for the study of public service change: what role does the development of leadership capacity play in public service reform?

Contribution. The aspect of this question that we address is the role of major leadership development interventions in facilitating the implementation of regulated marketization reforms and, in recent years, austerity measures for public services. We develop a critical explanation of the foundational contribution that national leadership development interventions, mounted around two decades ago in England, have made to the emergence, proliferation, and normalization of leadership development provision for public services. Our account is based on findings from large-scale qualitative research on three national leadership development interventions: for school education, healthcare, and higher education. We examine the contemporary legacy of these interventions within the burgeoning international movement to develop senior staff in public service organizations as leaders, illustratively comparing interventions for our three focal service sectors in five Anglophone countries: the USA, Canada, Australia, New Zealand, and England. We reflect on the diffuse impact of the foundational interventions and their legacy in England for the regulated marketization of public services and their contribution to wider social change, and point towards promising starting-points for rethinking developmental support for the coordinated effort that public service provision entails.

Explanation. Ten headline claims are that:

- Powerful groups in and around the United Kingdom (UK) Labour government harnessed leadership development as a means of furthering the neoliberalization, or marketization, of public services by applying regulated market principles to public service provision.
- Government politicians deemed it essential to sustain the cooperation of senior staff in public service organizations, because the government depended on them to put into practice reforms to extend the regulated marketization of public services.

- Governmental investment in national leadership development interventions was directed towards acculturating senior staff in public service organizations as leaders, committed to acting as the government's agents in spearheading the translation of reform policies into practice within their organizational and community jurisdictions.
- However, provision within these interventions focused on generic leading activity, diluting the government's envisioned link with change agency for reforms.
- This provision was relatively ineffective for acculturation, failing to overlay the service professional culture to which most participants already subscribed, but they valued the record of participating as a source of credentials for their career advancement.
- The provision and associated credentials contributed towards the professionalization of public service leadership, since expertise in leading activity could be gained through this specialized training.
- Being a leader legitimated senior staff expressing their service professional values in shaping the direction of public service provision, but the government circumscribed its parameters through reforms specifying expected service outcomes and increasing the accountability of senior staff for their achievement, enforcing compliance and pre-empting resistance.
- Over time, subsequent iterations of these interventions have gradually brought greater acculturation of senior staff as leaders, though not necessarily their commitment to acting as change agents for reforms and austerity measures that further the neoliberalization of public services, while accountability measures continue to pre-empt concerted resistance by identifying individual under-performers and applying and publicizing negative sanctions.
- The interventions, alongside other factors, have informed interventions elsewhere as part of the international expansion and consolidation of public service leadership development.
- They have made a more indirect, diffuse contribution to furthering the neoliberalization of public services, changing the nature, quality, and availability of providers and their provision, in turn shaping public expectations about public services as societal institutions—but there are possibilities for altering the nature and focus of developmental support.

These unqualified summary claims can scarcely do justice to the complexity of the phenomenon we investigated or the depth of explanation we have attempted. The contextualization of these claims, their elaboration, and their justification—empirical, conceptual, theoretical, metatheoretical, axiological—take up the entire book. Greater investment in reading it promises a fuller grasp of our argument; more prosaically, you haven't read the book till you've read it. Chapter 1 contains more information on the book's content: the concluding sections of this introductory chapter introduce our three-part structure and indicate how chapters within each part sequentially develop our argument.

Acknowledgements

Our research project lies at the heart of this book. We would like to acknowledge the valuable guidance offered by our steering group: Nick Abercombie, John Clarke, Mike Davies, Louise Fitzgerald, Ron Glatter, Toby Greany, Bob Hudson, and Kath Thompson. We are indebted to Paula Mullins, our project manager, for her calm efficiency and reliability. Jenneth Parker conducted most of the HE interviews. We are grateful to all our interviewees for their willingness to participate in the research during a turbulent time. Cardiff Business School gave Mike Wallace research leave in 2019–20 to work on the book, and Alison Wray contributed ideas and wordsmithing expertise that were instrumental in bringing it to fruition. Kristy Barker's expert copy-editing of the manuscript greatly improved the readability of the text. We would like to extend our special thanks to Karthiga Ramu, Senior Project Manager at Integra Software Services, for the highly professional way in which she guided the book through every stage of the complex production process with courtesy and meticulous attention to detail. The project was funded by the Economic and Social Research Council (ESRC), award number RES-000-23-1136-A. The ideas expressed in this book are those of the authors, and do not reflect the view of the ESRC.

Contents

III.   DEVELOPING PROFESSIONALIZED LEADERS FOR NEOLIBERALIZED PUBLIC SERVICES

List of Figures

List of Tables

List of Acronyms and Abbreviations

ABS	Association of Business Schools
ACE	American Council on Education
ASCL	Association of School and College Leaders
BAME	Black, Asian, and minority ethnic heritage
BAMM	British Association of Medical Managers
BIEL	Bastow Institute of Educational Leadership
CCG	Care Commissioning Group
CCHL	Canadian College of Health Leaders
CDA	Critical discourse analysis
Centrex	Central Police Training and Development Authority
CEO	Chief Executive Officer
CHERD	Centre for Higher Education Research and Development
COVID-19	Coronavirus disease
CPD	Continuing professional development
CTC	City Technology College
CUC	Committee of University Chairs
CV	Curriculum vitae
CVCP	Committee of Vice Chancellors and Principals
DBIS	Department for Business, Innovation and Skills (2009–2016)
DCSF	Department for Children, Schools and Families (2007–2010)
DES	Department of Education and Science (until 1992)
DfE	Department for Education (1992–1995; 2010-)
DfEE	Department for Education and Employment (1995–2001)
DfES	Department for Education and Skills (2001–2007)
DHSS	Department of Health and Social Security (until 1988)
DIUS	Department for Innovation, Universities and Skills (2007–2009)
DoH	Department of Health (and Social Care) (1988–)
FE	Further Education
GP	General practitioner (primary care)
GuildHE	GuildHE (for higher education)
HE	Higher education
HEADLAMP	Headteachers Leadership and Management Programme
HEFCE	Higher Education Funding Council for England
HESDA	Higher Education Staff Development Agency
HMIC	Her Majesty's Inspectorate of Constabulary
HR	Human Resources
HRC	Humanities Research Council
ICT	Information and communication technology
IDeA	Improvement and Development Agency

IHM	Institute of Health Management
LEA	Local Education Authority
LEADS	Lead self, Engage others, Achieve results, Develop coalitions, Systems transformation
LFHE	Leadership Foundation for Higher Education
LGA	Local Government Association
LHMI	L H Martin Institute
LMS	Local management of schools
LPSH	Leadership Programme for Serving Headteachers
MASHEIN	Management of Small Higher Education Institutions Network
MBA	Masters degree in Business Administration
MP	Member of Parliament
NAHT	National Association of Headteachers
NCHL	National Center for Healthcare Leadership
NCLSCS	National College for Leadership of Schools and Children's Services
NCSL	National College for School Leadership
NCTL	National College for Teaching and Leadership
NDC	National Development Centre for School Management Training
NHS	National Health Service
NHSIII	NHS Institute for Innovation and Improvement
NHSLC	NHS Leadership Centre
NHSTA	NHS Training Agency
NLC	National Leadership Centre
NLDB	National leadership development body
NPM	New Public Management
NPQH	National Professional Qualification for Headteachers
NSS	National Student Survey
NYC	New York City
NZMoE	New Zealand Ministry of Education
NZMoH	New Zealand Ministry of Health
NZUWiL	New Zealand Universities Women in Leadership Programme
OCT	Ontario College of Teachers
OECD	Organisation for Economic Cooperation and Development
OED	Oxford English Dictionary
OfS	Office for Students
Ofsted	Office for Standards in Education
OME	Ontario Ministry of Education
OPSR	Office of Public Services Reform
PCG	Primary care group
PCT	Primary care trust
PEC	Professional executive committee
PFI	Private Finance Initiative
PHLP	Public Health Leadership Programme
PQP	Principals Qualification Programme
PSLA	Public Service Leadership Alliance
PSLC	Public Service Leadership Consortium

PVC	Pro vice chancellor
QAA	Quality Assurance Agency for Higher Education
QOF	Qualities and Outcomes Framework
RAE	Research Assessment Exercise
SCOP	Standing Conference of Principals
SCV	Safer Care Victoria
SHA	Strategic Health Authority
SOLACE	Society of Local Authority Chief Executives and Senior Managers
SPAD	Special political adviser
TEF	Teaching Excellence and Student Outcomes Framework
TMP	Top Management Programme
TTA	Teacher Training Agency
UCoSDA	Universities and Colleges Staff Development Agency
UK	United Kingdom of Great Britain and Northern Ireland
UNZ	Universities New Zealand
UUK	Universities UK
USA	United States of America
VDET	State of Victoria Department of Education and Training
VDHHS	State of Victoria Department of Healthcare and Human Services

PART I

DEVELOPING PUBLIC SERVICE LEADERS

AN ELITE POLICY 'META-LEVER'?

1
Leadership development for public services as a growth industry

The final decades of the twentieth century witnessed a steady expansion in the engagement by the United Kingdom's (UK) Conservative government with training senior staff from public service organizations as managers, connected with its ambition to reform the public sector on private sector lines. Then, in the space of just six years, the successor Labour government eclipsed that endeavour through its own investment, on a scale without international precedent. Ministers launched, reconfigured, or financially supported a cumulative suite of centralized, national-level interventions to develop senior staff from organizations providing each public service—as leaders. The formality of these interventions, framed as 'leadership development', contrasts starkly with the informal, often incidental, learning process whereby those who occupy positions carrying management responsibility for the work of other staff generally develop their capability through workplace practice and reflection. What contextual factors prompted such a major commitment? Why develop senior staff as *leaders*, not managers or administrators? Why opt for national interventions? What forms did the interventions take and how did they operate? What impact did they achieve in reaching target groups and influencing their thinking or practice, and why? How might they have contributed to wider changes in the nature and operation of public services? Does the legacy of these interventions, several governments and two decades on, demonstrate whether they were a passing management fad or an influential contributor to something bigger, enduring, normalized, perhaps emulated?

Prompted by these questions, the book has two aims. First, we seek to explain why and how the interventions occurred, and what their contemporary implications are. Our starting-point will be to examine the ideological and economic context behind these interventions to promote more and better public service leadership, in the eyes of their governmental architects or underwriters. We then examine discursive and practical training antecedents on which the interventions built; their orchestration through coordinated implementation activity amongst those charged with operational responsibility; the leadership development practices entailed; links

Developing Public Service Leaders. Wallace et al., Oxford University Press. © Mike Wallace, Michael Reed, Dermot O'Reilly, Michael Tomlinson, Jonathan Morris, Rosemary Deem (2023). DOI: 10.1093/oso/9780199552108.003.0001

between the interventions and politically driven reform of public service governance and provision; and their intended outcomes, legacy, and indirect outcomes in contributing towards wider societal change. We will draw on findings from substantial qualitative research on interventions for the public-funded services of school education and healthcare in England, and, as an outlier, the intervention for partly public-funded higher education (HE), UK-wide. Despite greater central regulation in recent years, HE is more autonomous from government than school education and healthcare. The status of HE as a public service, rather than a set of charitable or private sector enterprises, has become increasingly contestable as fees for student teaching rise.

Our second aim is to locate these national-level interventions and their direct legacy (in England and the UK, as appropriate) within the international movement to establish and consolidate forms of leadership development for public services. Special attention is paid to Anglophone industrialized countries, where leadership development interventions of varying scope are integral to contemporary public service management.

Since leadership and its development are burgeoning fields of enquiry, we need to clarify what this book is and is not about. It is about the complex change process embodied in an 'extreme' case (Yin, 2003), unique in scope at the time, of serial, large-scale, centralized national leadership development interventions across a national system of public service provision. In pursuing our first aim, we anticipate that the factors rendering this case so extreme are likely to reveal more of the underlying causal mechanisms at work than a typical case might do. In connection with our second aim, it also offers a 'critical case' (Flyvjberg, 2001, p. 78) of 'strategic importance in relation to the general problem', explaining how public service leadership development may contribute to societal change. The architects of our extreme case intended each intervention to generate more leadership of a kind they valued and to achieve outcomes they desired for the relevant public service sector. These interventions targeted individual professional staff in top and senior positions of management responsibility, or 'groups of individuals bound by some purpose' (North, 1990, p. 4), from organizations providing a public service, exclusively or within their portfolio of activities. Leadership development provision offered by most interventions gradually extended to individuals in more junior management positions, construed as 'middle leaders', and early career staff, as 'future leaders'. Typically, those targeted were responsible for the work of other professionals providing services to citizens, or to local or central government.

The context of the UK state sets parameters for this extreme case. For historical reasons, national-level interventions may serve different devolved governmental jurisdictions within the unitary state constituting the UK. In 1998, the UK government established devolved governments for Scotland and Wales, plus the Northern Ireland Executive. Each is responsible for most public services within its jurisdiction, including education and healthcare. The UK government retains responsibility for public-funded school education and healthcare in England; for policing in England and Wales; for defence UK-wide; and for the Home Civil Service in England, Wales, and Scotland (the Northern Ireland Civil Service is separate). We focus on interventions for each public service sector covering England, and sometimes also other jurisdictions, whose scope is greater than any parallel national-level interventions mounted by the devolved governments for their public services. Universities and HE colleges are private organizations, government-regulated and partially government-dependent; most are constituted as charities. The UK government and national devolved governments together regulate HE and allocate contributory funding for some teaching and research, with the UK government offering most research funding. Agencies of all these governments provided funding to support the national leadership development intervention for HE.

Equally salient is the UK distinction between public services and the government civil service, also for historical reasons. The term 'public services' covers services for citizens funded by a national government through taxation and provided by state-administered organizations in the public sector, as with local government administration, or by commissioned private or voluntary sector organizations (Burton, 2013). National governments employ civil service officials to administer executive activity. Civil service responsibilities include central administration of the implementation and operational oversight of UK government policies for local public service provision, including school education, healthcare, and HE. Therefore, civil servants contribute to administering government-initiated, or otherwise financially supported, leadership development interventions for senior staff in organizations providing public services—including leadership development for the civil service itself. In some countries the employment status of professionals in organizations providing public services is that of a civil servant. In others, government civil services are called 'public services' (as in Canada, Australia, and New Zealand). For consistency, we reserve the term 'civil servant' to denote staff employed within a permanent central government executive apparatus.

The book is also about practices construed as leadership development, however consistent (or not) with expert definitions, say, 'expanding the collective capacity of organizational members to engage effectively in leadership roles and processes' (McCauley, Moxley, & Van Velsor, 1998). This definition does not specify what counts as leadership. Instead, it foregrounds the formal and informal processes for identifying individuals or groups, and for promoting individual and collective learning to enact roles embodied in the contextualized group influencing process of leadership, irrespective of whether those involved are authorized to influence others. The interventions in our investigation concentrate on individuals who, as leaders, influence others, more accurately termed 'leader development' (Day, 2001, 2011). By contrast, the development of collective leadership, as within teams, embodies often unequal, yet still mutual, influencing activity. Except where indicated otherwise, we will follow the terminology adopted by those whose views we report. From Day's perspective, much that is undertaken in the name of (collective) leadership development amounts to (individual) leader development, with consequences for the development of individual leaders and the collectivities of which they are members.

However, this book is not about leadership, as such. We remain agnostic about what leadership is, beyond construing the phenomenon as relational, often asymmetrically so: a contextualized group influencing process entailing some measure of voluntary contribution or acquiescence amongst those involved, connected with the pursuit of some group task, and variably linked with individual social identities. Our definition excludes group influencing processes reliant on psychological or physical coercion, and individual self-influencing processes, say, 'self-leadership' (Stewart, Courtright, & Manz, 2011), focusing on internal self-motivation and monitoring. While our construal emphasizes the collective nature of leadership as a group phenomenon, an ambiguity integral to the concept lies in its linguistic form, certainly in the English language. Semantically, leadership denotes:

- An individual quality comprising the skilled activity of influencing others to engage cooperatively in some group task; in other words, to follow the leader. The suffix '-ship' denotes leadership to be a skilled activity, carried out with varying effectiveness. This meaning of leadership, or more accurately 'leader-ship', is *leader-centric*: attention is drawn towards the quality of skilled activity carried out by someone as a 'leader', whether or not so designated.
- The individual or collective social positioning of designated leaders, as where someone 'takes on the leadership of this university' or reference is made to the (corporate) 'leadership of this university'. Here, attention is drawn to a designation that legitimates leading activity to influence others within a jurisdictional remit.

- The group process of attempting to influence and accepting influence embodied in working cooperatively to achieve some group task.

Leadership simultaneously denotes a leader-centric skill, designated position as a leader, and group process. That it means more than the skill of leaders is exemplified by the statement: 'Excellent leadership by the senior leadership team; pity none of the others followed.' This statement is meaningful only if the speaker is being ironic (using 'excellent' to mean 'terrible' or even 'no' leadership). Beyond the skill of leaders in leading, leadership is about the legitimation of leaders in doing so, and their assumed influence on the contribution that others within a group make towards a collective task. The relative weighting between the three denotive aspects of leadership varies in use, causing an inherent degree of ambiguity in the meaning of leadership. The dominant usage of politicians, academics, trainers, and practitioners featuring in our study is leader-centric, encompassing the leader's 'leader-ship' alone. We shall see how this leader-centricity impacts on leadership discourse and leadership development practice, with implications for public service provision.

Another reason for the relative ambiguity of leadership is its inherently metaphorical character, alongside that of associated terms such as 'leader' and 'leading'. They offer simple proxies for the complex and less tangible experiences, perceptions, and actions they encapsulate (Alvesson & Spicer, 2011; Hatch, Kostera, & Kozminski, 2006; Hoyle & Wallace, 2005, 2007). Our interest lies in the articulation of metaphors within the discourse of different protagonists, serving their ends-in-view; why and how some metaphors become dominant; and how they frame prescriptions about leadership, developmental activities for leaders, and the perceptions and reported practices of recipients.

The scope and contemporary significance of this extreme case

The suite of national interventions to develop public service leadership was a 'world-first' in terms of centralization and scope; its legacy forms part of the expanding international movement to develop public service leadership capacity. This movement includes other groups with a material interest in leadership capacity-building: from national representative bodies for senior staff in public service organizations to staff responsible for human resource management in public service organizations. Table 1.1 shows the scale of

Table 1.1 UK Labour government involvement in establishing, reconfiguring, or financing national leadership development interventions, 1997–2010

National leadership development body (NLDB)	Public service sector	National jurisdiction	Formal relationship with a department of the UK government, reflecting the extent of central regulation	Year of launch/ reconfiguration
Academy for Executive Leadership	Local government	England, Wales	**Distanced:** formed as part of the Improvement and Development Agency (IDeA), owned by the Local Government Association (LGA), a representative body for local authorities and independent of central government	1999
Centre for Management and Policy Studies	Civil service	UK	**Close:** established by the UK government following a review, located in the Cabinet Office, and incorporating training provided by the predecessor Civil Service College. A unit within the **Cabinet Office**	1999
National School of Government			**Close:** successor body in the **Cabinet Office**. A non-ministerial government department	2005
National College for School Leadership *	School education	England	**Close:** established by the **Department for Education and Employment** (DfEE), received an annual remit letter. A company and non-departmental public body	2000
National College for Leadership of Schools and Children's Services	School education, social services		**Close:** remit extended by the **Department for Children Schools and Families** (DCSF) to leaders of services for children	2009
NHS Leadership Centre	Health	England	**Close:** established by the **Department of Health** (DoH). A unit within the NHS Modernisation Agency, a DoH executive agency	2001

NHS Institute for Innovation and Improvement*			Close: successor body created with a wider remit including leadership development, funded by the DoH after an 'arm's length bodies' review. A Special Health Authority (arm's length)	2005
Social Care Institute for Excellence	Social services	England, Wales, Northern Ireland	Moderately close: established by the National Institute of Social Work, the DoH, and the Welsh Assembly. Became an independent charitable company, contributory funding from the DoH and governments of the devolved jurisdictions	2001
Defence Leadership Centre	Defence	UK	Close: The Defence Leadership Centre was established within the Defence Academy by the UK government, following the 2001 Defence Training Review. Remit letter from the Ministry of Defence. An executive agency	2002
Leadership Academy for Policing	Police	England, Wales	Close: within Centrex, the Central Police Training and Development Authority established by the Home Office to replace National Police Training, a Home Office department. Centrex was a non-departmental public body	2002
National Policing Improvement Agency			Close: reconfigured as part of the National Policing Plan following a review. Remit letter from the Home Office. A non-departmental public body	2007
Centre for Excellence in Leadership	Further education	England	Close: established by the UK government's Department for Education and Skills (DfES) as a national agency, operating from 2006 through a charitable trust formed by its operating company	2003

Continued

Table 1.1 *Continued*

National leadership development body (NLDB)	Public service sector	National jurisdiction	Formal relationship with a department of the UK government, reflecting the extent of central regulation	Year of launch/ reconfiguration
Learning and Skills Improvement Service			**Moderately close:** reconfigured with a wider remit as a sector-owned public body following a review. A non-profit company and charity, contributory funding from the **DCSF**	2008
Leadership Foundation for Higher Education *	Higher education	UK	**Distanced:** established by Universities UK (UUK) and the Standing Conference of Principals (SCOP) representing universities and colleges, endorsed by the **DFES**, contributory funding from UK HE funding councils. A charity and non-profit company	2004
Leadership Centre for Local Government	Local government	UK	**Distanced:** initiative of the local authority representative body the Society of Local Authority Chief Executives and Senior Managers (SOLACE), contributory funding from the **Office of the Deputy Prime Minister**. SOLACE became a charity in 2008	2004
Centre for Leadership	Fire and rescue service	England	**Close:** established by the **Office of the Deputy Prime Minister** within the Fire Service College following a review. An executive agency and trading fund	2006

* The shaded NLDBs were investigated in our research (discussed in Part II).

the UK Labour government's engagement in national-level interventions throughout its tenure (1997–2010). The table lists national leadership development bodies (NLDBs) for different public services, in chronological order of their establishment or reconfiguration by the government or their creation by national representative bodies for senior staff with UK government financial support. The second column indicates the sector served by an NLDB. The third summarizes the NLDB's remit within the UK. The fourth categorizes the formal relationship between an NLDB and the UK government department responsible for that public service, depending on the extent of governmental regulation and oversight, with a note to warrant our categorization of this relationship as 'distanced', 'moderately close', or 'close'. The final column gives the year of an NLDB's official launch or reconfiguration.

All interventions were subject to some degree of UK government control except the Academy for Executive Leadership, established by the Local Government Association (LGA), a representative body for local authorities, with no UK government contributory funding. Government politicians directed the Cabinet Office, the cross-government department responsible for coordinating the pursuit of government objectives through other departments, to prioritize leadership development across all public services (Performance and Innovation Unit, 2001). What transpired was a separate NLDB for each public service sector in England, sometimes also covering one or more devolved government jurisdictions. By 2007, seven government departments responsible for specific services had set up either one or two NLDBs and were overseeing and financing them through departmental budgets. Civil servants from several of these departments, including education (Bolam, 2004), had prior experience of department-level initiatives to develop management capacity. Yet each national leadership development intervention was mounted independently.

Some interventions were entirely new; others overlaid or ignored past management development initiatives; existing NLDBs were reconfigured. Illustratively, the Police College had provided officer training since 1948, mainly preparation for promotion (Harris, 1949). The Central Police Training and Development Authority replaced it in 2002, with the working name 'Centrex'. Couched within Centrex's 'core responsibility for setting police doctrine and providing support for operational policing matters' (HMIC, 2003, p. 5) was the new 'National Police Leadership Centre', offering leadership development programmes for senior officers. Times could be turbulent for NLDBs whose formal relationship with the UK government was close: government departments subsequently reconfigured this NLDB for the police service, plus those for the civil service, school education, and healthcare. The NLDB for further education was also reconfigured, and its formal relationship with government was loosened while retaining government financial support.

During the period 2007–8 we investigated the three NLDBs shaded in Table 1.1: two were the versions of the NLDBs, at that time, for the public-funded service sectors of school education and healthcare in England: respectively, the National College for School Leadership (NCSL), and the National Health Service (NHS) Institute for Innovation and Improvement (NHSIII). The NHSIII was established by reconfiguring its predecessor, the NHS Leadership Centre (NHSLC). Some of its provision was incorporated within the NHSIII's wider brief to develop and provide guidance on innovation. The third national body (our outlier) was the Leadership Foundation for Higher Education (LFHE), amongst three national bodies launched by representative bodies for senior staff with initial UK government financial support. The LFHE covered partly public-funded HE, UK-wide.

The lasting significance of this extreme case is twofold, to be discussed in Part III: both a direct legacy and a more diffuse international legacy as one of many sources informing policy and practice elsewhere. Accounts of interventions are disseminated through international advice literature designed to inform governments and other stakeholder groups. A key contributor is the Organisation for Economic Co-operation and Development (OECD), by 2021 representing thirty-six industrialized democratic countries. The OECD has championed national-level leadership development interventions since the advent of the UK Labour government. Publications focus on experimentation with interventions and advocate expanding provision, especially for government civil services since they are integral to governmental executive operation. An early report on interventions for senior civil servants hinted at an inherent risk for governments (OECD, 2001, p. 9):

> . . . developing an elite leadership cadre has many advantages . . . [but] if a group of leaders begins to pursue their own interests rather than the national interest . . . [it] may become closed and insufficiently responsive to wider changes in society. So, new issues on the agenda are how to build a leadership cadre that is more responsive or representative, and also, how to re-orient and refresh existing cadres if they have begun to get out of step with the society they represent.

The imperative to 'build' tomorrow's 'cadre' and 're-orient or refresh' civil servants, as leaders, implies acculturating them towards government agendas. 'Acculturation' is a process of cultural interchange whereby individuals or groups come to embrace beliefs, norms, and values of another culture (Berry, 1997). This OECD report acknowledged the challenge of attempting to engineer a new culture: 'any successful leadership strategy involves culture change. We know that culture change is very difficult, and that where it does take place it is over a long period and in response to a variety of powerful pressures' (p. 29). Interventions from fifteen OECD countries received mention, with approaches ranging from centrally directed initiatives (in the UK) to an emergent, loosely coordinated marketplace for provision. Within a decade, global economic growth had subsided into financial crisis. Informed by that experience, OECD advocacy shifted towards national strategies for administrative system-wide leadership capacity-building to 'make reform happen' in this exceptionally hostile economic environment. Cross-administrative level leadership was now identified as a lesson from government-driven structural reforms fostering political and executive acceptance and support to ensure faithful implementation (OECD, 2010, pp. 17–18):

> Leadership is critical . . . whether by an individual policy maker or an institution [implying organizations] charged with carrying out the reform . . . the call for strong leadership should not be read as endorsing a top-down approach to reform or suggesting a preference for unilateral action by the executive. While unilateral reforms are sometimes the only way forward and reformers may need both toughness and political cunning when dealing with opponents . . . successful leadership is often about winning consent rather than securing compliance. This is particularly the case where those directly affected by a reform will play a role in implementing it.

Comparative research on leadership development for top government civil servants in fifteen OECD and four non-OECD countries (Van Wart, Hondeghem, & Schwella, 2015) confirms the expanding reach of governmental investment in major interventions. Seemingly, their aim is to 'win consent' of top civil servants, on whose cooperation governments depend to operationalize public service reform policies. According to the OECD (2010, p. 222), leadership development can help solve a 'key challenge in implementing reform ... locating or creating the necessary capacities, first, to implement the reform, and then, to function in the new environment and to address the new tasks assigned to civil servants and/or levels of government'.

Advocacy has continued during the subsequent decade, characterized by government-imposed austerity measures in many OECD countries (Anderson & Minneman, 2014). Shortly before the coronavirus disease (COVID-19) pandemic erupted in 2020 the OECD (2019a) announced a formal recommendation, carrying 'great moral force as representing the will of Adherents' (all OECD countries) and 'the expectation that Adherents will do their utmost to fully implement' it. OECD countries were tasked with 'building leadership capacity' through investments that included 'developing the leadership capabilities of current and potential senior-level public servants' by 'encouraging and incentivising employees to proactively engage in continuous self-development and learning, and providing them with quality opportunities to do so' (OECD, 2019b, pp. 6, 8). The OECD stepped beyond advice to assert a moral imperative supported by all member countries, suggesting that leadership development interventions for government civil services are set to increase.

Significant OECD attention to school education entailed a study of leadership development across twenty-two education systems within nineteen countries (Pont, Nusche, & Moorman, 2008). The HSBC Education Trust contributed to funding the work, reflective of private sector interest in supporting public service management. Leadership development, especially for headteachers (principals), was identified as a major 'policy lever' for governments. The report evidences variable 'professionalization' (implying specialist training) of leadership development for headship, with all systems catering for one or more of the preparatory, induction and in-service stages. Attention was drawn to the NCSL's provision in England.

Commercial advice literature on healthcare includes a report from the multinational auditing company network KPMG (2016), promoting leadership development as a route to healthcare productivity gains. The evidence base included six reputationally 'innovative and successful case studies of management and leadership development in the health industry' (p. 7) from five Anglophone countries. Of four case studies focusing on public service interventions, only the NHS Leadership Academy in England (a successor to the NHSIII) operated nationally as 'one of the largest healthcare management and leadership development programs in the world' (p. 21). Healthcare provision in England is unusual amongst Anglophone countries in comprising a national public service funded through taxation rather than insurance, offering the financial basis for a large-scale, centralized intervention.

Private sector-based advice literature extends to HE. More than a decade ago, the UK's LFHE commissioned a management consultant to conduct a 'global study' of leadership development in this sector. The report (Fielden, 2009, p. 3) examined the programmes of twenty 'leading providers throughout the world' (all but one still offered the same or similar programmes at the time of writing). The formal relationship between these providers and the government of their country varied widely; indicatively, only two were located within a government department (Malaysia and China) but seven were mounted by representative bodies for universities (including LFHE). The rarity of government oversight and financial support for interventions confirms the LFHE as an outlier compared with public-funded services such as school education and healthcare. Most programmes catered for senior university staff, with over half of providers engaging in entrepreneurial internationalization by offering places to participants from other countries.

Advice literature evidences the ongoing international spread of external leadership development interventions since the UK Labour government's landmark initiative. These sources imply that external interventions remain on the rise, for some public services at least; many have endured, even if reconfigured; and their reach now extends beyond western industrialized countries. They also confirm how extreme the suite of UK Labour government interventions was. One reason government politicians could mount such a large-scale initiative is their unrivalled scope for experimental intervention in public services compared with their counterparts in many other western democracies, thanks to 'British exceptionalism' (Pollitt, 2007, p. 529). Facilitating factors include the majoritarian and adversarial political system; a first-past-the-post election protocol, often producing a substantial majority of Members of Parliament (MPs) within the political party forming the government, with extensive control over parliamentary votes required to pass legislation; and an electoral cycle of up to five years, long enough for radical and unpopular policies to be launched early in the cycle, with little immediate threat of the electorate holding government ministers to account. The period of Labour government lasted thirteen years. The Labour Party won three successive general elections (1997, 2001, 2005), through with a smaller majority of parliamentary seats each time. So government politicians were well positioned to undertake this innovative experiment.

However, arguably the most important contextual factor motivating investment in a suite of national leadership development interventions was economic, underpinned by ideology (to be examined in Chapter 2). The incoming Labour government endeavoured to improve the economic situation inherited from the outgoing Conservative government, according to Labour Party political and economic values, framed by the ideological commitment to a social democratic variant of neoliberalism: 'the extension of competitive markets into all areas of life, including the economy, politics and society' (Springer, Birch, & MacLeavy, 2016, p. 2). The government's economic strategy for enhancing prosperity included radically changing public service provision through regulated marketization reforms featuring a social democratic emphasis on social justice. The reform strategy built on embedded Conservative reforms driven by that government's more entrepreneurial variant of neoliberalism. Leadership development offered Labour government ministers a means to support part of their economic strategy, facilitating the implementation of public service reforms and the operation of reformed services.

An elite 'policy meta-lever'?

The OECD study on leadership development interventions for senior school staff introduced earlier hints at the potential payoff for central government politicians. Pont et al. (2008, p. 28) claimed that:

> Developing the workforce of principals [headteachers] promises to be a highly cost-effective human capital investment, as quality leadership can directly influence the motivations, attitudes and behaviours of teachers and indirectly contribute to improved learning of their students. The fact that such a small group of people can potentially have an impact on every student and teacher in the country makes principals a key policy lever for educational improvements.

Where 'improvements' include those sought by a national government, as with regulated marketization reform of public services inspired by neoliberalism, a leadership development intervention might enhance the potential for governmental influence on all organizations whose senior staff have been developed as leaders in this way. Launched at scale and targeting senior staff, such a national intervention to develop public service leaders could aim to increase their capability to lead and commitment to act as a conduit for the implementation of the government's public service reforms, alongside any local improvement efforts. Once developed as public service leaders, headteachers are construed here, metaphorically, as a 'key policy lever' for architects of the leadership development interventions to deploy. It would remain available for ministers from that government to use, and conceivably for successor governments, of whatever political complexion. However, the leadership development interventions themselves may offer even greater potential as a generic, facilitative 'policy meta-lever', engendering a readiness amongst those developed as public service leaders to implement any present or future policy agenda for their service sector.

We have coined the term *meta-lever* to denote a hierarchically ordered means of facilitating the operation of other policy levers to secure the implementation of specific policies. Alongside the policy lever concept employed by Pont and colleagues (see also Steer et al., 2007), the metaphorical concepts of 'governing instruments' (Kooiman, 2003), 'tools of government' (John, 2011), or 'policy instruments' (McDonnell & Elmore, 1987) all draw attention to some amplificatory linkage, converting a policy into new or modified practices of implementers across targeted settings. Policy levers can be understood (also metaphorically) as 'carrot and stick' strategies at the disposal of governments to foster or enforce the transmission of policy goals into practice. Government resources may be selected, individually or in combination, for strategies offering different sources of leverage. McDonnell and Elmore (1987) distinguish between:

- mandates: formulating rules (regulatory and priority-setting, often through targets) governing action to ensure compliance, frequently enforced through monitoring or targeted surveillance alongside punitive sanctions for non-compliance or under-performance;
- inducements: offering financial rewards or other forms of advantage in return for specified actions (optional, or technically so but obligatory in practice where those targeted depend on these rewards or advantages);
- capacity-building: allocating money for procurement or investment in developing some desired capability (as conceived in the OECD study discussed, though leadership development interventions may be designed as a meta-lever to facilitate the deployment of individual policy levers);
- system-changing: establishing or reconfiguring the balance of authority between organizations within a hierarchical system, typified by public services (witness 'hollowing out' since the 1980s—reducing the role of local government in the administration of English public services (Clarke & Newman, 1997)).

More recently identified strategies (John, 2011) include persuasive communication to influence the disposition of service providers and citizens towards cooperating, as with the coproduction of local services; and encouraging the development of inter-organizational networks and forms of governance that encourage collaborative working, exemplified by public–private partnerships. If national leadership development interventions could operate as a long-term policy meta-lever rather than just a short-term capacity-building policy lever, they could, in principle, create favourable conditions for implementing practices connected with other policy levers to promote the implementation of multiple policies within the current reform agenda, or putative future agendas.

Since major leadership development interventions for public services are available only to those powerful enough to mount them, they might constitute an *elite* policy meta-lever. The change process such interventions entail is endemically pluralistic, since power to realize perceived interests is distributed, however unequally. Central government politicians top the power hierarchy in respect of many leadership development interventions for public services, illustrated by the Labour government's ability to establish or financially support all but one of the interventions listed in Table 1.1. Yet, as already noted, government politicians depend on senior staff in public service organizations as conduits for their incremental improvement or radical reform agendas, and ultimately on service professional staff responsible for provision itself. Equally, these politicians depend on the expertise and cooperation of directors and other senior staff in the NLDBs to commission or provide leadership development programmes. Therefore, it is impossible simply to 'read off' the outcome of a leadership development intervention, just as it is to assume that a public service reform will be implemented as government ministers intend.

Conversely, some groups hold considerably more power than others, giving them the potential to wield it (Scott, 2008). They may also exercise this power to realize their interests despite opposition, and to keep issues off the agenda. Elites may even engage exploitatively in channelling the perceptions and associated values of others (Lukes, 2005), deflecting them from perceiving where their own interests lie. The 'manufacture of consent' (Lippmann, 1922) to be governed by elites rests on non-elites perceiving that elite interests are in the common interest, so it is in their interest to comply. This power differential may be conceptualized by focusing on 'ruling minorities' (Scott, 2001, p. 36), construed as elites 'in positions to make decisions having major consequences. Whether they do or do not make such decisions is less important than the fact that they do occupy such pivotal positions: their failure to act, their failure to make decisions, is itself an act that is often of greater consequence than the decisions they do make' (Mills, 1956, p. 4).

The authoritative position of central government politicians, with their constitutionally enshrined power of decision over policy directions and resource allocation, marks them out as elites. Other groupings at the national and more local levels of a public service administrative system also have significant power of decision within their jurisdiction. Elected councillors within the local education authorities (LEAs) of local government have some decision-making powers over public-funded schools in their area; elected board members of representative bodies for senior staff in public service organizations have decision-making powers for activities related to their membership—instrumental in establishing the national leadership development intervention for HE. Authoritative power of decision within a jurisdiction may also confer licence to influence by contributing towards decisions beyond its boundaries, as ministers enjoy within cabinet government. Subsequent chapters will examine uses of power by elites involved with the national leadership development interventions in our extreme case; consider what potential the interventions had to operate as an elite policy meta-lever and how much was realized; and review what potential their contemporary legacy interventions may have, alongside broadly parallel interventions in other Anglophone industrialized countries, and so whether such interventions are capable, in principle, of constituting an elite policy meta-lever to facilitate the deployment of other policy levers by a present or future government.

Building up the argument

There are three parts to the book. Part I examines contextual factors framing the UK Labour government's engagement, alongside representative bodies for senior staff from public service organizations, in major leadership development interventions for different public services; the complex, elite-driven change process these interventions entailed; and the main construals of leadership on which they were founded. Part II explores elite contributions to the three national leadership development interventions within our extreme case to explain why and how the suite of interventions came about, operated as it did within each service sector we investigated empirically, and produced a mix of intended and unintended immediate outcomes. Part III broadens the focus: reviewing the contemporary legacy the suite of interventions has left, with special attention to school education and healthcare in England and HE across the UK; comparing these interventions with major national or regional examples in other Anglophone countries; and considering the indirect outcomes of national leadership development interventions covering England in contributing towards ongoing neoliberalization and associated changes in public services as institutions—taken-for-granted sets of rules and expectations about the purposes and provision of services for citizens, perpetuating the control that elites within the UK government exert over public service providers and citizens alike.

The rest of Part I completes the overview begun in this chapter. Chapter 2 focuses on the evolution of economic and ideological factors influencing the UK Labour government's ambition to build up a suite of large-scale leadership development interventions for individual public services. We consider further the choice of alternative means open to governments for promoting policy implementation, and the attraction of leadership development interventions for bringing senior staff in public service organizations 'onside' as willing, or at least compliant, conduits for policy implementation and operation, whatever the agenda at hand.

In Chapter 3 we outline the critical realist meta-theoretical position framing our theoretical and empirical endeavours, considering the implications of this position for interpreting social reality through endemically metaphorical language. Critical realism provides an ontological foundation for explaining why and how our focal leadership development interventions occurred as they did, and how they drew on and have become part of a wider, and increasingly institutionalized, international movement to develop public service leaders. To grasp the process and outcomes of mounting and consolidating the leadership development interventions, the analysis centres on unequal workings of power across administrative system levels. We then introduce our theoretical perspective, foregrounding uses of power amongst elites and other groups as they engage, within and between administrative system levels, in leadership development interventions and in enacting leadership within public service reforms. We link elite theory to the change process through the metaphor of 'orchestration', embracing both overt and behind-the-scenes elite activity to translate leadership development policy into practice.

Chapter 4 traces the sequence of metaphorical concepts, mostly from the United States of America (USA), contributing to the international spread of leadership discourse that informed the UK Labour government's engagement in leadership development interventions for public services. We explore how theories of visionary leadership influenced the emergence of this discourse, partially displacing what was hitherto construed as management, and document the elite appropriation of a leader-centric form of visionary leadership discourse connected with politics and business, then public services. Elites in the UK Conservative government, civil servants, and Labour Party politicians began employing this discourse prior to the election of the Labour government in 1997, creating favourable conditions for elites from the Labour Party to harness it towards national leadership development interventions for each public service sector.

Within this context of public service reform, inspired by neoliberalism and emergent leadership discourse, Part II examines in depth the elite orchestration of the Labour government's national interventions for school education and healthcare, and its support for the HE equivalent. Chapter 5 introduces our empirical research, setting the scene for presenting the findings. Our theoretical perspective informs the conceptual framework for the investigation, including our heuristic concept of 'leaderism', an emergent ideological discourse underpinning the leadership development interventions. The origins of leaderism lie in US visionary leadership theory and business practice.

Our findings on the discursive framing of the three interventions are discussed in Chapter 6, portraying how elites in and around the UK government spread the discourse of leaderism, an extension of longstanding managerialism. Leaderism was expressed in promoting the development of greater leadership capacity. It was allied with garnering support from senior and service professional staff in public service organizations for regulated marketization reforms, within the political project pursued by government elites to further public service neoliberalization. We then explore how the national leadership development interventions were viewed as a means of building and sustaining the desired leadership capacity, and so as part of reform and, potentially, reformed provision. We show how elites incrementally initiated or reconfigured leadership development interventions involving an NLDB for school education, healthcare, and HE, and how the different patterns of elite orchestration linked to the formal relationship between each NLDB and central government. We also point to the role of NLDB specifications and regulatory arrangements in bounding the scope for manoeuvre afforded to senior NLDB officials. The chapter concludes by identifying linked causal mechanisms explaining the findings presented so far.

In Chapter 7 our focus shifts toward responses to their brief amongst elites tasked with NLDB executive operation, harnessing scope for moderate mediation of the government discourse of leaderism and greater mediation of the envisaged NLDB provision within bounds imposed by the regulatory arrangements. Leadership development activities only loosely linked leadership with implementing reforms, while offering credentials participants could use for career advancement. This move accorded with the advocacy of representative bodies for senior staff in public service organizations to support the professional and career development of their members as professional *leaders*, rather than senior service professionals or administrators. The disparate origins of the three NLDBs we studied were reflected in the efforts of senior NLDB officials to preserve an NLDB for each service or sector within it, despite some duplication of provision and government initiatives to promote collaboration and minimize competition between NLDBs. The account of explanatory causal mechanisms is extended to explain these NLDB responses.

Chapter 8 compares responses of senior staff from the different public service organizations, as members of local elites or close associates, to their experiences of leadership development provision offered by NLDBs and other providers. NLDB provision was experienced as largely generic. Current reforms were discussed as challenges to be addressed, but senior staff were not pressured to accept leading the implementation of present and possible future government-driven reforms as their responsibility. Senior staff did perceive themselves as leaders, though their leadership discourse only partially aligned with the central government discourse of leaderism linked to regulated marketization reforms. They felt entitled, as leaders, to shape the direction of change in line with their service professional values, rather than those of government ministers. A significant minority of senior staff were motivated to participate in NLDB provision, either as a professional development opportunity or to acquire the credential offered by the record of their participation (and, for one NLDB, a formal qualification). Their motivation accorded with advocacy by representative bodies for senior staff to enhance, through this formal training, the status of senior staff as professional leaders. Immediate outcomes of the national leadership development interventions suggest that central government regulatory measures circumscribed the orchestration and moderate mediation or relatively autonomous operation of these interventions. The accountability regime proved more potent in securing senior staff compliance than the potential meta-lever of leadership development did in securing any commitment to implementing present or future government-driven reform agendas. The account of causal mechanisms is completed, explaining how these immediate outcomes were generated.

Part III examines the contemporary legacy of the foundational interventions in England (UK-wide for HE), locating it as part of the wider international movement amongst governments and other stakeholders, especially representative bodies for senior staff in public service organizations, to direct or support large-scale leadership development interventions. We consider their varying potential, realized or not, as a facilitative elite policy meta-lever. The focus then broadens to consider the wider implications of our investigation for elite engagement as leaders in pursuing further neoliberalization of public services, within the bounds imposed by regulatory regimes that serve to sustain the domination of central governments over providers, and over citizens as users of public services.

Chapter 9 reviews what has happened to the suite of foundational leadership development interventions since the advent of Conservative-dominated governments from 2010. We offer an update of the unfolding political and economic context over the decade since, until the pandemic forced the suspension of much leadership development activity. This context was characterized by a reversion to more individualized and entrepreneurial regulated marketization of public services, complemented by stringent austerity measures. All the national leadership development interventions survived in some form, and the suite had been augmented by a new cross-public service intervention. We cite indicative evidence from recent research on the experiences of staff in schools, healthcare, and HE to highlight the extent to which regulated marketization reforms since the time of our study are altering the nature of public service provision and its leadership, and the possible contribution of leaderism and leadership development to the contemporary situation.

In Chapter 10 the focus broadens. We compare the interventions for school education, healthcare, and HE in England with an illustrative group of national or regional leadership development interventions for these service sectors in the USA, Canada, Australia, and New Zealand, drawing on public website and documentary evidence. All countries feature substantial investment by governments or representative bodies for senior staff in this form of intervention, though contextual differences affect the degree to which each service is public-funded, and so subject to governmental regulative control. These country-specific factors affect which elite groupings take the initiative to orchestrate each leadership development intervention, and so its potential as an elite policy meta-lever, while also offering a means of career advancement for participants in provision. The case of England remains extreme, though less so than at the time of our research.

Chapter 11 considers implications of the extreme case, its contemporary legacy, and our comparison with interventions in other Anglophone countries for understanding the emergence, consolidation, and institutionalization of public service leadership development. We mount an explanatory interpretation of the contribution that national leadership development interventions make in England to sustaining the domination by government elites of senior staff in public service organizations and their representative bodies, empowering the government to extend public service neoliberalization through regulated marketization reforms and austerity measures. Our three focal interventions are then located within the wider international movement to develop public service leaders. We reflect on alternatives to leader-centric construals of leadership; the extent to which the national leadership development interventions covering England have realized their high potential 'on paper' as a meta-lever, alongside multiple policy levers, to ongoing public service neoliberalization and societal change; and limitations of the heavy reliance most interventions place on training individuals away from the workplace.

'Spoiler alert': explaining the initiation, implementation, and outcomes of national interventions

For ease of reference, Appendix 1 offers a schematic summary of the explanation we construct chapter by chapter in Parts II and III: the elite orchestration of national leadership development interventions for our three focal services (Chapter 6); elite orchestration of their provision (Chapter 7); elite responses amongst participants and others and the immediate outcomes (Chapter 8); the legacy of the NLDBs in England (Chapter 9) and internationally (Chapter 10); and indirect outcomes related to public service neoliberalization within wider societal change (Chapter 11). We refer to relevant elements of this summary towards the end of Chapters 6–11, building incrementally towards our overall attempt at an explanation incorporating a complex set of interacting causal mechanisms, plus proximal and ultimate outcomes.

2
Leadership development interventions in context

Public service neoliberalization

What contextual factors prompted the UK Labour government to make its unprecedented commitment to developing public service leaders? We examine aspects of the economic and political context influencing the emergence and scope of public service leadership development interventions that constitute our extreme case, framing the purposes of initiators within central government and bodies representing senior staff from public service organizations. We previously pointed to contextual factors flowing from the UK's political history. Two affect the focus and boundaries of these interventions: the UK government's jurisdiction over most public services had become largely confined to England by the time of our research; and, despite the term 'civil' in the title of the UK government civil service, it is a public service, included within the suite of national leadership development interventions. The third contextual factor, British exceptionalism, explains why the UK government's unusual scope for unilateral action positioned it to mount interventions on this scale.

However, the most significant factor was both ideological and economic. Leadership development interventions are instrumental: direct or indirect means to an economic end, itself a means of realizing the interests and thereby expressing the economic, political, and social ideologies of the powerful. Here we build on our earlier claim that the UK Labour government alighted on leadership development primarily to facilitate the implementation and consolidation of its public service reforms, extending the regulated marketization of public services begun by the predecessor Conservative government. The Labour government's reform agenda was driven by a similar economic, political, and social ideology, but directed towards a different balance of political and social ends. The 'Third Way' between traditional socialism and capitalism (Giddens, 1998) aimed to reconcile a novel conception of socialism, as an ethical commitment to equal opportunity and

Developing Public Service Leaders. Wallace et al., Oxford University Press. © Mike Wallace, Michael Reed, Dermot O'Reilly, Michael Tomlinson, Jonathan Morris, Rosemary Deem (2023). DOI: 10.1093/oso/9780199552108.003.0002

social justice promoted through social welfare, with capitalism, founded on entrepreneurship. Pursuing this aim implied economic policies where 'the enterprise of the market and the rigour of competition are joined with the forces of partnership and co-operation', incorporating a 'thriving public sector and high quality services, where those undertakings essential to the common good are either owned by the public or accountable to them' (Adams, 1998, pp. 144–145). The marketization emphasis of public service reform was expanded by continuing to promote competition between service organizations, while also fostering local collaborative service provision through service organization networks, often involving some level of public participation. We will explore how the ideological and economic background precipitated this reform agenda, and so the Labour government's dependence on senior staff in public service organizations to put reforms into practice. This dependence prompted the government's move to develop senior staff as leaders who would act as conduits for the regulated marketization reforms and operators of the 're-formed' services. Now, down to business, beginning with an anecdote.

'It's the economy, stupid!' Neoliberalism and the Keynesian public sector

The slogan quoted in this heading was coined by a strategist for the US Democratic Party during the 1992 United States (US) presidential election campaign, prompting campaigners to emphasize the economy and wealth creation on the grounds that financial wellbeing matters most to voters. Informed by private sector practices, Bill Clinton, the incoming president, engaged in public service reforms to reduce the tax burden for citizens and improve efficiency. They included overhauling the federal civil service. Inspired by business experience, Vice-President Gore (1993, p. 1) undertook a 'National Performance Review', identifying principles for 're-inventing the federal government's operations . . . cutting red tape, putting customers first, empowering employees to get results, and cutting back to basics'. Private sector practices were assumed to be most efficient, and transferable to the federal civil service within the public sector.

The resultant efficiency drive produced new legislation and interventions: downsizing the workforce; introducing performance-related pay; shifting responsibilities from federal to state and local levels; and requiring federal agencies to prepare plans, identify goals, and report performance in achieving these goals (Kamensky, 1999). Economic concerns impelled this reform, yet it was also politically driven, bringing social consequences through its nationwide impact on federal administration and public service provision. Recourse to private sector practices as a model for improving public services through Clinton's version of a 'Third Way' (Skowronek, 1997, pp. 448–463) was mirrored in many western countries, where private sector practices were also subject to reform. A key motivator was neoliberalism, the ideology underpinning political experimentation to implement neoliberal principles across all economic sectors, including the US federal government civil service. Neoliberalism had profoundly influenced US public policy under the presidency of Ronald Reagan (1981–9) and UK policy under the premiership of Margaret Thatcher (1979–90), and was beginning to affect Deng Xiaoping's China (Harvey, 2007). It was subsequently to influence the emergence of public service leadership development interventions in the UK and elsewhere.

Use of the concept 'neoliberalism' has proliferated in recent years (Boas & Gans-Morse, 2009). The definition offered by Springer, Birch, and MacLeavy (2016) in Chapter 1 covers a commonality across neoliberal thought since the 1930s (Mirowski & Plehwe, 2009): to extend the application of competitive market principles across all domains of society. Its achievement in contemporary states requires political support and has consequences for citizens, as market participants. So neoliberalism implies more than the economic principle at its core. What makes neoliberalism an ideology? In broadly Marxist terms, the concept of ideology implies a configuration of ideas embodying assumptions, normative beliefs, and values, representing a view of the social world and how it should be. Ideologies promote a group interest and its acceptance by other groups through relations of domination; power is structured into enduring relations of authoritative control by some groups over others (Deem & Brehony, 2005; Fairclough, 2015; Scott, 2008). Interests, following Weberian usage, constitute wants motivating instrumental actions to fulfil purposes and promote wellbeing (Swedberg, 2005). Interests may be material, as in seeking economic gain through market transactions within a capitalist economy, and ideal, as in valorizing individual freedom; these interests combine in prompting the search for political advantage through action to maximize the scope for entrepreneurship. Neoliberalism is a configuration of ideas founded on interests: material in seeking, say, to marketize public services, and ideal in seeking to increase individual freedom from constraints and freedom to innovate through expanding opportunities for entrepreneurship within public service provision.

Ideologies rest on assumptions—often implicit—about human nature and its consequences. The ideology of neoliberalism assumes people to be individualistic, self-interested, competitive, possessing unequal ability to achieve their purposes and unequal access to resources; so an inevitable consequence of competition is to generate winners and losers in society (McGuigan, 2014). However, since any ideology constitutes a configuration of ideas to which people may subscribe, the relative weighting of these ideas and boundaries of the entire configuration are neither absolute nor immutable. The version of neoliberalism underpinning the UK Labour government's public service reform agenda emphasized regulation and local collaborative provision within marketized public services more than that of the predecessor Conservative government. Ideologies are expressed through discourse, socially conditioned patterns of language influenced by other aspects of society, including unequal power relations between groups (Fairclough, 2015). Ideological discourse has social effects, as where members of a group are persuaded to accept their subordinate position within a relationship of domination. Neoliberalism began as an ideology underlying the discourse of early protagonists, and inspired diverse practices once powerful groups subscribing to this ideology were positioned to realize their material interest in intervention to generate economic change.

The 'neo' in neoliberalism signals its origin in reaction against earlier ideologies of classical 'laissez-faire' liberalism advocating free engagement in markets, unfettered by state regulation and collectivist social planning where resources are allocated centrally to socially owned organizations responsible for economic production (Plehwe, 2009). Neoliberal economists blamed classical, unregulated liberalism for precipitating the unemployment and poverty of the Great Depression in the 1930s. The increased government intervention entailed in post-Second World War social planning to promote economic recovery in the USA, and the socialist government in the UK, were held to deny individual freedom viewed as foundational to liberalism. One advocate (Hayek, 1944, p. 77) believed that centralized planning would generate totalitarianism by requiring that 'the will of a small minority be imposed upon the people'. A middle ground was to promote marketization regulated by a small, strong state. Some advocates, including Hayek, argued for minimal state intervention, solely to facilitate market participation. Others, notably Friedman (1962, p. 15), supported a proactive, supervisory, interventionist state:

> government is essential both as a forum for determining the 'rules of the game' and as an umpire to interpret and enforce the rules decided on. What the market does is to reduce greatly the range of issues that must be decided through political means, and thereby to minimize the extent to which government need participate directly in the game.

The 'umpire' state should create rules of market participation to pre-empt market failure, engaging only in provision of whatever residual element of social welfare was not amenable to full marketization as an individual private good.

During post-war reconstruction, neoliberalism remained the fringe ideology of a loose international grouping of economists, incompatible with the Keynesian economic regimes established from 1945 and predominating in western countries for three decades. The ideological underpinnings of these regimes justified state control of national economies to sustain full employment, alongside extensive welfare provision funded by the tax base that full employment could generate. In the UK, an influential government report (Beveridge, 1942) recommended replacing what was a fragmented system of locally based public services, uneven in quality and accessibility, with a national welfare system. It should offer universal access to high-standard, state-provided services, funded mainly through taxation, reflecting the principle of need rather than ability to pay. These recommendations were implemented in 1945, expanding the domain for state intervention within the 'Keynesian welfare state' (Jessop, 1994, p. 17) founded on incremental expansion of mass production and consumption. Hallmarks of Keynesian economic management included frequent government intervention to sustain full employment by stimulating or dampening inherently unstable aggregate demand for goods and services; state ownership of industries and services, including transport; institutionalized collective bargaining with labour unions, delimited by the imperative of full employment promoting mass consumption; and a form of welfare state comprising, in the UK, a large public sector funded through high taxation, providing extensive citizen welfare benefits to sustain the workforce and consumer base on which future prosperity depended (Fletcher, 1989).

The emergence of professionalism in the public sector

The 'bureau-professional' regime for coordinating public service provision within the welfare state combined two forms of coordination. The first was bureaucratic administration: officials implemented central government policies as appropriate to the administrative structure of the service and that of local government or regional administrative authorities, impartially conducting routine administration of the service. Bureaucratic administration was complemented within public service organizations by professionalism: making expert judgements within non-routine situations entailed in serving individual citizens, students, or clients. Service organization staff, as professionals, were entrusted with considerable autonomy, justified on the grounds of needing freedom to exercise that judgement (Clarke & Newman, 1997).

Over the lifetime of the UK Keynesian welfare state, representative bodies for different public service occupational groups had sought to enhance the status and working conditions of their members as a profession. Representative bodies engaged in a project of *professionalization*, focused on occupational characteristics meeting criteria that had long distinguished the high-status occupations of medicine and law as fully fledged professions (Evetts, 2012; Hoyle, 2001). These criteria spanned expert knowledge based on lengthy specialized training; a strong boundary surrounding entitlement to professional membership; autonomy as a practitioner, subject to occupational self-regulation through a governing body administered by representatives of this profession; and a commitment to serving the interests of clients.

Implicit in professionalization projects lay the promotion of values including altruism, embodied in the commitment to serving clients (rather than a self-serving orientation). Such values were explicitly sedimented in formal rules, notably professional codes of ethics, and in the advocacy of norms: informal expectations guiding acceptable behaviour for members of a profession, such as exercising autonomy in their work and acting as trustworthy experts within their practice domain. Should such rules and norms become so entrenched as to be taken for granted society-wide, the professions themselves would amount to emergent societal *institutions*. North (1990, p. 3) defines institutions as 'the rules of the game in a society' (echoing Friedman's usage noted earlier, construing the state as arbitrator of the 'rules' governing marketization). Institutions may comprise explicit formal rules, such as constitutions and laws enforced by the state, and informal, often tacit, constraints such as 'codes of conduct, norms of behaviour, and conventions' (p. 36), enforced by members of the relevant group. Together these rules and norms frame shared expectations about the range of organizational, group, and individual activity that typically occurs, and the proportion of this activity deemed acceptable. Amongst the societal institutions identified by Thornton, Ocasio, & Lounsbury (2012), most relevant to our focus are professions, the market, and the state.

Professionalization may be construed as comprising two components, whose relative weighting varies (Hoyle & Wallace, 2005). The *institutional* component embraces the process whereby an occupation increasingly meets criteria reflecting assumptive or formal rules underlying a profession as a societal institution; the *service* component refers to 'acting professionally', a commitment towards ethical practice in providing an effective service for each client through attention to meeting their needs. Rationales behind the institutional professionalization of public service occupations, or maintaining their status as professions, constitute an ideology of professionalism. It is promoted through a discourse of service quality supporting the material interests of these groups by justifying their remuneration and protection of their occupational jurisdiction, and their ideal interest in freedom to exercise expert judgement (Abbott, 1988; Larson, 1977). Insofar as service professionalization is also promoted within an occupational group, the ideology of professionalism is part-directed towards serving the material interests of clients through the value placed on service quality and improvement.

The varying degree of professionalization achieved by different occupational groups in the public sector was significantly gendered. School teaching and nursing within healthcare, staffed mainly by women, were widely construed as 'semi-professions' (Etzioni, 1969). Specialized expertise was less extensive, requiring less training than medicine or law. Teachers and nurses in the public sector were state employees, regulated by government. By contrast, doctors employed by the National Health Service (NHS) were regulated by the General Medical Council, a statutory licensing body, and accorded extensive autonomy. The professionalization of UK academics—though not other HE employees—was even greater. Academic knowledge was accepted as highly specialized. Accordingly, academics also enjoyed extensive autonomy. Prior to 1987, many were appointed to tenured posts that could not normally be terminated, protecting their academic freedom. (However, from 1987 existing tenured status was forfeited if an academic achieved promotion.) Academics were regarded as members of a 'key profession' and accorded high status as 'the educators and selectors of the other professions', inculcating the foundational expert knowledge of 'the graduates they produce for service in the schools, colleges, central and local government, hospitals, law courts, and all the other institutions of modern society' (Perkin, 1969, p. 1).

Classroom autonomy for UK teachers had long been justified on the assumption that 'teacher knows best' how to educate children, so should be trusted to decide what and how to teach. During the 1970s, a minority of teachers harnessed this autonomy towards experimentation with student-centred 'progressive' approaches that soon generated controversy. Pressure mounted from Conservative politicians and their advisers for public service professionals to be made more accountable for their work to central government and clients, implying stronger external regulation. However, by then the regulation of economic activity, including public sector provision, had loosened. A tradition of 'club regulation' (Moran, 2007, p. 4) had evolved, whose 'operations were oligarchic, informal, and secretive', serving the interests of powerful groups, including business and the medical profession, with little state engagement. There was an 'elite acquiescence in allowing a large amount of self-regulation, with a light touch by regulatory institutions and legal instruments' (Page, 2008, p. 222). For the public sector, a hallmark of club regulation was reliance on staff in service organizations regulating their own practice, with little oversight. Regulating public services contradicted the institutionalized expectation that staff should have extensive autonomy over service provision. Thus, while schools were subject to inspection by central government or local education authorities (LEAs), the local government bodies responsible for school education within their jurisdiction, inspections were rare. They typically culminated in friendly advice, and judgements of inspectors were not made public (Rhodes, 1981). We noted above how NHS doctors were subject to the medical profession's system of self-regulation, and universities were subject to little accountability over funding secured from central government. By the 1970s, Keynesian economic regimes faced enduring economic problems (Foster & Plowden, 1996). In the UK the rising cost of welfare provision within a burgeoning public sector threatened to outstrip the capacity of a mass production-based private sector to sustain this cost in a context of low productivity, demands for better pay and conditions from unionized workforces, and mounting international economic competition.

The adoption of neoliberalism within the UK Conservative Party

These chronic economic crisis conditions favoured the revival of neoliberal ideology, with politicians sympathetic to it positioned to realize their interest in translating neoliberal ideas into government policy as the intellectual basis for economic reform, extending to the public sector. Friedman's ideas influenced the UK Conservative Party politician Margaret Thatcher and Sir Keith Joseph, the intellectual architect of 'Thatcherism'. He claimed that state bureaucracy and union power, plus private sector taxation to subsidize the ever-expanding public sector, inhibited the private sector's wealth generating potential. His solution was 'the essential reduction of the state sector and the essential encouragement of enterprise. We are over-governed, over-spent, over-taxed, over-borrowed and over-manned [sic] ... We must also have substantial cuts in tax and public spending and bold incentives and encouragements to the wealth creators' (Joseph, 1976, p. 17).

This solution has been variously pursued ever since the election of a Conservative government, with Thatcher as prime minister, in 1979. Neoliberalism here and elsewhere has reached beyond ideology and associated discourse, becoming an ideologically driven and multifarious process of evolving practice. Characteristics include diverse ensembles of interventions within parameters afforded by the principle of regulated marketization; incessant 'creative destruction' (Schumpeter, 1942, p. 83) wrought by permanent product and process innovation affecting the production of goods and services; country-specific trajectories of cumulative experimentation and retrenchment; and international policy-borrowing (Whitty, 2012). The circumscribed diversity of this process is captured geospatially by the term 'variegated neoliberalization' (Brenner, Peck, & Theodore, 2010, p. 207), described by Peck and Theodore (2019, p. 246) as

> an emergent mode of regulation ... cumulatively embedded across multiple sites and spaces such that it increasingly defines the rules of the game and the terrain of struggle, even if never acting alone or monopolizing that terrain. This approach is grounded in the following analytical principles: first, insistence on a processual understanding of neoliberal*ization* [original italics] as a restructuring ethos, proactive and frontal in form and programmatically transformative in scope and ambition, and as a result in an ongoing state of contested reconstruction; and second, recognition of the necessarily variegated character of programs and projects of neoliberalization, the uneven spatial development of which is constitutive and not a way station on a path to completeness, its reactionary face always being consumed (if not defined) by context-specific struggles, rollbacks, and flawed experiments.

This depiction emphasizes the *processual* and open-ended character of neoliberalization: intervention to achieve radical change may provoke iterative contestation and reconstruction, not settlement. It also highlights variation in the *content* of changes pursued, and over what transpires in different contexts. This processual, context-sensitive approach enables any intervention framed by tenets of neoliberal ideology to be located within policies and practices undertaken in different countries and economic sectors.

Illustratively, our vignette of US government experimentation to reform its federal civil service comprises one variant of neoliberalization, specific to a country, time, economic sector, and public service. Features of the neoliberalization process mentioned include the government strategy of conducting a review to inform and justify subsequent intervention. The content of the change sought here promotes regulated marketization through putting the citizen 'customer' first and empowering civil servants to get results, combined with private sector-derived regulation through goal setting and performance reporting. Conditions favouring marketization are fostered by 'cutting red tape', removing regulatory practices inhibiting civil servants from acting entrepreneurially; and by downsizing, confining the market niche of the residual service to what other agencies cannot do more economically. The emphasis on variegation foregrounds how any intervention may be situated locally, nationally, and internationally within an assemblage of interactively evolving interventions.

Variegation encompasses the relative emphasis governments place on engaging in regulated marketization. Comparative research on Organisation for Economic Cooperation and Development (OECD) member states early in the period of UK Labour government implies that the UK was towards the high end of the engagement continuum, alongside other Anglophone countries (Hall & Soskice, 2001, p. 19). The UK, USA, Australia, Canada, New Zealand, and Ireland were categorized as possessing 'liberal market economies', with private sectors reliant on competitive relationships between companies (rather than collaboration between, say, suppliers and manufacturers) and offering relatively low employment protection for workers.

Regulated marketization interventions have spread beyond the private sector, applying market discipline to public and voluntary sectors. A multiplicity of technocratic policies draws selectively on marketization and regulation mechanisms, commonly termed New Public Management (NPM) (Ferlie, Ashburner, Fitzgerald, & Pettigrew, 1996; Hood, 1991), and later 'governance' (Osborne, 2010), including 'network governance' (Klijn & Koppenjan, 2016; Newman, 2001). According to Pollitt and Bouckaert (2017, p. 12), 'all the leading NPM countries are predominantly Anglophone (Australia, New Zealand, the UK, and the USA)'; they note that NPM reforms have also been promoted in Canada, with limited implementation (p. 262). Under NPM, 'citizens and clients were recast as consumers, and public service organisations were recast in the image of the business world' (Newman, 2000, p. 45). Private sector practice was (and is) widely valorized as a model for more effective public services, with private sector organizations increasingly contributing to public service provision.

Variegated neoliberalization of public services: economic regime change, by stages

Scope exists for variants of neoliberalization to incorporate moderately tangential practices, delimited by core ideas within the ideology of neoliberalism. One micro-level example is where headteachers of neighbouring schools subvert conditions created by central government encouraging them to compete against each other for students by operating as a collective, collaboratively marketing their joint provision (Wallace, 1998). However, any practices that are inimical to these core ideas—say, outright refusal by headteachers to engage with prospective parents—fall outside the limits and risk attracting sanctions.

At the macro level of analysis, limits to variation make it feasible to place in sequence groups of actions and events characterizing some focal aspect of neoliberalization. Jessop (2019) offers a periodization comprising sequential stages in the process of economic regime shifts in the USA and UK, focusing primarily on financial capital but including implications for public service neoliberalization. Applying the first five stages to the UK context takes us up to the Labour government's unprecedented investment in national leadership development interventions for each public service. (We will introduce in Chapter 9 two further stages covering the years since our research.) Labels for stages are ours, drawing on Jessop's account:

- *Stage 1: pre-history*, the emergence of an intellectual and ideological movement and its evolution into a political movement, culminating in the likelihood of a political party committed to neoliberal policies forming the national government;
- *Stage 2: consolidation*, where senior government politicians worked to establish control of parliament and the government civil service, and to pre-empt or overcome resistance from inside government or elsewhere. The goal was to achieve cultural hegemony, enduring domination over other groups based on their acceptance or compliance, to facilitate the government's pursuit of its neoliberal political project;
- *Stage 3: rolling back the existing economic regime* (overlapping with stage 2). Activity entailed systematically removing obstacles to the political project by dismantling the institutions and practices of the Keynesian regime, including the welfare state and public sector organizations within it. Government politicians also translated the ideological discourse of markets and the liberal state into policy initiatives, including regulated marketization reforms for the remnant of the public sector;

- *Stage 4: rolling forward neoliberal institutions*, where senior government politicians changed the 'rules of the game' through policy initiatives supported by legislation, resourcing, training, and advocacy, to expand the domain of markets into all economic sectors, including public services. Incremental sedimentation of legislation, organizations, and practices in what became the new institutional order consolidated the economic regime shift, making its reversal difficult to achieve for any future government driven by some incompatible ideology;
- *Stage 5: blowback and adjustment to maintain the neoliberal momentum*, where resistance built as consequences of the economic regime shift for disadvantaged groups became apparent, prompting sufficient compromise and mitigation to maintain existing momentum.

Stage 1 resonates with our account of neoliberalism's emergence as a configuration of ideas amongst US economists reacting against classical liberalism; the revival of neoliberalism in the UK and its translation into a political movement by senior members of the Conservative Party, reacting against problems with the prevailing Keynesian economic regime, including its costly welfare state; and the election of the Conservative government in 1979. Later, we portray how stages 2–4 cover the Conservative government's pursuit, within its variant of neoliberalization, of reforms for school education, healthcare, and higher education (HE). Stage 5 covers the Labour government's followthrough, including its national leadership development interventions for these public services.

Managerialism in support of variegated neoliberalization

The imposition of private sector management practices on public service organizations has recast public services in 'the image of the business world'. This move reflects the subscription of government politicians to 'new' managerialism, another evolving ideology, associated discourse, and set of practices supporting public service neoliberalization (Clarke & Newman, 1997; Deem, 2017; Deem, Hillyard, & Reed, 2007; Shepherd, 2018). What is novel in 'new' managerialism is first, the appropriation by government politicians of managerialism as a dominant ideology, discourse, and practice in the private sector (Klikauer, 2015); and second, its extension to the public sector in facilitating the regulated marketization reforms of neoliberalization. The organizational ideology of managerialism is instrumental, valorizing managerial engagement in rational planning, coordination, and controlling work within the organization as an efficient means of serving a collective purpose; managers should have primacy over workers, owners, or shareholders in setting this purpose and the direction of activity to achieve it. Therefore, managers should be given sufficient freedom—'the right to manage'—to make decisions, set goals, allocate resources.

Managerialism had been enacted within the private sector before the 1980s to increase managerial control over business organizations in the service of neoliberalization. Managerialism is organizational, devoted to the managerial good, spanning top executive remuneration and the achievement of a market monopoly; neoliberalism is political, devoted to the economic good for those able freely to engage in competitive markets for goods and services. Private sector enactment of managerialism included initiatives to de-unionize and casualize the labour force, enabling the reduction of production costs. Such practices informed the politically driven enactment of managerialism within public services, as the 'organisational arm of neoliberalism' (Lynch, 2014, p. 1). Many UK Conservative government politicians harboured a managerialist belief in the superiority and generalizability of private sector management; one cabinet minister (Heseltine 1980, quoted in Pollitt, 1993, p. vi) opined that 'efficient management is the key to the [national] revival . . .. the management ethos must run right through our national life—private and public companies, civil service, nationalised industries, local government, the National Health Service'.

Managerialism is not intrinsically concerned with government politics. Yet the enactment of managerialism by the Conservative government offered powerful support for its political project of public service neoliberalization through regulated marketization reforms. Public service organizations were the main target of managerialism, to make them more business-like and so more efficient. Organizations included public-funded schools and hospitals, and partly public-funded universities and colleges (Vernon, 2018). Managerialism supported neoliberalization through reforms designed to change public service organizations *as* organizations, establishing proxies for private sector parameters and management practices. Some created conditions favouring competition for 'customers', externally imposing the content of services alongside performance and accountability measures. Others imposed or encouraged private sector management practices including appraisal, performance-related pay, and operational budgeting.

The generic ideology of managerialism has spawned complementary forms implicated in public service neoliberalization. Each extrapolates from core ideas about the legitimacy and value of organizational management. Table 2.1

Table 2.1 Three ideal types of managerialism supporting public service neoliberalization

Characteristic of managerialism	Ideal type of managerialism		
	Neo-Taylorism	Entrepreneurialism	Culture management
Organizational control focus	Internal: control staff providing the service	Internal: control staff providing the service	Internal: control staff providing the service
		External—seek individual organizational advantage over competing organizations	External—seek collective advantage with collaborating organizations
Means of control	Direct, overt: instructing staff and providing incentives to comply, including potential sanctions	Indirect, covert: encouraging staff to compete internally, and attracting 'customers' to choose this organization over competitors	Indirect, overt and covert: nurturing staff commitment to goals and practices specified by organizational managers, and nurturing collaboration with other organizations
Minimum response required	Behavioural compliance	Behavioural compliance or positive choice	Beliefs and values motivating voluntarily supportive behaviour
Trust relationship between managers and other staff	Low trust, due to potential for evaluation of staff practice and sanctions	Low trust, due to some staff gaining advantage over others, potential for 'customer' evaluation of staff practice and withdrawal of custom	High trust, due to reliance on shared beliefs and values motivating voluntary compliance and collaboration, tempered by occasional verification, potential for withdrawal of commitment
Examples of generic management practices enacting managerialism	Allocating tasks, identifying performance indicators, surveillance, sanctions	Incentives to compete, establishing a market niche, financial penalties for non-competitiveness, empowering consumer choice	Consulting on decisions about organizational vision and goals, exemplifying desired behaviour, rewarding commitment and sanctioning lack of it

summarizes three Weberian 'ideal types', abstractions constructed by selecting essential elements that fit rationally together. Each offers a heuristic, drawing attention to the characteristics of that form and contrasts between the different forms (Swedberg, 2018). Empirically, practices may span forms; distinctions between them may be less clear-cut than the typology depicts. All three ideal-typical forms promote managerial control within an organization. The left-hand column indicates key contrasts:

- seeking managerial control solely inside the organization or also in relation to other organizations that may be competing or collaborating to gain collective advantage within the marketplace;
- reliance on direction or persuasion as means for maintaining control;
- the minimal response of workers for control to work, from a managerial perspective;
- the degree of trust characterizing the relationship between managers and workers that the means of control engenders.

Neo-Taylorism is an evolution of Frederick Taylor's foundational 'scientific management' from the 1900s, retaining a strong 'top-down' hierarchical orientation. It is enacted by concentrating directive and potentially punitive power in the hands of managers. Neo-Taylorism operates through detailed specification of who must do what to achieve outcomes specified by managers, backed by surveillance and accountability measures to ensure compliance. Workers need neither agree with managerial imperatives nor trust that managers have their wellbeing at heart, but they must carry out specified tasks or risk incurring sanctions.

Entrepreneurialism is more subtle, enacted by creating conditions favouring competition: between workers, against other organizations in the marketplace by seeking to attract and retain customers, or both. Again, workers need neither believe in competing nor trust the intent of managers, but their continuing employment depends on conformity in obtaining a sufficient share of internal resources or generating and meeting adequate customer demand for organizational survival.

Culture management is most subtle, embracing a combination of transparency and unspoken intent behind practices that include symbolic actions, such as 'Management by Walking About' (Packard, 1996, pp. 155–156), where managers openly demonstrate interest in workers while covertly monitoring them. Where focused internally, these practices encourage workers to trust managers and commit themselves to pursuing organizational goals defined by managers. Where focused externally, members of other organizations are encouraged to commit themselves to collaborative working for collective advantage. The minimum response required for operational success is higher than for the other forms of managerialism because it relies on persuasion, so the response must be wholly or partly voluntary. The ideological character of culture management relates to its contribution towards furthering an enduring relationship of domination, where workers come to accept it as natural that managers should determine organizational goals and workers should support managers. Part II will consider how this form of managerialism resonates with the discourse of culturally oriented forms of leadership promoted by the UK Labour government, underpinning its suite of national leadership development interventions. Culture management and leadership both concern 'winning consent rather than securing compliance' (OECD, 2010).

Private sector management practices inspired managerialism, supporting the public service reforms that directly promoted marketization. They were complemented by governmental marketplace regulation, remotely delimiting the practices of professionals responsible for service provision, consistent with the exhortation of US management gurus Osborne and Gaebler (1992, p. 35) to 'separate policy decisions (steering) from service delivery (rowing)'. The UK government's variant of public service neoliberalization, supported by managerialism and informed by developments in other Anglophone countries, epitomizes 'steering, not rowing'. Neoliberalization is characterized by serial experimentation with highly regulated marketization of the previously monolithic, state-funded, and professionally staffed public sector responsible for the provision of different services, especially in England. Internationally, experimentation lies within broad parameters sedimenting as institutional constraints (the 'rules of the game').

These 'rules' include subordinating social welfare to labour market flexibility as the Keynesian welfare state is replaced by the creatively destructive 'hollowed-out Schumpeterian workfare state' (Jessop, 1994, p. 24). Entitlement to welfare benefits is rendered conditional on undertaking training or demonstrably seeking work through 'a range of compulsory programs and mandatory requirements for welfare recipients with a view to *enforcing work while residualizing welfare*' [original italics] (Peck, 2001, p. 10). The logic is to reduce welfare dependency and increase employment in jobs with chronic vacancies that are often caused by low pay and poor working conditions. Workfare regimes 'privilege transitions from welfare to work, typically through the combined use of "carrots" in the form of work activities and job-search programmes and "sticks" in the form of benefit cuts for the non-compliant' (Peck & Theodore, 2010, p. 429). The UK government civil service retains responsibility for workfare provision in England, in contrast to other public services provided by staff from specialist occupations. While our focal public service sectors did not relate directly to social workfare payments, all three were affected by the same underlying principle of minimizing public expenditure and maximizing the marketization of public services. In HE, the replacement of tax-funded student grants with tuition fee charges levied on students as 'paying customers' clearly follows this principle.

Neoliberalization of school education and healthcare (England), and HE (UK)

Creative destruction is a prerogative as much of central government ministers as of private sector entrepreneurs. Once the Conservative Party won the 1979 general election, Margaret Thatcher's government embarked on public service regulated marketization reforms within its UK context-specific variant of neoliberalization. Successive Conservative governments proceeded through stages 2–4 and entered stage 5 of the periodization introduced earlier.

Stage 2 (consolidating power over the government apparatus) was swift. Commitment to neoliberalization among government ministers and the government's parliamentary majority minimized resistance from the Labour Party and other parties in opposition. Civil service reform began immediately with the appointment of Derek Rayner (then joint managing director of the retailer Marks and Spencer) as government adviser and director of its new Efficiency Unit (Haddon, 2012; Lowe, 2011), with a remit to seek ways of saving civil service expenditure, in part by introducing private sector management practices to increase efficiency. The radical 'Next Steps' report (Efficiency Unit, 1988) resulted in the devolution of much policy delivery, or 'rowing' (as Osborne and Gaebler put it), to arms-length agencies. Government still did the 'steering'. Stage 3 (rolling back the Keynesian economic regime) included downsizing the public sector by privatizing transport and utilities and selling off local government-owned low-rental housing, alongside dismantling the local government 'steering' role for schools and other services. Stage 4 (rolling forward neoliberal institutions) entailed reconfiguring the residual public services.

Stage 5 (blowback and ameliorative adjustment) gained traction during the 1990s once it became evident how neoliberalization was impacting on different social groups. Significant disaffection emerged amongst 'semi-professional' and professional staff directly responsible for public service provision. Teachers had lost their classroom autonomy and negotiating rights over pay and conditions (Lowe, 2007); nurses were experiencing a lack of resources, chronic understaffing, and low pay (Meadows, Levenson, & Baeza, 2000); HE academics were losing their autonomy due to managerial intervention prompted by external factors, including cuts within central government funding sources, increasing student numbers, and pressure for responses to the needs of students and employers (Deem & Brehony, 2005; Willmott, 1995). Public concern over access to and the quality of public services was stark within healthcare: surgery waiting times could exceed a year (Devlin, Harrison, & Derrett, 2002). Satisfaction with the NHS, and especially hospitals, had long been relatively low (Judge, Solomon, Miller, & Philo, 1992).

Labour Party manifesto promises for the 1997 general election implied significant ameliorative adjustment of the Conservative government's radical experiment with economic neoliberalization. Public service improvement was central. A message from party leader Tony Blair (Labour Party, 1997, p. 1) opened the manifesto: 'I believe Britain can and must be better: better schools, better hospitals, better ways of tackling crime, of building a modern welfare state.' The Labour Party achieved a landslide victory with a huge parliamentary majority. From 1997 to 2010, the 'public service modernization' agenda pursued by successive Labour governments maintained some elements of the inherited neoliberalization trajectory, notably welfare-to-work initiatives, while moderately modifying others. They included innovations expanding marketization, supported by importing private sector management practices; fostering market-compatible collaborative working, especially between schools within local networks or federations (Muijs, Ainscow, Chapman, & West, 2011); and radically extending centralized regulatory arrangements circumscribing service provision.

Grasping the contextual reasons why Labour government innovation might extend to national leadership development interventions for each public service requires an understanding of how previous public service neoliberalization had generated a platform for adjustment and further experimentation; how the ministerial modernization agenda then pursued public service neoliberalization along a more social democratic trajectory; how central government dependence on senior staff in public service organizations to implement reforms and operate 're-formed' services prompted intensive efforts to persuade them to endorse and engage proactively with these reforms; and why representatives from senior staff representative bodies might support or seek government investment in developing senior staff as leaders.

In economic terms, a regulated market form of public service may comprise customers with a choice of alternative providers, informed about the service on offer; service providers competing for customers and marketing their service provision; the service itself as a commodity that different providers are capable of offering; and regulators who make rules, keep market operation under surveillance, enforce these rules, and, if necessary, act to prevent market failure. Central governments are uniquely placed to drive the neoliberalization process embodied in regulated marketization to attain this form of public service provision. Variegation of neoliberalization processes arises here: scope exists for experimentation with different aspects of public service provision when overlaying the existing public sector arrangements with some proxy for the consumption of services offered by competing private sector providers. Figure 2.1 depicts a regulated marketization heuristic for analysing the dynamics of neoliberalization, supported by managerialism, in such contexts. *Central government*, in the middle of the diagram, is the prime mover of public service neoliberalization, promoting marketization and imposing its regulation, to generate and sustain a market with three components:

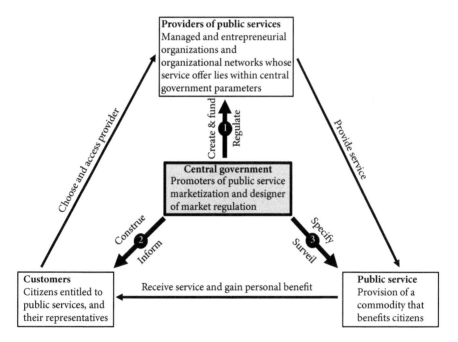

Figure 2.1 Modelling the neoliberalization of public services through regulated marketization

- Citizens construed as *customers*, entitled to receive a public service themselves (e.g. patients, students); otherwise citizens responsible for customers (e.g. parents, carers) or professionals (e.g. healthcare commissioners) who arrange for provision on behalf of customers;
- Business-like *providers of public services*, capable of acting entrepreneurially and designing a service offer, delimited by central government funding and regulation;
- *Public services*, encompassing, in our extreme case, the content and quality of education or healthcare as a service commodity offered by different public service providers.

Each market component interacts with the others through dominant directions of influence, indicated by arrows. The three heavy arrows show how central government may influence the other three elements through:

1. creating new forms of provider, approving and funding their provision, and regulating their operation;
2. promulgating a discourse, relayed through the mass media, construing citizens as customers and informing them or their representatives about the entitlement to choose, or express a preference for, their preferred provider and service offer;
3. specifying service content, standards of quality, and targets for achieving them, while simultaneously creating arrangements for assessment, surveillance, and dissemination of the results, potentially informing customer choice.

The remaining arrows depict the sequence whereby customers, or citizens or professionals responsible for them, make their informed choice and access their preferred provider. The latter provides the service that customers receive.

The variant of public service neoliberalization pursued by the UK Conservative government

This heuristic guides our ordering in Table 2.2 of public service neoliberalization elements that the UK Conservative government harnessed towards the regulated marketization of school education, healthcare, and HE within stages 3 and 4 of the neoliberalization variant pursued in the 1980s–90s. We have inserted, in brackets and bold type, our interpretation of the main impact each element exerted on service marketization, market regulation, or

Table 2.2 Conservative government neoliberalization of school education, healthcare, and higher education 1979–1997 inherited by the UK Labour government *

Elements of neoliberalization introduced by UK Conservative governments, impact on marketization and/or regulation	Regulated marketization reforms and year of implementation		
	School education (England)	Healthcare (England)	Higher education (UK)
Construe service recipients as customers, or purchasers on behalf of customers (**marketization**)	Parents construed as proxy customers for their child's school education (1981)	Government-financed internal market where purchasers, e.g. health authorities, buy services from providers, e.g. hospitals, on behalf of patients (1990)	Overseas students construed as customers, fee subsidies abolished (1980) Government-owned Student Loans Company, providing top-up loans for student maintenance costs (1990)
Promote customer choice between alternative service providers (**marketization**)	Parental right to choose a child's school and appeal if not offered their choice (1981) Open enrolment of pupils (1988)	General practitioner (GP) practices encouraged to become fund-holders, commissioning services, e.g. from hospitals (1991)	Polytechnic and higher education colleges able to apply for university status, if successful become eligible to award university degrees (1992)
Inform customer choice about service providers and their quality of service (**marketization**)	Publication of league tables based on national examination results (1992) Office for Standards in Education (Ofsted) created to oversee regular inspections, mostly by successfully tendering private sector teams, results published (1993)		Regular assessment of university research by central government agency, linked to research funding and published quality rankings (1986, 1989, 1992, 1996) Teaching quality review by central government agency, regular cycle (1993)

Continued

Table 2.2 *Continued*

Elements of neoliberalization introduced by UK Conservative governments, impact on marketization and/or regulation	Regulated marketization reforms and year of implementation		
	School education (England)	Healthcare (England)	Higher education (UK)
Create alternative forms of service provider (**marketization**)	Option for schools to become grant-maintained, funded directly by central government (1988) City technology colleges (CTCs) established, funded by central government and business (1988)		Enabling polytechnics and university colleges to apply for university status (1992)
Promote private sector management practices, impose greater efficiency requirements, encourage service providers to operate like businesses within a regulated service market (**managerialism in support of marketization and regulation**)	National provision of senior school staff management training (1983) National curriculum development planning (1988) Local management of schools (LMS), operating budget based on number of pupils (1988) Teacher and headteacher appraisal (1991)	General management of hospitals, promotion of clinician participation, more pay for managers (1983) New GP contract, more pay (1990) Providers (e.g. hospitals) became trusts with a board of executive and non-executive directors	Central government grant to universities cut by 10% (1981) Expansion in student numbers plus reduced government funding per student (1989) The semi-autonomous University Grants Committee replaced by the Universities Funding Council, directly responsible to central government (1989)
Promote market entry for private sector organizations as service provider sponsors, providers (**marketization**)	Business sponsors for CTCs (1988) Privatized inspection teams (1992)	Compulsory competitive tendering by health authorities to outsource ancillary services, e.g. hospital cleaning (1986)	University College at Buckingham granted university status as the first UK private university (1983)

	Higher education	Health	Schools
Remove administrative market barriers (marketization and regulation)	Enabling polytechnics and university colleges to apply for university status (1992)	Reduced hierarchy of administrative tiers: abolished Area Health Authorities (1982), reduced number of Regional Health Authorities (1994)	Reduced LEA administration of schools (from 1988), e.g. via open enrolment, LMS, schools funded by central government, Ofsted inspections replacing those conducted by Local Education Authorities (LEAs)
Specify service content (regulation)			National curriculum (1988)
Specify service standards (regulation)		Patients' charter stipulating rights and care standards, e.g. waiting time targets for operations (1991)	Standard assessments (1988); Ofsted inspection foci (1993)
Monitor and publicize providers' standard of service (marketization and regulation)	Research assessment exercises (from 1986); Teaching quality review (from 1993)		Ofsted inspections (1993); School league tables 1992
Intervene if standard of service unacceptable (regulation)			Failing schools identified by Ofsted subject to special measures (1993)

* Main sources (each with links to primary sources): Gillard (2018); Nuffield Trust (2019); Rivett (2019); chronology in Brown and Carasso (2013)

both. Each element is consistent with one or more dominant directions of central government influence outlined in the model:

- promoting informed customer choice of service;
- creating alternative forms of provider to offer choice, and rendering them more business-like and entrepreneurial by introducing private sector management practices and promoting market entry for private sector providers;
- hollowing out the national service system by removing barriers to marketization posed by a middle tier of government or service administration between the centre and the service organization level;
- specifying service content and standards, coupled with surveillance, assessment, and publication of results;
- intervening in the market to correct service provision deemed substandard.

Reforms appear under one or more elements of neoliberalization, as appropriate to the reform or its impact on regulated marketization. The remaining columns compare major central government-driven reforms and the year of their implementation (often long after their announcement), categorized by element of neoliberalization, for each of our focal service sectors. Since we are concentrating on the inception of reforms, we have not indicated where any reform was subsequently revised or abandoned.

Neoliberalization of school education was most comprehensive, with all elements represented. Healthcare reform focused more narrowly on hollowing out the multiplicity of administrative layers, while creating a system-wide internal market with services 'purchased' from hospitals and other care organizations on behalf of patients by representative bodies created or refashioned for the purpose. The 'providers', mainly hospitals, were subjected to private sector management practices, including their reconfiguration as trusts managed by a board of directors. There was less emphasis on promoting individual customer choice or monitoring service provision. Neoliberalization of HE, already partly public-funded, concentrated on the construal of students as customers and investors, typically required to take out a loan towards their maintenance costs while studying in return for the benefit of a university education. Simultaneously, the range of providers was expanded by allowing market entry for historically more vocationally oriented polytechnics and colleges that offered HE courses. They could apply for university status, bringing the entitlement to award university degrees. Occasional and increasingly regular assessment of university research, then teaching, alongside publication of results enabled differential allocation of the central government contribution to research and teaching. Published assessment results came increasingly to inform student choice of university or college, precipitating competition between them to obtain high ranking, for funding and reputational reasons.

Reforms enacting managerialism—especially entrepreneurialism—through the introduction of private sector management practices featured in both public-funded services. Ministers looked to private sector management experts to advise on these reforms. The management consultants Coopers & Lybrand (1988, p. 7) were commissioned to guide the devolution of local government school budgets direct to each school, asserting that business management is both best and generalizable:

> Good management requires the identification of management units for which objectives can be set and resources allocated: the unit is then required to manage itself within those resources in a way which seeks to achieve the objectives; the performance of the unit is held to account for its performance and its funds. These concepts are just as applicable to the public sector as they are to the private sector.

Sir Roy Griffiths, a director of the Sainsbury's supermarket chain, was an influential private sector adviser commissioned to report on NHS management (DHSS, 1983). He recommended introducing 'general management' to replace a cumbersome regime of consensus decision-making by multidisciplinary teams of chief officers. Business-style practices for these general managers spanned short-term contracts, performance review, and performance-related pay (Pollitt, Harrison, Hunter, & Marnoch, 1991). HE reforms imposed conditions remotely, through funding cuts alongside expansion in student numbers, forcing senior staff to seek greater efficiencies (Willmott, 1995) and encouraging them to adopt private sector management practices.

Further variegation by the UK Labour government to maintain the momentum of neoliberalization

In 1997 the incoming Labour government inherited the cumulative neoliberalization of these and other public services, forming part of the context on which their own public service reform programme was to build. Key motivations behind the central government turn to national leadership development interventions, coupled, for HE, with the advocacy of senior staff representative bodies, were ensuring that senior staff in public service organizations continued to comply with existing regulation by operating previously reformed aspects of service provision, and the consequent need for Labour government ministers to prompt and support them as implementers of the new agenda for further neoliberalization.

Blair (2010, p. 284), the new prime minister, 'began to look for ways, all ways, of getting business ideas into public service practice'. Table 2.3 summarizes how successive Labour government agendas unfolded during stage 5 of neoliberalization, as the thrust shifted in emphasis. The table depicts the gradual overlaying of the 1997 neoliberalized context by more reforms, ordered by the same sequence of neoliberalization elements for the three services (though promoting customer choice between alternative service providers did not feature). Labour governments reversed few of the reforms introduced by their predecessors. While grant-maintained schools were abolished, the creation of increasingly diverse forms of school soon filled their market niche. Ministers retained most elements introduced by Conservative governments, extending some, reworking others. School education exhibited a dual emphasis on marketization: first, creating an even wider range of service providers to serve parental choice; second, involving the private sector as sponsors for some forms of school and as financers of a major school building and refurbishment programme. Further regulatory measures included prescribing how literacy and numeracy should be taught in primary schools; monitoring the performance of schools in achieving 'tough targets' set by the government for standard assessment and exam results, maximizing school attendance, and minimizing pupil exclusion; and intervention to close failing schools and re-open them in a new form.

Alongside promoting entrepreneurialism within marketization, managerialism was enacted in other ways. First, the national leadership development interventions (Chapter 1) embodied culture management of participants within the developmental programmes, encouraging them, as leaders, to deploy culture management within their service organizations. Second, neo-Taylorist principles were reflected in enhanced regulation imposed on schools, involving centrally specified performance targets, surveillance through published assessment results and inspections, and sanctions for failing to achieve these targets or a positive inspection judgement. Favourable conditions were created for neo-Taylorist practice amongst senior staff to prioritize achieving targets and demonstrating that inspection criteria were fully met. Statutory performance measurement and management, incorporating

Table 2.3 Further neoliberalization of school education, healthcare, and higher education by UK Labour governments 1997–2010 *

Elements of neoliberalization introduced by UK Labour governments, impact on marketization and/or regulation	Regulated marketization reforms and year of implementation		
	School education (England)	Healthcare (England)	Higher education (UK)
Construe service recipients as customers, or as purchasers on behalf of customers **(marketization)**		GP fundholding abolished (1997), Primary care groups (PCGs) created, including GPs, to commission health services from hospitals and other providers, and manage local community healthcare (1999) Most PCGs became Primary care trusts (PCTs) (2000) GP practices commissioning healthcare with PCT support (2005)	Students to pay tuition fees, entitled to maintenance and tuition fee loans, maintenance grants for poorest students, government sold loan portfolio to private sector investors (1998) Student loans included university tuition fees (2006) Promoted HE expansion and more inclusive participation (2001)
Inform customer choice about service providers and their quality of service **(marketization)**	'Naming and shaming' of schools judged by Ofsted inspections to be failing (1997)	National improvement targets for public health priority areas, local targets for improving public health (1999)	Research assessment by Higher Education Funding Council for each country, commercial league tables of results (2001, 2008)

Continued

Table 2.3 *Continued*

Elements of neoliberalization introduced by UK Labour governments, impact on marketization and/or regulation	Regulated marketization reforms and year of implementation		
	School education (England)	Healthcare (England)	Higher education (UK)
		Publication of NHS Constitution, enabling informed choice by patients (2009) National assessment of hospital performance and publication of results (2001)	Quality Assurance Agency for Higher Education (QAA) created, introduced audit for English universities, six-year cycle, results published (1997) Annual National Student Survey (2005)
Create alternative forms of service provider (**marketization**)	Grant-maintained schools abolished, foundation schools created with control over pupil admissions (1998) Many secondary schools became specialist colleges with business sponsorship, could select <10% of pupils for specialist subject (2000) Increase in faith schools, e.g. Islamic secondary school for girls (2001) City academies replaced failing schools, funded directly by central government with business, charity or faith group sponsorship and governance, could select <10% of pupils (2002) Federations for shared governance established between schools (2002)	Hospitals could apply to become more autonomous foundation trusts, board of governors including staff and local people, working with a board of directors (2004)	

Promote private sector management practices in service provider organizations (**managerialism in support of marketization**)	Performance management, incorporating appraisal, performance-related pay (2000) Leadership development provision promoted by the National College for School Leadership (2000)	National leadership development provision promoted by the NHS Leadership Centre (2001), then NHS Institute for Innovation and Improvement (2005)	Funding support for national leadership development provision from the Leadership Foundation for Higher Education (2004)
Promote market entry for private sector organizations as service provider sponsors, providers, financers (**marketization**)	Education Action Zones—grants and business sponsorship for schools in deprived areas (1998) Secondary school specialist colleges with business sponsorship (2000) Privatization of LEA support services for schools provided by LEAs judged to be failing (1998)	Hospital building programme part-financed via the Private Finance Initiative (PFI) (from 1997) Commissioning of independent treatment centres for specified operations including private sector providers (2003)	

Continued

Table 2.3 *Continued*

Elements of neoliberalization introduced by UK Labour governments, impact on marketization and/or regulation	Regulated marketization reforms and year of implementation		
	School education (England)	Healthcare (England)	Higher education (UK)
	Building schools for the future: building programme part-funded via PFI (2005)		
Remove administrative market barriers (**marketization and regulation**)	Privatization of failing LEA support services (1998)	Reduced administrative tiers: District Health Authority administrative tier replaced by Strategic Health Authorities (SHAs) for regions (2000), number of SHAs and PCTs reduced (2006)	
Specify service content (**regulation**)	National primary schools literacy strategy, related LEA and national improvement targets (1998) National primary schools numeracy strategy (1999), LEA and national improvement targets		
Specify service standards (**regulation**)	LEA and national improvement targets for national literacy strategy (1998) Targets for school attendance and pupil exclusion (1998)	National Service Frameworks setting national standards for areas of care, e.g. cancer, mental health (1998)	QAA specification of standards for undergraduate and postgraduate degree programmes (1997)

Monitor and publicize providers' standard of service (**marketization, regulation**)	LEA and national improvement targets for national numeracy strategy (1999)	National Institute for Health and Clinical Excellence established to provide quality guidance (1999) Quality and Outcomes Framework to measure care quality of GPs (2004)	QAA audit of university and college teaching programmes (1997)
	'Naming and shaming' of failing schools (1997)	Commission for Health Improvement created to assess clinical performance of hospitals and publish results (2001), replaced by Healthcare Commission (2004), Care Quality Commission (2009) Monitor (NHS) created to authorize and monitor foundation trusts (2002)	
Intervene where providers' standard of service judged unacceptable (**regulation**)	LEA and central government intervention in 'schools causing concern', potential for closure (1998)		

* Main sources as for Table 2.2

annual appraisal, mandated a complementary internal procedure for setting individual priorities, monitoring progress, and providing rewards or sanctions.

Healthcare underwent serial government-imposed 're-disorganization' of the internal market (Pollitt, 2007), changing commissioning bodies and adding another form of provider by creating 'foundation trust' hospitals, with greater autonomy to manage service provision. Tightened regulation through specifying service standards, monitoring performance and publishing results informed patient choice, while financing a hospital building programme and contracting private sector provision for certain medical operations generated a degree of NHS privatization.

For students, HE became increasingly a private investment, with each university or college charging tuition fees within government-set parameters. (Arrangements in Scotland and Wales differed after their devolved governments were established in 1999, with jurisdiction over most domestic policy.) Student loans were extended to cover both maintenance and tuition. Marketization measures included informing student choice through research and teaching assessment, including an annual national survey of final-year undergraduate students, coupled with publication of results and the commercial publication of university league tables. Consistent with the more autonomous status of universities and colleges, HE was subject to less direct central government regulation than the public-funded services of school education and healthcare. Nevertheless, in all three service sectors the regulated marketization reforms reinforced pressures for efficiency and accountability that the Labour government inherited, favouring further senior staff engagement with private sector practices enacting managerialism.

Mitigating central government dependence on senior staff in public service organizations

Achieving the Labour government's agenda of further public service neoliberalization relied on the response of senior staff in public service organizations, the implementation sites for the evolving reform programme. Blair's foreword for a pamphlet outlining the government's reforms (OPSR, 2002, pp. 2–3) acknowledged the government's dependence in stating that these reforms could 'only be brought about through the efforts of skilled, dedicated and highly motivated public servants . . . My colleagues can—and will—play our full part but, in the end, you are the people who will deliver.'

Leadership development was a key form of support. Table 1.1 (Chapter 1) showed how central government investment in leadership development interventions involving a national body was well advanced by 2002. A second pamphlet confirms how government discourse linked the effectiveness of public service leadership with proactively implementing government-driven reforms, as fostered through national leadership development interventions: 'More effective leadership, as a driver for reform, is being encouraged through, for example, the National College for School Leadership [NCSL] set up in Nottingham, and the NHS Leadership Centre' (OPSR, 2003, p. 11). Senior staff in public service organizations were now construed as leaders, with leadership development interventions designed as means for securing the implementation and operation of the Labour government's public service reform programme. This investment promised to yield the return of additional ministerial leverage over the implementers on whose cooperation government ministers depended.

Government dependence on senior staff in the more autonomous HE sector to accept, implement, and operate within conditions set by regulated marketization reforms was paralleled by a confluence of ministerial interests with those of representative bodies for senior staff, especially vice chancellors and chairs of university governing bodies. Both government and representative bodies sought to further the neoliberalization of HE, incorporating managerialism, to compete successfully within an increasingly global market for students and research funding. The representative bodies were prompted to propose the Leadership Foundation for Higher Education (LFHE, discussed in Chapter 6), advancing a 'business case' construing HE's role in terms resonant of the private sector, highlighting its 'contributions to economic growth, research quality, student satisfaction and employability' (UUK/SCOP, 2003, p. 1). The justification for 'additional investment' in the LFHE included the assertion, reflecting the managerialist ideology of entrepreneurialism, that 'higher education institutions are distinct, autonomous businesses with diverse missions and markets. The value of a dedicated Leadership Foundation is that it will be sensitive to different customer needs and market drivers as well as to the specific higher education context' (p. 3). The government announcement of financial support for the LFHE was included in a list of envisaged reforms for the sector: 'excellent leadership and management' was needed, including the capability to 'support links between higher education and business' (DfES, 2003a, p. 78). Provision of funding support served the interest of the government in mitigating its dependence on senior staff in universities and colleges to embrace its HE agenda by developing them as leaders of reform. Establishing the LFHE served the material and ideal interest of the representative bodies, and so senior staff, in developing their ability to manage their 'distinct, autonomous businesses' in a more business-like way.

Summing up, our answer to the question opening this chapter is that variegated neoliberalization, supported by managerialism, is the key contextual factor stimulating this major investment in the development of leadership capacity across the public services in England, and UK-wide for HE. The 'blowback and ameliorative adjustment' stage reached by the variegated neoliberalization process may have influenced UK Labour government ministers to mitigate their dependence on senior staff in public service organizations by seeking to develop them as leaders who would act as conduits for regulated marketization reforms in their organizations, and others with which they might forge collaborative links. We will examine that possibility in Part II. The UK Labour government was not only motivated but also socially positioned to undertake this unparalleled investment. The constitutional history and democratic institutions of the UK by the early 2000s provided the structural basis for 'British exceptionalism', and the large parliamentary majority enjoyed by the incoming Labour government gave ministers extensive scope for unilateral initiative-taking.

We now shift focus from context to framing. In the next chapter we set out the assumptions underpinning the kind of explanation we are attempting, and the main elements of our theoretical perspective focusing on the power and workings of elites across different administrative levels of a public service system.

3

Framing the enquiry

Critical realism, an elite perspective, orchestrating change

A truism of research is that the questions you ask depend on the assumptions you make about what could be there for the discovering, how you might be able to discover it, and why the effort of discovery is worth making. In Chapter 1 we heralded our goal as explanatory, tackling questions about why and how the United Kingdom (UK) Labour government's suite of national interventions to develop senior staff from public service organizations as leaders happened as it did, and how this initiative relates to the contemporary international movement embracing public service leadership development. Accordingly, we set out the foundational assumptions framing our explanatory purpose to indicate why we opted for the analytical perspective we employ. This theoretical orientation addresses elite engagement in the contextualized process of change embodied in the national interventions, generating both intended and unintended outcomes.

First, the critical realist metatheoretical position is outlined, informing the explanatory purpose, methodology, ethical grounding, and theoretical starting-point for our investigation. The critical realist view of explanation construes observable social phenomena as a surface manifestation of largely hidden causal mechanisms, to be inferred from empirical evidence of their effects. Second, we summarize the theorization of structurally based elites and elite networks positioned in and around the apex of hierarchically managed organizations at different social or administrative system levels. We focus on the mainly persuasive, contingently coercive workings of power whereby elites build and sustain domination over other groups (Chapter 2), subordinated by their acceptance of elite control. Third, we offer a conceptualization of the complex change process entailed in the introduction of leadership development interventions. We consider the role of elites in orchestrating change, openly and 'behind the scenes', to realize their interests within constraints bounding their room for manoeuvre. Finally, the notion of professionalization (Chapter 2) is harnessed to explain why senior staff

Developing Public Service Leaders. Wallace et al., Oxford University Press. © Mike Wallace, Michael Reed, Dermot O'Reilly, Michael Tomlinson, Jonathan Morris, Rosemary Deem (2023). DOI: 10.1093/oso/9780199552108.003.0003

from public service organizations, and those aspiring to these positions, may engage in the interventions as a source of credentials for individual career advancement. We conceive such leadership credentials, metaphorically, as a form of capital or source of advantage contributing to the professionalization of senior staff as leaders.

Critical realism: a philosophically informed metatheory framing social scientific enquiry

The philosophical position of critical realism (Archer et al., 2016; Edwards, O'Mahoney, & Vincent, 2014) embraces a philosophy of natural and social scientific enquiry grounded in ontology, a theory of existence (Fleetwood, 2004). The social world is held to differ from the natural world due to the 'double hermeneutic' (Giddens, 1993, pp. 9–15): objects of study are societies and people within them who have their own experience of the phenomenon being interpreted by social scientists; the findings of researchers may influence the perceptions and actions of the people being studied. Further, the social realm is intrinsically *social*: an emergent characteristic of human interaction, to be explained through reference to social structures and processes, and ideas people have about them. Reductionism, explaining a social phenomenon via another level of explanation in, say, biological terms, is rejected (Danermark, Ekstrom, Jakobsen, & Karlsson, 2002; Sayer, 2010). Tenets of the philosophical position underpin a 'metatheory' of natural and also social science, an account of 'domain assumptions' (Gouldner, 1971) concerning the nature of social reality and causation, how it can be known, and what values should inform the endeavour. This metatheory, incorporating a critical realist ontology, does not explain anything in itself; rather, it operates as a metaphorical 'under-labourer in clearing the ground a little, and removing some of the rubbish that lies in the way to knowledge' (Locke, 1690/1997, p. 11). The resultant set of assumptions informs the design of empirical enquiry, guiding the generation of empirical data and suggesting what kinds of theory may be capable of explaining it (Archer et al., 2016).

Critical realism originated in the 1970s (Danermark et al., 2002). A founding philosopher, Roy Bhaskar (1978, p. 13), posed the ontological question about social existence: 'what properties do societies and people possess that might make them possible objects for knowledge?' Social scientists inevitably harbour beliefs about the 'properties of societies and people': the nature of social order, structures, processes, people, causes, effects. Bhaskar's question invites social scientists to articulate these beliefs. A short critical realist answer is that a single, distinctively social reality exists, independently of our awareness. This social reality is partially unobservable; some aspects can only be inferred. An entity is deemed real if it has causal effects—it makes a difference (Fleetwood, 2014). The causal power of an entity may be tendential, or 'transfactual' in not always producing the causal effects of which it is capable. Many real entities will co-exist within any context, each with their own tendencies. Interaction between entities may result in some causing effects while others do not, in ways that are not reliably predictable. Human access to the external reality of things that make a difference is mediated by language; there is not a one-to-one correspondence between external objects and the concepts through which people describe them. So the relationship between a concept and the reality to which it refers is characterized by an inherent degree of ambiguity, or equivocality of meaning. Conversely, language is not arbitrary; it refracts external reality. Wishful thinking is just that because language is not sufficient unto itself; uncontrollable external reality intervenes.

Significant here is the intrinsically *metaphorical* character of language (Lakoff & Johnson, 2003), derived from aeons of people's embodied encounters with each other and with the natural world. Metaphor asserts some resemblance between concepts that are otherwise unrelated to generate a non-literal meaning, as in 'the leadership journey'. Most basic are positional metaphors such as 'up' and 'down', derived from the bipedal nature of human existence and sedimented in language, as in (non-literally) 'looking up to' someone who is respected and 'looking down on' on the opposite. Acknowledging human embodiment implies that there are essential characteristics of being human, including the capacity for language, loosely shaping and bounding human activity. Critical realist ontology encompasses '*weak* essentialism, in which the recognition of certain embodied capabilities places some constraints on human activity, but of a conditioning kind rather than a determining kind' [original italics] (Mutch, 2018, p. 244). Weak critical realist essentialism allows for the existence of real, and so causal, essences connected with human attributes, yet the effects of these essences are indeterminate. While they contribute to framing the scope for human agency (capacity to choose between alternative actions), they do so within wide limits.

Language refracts external reality through a web of metaphorical concepts, each comprehended by reference to others, leaving scope for relative ambiguity between a metaphorical concept and its referent. Take our term 'national leadership development body' (NLDB). An NLDB is a form of organization, not literally a *body*. We invented the term, using the concept of 'body' to convey a sense of internal coherence and fixity to something neither wholly material nor physically bounded. We will develop the idea of metaphorical concepts in Chapter 4 to analyse how leadership discourse emerged within public services, and why the UK Labour government chose national interventions to develop a leader-centric construal of *leadership*. Scope for multiple interpretation through language is multiplied, in turn, by the potential for social scientists to reinterpret the interpretations of people they study, and for the interpretations of social scientists to filter back via the double hermeneutic. So critical realism posits a single reality, subject to multiple and incomplete interpretations, amounting to more than people's interpretations, and not wholly observable. Yet in principle, the causal effects of hidden aspects may be detected empirically.

Sayer (2004, p. 7) distinguishes between the *construal* of social reality and its *construction*. Construal denotes interpreting the social world or creating a mental construction of it, presupposing that there is an independent reality to be construed, even if it cannot be directly apprehended without conceptualization. The interpreter's construal may be partial or mistaken, so while construal is not arbitrary, it can never be definitive. There is more to social reality than the language describing it. Construction of social reality implies materially creating a social entity rather than interpreting an existing one, sometimes by design, as with establishing an NLDB as a new organization. But the entity is assumed to be socially real, not merely a linguistic artefact. Once established, this organization gains relative independence from its constructors, those who subsequently work or experience being trained in it, or researchers who investigate it. The NLDB gradually sediments further construals and patterns of associated actions that come to pre-exist, framing possibilities and constraints for current interaction. The socially constructed NLDB becomes more than the sum of the ideas of people who designed it. This 'more' is real: an entity capable of causal effects that include shaping social practices and their interpretation.

A longer answer to Bhaskar's question elaborates the core ontological premise of critical realism, offering a sophisticated account of how the social world is that may direct the attention of researchers in discovering aspects of it. Fleetwood (2014, p. 182) offers a condensed version by listing key concepts: ontic (factually existing) properties of societies and people are 'characterized by stratified, emergent, and transformational entities, relations and processes'. This ontology has implications for the rest of the 'chain of metatheoretical concepts' framing enquiry: from aetiology, or assumptions about causation; through epistemology, methodology, and the role of substantive theory; to the form of explanation and mode of inference for its achievement.

The ontological position of critical realism on social reality: a basis for social scientific explanation

'Entities, relations, and processes' signal three linked foundational concepts that the adjectives 'stratified, emergent, and transformational' qualify. First, the overarching concept is *entities*, referring to distinguishable things existing independently of other things, say, 'leadership development intervention', 'training venue'. Entities that can cause effects and make a difference are assumed to be real, but the mode of that reality varies, and entities may straddle two or more modes. Physical entities existing independently of all people (say, the ground on which the training venue is built) are *materially* real. Conceptual entities (such as leadership) are *ideally* real, as are discourse, language, explanations. Social entities connected with human association (NLDB, leadership as a group influencing activity) are *socially* real, as are senior leadership teams, public service organizations, and social structures including government, public services, the state. Physical entities constructed by people (the training venue building, training documents, an online networking platform) are *artifactually* real. Social reality encompasses causal entities whose mode is social and those that are bimodal, as with leadership—an ideally real concept and social practice—or trimodal: NLDBs are artifacts combining entities that are materially real (NLDB training rooms), ideally real (the notion of training), and socially real (training activities). Importantly for explanation, ideally and socially real entities may exist independently of their identification by people. Social scientists may invent a new concept or identify a driver of social activity about which the people being studied are unaware.

Second, *relations* between real entities impinge on their ability to cause effects, as where 'leadership' links with 'leader', 'leading', 'follower', and 'following' to form a set of interrelated ideally and socially real entities. In Chapter 1 we highlighted the relational character of leadership as a group phenomenon to which all members contribute voluntarily in some degree. Their relationship is internal to leadership. As a group entity, leadership cannot exist with a leader and leading but no follower and following (and the reverse). Within this relationship, leading logically implies following. The ability of leaders to have causal effects by leading depends on having followers, sufficiently willing or compliant to follow the lead they are given. This relationship ranges along a hierarchical–equal dimension. At the hierarchical extreme, a designated leader leads by attempting to influence other members, cast as 'followers', who accept the leader's influence by following. At the equal extreme, all members participate as much in the role of 'leaders' as in that of 'followers', sharing attempts to influence each other by leading and accepting—or even facilitating—influence through following. The relational character of leadership, so the significance of the other entities for the ability of leadership to cause effects, raises a question over the causal efficacy of interventions within our investigation designed, leader-centrically, to develop individuals as 'lead*ers*' in the name of 'leader*ship* development'.

Third, social reality embodies entities capable of causal effects constituting *processes* that evolve through human activity. The timescale of significant change varies. Some entities are relatively static: an NLDB training venue may not change over a decade; what happens within it will. Other entities, such as leadership development provision, are fluidly processual and change continually in minor ways, as where training programmes are routinely revised. Processual entities may occasionally change in major ways. Chapter 1 summarized how one NLDB, the NHS Leadership Centre, was replaced and its leadership development provision incorporated into another, the NHS Institute for Innovation and Improvement. Chapter 2 portrayed the turbulent context in which national leadership development interventions constitute a complex change process nested within the process of public service reform, as part of the neoliberalization of public services, within the wider political project of economic neoliberalization.

Now for Fleetwood's qualifiers. The first two are the intertwined ontological assumptions that external reality is both *stratified* and *emergent*. We noted earlier how critical realism acknowledges a stratification between different explanatory levels, while rejecting reductionism: entities identified at one level of reality are explained in terms of those at another level. However, there is a relationship between different levels. The social world is rooted in the biological because people are also biological organisms; yet people amount to more than the aggregate of their biological parts, so social reality is irreducible to the biological, while being emergent from it. Reality within the social realm is similarly both stratified and emergent.

- At surface level is the observable *empirical* domain of human experiences and perceptions of events and actions. (In our research we analysed documents whose texts enshrined the perceptions of their authors, and asked informants about their experiences and perceptions.) The empirical level is emergent from and irreducible to:
- the observable *actual* domain of events and actions occurring in space and time, only some of which are experienced by those people who happen to be investigated empirically, and the totality of which does not necessarily coincide with what they believe it to be. Our access to the perceptions of informants based at different administrative levels

enabled us to build a 'second-hand' understanding of the operation and impacts of the NLDBs we investigated that reached beyond the perception or knowledge of any informant. The actual level is emergent from and irreducible to:

- the *real* or 'deep' domain of emergent, unobservable but inferable social structures, the cultural system, and causal mechanisms generating the events and actions of the actual domain that underlies the empirical domain of human experience and perceptions. Critical realist ontology avoids equating the existence of causal mechanisms with evidence of their enactment. Merely the potential structured into a social position for, say, applying punitive sanctions may be enough to cause the effect of self-disciplinary activity within the target group to mitigate the sanction threat. In Part II we will report how we inferred emergent generative mechanisms explaining why, within the context we studied, leader-centric construals of leadership became the focus of interventions, why the interventions were established as they were, and why some intended outcomes did not ensue while unintended ones did and produced outcomes that were neither expected nor acknowledged.

Deep explanation is about the (metaphorically) 'root' causes of the way things are and why they do or do not happen, requiring a double move beyond the empirically accessible domain of experiences and perceptions and the actual domain of patterns of events and actions, about which people may be unaware. The explanatory potential of critical realist enquiry lies in the inferential endeavour to identify generative mechanisms and understand their causal powers and effects within the context of the enquiry.

Analytical links between social structure and culture

Fleetwood's third qualifier foregrounds the ontological workings of social change by reference to the *transformational* character of external reality, according to ontological assumptions about the relationships between social structure, culture, and agency. All three entities are socially real; any aspects of which people are aware are also ideally real. The starting-point for Archer's (1995) 'morphogenetic' approach to understanding social reality and change, and how they might be explained, is the observation that society is intrinsically transformable; it has no essential form, and is produced, reproduced and changed through the actions of people. Archer conceives the dynamics between structure, culture, and agency as an unending sequence of

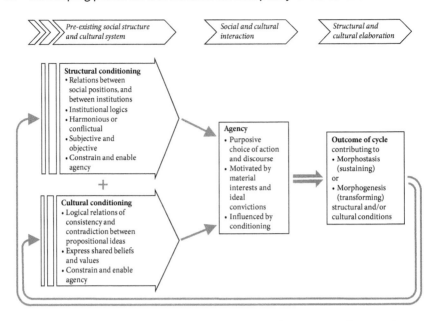

Figure 3.1 Modelling the relationship between social structure, culture, and agency within a morphogenetic cycle

morphogenetic cycles. The metatheoretical premise underpinning each cycle is that pre-existing structural and cultural circumstances within people's context have constraining and enabling effects, conditioning (but not determining) how people interact; the intended and unintended outcomes of their interaction contribute to reproducing or modifying these structural and cultural circumstances, and in so doing people remain as they are, or change. Figure 3.1 provides a schematic representation, informed by Archer's approach.

According to Archer (1995, pp. 15–16), relationships between social structure and agency and between the cultural system and agency may be explored through a methodological strategy of *analytical dualism*. Structural and cultural antecedents conditioning interaction are analysed first, and then the expression of agency in interaction and its outcomes contributing to the reproduction or changing of those structural and cultural conditions. Analytically isolating structural and cultural factors providing the context for agency makes it possible to examine how these factors shape subsequent interactions and, in turn, reproduce or transform the initial context. A morphogenetic cycle begins with the *pre-existing social structure and the cultural system* (on the left of the diagram), creating conditions influencing present interaction. The broken tail of the arrows depicting how structure and culture condition interaction represents their emergence from the cumulative aggregation and overlaying of outcomes from past (including long past) cycles. Social structure and the cultural system co-exist in a relationship of relative autonomy. They can be analysed separately, and the relative significance of each weighed as contributory contextual influences on interaction in specific settings.

Social structure, existing in the real or 'deep' domain, is conceived as the emergent, cumulative pattern of relations amongst the social positions people occupy (Porpora, 2013), giving people differential access to sources of power within the actual domain for realizing their material interests connected, largely, with economic, political, and social wellbeing. Awareness of relations between social positions varies. Some social positions exist both intersubjectively and subjectively, so socially and ideally, featuring in associated discourse. Thus, a team relationship exists where people occupying team membership positions understand what the team is, and what being a member involves for their contribution to it. Other entities exist where people occupy dominant and subordinate positions objectively, without necessarily being aware of this relationship and their contribution to it, as with relationships of domination (Chapter 2). If no one is aware of the socially real domination relationship, it remains non-discursive but, in principle, detectable, so capable of becoming both socially and ideally real. Other emergent and objective structural relations relevant for us include the objective relations of competition promoted by regulated marketization reforms for public services, and the dependency of government politicians on senior staff in public service organizations to implement and operate government-driven reforms.

Relational social positions may be influenced by emergent properties of one or more institutions (Chapter 2)—sets of rules and norms shaping perception and action, so influencing the workings of agency. These emergent properties include the degree of compatibility or incompatibility amongst rules and norms within each institution and between different institutions, affecting the options for actors over which rules and norms they express, prioritize, or downplay. Institutions are both socially and ideally real insofar as their constituent rules or norms are explicit. They vary in scale and degree of formality: from societal-level institutions including the state, the market, and professions, embodying many sub-institutions (here, the welfare or workfare state, encompassing state-funded or supported schooling, healthcare, HE, professional training and development), to largely informal and customary institutions such as celebrating birthdays. Most significant for our study is the impact of multiple societal institutions and sub-institutions on relations amongst social positions conditioning agency, and the possibility of successive morphogenetic cycles gradually generating institutional change. The UK Labour government's suite of national leadership development interventions and public service reform programme drew on rules and norms connected with all the institutions and sub-institutions just cited. We will consider in Part III the possibility that they have contributed to institutional change over the past two decades within the UK and internationally.

The multiplicity of institutions from different societal sectors, and the partial incompatibility between rules and norms within and between institutions, constitutes part of the social structure. Different institutional configurations of rules and norms are sedimented within a plurality of *institutional logics* that actors may bring to their present interaction: these logics constitute ways of thinking that draw on rules and norms from one or more relevant institutions in guiding action. Institutional logics have been defined as 'socially constructed, historical patterns of cultural symbols and material practices, including assumptions, values, and beliefs, by which individuals and organizations provide meaning to their daily activity, organize time and space, and reproduce their lives and experiences' (Thornton, Ocasio, & Lounsbury, 2012, p. 2). In our study, an institutional logic of training and development originated with government politicians, their advisers, and representatives of senior staff in public service organizations; it was augmented by professional trainers associated with each NLDB. This institutional logic related to the logics framing management and professional practice in the relevant service sector; it also drew on the market logic in respect of commissioning of training and other developmental activities. Rules and norms reflected in different institutional logics drawn upon by actors may be compatible, favouring stasis, or variably incompatible, generating tension and conditions for change. Within societal institutions, change may occur: first, very gradually, through shifts in rules and norms constituting one or more existing institutions, drawn upon in the institutional logics to which agents from a multiplicity of organizations subscribe and socialize incomers to share; second, through incremental hybridization between them; third, more rapidly within and between organizations, through the process of institutionalization as rules and norms become increasingly taken for granted; or fourth, through de-institutionalization, where previously accepted rules and norms are challenged.

The degree of compatibility or incompatibility between institutions and sub-institutions is itself an emergent structural property affecting relational social positions. Two ideal-typical institutional configurations identified by Archer, both featuring incompatibilities between institutions, are significant for our focus on national leadership development interventions and their linkage with public service reforms. First is the configuration of *necessary incompatibilities* between institutions that are internally and necessarily related (Archer, 1995, p. 222), creating conditions favouring compromise between groups with partially or wholly incompatible material interests, so tending to perpetuate the status quo. In Chapter 2 we described how, in the UK, the institutional configuration comprising the Keynesian welfare state, professions, state schooling, healthcare, and higher education (HE) lasted for several decades. Illustratively, the ever-growing expenditure demanded by the large public sector within the welfare state was met through high taxation, constraining entrepreneurial activity in the private sector since business profits were heavily taxed. Serial compromise perpetuated the economic system despite inherent incompatibility between the institutions of social welfare and the market and corporations, until the system foundered. Then the external factor comprising Thatcherite neoliberalization overturned the longstanding institutional logic of compromise.

Second is the configuration of *contingent incompatibilities*, creating conditions conducive to social transformation. A configuration of societal institutions and sub-institutions is incompatible with contingent external influences impinging on the pre-existing institutional order. Actors engage in competitive forms of interaction to realize their respective material interests, either as initiators and supporters of the external influence promoting change that will rework the institutional order, or as its preservers endeavouring to eliminate the external influence. From the 1980s, the contingent external influence of Conservative government public service reforms disrupted the Keynesian economic order relating to public services. 'Creative destruction' relied on expanding the scope of the market and corporations, the two institutions whose scope for profit had been constrained by the requirement to serve the high taxation needs of the welfare state. The market and corporations embodied rules and norms that were largely incompatible with those of the welfare state, alongside extant institutions including the state itself (encompassing government). Public service reforms promoted the gradual hybridization of institutions connected with individual public services, including state schooling, healthcare, and HE, within the 'hollowed-out Schumpeterian workfare state', in Jessop's (1994) terminology. This external influence was taken forward and moderately reshaped by the successor Labour government, in part through the national leadership development interventions.

In sum, social structure iteratively overlays the sedimented outcomes of past interactions between people and the ways in which they were influenced by their relational social positions and institutional logics, affected, in turn, by the emergent relationships of compatibility or incompatibility between institutions and external influences on them within the wider institutional order. The causal properties of social structure comprise the emergent or aggregate consequences of these cumulative past interactions. The effect of these consequences constitutes *structural conditioning* in the form of constraining or enabling influences on individuals and groups, dependent on their social positions, institutional logics, and material interests.

The *cultural system*, also existing in the real or 'deep' domain, is viewed as the system of emergent and cumulative logical relationships of mutual consistency or contradiction within and between propositional ideas and their combinations: theories and beliefs about the social, psychological, spiritual, and natural worlds, and associated ethical and preferential values. These theories and beliefs are shared within different groups and contribute to realizing their ideal interests. Such ideas constitute cultural components: collective products of thought, as distinct from meanings to which people may subscribe at any time. While the logical relationships between ideas exist whether perceived as such or not, within the actual domain people may causally influence the ideas to which others subscribe, whether consciously held beliefs, symbols, norms, and values or more subliminal, taken-for-granted codes of behaviour. Sets of cultural components are embodied in meanings that become shared amongst groups, occupying different social positions within the social structure related to their value commitments and idealistic convictions. The configuration of a contemporary culture will be influenced by the accretion of allegiances from past generations. Different groups may subscribe to contrasting and often contradictory, or mutually incompatible, cultural allegiances. Here, the contemporary cultural pattern may be characterized by awareness of both what different groups do share and what they do not. Most components of culture are both socially and ideally real since they are discursive, but people may be unaware of their implicit codes of behaviour unless, perhaps, their awareness is raised when those codes are transgressed by the behaviour of others.

The logical property of inconsistency between sets of ideas or doctrines is the basis for ideal-typical cultural relationships paralleling the two structural relationships of incompatibility between institutional configurations already described. They also create conditions conducive to perpetuation of the status quo or social transformation in terms of culture. First is the relationship of *constraining contradictions* (Archer, 1995, p. 230), paralleling the structural relationship of necessary incompatibilities. Groups subscribing to a doctrine that embodies contradictory beliefs and values face cultural tension, and attempt to reinterpret or downplay one or other belief or value, or else seek a middle ground between them to reduce the cultural dissonance. We saw in Chapter 2 how the emergent ideology of neoliberalism reflected a tension between Hayek's belief in minimizing market regulation and Friedman's contradictory belief in regulation by government, as market umpire, with contingent intervention to enforce its rules. The middle-ground position represented too much regulation for some, too little for others. This uneasy cultural compromise continued to play out in respect of public services in England years later as UK Labour government politicians leaned towards greater regulation of the public service market than the predecessor Conservative government.

Second is the relationship of *competitive contradictions* (Archer, 1995, p. 239), paralleling the structural relationship of contingent incompatibilities. Groups subscribing to one of two or more mutually contradictory sets of doctrinal beliefs and values take sides and support their doctrine against competitors. Chapter 2 indicated how beliefs within the emergent economic ideology of neoliberalism ran counter to those of laissez-faire liberalism and socialism. Subsequently the instrumental ideology of managerialism, in supporting neoliberalization, ran counter to the ideology of professionalism that had justified extensive individual autonomy for service practitioners.

Cultural conditioning parallels structural conditioning in contributing to constraining and enabling influences on actors, according to the logical relationships between cultural components embodied in cultural allegiances and associated beliefs and value commitments, who else shares them or subscribes to alternative cultural allegiances, and the compatibility between the cultural allegiances of different groups. Some cultural allegiances may reflect long tradition, exemplified by the widespread belief that people can be trained as effective leaders; the UK origins of this belief in the military sphere reach back two centuries (Smyth, 1961). Others have emerged recently, including the belief that senior staff in public service organizations are, or should be, leaders.

Structural relations between people occupying different social positions may be variably harmonious or conflictual; cultural allegiances within and between groups may be variably consistent or contradictory. While each is relatively autonomous from the other, social structure and the cultural system contribute, in varying measure, to the conditioning of interaction. The structure of relations between social positions lies partly outside the awareness of people; they contribute, largely unwittingly, to its perpetuation or change (as with domination). Logical relations within and between the propositional ideas underpinning the cultures to which different groups subscribe are more likely to surface when cultures collide, but their perpetuation or change is rarely the prime focus of discourse. Together, social structure and the cultural system constitute ever-present conditioning influences on (but not determinants of) human agency, and its iteratively reproduced or transformed outcome.

The interaction of structure and culture with agency

Central in Figure 3.1 is present *social and cultural interaction*, where (separately analysed but coexisting) structural and cultural conditioning influences the expression of human *agency*, which is socially and, where reflexive and discursive, also ideally real. Agency is expressed through actions within the actual domain, and by deliberately withholding from action. We noted earlier how agency refers to the capacity of individuals and groups, as human agents embodying individual capabilities and coherent selves, to choose between alternative courses of action; they could do otherwise as they intentionally, or habitually, pursue their material and ideal interests. Much choice is made reflexively through the 'internal conversation' actors have with themselves: 'agents have to diagnose their situations, they have to identify their own interests and they must design projects they deem appropriate to attaining their ends' (Archer, 2003, p. 9). Structural and cultural conditions are encountered by actors with varied scope, but always some residual latitude, to deploy their agency as they interact in the present, reflexively or more subliminally pursuing projects to realize, or else sacrifice, their material or ideal interests, in line with these conditioning influences or contrary to them.

Archer (1995, pp. 258–259) reserves the term *corporate agents* for groups who are powerful enough to change structural and cultural conditions because they are capable of acting 'corporately' in pursuing their shared interests: they are 'aware of what they want, can articulate it to themselves and others, and have organized in order to get it, can engage in concerted action to re-shape or retain the structural or cultural feature in question'. Central government politicians, as elites or ruling minorities (Chapter 1), are quintessential corporate agents. Their authoritative position as the elected government executive legitimates their 'corporate' capacity to bring about social and economic change, including the regulated marketization of public services and deployment of leadership development interventions as an elite policy meta-lever. By contrast, *primary agents* are those 'lacking a say in structural or cultural modelling', whose agency is 'uncoordinated in action and unstated in aim', but who, when responding in similar ways, can still, collectively, 'generate powerful, though unintended aggregate effects which is what makes everyone an agent'. The distinction between those whose combined agency offers a basis for their synergistic power and those whose agency remains largely individual draws attention to groups whose latitude for agency is greatest and who, collectively, are empowered to make the greatest difference to society.

To the right of the diagram is *structural and cultural elaboration* of the pre-existing social structure and cultural system. It is caused by interaction amongst primary and corporate agents as the present becomes the past, largely as an unintended consequence that adds to the aggregate of consequences flowing from past interactions. The upshot of this elaboration may contribute to *morphostasis*: reproducing the social structure, the cultural system, and actors' scope for agency. Alternatively, it may contribute to *morphogenesis*: changing the social structure, the cultural system, or both, through changes in the social positions and cultural allegiances of actors themselves, as agents, and so their individual and collective scope for agency. The elaborated structure and cultural system form the context for the next morphogenetic cycle (indicated by the arrows cycling back to what is now the pre-existing social structure and cultural system for the next morphogenetic cycle), generating the possibility that, through a series of further cycles, the social structure, cultural system, or both may become transformed.

Archer's morphogenetic approach bears out Marx's (1852) dictum that 'Men [sic] make their own history, but they do not make it as they please; they do not make it under self-selected circumstances, but under circumstances existing already, given and transmitted from the past'. 'Making history' implies that human agency can generate social transformation, but this potential is inherently conditioned (*not* pre-ordained) by the consequences of previous history. There is a temporal distinction between social structure plus the cultural system, as the emergent consequences of accreted past interactions, and agency, as the present ability (variable, but always existing) to choose between alternative courses of future action. Moreover, there is a massive temporal asymmetry between the stretch of history culminating in the pre-existing structure and cultural system influencing actors in the present, and the brief timespan of their current agentistic action and interaction. The present continually slips away into the past and elaborates the social structure and cultural system, contributing to their eventual reproduction or transformation. This temporal asymmetry explains why, say, entrenched relationships of domination may endure even if subordinate groups do question the social position in which they are placed. Deploying agency to resist confronts the emergent power of dominant groups to maintain the status quo resulting from perhaps generations of actors reproducing the relational structure of domination. Present members of dominant groups may perceive this relational structure as normal, interpreting resistance as an aberration, deploying their agency to resist the resistors and enforce compliance. Social transformation can be a protracted struggle.

The morphogenetic approach provides a sophisticated metatheory for grasping how social structure, culture, and agency inter-relate within the process of social reproduction and transformation. It points to key constituents of social reality and the sources and dynamics of social causation to be considered in explanatory investigations of substantive social phenomena, including the innovation of public service leadership development interventions. So far, we have covered the context for this initiative, our references back to Chapter 2 illustrating aspects of the pre-existing social structure and cultural system that constrained and enabled scope for agency amongst government politicians and representative bodies for senior staff in public service organizations.

Indicatively, the structural relationship of governmental dependence on senior staff in public service organizations to achieve their regulated marketization reforms reflected the social position of each group in respect of the other as it affected the pursuit of this interest, or resistance to it. Influencing the structural relationship was the contingent incompatibility between the pre-reform institutional order and institutions underpinning the efforts of the past Conservative and the successor Labour governments to reform public services. The dependence relationship and the institutional disruption were both emergent and causal. We cited illustrative evidence in Chapter 2 that government politicians were aware of their dependence, prompting the endeavour to mitigate it through the national leadership development interventions.

The cultural system was characterized by competitive contradictions, as described earlier, between incompatible sets of beliefs and values constituting alternative economic ideologies and between the instrumental ideologies of managerialism and professionalism. But these ideologies may also be internally inconsistent. Labour government politicians' commitment to the 'Third Way' constituted an emergent hybrid ideology, combining individualistic neoliberalism, supported instrumentally by managerialism, with a more socially oriented concern for citizen welfare supported through public services provided, residually, through a public sector. Part II will address how these pre-existing aspects of the social structure and cultural system affected the scope for and expression of agency amongst those who mounted and responded to the leadership development interventions. The upshot of agency was to elaborate the social structure, cultural system, and scope for agency itself, with some aspects becoming moderately transformed through iterative morphogenetic cycles.

Explaining social reality: to what end?

Commitment to ontological realism prioritizes the domain of the real as the primary focus for investigation; its emergent causal properties and associated generative mechanisms are fundamental to explaining conditions causing the social phenomena to occur in the actual domain of events and activities, within their context, and to produce the outcomes they do. However, the unobservability of the real means that all knowledge of it is inherently a product of interpretation by investigators (including us), situated historically, socially, and culturally, and influenced by their ideal convictions. Epistemologically, how we can know what we claim to know is inevitably relative to this positioning; there is no way of producing human-free eternal knowledge. But epistemic relativism does not mean anything goes; the ontological commitment to a single reality, multiply interpreted, leaves scope for *judgemental rationality* (Archer et al., 2016, p. 6): recourse to the application of conceptual and empirical research quality criteria for weighing up the convincingness of competing claims to knowledge. It is possible to make relatively well-justified claims about the unobservable causes of observable events, while accepting that these claims are historically located, contingent, and open to change.

Given the construal of social reality as stratified, emergent, and causally influenced by contextualized structural and cultural conditions interacting with indeterminate agency, the domain of the real constitutes an extremely complex, open system of interrelated causal powers and generative mechanisms. Their expression is highly contingent, and the system itself is susceptible to external influences. Causal powers are dispositions or capacities which may be 'possessed with or without being exercised and exercised with or without being actualised' (Fleetwood, 2004, p. 43). Consequently, the operation of causal influences is explained in terms of tendencies: generative mechanisms may tend to bring about particular effects without always doing so. They may exist transfactually, as we previously observed, even though not expressed in a specific context. Therefore, it is impossible reliably to predict their expression in all circumstances, though some prediction of tendencies may be feasible. Far from pursuing 'thin' descriptive empirical generalization, the goal of critical realist research is 'thick explanation' (Fleetwood, 2014, p. 209): the elucidation of causal powers and interacting generative mechanisms; their contingent expression or non-expression in a particular context;

and theoretical generalization by establishing concepts and their linkages capable of contributing to explanatory insights about social phenomena across multiple contexts.

A twofold explanatory logic links findings in the empirical domain through to the causal powers and generative mechanisms in the real domain (Danermark et al., 2002; O'Mahoney & Vincent, 2014). *Abduction* explains the empirical by inferring the real, often when analysing findings from a theoretically informed empirical investigation of a social phenomenon in a particular context. This mode of inference facilitates conjectural insight, abstracting from the details of empirical description those essential aspects offering a basis for causal explanation. It entails asking a 'why' question: 'What causal powers and generative mechanisms explain most plausibly why these key findings came about in this context?' *Retroduction* elaborates on the initial abductive inference by moving iteratively between the real and empirical, working back from the initial inference to determine parameters of the structural powers and generative mechanisms operating in this context, and whether they operate similarly or interact with other mechanisms in different contexts. This complementary mode of inference asks a more expansive 'why' question: 'What are the basic conditions that made the existence of these causal powers and generative mechanisms possible?' The explanation built up in Part II relies primarily on abductive inference, as our empirical research was a first move towards investigating and explaining an emergent social phenomenon in a specific historical, national, and public service context. Locating this 'extreme case' and its legacy within a contemporary international movement in Part III allows for very modest retroductive consideration of whether structural powers and any generative mechanisms we identified could also obtain in other national settings.

Critical realism engages with axiology, the study of values, and the articulation of a normative position: a set of ethical values framing the purpose, focus, and conduct of enquiry and the communication of its outcomes. The role for critical social science was conceived originally in terms of *social emancipation* (Danermark et al., 2002), freeing people from forces assumed to lie beyond human control that constrained their ability to control their lives. Social structures and generative mechanisms in the domain of the real were a core focus. Since they are socially produced and create pre-existing conditions constraining and enabling agency, in principle they are capable of being changed through agency. Exposing relations of domination or exploitation and their associated generative mechanisms can raise the awareness of dominated and dominators–the exploited and exploiters–to the constraints these relations impose, to any false beliefs sustaining them, and to related injustices for and avoidable suffering of the dominated and exploited.

Complementary attention has been paid more recently to the ontology of human flourishing and wellbeing, consistent with the weak essentialism in respect of human embodiment highlighted earlier, foundational for a more sophisticated ethical stance. Sayer (2011, p. 226) points to human properties reaching beyond freedom and including positive constraints: 'we are dependent social beings, only able to live through others, and reliant on the care of others for significant parts of our lives. Further, some constraints, such as those of responsibilities for and attachments to others, can enrich our lives.' Implicit in this conceptualization is a softening of the conventional distinction between facts and values, while allowing for the complexity, plurality, and variability of human properties—a 'cautious ethical naturalism' (Archer et al., 2016, p. 7). Social facts are value-laden; concepts such as 'development' embody assumptions about what it is to be human and ascribe a positive value to increasing human capabilities by this means. Conversely, as Gorski (2013, p. 543) points out, '*values are fact laden* [original italics] . . . our values have an experiential basis' and are 'open to empirical investigation'. Efforts to express an ethical value (say, wellbeing) based on experience of conditions conducive or antithetical to what is valued may generate contrary unintended consequences (say, unhappiness), prompting a change in value and practice. Our research is emancipatory in intent and underpinned by a cautious ethical naturalism. However, we are acutely aware that raising awareness through academic publication is far removed from informing public service policy or practice, let alone influencing their trajectory to take an emancipatory turn.

A structurally based elite perspective on the dynamics of domination and change

The critical realist metatheory sets parameters for theorization capable of explaining substantive social phenomena such as leadership development interventions for public services. Our perspective is founded on the theoretical approach developed and applied elsewhere by one co-author (Reed, 2012a, 2012b). Focusing on elites offers a potent basis for explanation by conceptualizing the relative social positioning and operation of corporate agents since they, collectively, possess enough power to transform social structures and the cultural system. Keys to elite groups holding and expressing power are, first, their superordinate social position within enduring relations that characterize a 'structure of dominancy' (Weber, 1978, p. 941), conditioning the expression of agency through interaction as it relates to the social phenomenon at hand; second, more contingently, their promulgation of persuasive discourse to build and sustain cultural acceptance for this positioning; and third, the forms of power they possess and how they express it.

Our starting-point is a more comprehensive *structurally based* construal of elites than Mill's foundational definition (Chapter 1). Scott (2008, pp. 32–34) confines the term to 'groups that hold or exercise domination within a society or within a particular area of social life . . . the term "elite" is most meaningfully and usefully applied to those who occupy the most powerful positions in structures of domination. Elites can be identified in any society by identifying these structural positions'. Linking power as domination with elites as occupants of the most powerful social positions aligns with the hegemonic aspect of power highlighted by Lukes (Chapter 1): elite domination may rest on persuading non-elites to accept their subordinate position and internalize their relative powerlessness. The resultant cultural hegemony, or increasingly intuitive acceptance of a hierarchical ordering of social positions as legitimate, protects elite economic, political, or social advantage by normalizing the stratification of social positions and inhibiting the consideration of alternatives.

Additionally, elite studies have pointed to less hierarchically differentiated sources of power, notably *characteristics of culture and discourse* (Du Gay, 2008; Warde & Bennett, 2008) and *relational networks* (Clegg, Courpasson, & Phillips, 2006; Useem, 1984). Wedel (2009) has coined the term 'shadow elite', drawing attention to the growing range of individuals and informal groups, often with a business or academic background, who act as government influencers while serving their personal agendas. They operate within social networks on which government politicians increasingly rely to inform policies connected with the pursuit of neoliberalization. Nevertheless, those identified as elites on cultural or network grounds tend to occupy an elevated social position somewhere within relations of domination, and even combine roles as, say, a business executive or consultant and donor to the political party in government, or a senior academic and government adviser. Culturally based and network sources of power are complementary to structural sources, yet insufficient in themselves to explain how ruling minorities operate and are reproduced, resisted, or transformed. The power of persuasion rests on readiness to listen amongst those who need to be persuaded. The ability to persuade is favoured by a powerful social position within domination structures. This advantageous position helps to predispose others towards accepting the operation of corporate agents as ruling minorities. The more powerful the social position corporate agents occupy, the greater their power of decision over:

- whether to articulate where they stand and who stands alongside them (to build and sustain their cultural allegiances);
- what they say (the form of discourse they use to persuade others to back or minimally accept their position);
- what they do to realize their material and ideal interests (in acting to achieve persuasive influence over others);
- who they do it with (other corporate agents in their positional nexus or wider network).

We have seen how the most powerful social position within a domination structure does not wholly determine interactional outcomes, whatever the timeframe; morphogenesis generated by resistance or more subtle subversion are always possibilities, however remote, because there is always some residual scope for agency. *Subversion* may be defined as the adaptive implementation of an externally initiated policy to express contradictory values to those underpinning that policy (Wallace & Pocklington, 2002, p. 66). Senior staff in an NLDB may subvert the government policy to establish it through adaptive implementation, so its leadership development provision supports the service professional values of participants, partially contradicting the economic and political values guiding central government policymakers responsible for the policy. Domination is inherently dynamic: processual and, in principle, transformable. To grasp these dynamics fully, it is necessary to incorporate attention to horizontal relational networks (Reed & Wallace, 2015; Savage & Williams, 2008) into the analysis of hierarchical power structures. The relative causal weighting between hierarchical and horizontal workings of power may vary in different contexts. In our extreme case, the hierarchical workings of power featured more prominently than horizontal relational networks within the domination structure, its impact on the complex change process entailed in the introduction or reconfiguration of national leadership development interventions, and their outcomes.

Stratified relations between corporate agents and others within domination structures are *asymmetrical relations of interdependence*, reflecting the variable scope for agency possessed by all parties. We have recounted how government politicians depend on senior staff in public service organizations to act as conduits for reforms that their superordinate social position, as senior executives of the democratically elected government, entitles them to mount. Hence the motivation to mitigate their dependence by mounting or resourcing national leadership development interventions. Senior staff, conversely, depend on government politicians for the opportunity to participate in this form of leadership development.

Holding power accompanying an elevated social position is not coterminous with exercising it. Pahl and Winkler (1974, pp. 118–119) warn that 'to begin with positions and their incumbents is to risk building a conclusion into one's methodology. Alternatives exist—to start with decisions or the places where they are made.' They construe 'action elites' (Pahl & Winkler, 1974, p. 114) as those who *exercise* the power they hold over the allocation of material and symbolic (ideal) resources, within or between organizations. Action elites represent the subset of corporate agents in elevated positions within any structure of dominancy engaged in making and implementing major decisions—a key focus for our research. This standpoint aligns with Scott's stratification of elites within relations of domination, and their potential for holding and exercising power relative to other actors at their level and at the other hierarchical levels of a social or administrative system, from the centre to the periphery, with whom they may engage in the endeavour to control the allocation of resources within their jurisdiction. Scott (2001, p. 25) distinguishes analytically between 'strategic', 'intermediate', and 'local' elite groupings, according to their elevated social position within the domination structures in which they are embedded and its associated potential for exercising power. The elevated social position of interacting elites may derive from the same or different and sometimes competing domination structures, affecting the power held or expressed by each group in relation to the others.

Strategic-level elite groups occupy positions at the apex of political and economic domination structures, enabling those within or close to government to express corporate agency in formulating and executing policy initiatives across areas of governmental responsibility, including public services. *Intermediate* and *local-level* elite groups occupy positions at the apex of expert professional groupings engaged in implementing and operating activities and programmes flowing from, or allowed by, policies that strategic-level elite groups have formulated. Regarding national or regional leadership development interventions for public services, the main political, administrative, management, and representative body (or professional association) groups who may be identified as elite members include:

- Strategic level: politicians within the central government and within regional governments in federal countries, the most senior government special political advisers (SPADs), top-tier government civil servants;

- Intermediate level: directors responsible for the implementation and operation of national or regional leadership development interventions, executives of representative bodies for senior staff in public service organizations;
- Local level: staff in top management positions in organizations providing public services (the primary target participants for many interventions).

More structurally dispersed intermediate and local-level elite groups deploy their individual and collective corporate agency in striving to turn the policy directives and initiatives of strategic-level elite groups into operational programmes and practices. Intermediate and local-level elite groups generally have some scope for agency in pursuing independent change agendas that are compatible with the agenda of strategic-level elite groups. Where intermediate-level and local-level elite groups collaborate, their corporate agency in working to realize their shared interests creates potential for the mediation of directives or advocacy coming from strategic-level elite groups. The power of elite groups to mediate (Brunetto, 2001; Ferlie, Fitzgerald, Wood, & Hawkins, 2005) the practices and dispositions that others are inviting or mandating them to adopt rests on deploying their corporate agency overtly to endorse, accept, comply with, modify, or resist these invitations or mandates, or more covertly to work around, subvert, or avoid them (Spours, Coffield, & Gregson, 2007).

The analytical demarcation between elite and non-elite is clear at the extremes, but more ambiguous around the demarcation between membership and non-membership of a ruling minority. The concentration of elite research on the players with the greatest power of decision in any organizational setting has meant paying less attention to conceptualizing the status of actors who work most closely with elite members. They may not possess power to make major decisions, but they do have scope to shape and implement such decisions, and they may be aspirants for appointment to a future top position. We will label these actors as *elite associates*. Elites employ many elite associates: indicatively, at the strategic level, SPADs and senior civil servants; at the intermediate level, senior NLDB administrators and trainers; at the local level, senior staff in public service organizations who do not occupy the top management role.

With respect to public services, elites and their elite associates variably engage with each other within and (our main concern in this study) across service system levels. Individuals may operate between these levels, as where they represent an elite grouping based at one level in governance or advocacy at another. Indicatively, the governance of intermediate elites responsible for directing national leadership development interventions may involve contributions from strategic-level elites representing government and business interests, other intermediate-level elites representing the interests, nationally, of staff in top and senior management positions in public service organizations, and local elites representing the interests of their professional grouping in their organization. Elite members also interact with non-elites in maintaining the status quo and orchestrating change.

Scott (2008, p. 32) offers a typology of elite ideal types based on the domination structures in which elites are embedded. Two ideal types are most relevant to our investigation, where elites primarily 'derive their power from the discursive formation of signifying and legitimating' that justifies who is entitled to control whom and why. Here, elite power is based on the occupation of an elevated social position, as with government politicians, in contrast to the control of allocative resources through physical coercion or inducements (whether positive rewards or negative sanctions). While each elite ideal type is identified by its main source of power, elite members may also have recourse to other sources. Thus, government politicians might have recourse to negative sanctions as a form of inducement (exemplified by the Labour government's policy of 'naming and shaming' schools judged by inspectors to be failing—see Table 2.3).

Building on Scott's elite typology, Reed (2012a) distinguishes *authoritative elites* as ruling minorities seeking monopoly control over the *regulation* of major social institutions, including the UK state, and the welfare state within it. Authoritative elites frame legitimate activity within and between the organizations over which they have jurisdiction. For the welfare state, organizations whose activity is so framed include the central government executive based mainly in Whitehall, schools, hospitals, and universities. Authoritative elites make and adjust the rules establishing and maintaining a social and political order, pre-empting threats to its effectiveness and legitimacy or defending it against such threats. For public services, authoritative elite members are typically government politicians. They occupy the topmost positions of bureaucratic hierarchies coordinating activity within government at the strategic level (national or federal government), and possibly intermediate level (regional or local government). Senior politicians from political parties forming the opposition to the party or coalition in government may be construed as 'aspirant authoritative elites'. Authority within their political party may transform into authority within government if their party wins a general election. Authoritative elites play a central role in framing and maintaining control of *command situations* (Scott, 1996, p. 41). Within domination structures, the stratified configuration of authoritative social positions and their relationships within and between the organizations may become institutionalized as regimes for their governance, legitimated and accepted as normal, 'common-sense'. The stability of command situations remains inherently vulnerable to any emergent internal struggles between elite factions, alongside external challenge from other elites.

Second, *expert elites* pursue monopoly control over the means of *acculturation*, shaping beliefs, norms, values, and codes of behaviour. They either possess specialized political knowledge, as with SPADs, or technical knowledge—often organized into professional structures and practices—and predominate in professionally staffed organizations and associated networks. Expert elites relevant to national leadership development interventions include top government civil servants providing administrative support for strategic-level authoritative elites (government politicians), intermediate-level NLDB directors, local-level headteachers, primary care trust (PCT) and hospital chief executives, and university vice chancellors. The operational complexity of government and public service organizations requires a 'double reflexivity': the capacity of elite members for self-monitoring and coordination alongside reflective expert practice within their sphere of responsibility, often involving a coordination role. The theoretical and technical knowledge involved is thus highly specialized; it is rationalized into various 'expert systems' on which government and public service organizations increasingly depend.

Close relationships developing between strategic-level authoritative and expert elites as interconnected networks of corporate agents are fundamental to the holding and expression of power. These elites seek to legitimate their dominant structural positions, establishing governance regimes reflecting their interests by articulating persuasive 'moral vocabularies of discourse' (Scott, 1996, p. 44); some may form 'advocacy coalitions' (Sabatier & Jenkins-Smith, 1993) promoting change to realize their overlapping interests through innovations in practice. However, their relationships with expert elites based at other levels may be more distanced.

Elite uses of power to shape culture and orchestrate change

Significant for our focus is elite recourse to cultural forms of persuasive influence, whether intentional, habitual, or subliminal. Intentional efforts at persuasion work by attraction. As Nye (2004, p. 5) explains, 'soft power—getting others to want the outcomes that you want—co-opts people rather than coerces them'. Soft power is founded on positive persuasion, using means that may be acculturative, to persuade implementers to believe in the policy; financial, to persuade them to change their behaviour in return for a reward; or credential, to persuade them to seek this gateway to career advancement. Studies of public service organizations suggest that professional cultures are not reliably amenable to managerial manipulation (Ashworth, Boyne, & Delbridge, 2009; Case, Case, & Catling, 2000; Wallace, O'Reilly, Morris, & Deem, 2011). *Acculturation* (introduced in Chapter 1) entails encouraging a target group to subscribe to managerially advocated beliefs and values, requiring the group's assimilation (Berry, 1997) of the managerial culture, so replacing aspects of the group's existing professional culture and altering its identity. Acculturation is difficult to achieve, but the potential payoff is high. Leadership development provision designed to acculturate participants as conduits for government-driven reforms incurs this difficulty and potential payoff for strategic-level elites in government.

Assimilative acculturation is a co-optative form of soft power, as Nye implies. Selznick (1949, pp. 13–15) construes co-optation as a pre-emptive 'process of absorbing new elements into the leadership or policy-determining structure of an organization as a means of averting threats to its stability or existence'. He distinguishes two forms of co-optation: *formal*, where power is not transferred to the co-opted group and its members are confined to operating within parameters set by the governing group; and *informal*, where power is transferred to the co-opted group, enabling its members to join the governing group and contribute to shaping its operation. Conditions favouring a move towards formal co-optation are, first, where the legitimacy of a governing group's authority is questioned, generating a need to win the consent of the governed, prompting the symbolic inclusion of other groups that might otherwise undermine the power of the governing group; and second, where there is a need in a large organization, administrative system, or state to establish forms of self-government capable of reaching and influencing people across the jurisdiction, on whom the governing group depends to sustain its power to govern. Formal co-optation offers a means of extending the organization-wide or state-wide reach of the governing group, while 'preserving the locus of significant decision in the hands of the initiating group'. This assertion resonates with Mills' definition of elites, suggesting that formal co-optation is an option for those in elevated social positions within a domination structure. By contrast, where a powerful external group poses a threat to the governing group's established authority, the governing group may attempt informally to co-opt the external group, incorporating it into the decision-making structure. Pressure to avoid acknowledging this move publicly may arise where doing so might undermine the legitimacy of the governing group with the governed.

Our primary concern is with a form of strategic-level elite formal co-optation that we term 'bounded empowerment'. Formally co-opted self-governing (or relatively autonomous) groups do have delimited power of local decision, contingent on outcomes and the process of their achievement lying within the bounds of acceptability to the governing group. In Part II we will explore the extent to which the UK Labour government's suite of national leadership development interventions operated as an authoritative elite policy meta-lever, employing bounded empowerment to mitigate the dependence of government politicians on local-level elites. Doing so successfully implies a cascade of positive influence from government politicians through to the professionals responsible for providing each public service:

- employing soft power, via national leadership development interventions, to extend the government's reach by getting senior staff in public service organizations (as local-level expert elites and elite associates) to want what government ministers want; through
- acculturating them as leaders committed to acting as conduits for the government's regulated marketization reforms; so they
- voluntarily deploy their bounded empowerment as local-level leaders to take associated initiatives within parameters acceptable to government, that include
- acculturating other staff in their organizations as leaders and service practitioners to want what senior staff want; so that
- all organization members voluntarily endeavour to implement government-driven reforms, operate reformed service practices, and engage in ongoing improvement efforts.

A second form of persuasive influence within a relationship of domination is *symbolic violence*, entailing some tacit collusion between perpetrators and recipients. Bourdieu and Passeron (1990, p. 4) coined this term to describe the ability of dominant actors to impose meanings on others, often unwittingly through corporate agency expressing shared norms and values, legitimating these meanings by concealing or ignoring the power differential forming the basis for their symbolic force. Symbolic violence helps to sustain domination by shaping perceptions and expectations of the dominated, so they are unlikely to notice this power differential or else will accept it as natural. The focal expression of symbolic violence within our study lies in the pursuit by strategic-level elites, through the national leadership development interventions, of their material interest in acculturating local-level elites and their associates (including aspirants for elite positions) towards implementing and operating government-driven reforms. The target groups would need persuasion to participate in large numbers, since take-up of leadership development provision was voluntary. It was technically so even where take-up amounted to 'an offer you dare not refuse', as in schools, where satisfactory completion of the preparatory leadership development programme became requisite for appointment to a first headship. Persuasion operated through strategic-level elites creating (for HE, financially supporting) opportunities to participate in leadership development mounted by intermediate-level elites in the NLDBs, supported by the advocacy of representative bodies for senior staff. Together they appealed to the material interest of individual target group members in their self-advancement through professional development (acquiring professional knowledge and skills) and career development (preparation for possible promotion). The record of participation in NLDB provision offered target group members a professional credential, helping to improve their present practice and, possibly, promotion prospects. Symbolic violence here would turn on *misrecognition* by local-level elites and their associates of the power-play at stake. Unwittingly, they would be colluding with strategic-level elites by participating in NLDB provision to empower themselves as local-level leaders of and within public service organizations, rather than to become acculturated as conduits for the implementation and operation of government-driven reforms.

The acquisition of such valued credentials may be examined through the notion of individual 'capital' (Bourdieu, 1986), or unequally possessed relational resources that actors use to attain a social position. Three relevant forms of capital are, first, accumulated bodies of knowledge and abilities comprising *cultural capital*, often denoted by formal qualifications symbolizing areas of valued competence. The credential noted above that accrued from participation in NLDB provision represents one form of cultural capital. Second are social resources acquired through relationships, including networks, enabling access to information and other forms of support, constituting *social capital*. All participants in NLDB provision stood to develop their professional network amongst other participants and trainers. Third, where cultural and social capital are recognized and endorsed, they confer significant *symbolic capital* on possessors, constituted by their 'reputation for competence and an image of respectability and honourability that are easily converted into political positions as a local or national *notable* [original italics]' (Bourdieu, 1984, p. 291). The requisite recognition and appreciation of the other forms of capital gives symbolic capital overarching status as a 'metacapital'

(Swartz, 2013, p. 112), an assemblage of relational resources that its posses-sors may harness towards attaining an elevated position within relations of domination. Here, credentials acquired by participating in NLDB provision and extending a professional network might be interpreted by selectors as symbolizing sufficient competence as a leader to merit appointment to a more elevated position within the hierarchical occupational order of their service, or specialism within it.

Such forms of capital become embodied in the dispositions or *habitus* of actors (Bourdieu, 1984): ways of thinking and propensities to act that contribute to conditioning their expression of agency in interaction. Partic-ipation in leadership development and the forms of capital it confers has implications for the habitus of local-level elites and associates as leaders. It may even contribute towards a change in habitus reflecting their profession-alization as experts within an emergent public service *leadership profession*, overlaying their pre-existing habitus as professionals with expertise in service provision who shoulder some responsibility for the work of their colleagues. So symbolic violence operates where strategic-level elites persuade senior staff in public service organizations to participate in NLDB provision. For senior staff, doing so is a means of acquiring forms of capital related to leading, shifting their habitus further towards being a leader, and sustain-ing or acquiring local elite status entitling them to lead. But what they become responsibilized for leading is the implementation and operation of government-driven reforms.

The metaphor of *orchestration* encapsulates the dynamics of elite interac-tion entailed in the change process for implementing public service reform, alongside other agendas. This term is employed figuratively, in line with the dictionary definition 'to arrange or direct (now often surreptitiously) to produce a desired effect' (Oxford English Dictionary, 2021). The definition indicates that the figurative meaning of the term 'orchestration' has shifted to embrace undeclared intentions, ulterior motives, and covert activity, along-side transparency and consistency of intent, motive, and action. Our con-ception of orchestration encompasses this mix in the interaction spanning elites and their associates across strategic, intermediate, and local levels, as they broker the acceptance and implementation of reforms or promote inde-pendent change. Orchestration is defined as 'coordinated activity within set parameters expressed by a network of senior leaders at different adminis-trative levels to instigate, organize, oversee and consolidate complex and programmatic change across part or all of a multi-organizational system' (Wallace, 2007, p. 25). The metaphor implies overt, unobtrusive, and possibly covert promotion by elites and their associates of a desired change trajectory, within the bounds of their scope for corporate agency; they maintain collective oversight, taking corrective action as necessary to sustain or modify the desired change. Orchestrating the suite of national leadership development interventions involves a chain of elite influence from the centre to the periphery of the administrative system: strategic-level elites engage with intermediate-level elites to establish or reconfigure and operate the NLDBs and monitor their provision; intermediate-level elites communicate with local-level elites to encourage their participation and provide leadership development support. Conversely, each elite grouping has some scope for corporate agency within their orchestration efforts to mediate the influencing efforts of elites based at the next level up the hierarchical chain of influence.

Elite orchestration of a specific change may incorporate, implicitly or explicitly, some form of change agency. *Change agents*, who possess generic expertise in facilitating change, are tasked with engaging proactively to help bring this change about. Change agents are 'the individuals or teams that are going to initiate, lead, direct or take responsibility for making change happen' (Caldwell, 2003, p. 140). As agents, they act on behalf of change orchestrators. They may also act on their own behalf for initiatives they take within their jurisdiction. National leadership development interventions offer the prospect of building cadres of change agents, acculturated towards fulfilling their duty to act voluntarily on behalf of the government with overall responsibility for public service provision, now and in the future. The more extensively these cadres become acculturated, the stronger will be their endorsement of government-driven reforms, and the more their change agency on behalf of policymakers will coincide with their change agency on behalf of themselves. How achievable this prospect is will be examined in Parts II and III.

Looking ahead

This structurally based elite perspective, incorporating a sensitivity to network and cultural relationships giving social advantage, offers a theoretical orientation capable of focusing on the interaction amongst powerful players across an administrative system entailed in orchestrating complex change. Major leadership development interventions for public services mounted by governments or representative bodies of the target groups constitute just such a complex change across multiple administrative system levels; achieving our explanatory aim will require examination of the power-play and ideological motivations for the interaction between elites based at each level. The critical realist metatheory offers guidance on where to look and how to infer linked generative mechanisms promising 'thick explanation' through our empirical investigation, underpinned by the elite perspective, in Part II; it forms the basis for examining, in Part III, the wider implications of our extreme case for public service leadership interventions and variegated neoliberalization today and tomorrow.

However, there remains more to do in contextualizing this set of leadership development interventions, contributing towards our second aim of locating the UK Labour government's initiative within the wider international movement. Chapter 4 will explore the cultural contribution made by the discursive evolution of metaphorical concepts for construing the coordination and control of organizational practice within domination structures surrounding the emergence and development of public services. We will seek to explain why the UK Labour government became an 'early adopter' of a leadership construal aligned with the concern of government politicians to acculturate senior staff in public service organizations as leaders committed to the government's present—and maybe future—reform agenda.

4
The translation of leadership discourse to public services

In Chapter 1 we introduced the possibility that leadership development interventions may offer government politicians some potential as an elite policy meta-lever for promoting the sorts of leadership activity they value in public service organizations, dependent on context. The leadership focus of developmental interventions for senior staff in such organizations is comparatively recent, contributing to what made the UK Labour government's investment in a suite of national leadership development interventions so innovatory at the time. But why go for the headline concept of *leadership* instead of, say, management or administration, both long-established terms in public service discourse? What kinds of leadership were government politicians advocating? In short, where did the initiators of these interventions get their leadership ideas?

These initiators, of whom we will hear more in Part II, were senior politicians and activists within the UK Labour Party whose early ideas for developmental interventions were hatched during the mid-1990s, when the Labour Party formed the official opposition to the Conservative government. Following the election of a Labour government in 1997, the initiators acquired corporate agency as authoritative elite government ministers and expert elite advisers. Now they were empowered to consolidate their focus on developing senior staff in public service organizations as leaders within a strategy for promoting the implementation of their regulated marketization reform agenda and the operation of reformed services. In establishing this focus, initiators drew selectively on discourses conceptualizing and justifying forms of organizational coordination and control. They had been generated through an evolutionary process of emergence, interplay, and dominance or decline in use of successive key normative concepts across different organizational domains over many years.

Coordinating and controlling activity is both socially and ideally real, so inherently subject to multiple interpretation through language, whose concepts are themselves metaphorical—as with leadership and leading (Chapter 1). Each concept foregrounds some aspects of a phenomenon while

Developing Public Service Leaders. Wallace et al., Oxford University Press. © Mike Wallace, Michael Reed, Dermot O'Reilly, Michael Tomlinson, Jonathan Morris, Rosemary Deem (2023). DOI: 10.1093/oso/9780199552108.003.0004

backgrounding or ignoring others, with implications for the framing of practice and developmental support. Language usage within discourse is socially conditioned. Metaphorical concepts foreground aspects of phenomena that are germane to the material and ideal interests of their proponents, initiators of leadership development interventions included.

Here we build on Chapter 2 in exploring another contextual factor impinging on our focal leadership development interventions: the emergence of a visionary construal of leadership in the USA, focused on bringing about change; its application to public services, first in the USA, then in the UK; and its adoption by senior politicians and their advisers within the UK Labour Party, engaged in developing policy proposals in preparation for the next general election campaign. US academics and consultants have featured centrally in the elaboration and formal definition of terms in general use, culminating by the mid-1990s in the widespread adoption of a novel leadership discourse. It embodied what was then a revolutionary idea: building a shared vision to motivate and guide collective improvement efforts. Burns (1978), a US academic, coined the notion of 'transforming leadership' by adding the adjective 'transforming' to the metaphorical concept of 'leadership'. Informed primarily by accounts of famous political figures, Burns conceived transforming leaders to be those who encourage followers to transcend their parochial self-interests by promoting a collective vision for radical improvement and collaborative efforts to achieve it, driven by a shared moral purpose of pursuing the common good. We examine how this morally grounded, visionary construal of leadership was translated to UK public services, in line with the neoliberalization trajectory, supported by a form of culture management within the instrumental ideology of managerialism. The dominant construal of leadership promoted within the Labour government's investment in national leadership development interventions still prevails, as we shall see in Parts II and III; it is informed by, or otherwise consistent with, Burns' formulation.

Historically, academics have stimulated discursive innovation and advocacy through journal articles and monographs. Journalists seek out such texts and selectively popularize ideas. Exceptionally, academics may act as 'public intellectuals' and 'opine to an educated public on questions of or inflected by a political or ideological concern' (Posner, 2003, p. 2) by writing for a general audience. A minority of academics in the USA and elsewhere have long promoted their normative ideas on policy issues or organizational practices through popular writing, public speaking, giving private advice to elite groups as advisers or consultants, and commenting publicly on what they have learned from doing so. With little quality control of this discursive output, the classic role of academics and other public intellectuals as qualified commentators has increasingly been overtaken by that of the 'thought leader', conceived by Drezner (2017, p. 9) as 'an intellectual evangelist. Thought leaders develop their own singular lens to explain the world, and then proselytize that worldview to anyone within earshot.' Politicians are a key audience, seeking new policy ideas that serve their material interests while aligning with their political and economic ideologies. The proliferation of leadership discourse in public service domains, and its differentiation from related concepts, may owe much to the efforts of thought leaders.

Our argument is developed in three sections. First, we outline our theoretical orientation, construing leadership and related concepts as fundamentally metaphorical. Second, we trace the emergence of leadership discourse in organizational practice and related academic study, and its translation to UK public services. Finally, we consider its take-up by strategic-level and intermediate-level elites and associates responsible for establishing the suite of national leadership development interventions in England.

Interpreting reality through metaphorical concepts and their entailments

We earlier claimed (Chapter 1) that leadership and related terms are metaphorical, offering a simple proxy for the more complex entities to which they refer. Following Lakoff and Johnson (2003), we regard such terms as *metaphorical concepts*: mental representations connoting a network of non-literal meanings, structured by one or more metaphors. Metaphor implies the endeavour to comprehend one concept in terms of another. A concept from the more unfamiliar or complex semantic domain (the target) is illuminated through reference to a concept from the more familiar or simple semantic domain (the source). The concept of 'transforming leadership' is metaphorical, implying that 'leadership is transforming'. The target is 'leadership', referring to a complex, relatively ambiguous, task-oriented, group-influencing process; it is illuminated by the source 'transforming', implying a generic, one-way process of *trans-forming*, the irreversible transition from one form to another. Attention is drawn towards some similarity between target and source; here, between leadership and transforming.

However, thought employing metaphorical concepts involves creative blending between aspects of the semantic network of non-literal meanings surrounding the target and the network of meanings surrounding the source. The meaning generated does not simply aggregate the selected aspects of target and source, but is in some degree novel (Cornelissen, 2005). The metaphorical concept of transforming leadership creates a blend whereby the group-influencing activity of leadership is connected with radical change as the means for achieving this transformational end. An initially conscious linking of source to target can rapidly become formulaic with repetition, and so subliminal. The metaphorical concept itself may then become the starting-point for further metaphorical linkages.

The innovative metaphorical foray of Burns proved profound. Many metaphors employed in popular management literature are superficial, designed to create a memorable image. Thus Dunford and Palmer (1996) recorded metaphors connoting corporate re-structuring which ranged from military/violence ('killing field', 'biting the bullet') to horticultural/nature ('pruning', 'slash-and-burn'). These images are not neutral. By inviting attention to some aspects of the target phenomenon, they divert attention from others. Our concern is with what are (metaphorically) termed 'root' metaphors, more constitutive of basic conceptual thought than stylistic embellishments. Take the metaphor 'leadership is strength', implicit in the claim that 'successful reforms need strong, high-level leadership' (OECD, 2010, p. 222). The complex concept 'leadership' (the target) is illuminated by the simpler concept 'strength' (the source). The source highlights, selectively, aspects of the target related to individual leading activity (leader-ship, rather than leadership as a group phenomenon). Such aspects might include risk-taking, forceful advocacy, direction-setting, and close oversight of others. But the source inevitably downplays other aspects of leading (plus the contribution of others in the group), say, exercising caution, consensus-building, delegating, encouraging others to take the initiative. The blending of leadership with strength generates new meaning by drawing attention restrictively towards only some aspects of the target. The metaphor is also normative. For the author of the cited quotation, strong leadership means good leadership, because it will enable valued reforms to be implemented successfully. The 'strength' source highlights certain aspects of leading (itself just one component of leadership as a group phenomenon), such as risk-taking. It foregrounds the selected aspects connoted by 'strength' as contributory aspects of effective leadership.

This source has the antonym 'weakness', forming the basis of the opposite (equally normative) metaphor: 'leadership is weakness'. Now the value-orientation becomes negative: weak leadership is, implicitly, ineffective leader-ship. Yet, depending on the context, aspects of leading highlighted by the 'weakness' source may not be the opposite of aspects foregrounded by the 'strength' source. Consider 'risk-taking'. Its opposite, 'avoiding risk' or 'exercising caution', may not be interpreted as weak leadership where leaders face adverse circumstances. In such a context, risk-taking may be judged negatively as reckless, despite its association with strong leadership. The metaphors structuring non-literal meanings of metaphorical concepts may both clarify intended meanings and render them more ambiguous: when is 'weak' leadership wise under the circumstances, and 'strong' leadership irresponsible? Metaphor is so deeply embedded in language that avoiding it and the imprecision it brings is impossible.

We will use this perspective to explore how the metaphorical concept of transforming leadership embeds more than just leadership and transforming. This concept is further structured by the metaphor 'transforming leadership is moral persuasion'. The language of transforming leadership involves a net-work of metaphorical *entailments*, expressions from the vocabulary of moral persuasion including inspiration, charisma, vision-building, moral purpose, fostering creativity, and developing others. The blending of such entailments structures thinking, so subliminally or consciously influences action. In this case, there is nothing intrinsically moral about the entailment of charisma. But when combined with entailments such as inspiration and moral purpose, charisma contributes to the 'persuasion' component of the 'moral persuasion' blend.

Metaphorical entailments highlight some aspects of the target concept while downplaying others that are inconsistent with the chosen sources. The 'moral persuasion' aspect of transforming leadership foregrounds the attempt to exert normative influence within a group by referring to ethical values. It also diverts attention from the contribution of those who are subject to such moral persuasion: their engagement in what we might call 'transforming followership', where they are receptive to this form of influencing activity and both endorse and facilitate it. In Chapter 1 we discussed how leadership simultaneously denotes a leader-centric skill (leader-ship), a leader-centric designated position as a leader, and a cooperative group process. The metaphorical concept of transforming leadership is not *all* about the leader. Yet the metaphorical entailments of the concept encourage leader-centricity: giving differential weight to the leader-ship contribution of the leader, whether designated as such or not, over the contribution of others in the group on whom the leader depends to achieve some task.

Analysing the metaphorical character of leadership and related concepts enables us to examine their emergence, interaction, shift in scope, and domination or decline as forms of discourse. General usage is equally a starting-point for academic theorizing and for appropriation by strategic-level elites for their economic and political purposes. We next review the disparate origins of metaphorical concepts, their emergence within academic enquiry or consultant advocacy, their application to public services, and their transatlantic evolution from the onset of public service neoliberalization in the 1980s to the advent of the Labour government, as proposed by academics and consultants and harnessed by strategic-level elites. The resultant discourse underlying leadership development interventions for public services in England since the mid-1990s, including school education, healthcare, and higher education (HE), has affinities with leadership discourse elsewhere.

Metaphorical refinement: from administration, through management, to leadership

Leadership, management, and administration are not neologisms. Each has served as a 'term of art' (a word with a specialized meaning within a particular field) to construe coordination and control activity in organizations. Their meanings are relatively stable within a national context, though never fixed, and usage may differ between Anglophone countries. The Oxford English Dictionary (2021), or OED, attests to their long pedigree in the English language. Table 4.1 summarizes usages of the most salient concepts for our public service focus. All appeared in the lexicon of governance, military activity, or trade long before these phenomena became the focus of academic study in the late nineteenth century.

Early US academic usage of the term *administration* included implementing government policy across emergent public sectors, stimulating the establishment of 'public administration' as a field of enquiry. Wilson (1887, p. 198), who later became US president, defined administration as 'government in action', claiming (p. 197): 'It is the object of administrative study to discover, first, what government can properly and successfully do, and, secondly, how it can do these proper things with the utmost possible efficiency and at the least possible cost either of money or of energy.' His claim suggests that metaphorical entailments of administration have long embodied the twin values of public service efficiency and economy within endeavours to improve provision. The field of business *management* was becoming established in the USA by the early twentieth century, as professional bureaucrats increasingly staffed the complex organizations created by industrialization (Grint, 2011), with a dominant focus on business organization structures and processes. Perhaps the most ambitious early formulation was advanced, not by an academic, but by the engineer and pioneer consultant Frederick Taylor (1911, pp. 5–7). He asserted that 'the best management is a true science,

Table 4.1 Organization-related meanings and usage of leadership and associated concepts

Concept	OED definition of usage relevant to contemporary organizations	Earliest OED quotation	Indicative pre-nineteenth century domains
Leadership	The dignity, office, or position of a leader, especially of a political party; ability to lead; the position of a group of people leading or influencing others within a given context; the group itself; the action or influence necessary for the direction or organization of effort in a group undertaking	1821	government, military
Management	Organization, supervision, or direction; the application of skill or care in the manipulation, use, treatment, or control (of a thing or person), or in the conduct of something	1598	business
Administration	The action of carrying out or overseeing the tasks necessary to run an organization, bring about a state of affairs, etc; the process or activity of running a business, organization, etc. In later use frequently with the implication of being a support-ing or subordinate component of a system (rather than directing or controlling it).	c1380	governance, government

resting upon clearly defined laws, rules and principles'. As metaphorical entailments, 'laws, rules, and principles' resonate with the implicit metaphor 'management is precision control'.

The study of *leadership* as an academic field built on the work of nineteenth-century historians. The dominant conceptualization was leader-centric (Thomas, Martin, & Riggio, 2013), construing this group phenomenon largely in terms of personality characteristics or 'traits' of individuals posi-tioned as formal leaders. The metaphorical entailments of leader-ship were traits such as 'intelligence', 'initiative', 'persistence' (Stogdill, 1948), and, reflecting the (largely male) empirical base, 'dominance' and 'masculinity' (Mann, 1959). The underlying leadership metaphor was along the lines of 'leadership is forceful personality'. Stogdill (1948, p. 66) drew attention to additional factors, including 'a working relationship among members of a group, in which the leader acquires status through active participation and demonstration of his [sic] capacity for carrying cooperative tasks through to completion'. Stogdill's realization helped to stimulate more sophisticated approaches to leadership research (Northouse, 2019; Yukl, 2013), including a focus on the contingent effectiveness of the behavioural style expressed by leaders in different contexts in adapting to circumstances, rather than changing them. The underlying metaphor was more akin to 'leadership is a good match' than to the 'leadership is forceful personality' metaphor of the trait approach.

The translation of metaphorical concepts to public services

The dominant value-orientation originally shared by scientific management and public administration influenced practices in US public services during the early twentieth century, as Callaghan (1962) illustrates in his critical account of what he dubbed the 'cult of efficiency' in public-funded schools, whereby they were operated on business lines. But pursuing the instrumental value of service efficiency transgressed the intrinsic value of service effectiveness. This early experiment in public service reform dissipated by the 1930s, though the concept of management endured in the USA as a term of art for coordinating business organizations. Academic studies of management tended to imply that practices are similar in all contexts, generalizing theories and findings to private and public service organizations (Rainey, 2014). Public service management was thus widely construed as a specific setting for generic means of coordination and control.

The study of US public services shifted by the mid-twentieth century towards articulating a desirable relationship between administration and leadership. Illustratively, Appleby (1947, p. 95) claimed that public administration was 'not merely "management" as ordinarily treated in technical terms, or "administration" as ordinarily treated with only a slightly broader meaning. It is public leadership of public affairs directly responsible for executive action . . . in terms that respect and contribute to the dignity, the worth, and the potentialities of the citizen.' The underlying metaphor might now be 'public administration is leadership to serve citizens', with metaphorical entailments of leadership, here the direction of executive action and citizen service, creating the blend that constituted Appleby's expanded compass for the term administration as his root metaphor.

Academic study of public service administration and management was still nascent in the UK when the welfare state was established (Chapter 2). The terms administration and management had entered practitioner discourse in healthcare. 'Hospital management committees' were created as part of the original National Health Service (NHS) coordination structure; members included an 'administrator', and a national administrative training scheme was established in 1956 (Edwards, 1993). 'Administration' (a narrower conception than Appleby's) held two main connotations: administration *within* service organizations, the routine paperwork or 'admin' to maintain provision; and administration *of* service organizations, the local government or NHS regional or area body oversight and coordination of provision.

Interest in applying business management ideas to state-funded schooling grew amongst practitioners and academics when central government policy of the 1960s spawned 'comprehensive' secondary schools, of unprecedented size (Hoyle & Wallace, 2005). Initial equivocation over treating schools as 'business-like', reflected in the refrain that 'schools are not factories', gave way to support amongst senior staff, their professional associations, and academics, such as the promotion by Glatter (1972) of 'management development' for improving school management practice. Then relatively novel in business organizations, management development entails ensuring the sustainable development of effective management practice organization-wide (Mumford, 1989). Elements include selecting managers, identifying their development needs, providing a training programme, and succession planning to support their collective career-long development. Momentum for this movement in schools was directed towards school-focused development (Bolam, 1982), where school staff, supported by academics, experimented with pedagogic, curriculum, and managerial innovations (Hoyle & Wallace, 2014) during the twilight years of 'club regulation', with minimal government oversight.

The NHS saw the inauguration of regional in-service management training courses for senior administrative and nursing staff in the 1960s (King's Fund, 1975). A series of reports on NHS operation called for clinicians to become more involved in management (King's Fund, 2011), with the 1974 reorganization ushering in 'consensus management' through multi-disciplinary management teams. At hospital level, they comprised the unit administrator, director of nursing, and unit medical representative. However, the Conservative government's introduction of general managers in the 1980s (Chapter 2), inspired by the ideology of managerialism, prompted the completion of a discursive shift from administration to management (Learmonth, 2005): metaphorically, management is not 'precision control' but 'giving direction', legitimating practices to tighten managerial oversight of professionalized clinical consultants (Harrison & Ahmad 2000).

Similarly, in HE, occasional reference to management included importing business practices. Thus, Shattock (1970, p. 318) advised: 'Concurrently with rationalizing and realigning the administrative organization of our universities, consideration needs to be given to some kind of management development programme to maximize the expertise and effectiveness of the men [sic] who operate it.' An indirect impact of Conservative government policies was pressure to 'deliver' more with fewer resources, prompting a discursive shift towards management accompanying the expansion of 'manager-academic' and career administrator roles (Deem, 1998). Subsequently, hybridization continued with the proliferation of combined administrative and academic roles, including research managers and learning technologists (Whitchurch, 2013). Overall, the administration of, and within, public service organizations became increasingly construed as a component of system or organizational management, embracing the coordination and control of ongoing activities and change.

The emergence of visionary leadership

Back in the USA, intensifying global competition during the 1970s threatened business profitability. Senior managers faced the unprecedented task of orchestrating radical change connected with downsizing while ameliorating its negative impact on employee morale by fostering commitment to performance improvements sought by managers (Conger & Kanungo, 1998). One response in university business schools was to posit a role for leadership in addressing these challenges. Thought leaders included Zaleznik (1977), who, focusing primarily on business practice, opined that leaders and managers are different sorts of people, whose personality traits derive from contrasting life experiences. Bennis and Nanus (1985, p. 21) adopted a behavioural distinction, based on research into the perceptions of private and public sector senior executive staff deemed 'successful', encompassed in the slogan 'managers are people who do things right and leaders are people who do the right thing'. Management is held to be restricted to operational matters (consistent with Appleby's earlier usage) within the value-framework set by leaders, while leadership is driven by values underpinning the orchestration of change. Kotter (1988), another influential academic and consultant, conceived leadership and management more moderately as distinct processes, not necessarily expressed by different types of people. The entailments of both metaphorical concepts had long overlapped, but they were now divorced. Leadership increasingly connoted change (metaphorically, say, 'leadership is changing for the better'); management was relegated to maintenance activity, which included keeping on track changes instigated by leaders (metaphorically, maybe, 'management is operational control)'.

Times were also tough in politics, with the Watergate scandal exposing presidential complicity in bugging the offices of political opponents. Enter Burns (1978), bringing moral values to the fore, considering both ends and means of the influencing process within his conception of 'transforming leadership' in a radical departure from the prevailing adaptive contingency approach within generic leadership theory. Burns distinguished transforming leadership, the synergistic effort to achieve a collective moral purpose, from 'transactional' leadership: the more prosaic individual exchange relationship on which previous leadership theories focused. Transactional leadership occurs when 'one person takes the initiative in making contact with others for the purpose of an exchange of valued things' (p. 19). But 'the bargainers have no enduring purpose that holds them together . . . in a mutual and continuing pursuit of a higher purpose' (p. 20). The metaphor here might be 'transactional leadership is barter'. Leaders rely on positive or negative sanctions in persuading followers to comply. By contrast, transforming leadership occurs when

> one or more persons *engage* with others in such a way that leaders and followers raise one another to higher levels of motivation and morality . . . Their purposes, which might have started out as separate but related, as in the case of transactional leadership, become fused. Power bases are linked not as counterweights but as mutual support for common purpose . . . transforming leadership becomes *moral* in that it raises the level of human conduct and ethical aspiration of both leader and led, and thus it has a transforming effect on both. (p. 20) [italics in original]

So transforming leadership is more effective than transactional leadership because it is *visionary*, with potential for gaining the enthusiastic support of followers through garnering their commitment to achieving it (pp. 202–203):

> The birth of the idea or vision that impels the revolution and its adoption by a decisive number of persons are probably the most crucial steps towards transformation . . . The source of that idea or that vision in a leader, or in a small group of leaders, may be as mysterious as the sparks of creativity in an artist or writer . . . leaders must be absolutely dedicated to the cause and able to demonstrate that

commitment by giving time and effort to it . . . Too, the revolution, like all genuine leadership, must address the wants and needs and aspirations of the populace—motives that may not be felt by followers at the time but can be mobilized through propaganda and political action . . . there must be a powerful sense of mission, of end-values, of transcending purpose.

Leaders have primacy in determining the content of the vision within the moral imperative of addressing the 'wants and needs and aspirations' of followers, whether or not the latter initially perceive their interests in these visionary terms. Burns implies that all 'wants and needs and aspirations' can be addressed through a unifying vision that dissolves any incompatible interests, transcending them through collective allegiance to the shared moral purpose. There is an understandable appeal of a metaphorical concept whose entailments (shared vision, inspiration, moral purpose) connote that politicians and senior staff in service organizations can empower themselves to transform a nation's public services. They can hold the moral high ground while securing unified commitment to a shared, mutually transformative, political goal.

This construal of leadership certainly transformed academic research. Bass (1985) softened the distinction between transforming and transactional leadership, conceiving them to lie along an effective–ineffective continuum. What he calls 'transformational' leadership (the label that has stuck) lies at the effective extreme, and his addition of 'laissez-faire' or non-leadership marks the ineffective extreme (Table 4.2). Normative metaphors underpin these distinctions: altruistic 'transformational leadership is shared moral purpose' trumps self-centred 'transactional leadership is barter', and both trump laissez-faire leadership's dereliction of moral duty; its implicit metaphor might be 'non-leadership is anything goes'.

An adjunct was 'charismatic leadership' Conger and Kanungo (1998), more restrictively focused on leaders articulating a vision and inspiring followers to identify with it and work towards its realization. This theory draws on 'charismatic authority' as conceived by Weber (1947, pp. 358–359), where the holder of charisma is 'set apart from ordinary men [sic] and is treated as endowed with . . . exceptional powers and qualities . . . regarded of divine origin or as exemplary, and on the basis of them the individual is treated as a leader'. The basis of charismatic authority lies in motivating others to follow by fostering their belief in the leader as exceptional and exemplary, empowering charismatic leaders to wield influence; charismatic leadership *is* (almost) all about the leader. The implicit metaphor here could be 'leadership is attracting followers'; its entailments (special gifts, emotional engagement)

Table 4.2 A continuum from transformational, through transactional, to laissez-faire leadership

Behaviour of leaders	How leaders interact with and influence followers
Transformational leadership	**Leaders encourage followers to transcend their self-interests by embracing a collective goal promoted by leaders**
Idealized influence	Leaders are charismatic, act as a role model for followers, have high ethical standards that win them trust and respect, and give followers a sense of collective purpose
Inspirational motivation	Leaders communicate high expectations, engage followers in committing themselves to achieving a shared vision of a desirable future that transcends their self-interest
Intellectual stimulation	Leaders encourage followers to be creative and innovative, to challenge their assumptions and those of leaders, and collaboratively to solve problems
Individualized consideration	Leaders create a positive climate and nurture the individual development of followers, encouraging them to identify their needs and facilitating their efforts to meet these needs
Transactional leadership	**Leaders create situations where doing what leaders desire lies within followers' self-interest**
Contingent reward	Leaders offer specific rewards in exchange for the contribution of followers, negotiating what they must do and the payoff for their support
Management by exception	Leaders make corrective criticisms, continually monitoring whether followers comply with their requirements and reactively intervening after any problems have arisen
Non-leadership	**Leaders adopt a 'hands off' approach with minimal leading activity**
Laissez-faire	Leaders abdicate responsibility for the group, avoid decisions, give followers no feedback, and make no effort to meet the needs of followers

are not inherently connected with moral purpose. Yet both charismatic and transformational leadership theories are normatively concerned with the characteristics and visionary actions of leaders who are capable of 'winning hearts and minds', whether for reasons of identification or moral persuasion, so gaining voluntary support from followers in achieving goals set by leaders. The significance soon attached to visionary leadership in US presidential politics is exemplified by a journalist's account (Ajemian, 1987) of George Bush Senior's failure in this regard while a presidential contender:

Colleagues say that while Bush understands thoroughly the complexities of issues, he does not easily fit them into larger themes. This has led to the charge that he lacks vision. It rankles him. Recently he asked a friend to help him identify some cutting issues for next year's campaign. Instead, the friend suggested that Bush go alone to Camp David for a few days to figure out where he wanted to take the country. 'Oh,' said Bush in clear exasperation, 'the vision thing'.

The advent of 'the vision thing' in leadership theory resonated with the parallel 'cultural turn' in management theory: harnessing organizational cultures towards managerial goals by manipulating symbols to mobilize organization-wide support. Effective managers are held to create a 'strong' corporate culture using symbolic strategies: telling stories, relaying corporate myths and legends, celebrating company heroes and heroines (Deal & Kennedy, 1982). These ideas were elaborated by thought leaders whose books and presentations impacted on practitioners, including Peters and Waterman (1982), Here, culture is viewed instrumentally: a managerial creation, not an emergent feature of organizational practices (the basis for our ideal type of 'culture management' within the ideology of managerialism (Chapter 2)). The distinction drawn by Smircich (1983) between culture as what an organization *has* or as what an organization *is* encapsulates how the former assumption underpinned the cultural turn. If organizations have a culture, it may be managerially manipulable. If they are a culture, then cultural change implies altering the entire social construct that the organization constitutes, beyond the scope of managerial control. While 'cultural turn' consultants do not foreground transformational leadership, it is viewed as complementary to culture management (Peters & Waterman, 1982, pp. 81–84). Both transformational and charismatic leadership are centrally concerned with shaping the culture of followers; their expression in practice, therefore, constitutes an acculturative and co-optative form of soft power.

The academic and consultant Schein (2010, p. 3) asserts that 'culture is ultimately created, embedded, evolved, and ultimately manipulated by leaders'. However, the relationship between leaders and culture is dynamic and not wholly manipulable, since

with group maturity, culture comes to constrain, stabilize, and provide structure and meaning to the group members even to the point of ultimately specifying what kind of leadership will be acceptable in the future. If elements of a given culture become dysfunctional leaders have to surmount their own culture and speed up the normal evolution processes with forced managed culture change programs.

Beyond this nod towards culture being what an organization is, and therefore emergent in unpredictable ways, culture is regarded as what an organization has. Fostering a 'strong culture' offers a means of exerting normative control over employees through manipulating them to accept what might not necessarily be in their interest (Kunda, 1992; Tourish & Pennington, 2002). While not centre otago, Schein includes 'a compelling positive vision' (p. 305) amongst ways in which leaders engender cultural shifts to create 'psychological safety' for members learning to implement major change. The metaphorical underpinning for 'cultural leadership' is explicit (p. 3): 'These dynamic processes of culture creation and management are the essence of leadership and make you realize that leadership and culture are two sides of the same coin.' For Schein, 'leadership is culture management': metaphorical entailments from 'compelling positive vision' to 'culture change programs' foreground influencing activity that elides leadership with management directed towards controlling cultural change in organizations.

Figure 4.1 offers a simplified 'gestalt' of the shifting relationship between the three root metaphors in the USA and the UK from the 1980s to the 2000s. The double-headed arrow along the top of the diagram indicates our main point of comparison: the relative focus of each metaphor on generating and implementing organizational change (including radical transformation), and on maintaining the operation of an organization, group of organizations, or

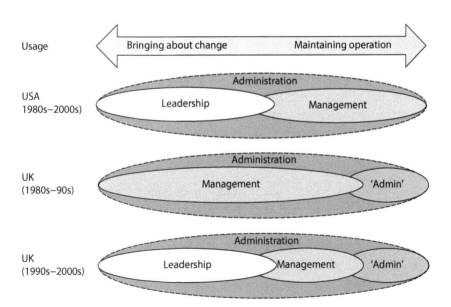

Figure 4.1 Recent evolution of metaphorical concepts relating to organizational coordination and control in the USA and UK

organizational system. The first row shows how, in the USA, the formal term 'administration' covered organizational governance and oversight, relating both to change and to maintaining operation. With the advent by the 1980s of visionary 'leadership', focusing on stimulating and influencing the direction of change, the compass of 'management' became more restricted to coordination and operational control. The second row indicates how, in the UK during the 1980s and 1990s, 'administration' was used similarly, but the within-organization variant 'admin' typically referred (as now) to routine technical work to maintain operation. Management still covered change and operation. The final row depicts the inroads made by visionary leadership, squeezing the compass of management in the 1990s, and so pre-dating the Labour Party's accession to government.

Visionary leadership enters (and distributed leadership emerges in) UK public services

The lower two rows of Figure 4.1 cover the period during which the UK followed the USA in adopting the metaphorical concept of leadership, with its novel visionary and charismatic entailments, in academic and practitioner discourse relating to public services. The central concern of leadership with bringing about change gradually resulted in management being confined to the maintenance of operational coordination and control, consistent with the formulation of Bennis and Nanus. Indicatively, interest in school leadership among North American academics expanded in response to marketization. Re-structuring initiatives extended school-level autonomy, steered by central government: Leithwood, Chapman, Corson, Hallinger, and Hart (1996, pp. 4–5) articulated the shifting compass of the three metaphorical concepts, also hinting at a need for leadership development, in noting how the new 'ideal educational organization' is

> less in need of control and more in need of both support and capacity development. Organizational needs such as these seem more likely to be served by practices commonly associated with the concept of leadership, as the term is used in North American literature, or 'management' as that term is used in much of the European literature, than by practices commonly evoked by the term administration.

The term 'leadership' and its now dominant metaphorical entailment of transformational change was increasingly distinguished from the more diffuse, less change-specific term 'administration' in North America, consistent with the claim of Appleby cited earlier. Research was beginning on transformational leadership in schools (Leithwood, Tomlinson, & Genge, 1996); its advocacy followed, soon reaching the UK (Southworth, 1998).

A challenge to the leader-centrism and largely one-way influence of transformational leadership on followers, initially in schools, subsequently in healthcare and HE, was posed by the notion of 'distributed leadership' (whose underlying metaphor might be 'leadership is mutual influence'). Years earlier, Gibb (1954, p. 884) had called attention to leadership 'as a group quality, as a set of functions which must be carried out by the group'. He proposed that distribution could be viewed as the aggregate of individual contributions or, more holistically, the pattern of combined contributions in fulfilling some function. Gronn (2000) resurrected this idea, allowing for a continuum between relatively hierarchical and more horizontal multi-way influence. Independently, Spillane, Halverson, and Diamond (2001) construed distributed leadership (in US schools) in terms of co-enacting tasks through contextualized thinking and acting amongst those in both formal positions and informal relationships based on individual expertise. Distributed leadership was viewed as being 'stretched over' the collectivity of actors involved, rather than individuals being conceived as leaders or followers. More radically, Gronn (2002, p. 429) asserted that distributed leadership was characterized by 'concertive action, rather than aggregated, individual acts'. Synergistic, combined influence towards a shared goal generated by concertive action can achieve more than the aggregated agency of the individual contributors acting alone.

Academic engagement with collective notions of leadership (Denis, Langley, & Sergi, 2012) and the related concept of 'distributed change agency' (Buchanan, Addicot, Fitzgerald, Ferlie, & Baeza, 2007) highlights how collaborative mutual influencing can maximize the potential for groups to achieve shared tasks. Literature reviews and research on distributed leadership have been conducted in school education (Bennett, Wise, Woods, Philip, & Harvey, 2003; Leithwood et al., 2007); healthcare (Currie & Lockett, 2011; Fitzgerald, Ferlie, McGivern, & Buchanan, 2013), and HE (Bolden, Petrov, & Gosling, 2009)—though a disjunction was found between the discourse of distributed leadership and hierarchical, siloed, or non-influencing experiences (Gosling, Bolden, & Petrov, 2009). Discourse and practice are not necessarily coterminous, but both transformational and distributed leadership are aspirational about the directions and sources of influence, and both conceptions of leadership have been available to inform politicians for two decades.

The tipping-point for the discursive shift from management to leadership amongst politicians and practitioners in UK public services came in the mid-1990s. Publicly available documents give a reasonable indication of how reference to management amongst key stakeholder groups was infiltrated by reference to leadership prior to the Labour Party's election to government. Conservative government reforms were still characterized by reference to management, reflecting receptivity to the prevailing business discourse. We consider indicative documents connected with school education, healthcare, and HE.

School education. During the 1980s, a national management training initiative for senior staff included an early reference to leadership (DES, 1983, para 83):

> Headteachers, and other senior staff with management responsibilities within the schools, are of crucial importance. Only if they are effective managers of their teaching staffs and the material resources available to them, as well as possessing the qualities needed for educational leadership, can schools offer their pupils the quality of education they have a right to expect.

The National Development Centre for School Management Training (NDC), a collaborative project between one university's education department and another's business school, supported government-funded training courses offered by approved universities and colleges. The NDC's project brief from the Department of Education and Science (DES) included exploring the relevance of management training ideas in business and elsewhere outside education (Bolam, 1986). The NDC adopted the broader metaphorical concept of management development to frame its guidance. A list of management tasks was generated for identifying management development needs (McMahon & Bolam, 1990; cited in Wallace, 1991, p. 28). Within ten 'management task areas' were two references to leadership: 'communication, organization and decision-making structures and roles' entailing the expression of a 'leadership and management style', and 'self-development', where 'personal leadership style' was a sub-task. So leadership was subordinated (leadership *within* management). Within a few years, the annual report of Her Majesty's Chief Inspector of Schools (Ofsted, 1997, p. 8) was to state:

> Issues of school management have been thrown into sharp relief by this year's inspection findings. Most schools are well led, but leadership is poor in one in seven primary and one in 10 secondary schools. The weakest schools are invariably the victims of poor management and weak leadership; the converse is true in successful schools.

The metaphorical concept of leadership was unelaborated, but entailments like 'poor' and 'weak' point to the normative reason for introducing the term. Leader-centrically, leadership was construed as the province of headteachers, extending in secondary schools to the whole senior management team and 'middle managers', typically heads of subject department. The report referred to a new national training scheme, the Headteachers Leadership and Management Programme (HEADLAMP). It was introduced in 1995 by the Teacher Training Agency (TTA), created to oversee teacher training and professional development in England, including headteacher training (Brundrett, 2001). The scheme's title now put management and leadership on an equal footing ('leadership *and* management'), consistent with usage in the US academic world.

The TTA had been tasked with developing 'national standards' for headteachers to frame new, central government-regulated training to include HEADLAMP for newly appointed headteachers, a preparatory National Professional Qualification for Headteachers (NPQH) for aspirants, and a Leadership Programme for Serving Headteachers (LPSH). Reflecting the managerialist assumption that 'business knows best', the TTA commissioned the management consultancy Hay McBer to conduct research on the 'characteristics of effective leaders'; the resulting evidence base comprised thirty-four interviews with reputationally 'highly effective headteachers' (Select Committee on Education and Employment, 1998 para 18). Reported characteristics included 'creating the vision' through 'strategic thinking' and a 'drive for improvement', and 'planning, delivering, monitoring, evaluating and improving' through 'transformational leadership'. In submitting evidence on the role of headteachers, a Hay McBer representative claimed (para 19):

> Excelling heads . . . create a vision, a very vivid vision, of what it is they want to do. They then move on to actually building commitment around that vision by involving people, the other teachers in the school, the parents, the governors, in actually planning for the delivery of that vision. Then the whole process is one of monitoring and evaluating of progress and then modification of the vision if necessary.

Headteachers choose the vision, then 'sell' it, rather than developing a shared vision through consultation, as implied by Burns' conception of transforming leadership. Discursive co-optation had occurred, labelling as 'transformational leadership' a practice that departed significantly from what Burns had in mind. (Implicit metaphorical entailments of the Hay McBer version might be 'leaders envision' and 'followers deliver'.) The initial version of the National Standards construed the key responsibilities of headteachers as five 'leadership and management' tasks (TTA, 1998). Leadership had entered the lexicon of policymakers, though its metaphorical entailments and relationship with 'management' had yet to become the new orthodoxy.

The term 'distributed leadership' did not appear, yet received brief mention in the revised version (DfES, 2004a, p. 9), where the professional qualities of headteachers include being 'committed to distributed leadership and management'. How such a commitment might be enacted was unelaborated, suggesting that transformational leadership remained the dominant metaphor informing Labour government expectations.

Healthcare. The introduction of general management after the Griffiths report of 1983 (Chapter 2) reflected the domination of management, perpetuated into the 1990s. Illustratively, a report foreshadowing the systemic reorganization of regional bodies for coordinating and commissioning local healthcare provision was entitled *Managing the New NHS* (DoH, 1993). Government attention to management training came later for healthcare than for school education. Local initiatives steadily expanded, one survey of hospital consultants reporting that 45 per cent of respondents had experienced management training in the previous five years (Horsley, Roberts, Barwick, Barrow, & Allen, 1996). Training provision often involved business schools as partners (e.g. Smith, 1992). The NHS Training Authority (NHSTA), established by the Department of Health (DoH) in the early 1980s, subsequently pursued the agenda heralded by Griffiths of engaging clinical consultants in contributing more to organizational management within the new regulated marketplace (NHSTA, 1988). Its proposals resonated with the NDC's promotion of management development for schools, the term now gaining currency amongst healthcare organizations (Loan-Clarke, 1996). Funding initiatives included inviting applications from Regional Health Authorities for development programmes, ranging from places on private sector-oriented business school courses to bespoke, context-sensitive modules (Newman & Cowling, 1993). Modest academic advocacy of leadership, directed at practitioners (e.g. Stewart, 1989), was complemented by reference to leadership amongst practitioners: (Rafferty, 1993) reported how senior nurses perceived themselves as having leadership roles; chief executives whom Learmonth (2005) interviewed in 1998 regularly mentioned leadership. Yet management continued to hold sway as the term of art.

Higher education. Management also dominated within policy documents. The 1992 Further and Higher Education Act that enabled a wider range of higher education providers to apply for university status made copious reference to management, none to leadership. Within a few years, however, the major review of higher education headed by Sir Ronald Dearing (National Committee of Enquiry into Higher Education (1997), p. 240) was employing the term, without elaboration, exemplified by the claim: 'governing bodies need to ensure that the vice chancellor is enabled to be fully effective in the leadership of the institution, has clear objectives and is held accountable for their achievement.' The Universities and Colleges Staff Development Agency (UCoSDA) was established in 1989 by the Committee of Vice Chancellors and Principals (CVCP), an advocacy body for vice-chancellors, to conduct research and promote academic continuing professional development. A UCoSDA (1994) report proposed the introduction of a national framework for management and leadership preparation and development. The term leadership was still an adjunct of management. Recommendations included the adoption of an inclusive approach to management development for all staff, from induction through to regular, career-long programmes for updating management skills.

During this period, academic surveys of management training provision (e.g. Bone & Bourner, 1998; Middlehurst, 1989) found the availability of opportunities to be patchy. In contrast to the comprehensive approach implied by management development, Middlehurst (1993, pp. 1–2) noted that initiatives were undertaken at university or college level and delivered by staff or external consultants. There was little needs identification or follow-up support. She raised the profile of leadership in her book *Leading Academics*, answering (in the affirmative) the question: 'is the concept of leadership appropriate and useful for non-profit, professional organizations such as universities?' By 1998, the research of Deem, Hillyard, and Reed (2007), noted earlier, was reporting how 'manager-academics' distinguished management (routine operation) from leadership (shaping change), consistent with emerging discourse in the other sectors.

Leadership discourse emerges within the UK Labour Party

Our illustrative sources highlight how, by the late 1990s, leadership discourse circulated through all three services, amongst both elites in and around government and public service professionals. In the preceding years, senior politicians from the Labour Party had attempted to amend Conservative government legislation, so were conversant with relevant documentation. Equally, Members of Parliament (MPs) and activists from the Labour Party were engaged in articulating an alternative political agenda, aiming to render

Labour electable after defeats in four consecutive general elections. Texts in the public domain illustrate the Labour Party's incremental adoption of visionary leadership discourse.

A school education example is the policy document 'Opening Doors to a Learning Society' (Labour Party, 1994, p. 3): 'Labour's vision is of an educated democracy in which good education... becomes the very basis for economic, political, and cultural success ... To achieve this vision we must start to advance the importance of education. Government cannot do this alone. What it must do is provide inspiration and leadership.' The Labour Party is construed as the corporate leader of nationwide educational advancement. Metaphorical entailments of (implicit) transformational leadership are 'vision', whose content is selected by the corporate leader; 'inspiration'; and 'leadership' itself, or, more accurately, leading. However, leading is to be hierarchically shared with the organizations promoting educational advancement: 'Schools must develop strong corporate identities founded on and supported by cooperative and purposeful leadership' (p. 10). The metaphorical entailments 'cooperative' and 'purposeful' are consistent with a truncated form of transformational leadership where senior politicians who aspire to form the next government, exclusively, provide the vision.

Labour Party election manifestos indicate how the discursive innovation of depicting government politicians collectively as leaders of reform emerged after 1992. Blair became party leader in 1994, shortly before the policy document above was published. The 1997 election manifesto, of which Blair was a key architect, suggests that he was instrumental in promoting leadership discourse. The previous Labour Party (1992) manifesto made no reference to a Labour government leading envisioned policy changes. Yet prior to the next general election, the Labour Party (1997) manifesto made 18 such references, employing metaphorical entailments of transformational leadership, including 'give a moral lead' and 'clear vision'. Documents proposing plans for specific services continued to convey the message that politicians in a putative Labour government would act as the corporate leader of nationwide public service improvement, as with healthcare (Labour Party, 1996, p. 283): 'Leadership. Labour offers a coordinated approach to the planned improvement of health, both in the community and at work.'

Blair's speech on school education delivered several months before the 1997 general election shows his commitment to this message, and to the corollary we highlighted (Chapter 2) reflecting the dependence of government on senior staff in public service organizations to implement its policies. Blair (1996a) implicitly acknowledged the contribution of local leaders when speaking of headteachers from 'good well-led' schools: 'While much of educational success can be attributed to the skills, knowledge and commitment of individual teachers, good leadership is critical.' Subsequently in this speech Blair positioned his aspirational self as prime minister at the apex of a future Labour government, leading the corporate leaders:

> The third component of successful education reform, after good policy and the engagement of the teaching profession, is strong leadership from the centre. This means the prime minister must maintain an interest, and I will, to ensure that when strategic decisions need to be taken, it is not just the education secretary speaking for education.

Following the Labour Party's victory in the 1997 general election, transformational leadership explicitly entered the government lexicon. An account of the UK civil service reform initiative launched by the incoming government in 1999 (OECD, 2001, p. 35) stated that the Head of the Civil Service's report to the Prime Minister that year

> called for transformational leaders throughout departments and agencies who set an example of the kind of behaviour required, work corporately and across institutional boundaries to deliver the outcomes the government is seeking, and who are able to articulate and gain commitment to a vision of the direction in which their organisation is heading.

Advocating that 'transformational leaders' across the civil service were needed to 'deliver the outcomes the government is seeking' reflects a stunted, instrumental version of Burns' conception of transforming leadership. The choice of vision rests with government politicians, not their 'transformational leader' government civil servants (seemingly construed, implicitly, as 'followers' led by government politicians). Further evidence is implicit in the quotation (Chapter 2) from Blair's foreword for the Labour government's reform programme document (OPSR, 2002): the government is responsible for 'providing an overall vision of where we must go'; civil servants and staff in public service organizations are 'the people who will deliver'. Senior staff appear to be construed as transformational leaders, but whose choice over the direction of transformation amounts to 'any vision you like, as long as it's ours'. If government politicians position themselves as transformational leaders exclusively entitled to articulate the 'overall vision of where we must go', then staff in public service organizations are subordinated as *transmissional* leaders—so, say, headteachers 'find themselves in a uniquely high risk position, piggies-in-the-middle between central government and its agencies on the one hand, and their staff colleagues, governors and other community stakeholders on the other' (Hoyle & Wallace, 2005, p. 136). Positioned as transmitters of the government's overall vision, staff in public service organizations are expected to articulate an allied organization-level vision and realize it through the implementation of public service reforms and the operation of reformed provision. Authoritative elites in the incoming UK Labour government pursuing 'the vision thing' through this construal of transformational leadership is not an inevitability. It is a choice of strategic-level corporate agents, serving their material interest in furthering the regulated marketization of public services and their associated ideal interest in brokering acceptance of a government-inspired vision for public service provision, underpinned by a social democratic variant of neoliberalism, and backed by managerialism.

Our account suggests that initiators of the national leadership development interventions obtained their leadership ideas from two main sources. First was their socialization into the discursive heritage of politics, embracing terms such as 'party leadership' and 'leader of the country'. 'Leadership' was already within the political lexicon. Hansard (2020), comprising official transcripts of UK Parliamentary debates, evidences growing use of the term 'leadership' by politicians during and after the Labour government's tenure. Figure 4.2 summarizes the number of times the word 'leadership' occurs across transcripts of the debates, year-on-year (except 2005–6, for which digitized transcripts were unavailable). This occurrence increased only slightly before and during the prior period of Conservative government. Yet during Labour's period in office, usage of the term 'leadership' more than doubled. Since then, it has continued to rise; leadership has become central to the political lexicon.

Second was the public output of academics. Intellectuals (most notably Burns) invented, refined, or remixed conceptual metaphors and their entailments; practice-oriented academics, often working as consultants and advisers, acted as thought leaders in promoting the operationalization of conceptual metaphors through developmental interventions or advocating their translation between countries or sectors (especially from business to public services); empirical researchers published findings on leadership and related social phenomena, often including recommendations to inform policy.

Other sources were more diffuse. They spanned management consultants, also acting as thought leaders, who popularized metaphors originating in the private sector, applied them to public services, or investigated public service practice as the basis for their advice; mass media output, including

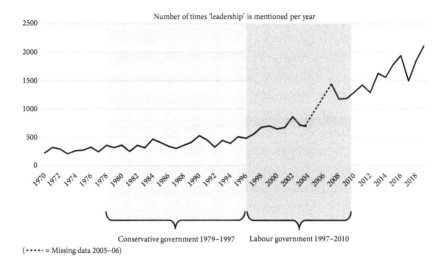

(••••• = Missing data 2005–06)

Figure 4.2 Increasing use of the term 'leadership' in UK Parliamentary debates recorded in Hansard, 1970–2019

political coverage and specialist newspaper articles or policy-focused programmes; and interaction with elites from governments of other countries and efforts to learn about policy initiatives elsewhere, facilitated by international agencies including the Organisation for Economic Cooperation and Development (OECD).

The content of discourses emanating from such sources incorporated the cumulative international legacy of the evolving interplay we have outlined between the conceptual metaphors of administration, management, and leadership, and their application to public services in the UK. Transformational variants of leadership proved attractive to senior politicians in the UK Labour Party, perhaps because their metaphorical entailments, especially vision and moral purpose, could be harnessed towards the public service reform agenda. There was little discursive evidence of distributed leadership, possibly because it promised less than visionary leadership for 'winning the hearts and minds' of senior public service staff (and government civil servants) for this reform programme and carried more risk of prompting concerted resistance by those whose hearts and minds had not been won.

Finally, we noted at the beginning of the chapter how experiencing and communicating about the socially and ideally real phenomenon of organizational coordination and control entails multiple interpretation through language embodying metaphorical concepts. Each term used to construe the phenomenon foregrounds some aspects while backgrounding others, endemically creating some ambiguity over the nature of the phenomenon itself. Our reliance on illustrative textual sources means our account can be only suggestive, but it gives a sense of how the leadership discourse informing the national leadership development interventions of focal concern represented the state of play within an evolutionary cultural conditioning process, by that time, and in that national setting. This process centres, first, on the unfolding interaction between the three root metaphorical concepts of administration, management, and leadership, and their respective entailments; and second, on the transatlantic migration of these root metaphors from the US and translation into UK public services. Emergent and sometimes shifting relationships of consistency and contradiction exist between these concepts and between variants of each, resonant of Archer's (1995) ideal-typical cultural relationship of constraining contradictions (Chapter 3): groups subscribe to a set of beliefs and values that at least partially contradict, prompting efforts to reduce cultural dissonance by reworking or trying to reconcile beliefs and values that sit uneasily alongside each other, so creating conditions favouring cultural perpetuation.

Here, the root metaphors do not encompass discrete aspects of the phenomenon. Management, long the dominant term of art covering coordination and control, including the 'management of change', has been downsized. Generating and implementing change has become the province of leadership. Yet ambiguity remains over the boundary between leadership and management. Is activity to sustain the momentum and direction of change to count as leadership or as management? How routine and modest must a change be (say, annual staff turnover) before it is construed as part of management? Different construals of administration, management, and leadership are not entirely compatible. Witness scientific management (metaphorically, 'management is precision control' with little consideration of the needs and interests of employees) and human resource management (focused on such needs and interests and their managerial manipulation); or, indeed, transformational leadership (metaphorically, 'leadership is shared moral purpose' promoted by the designated leader) and distributed leadership (metaphorically, 'leadership is mutual influence', implying equal ability to shape leading activity). To the extent that a cultural relationship of constraining contradictions does obtain, ambiguity over the compass and interrelationship of the root metaphors is set to continue, as are scholarly and practitioner attempts to rework them.

Taking stock (metaphorically)

Pursuing our first aim in Part I has begun to establish why these interventions may have happened as they did. Chapter 1 highlighted historical and constitutional conditions resulting in 'British exceptionalism', giving UK governments unusual scope for unilateral manoeuvre. Chapter 2 revealed how the interventions were prompted by the UK Labour government's welfare-oriented social democratic variant of public service neoliberalization, supported by managerialism, alongside acknowledged ministerial dependence on senior staff in public service organizations to implement and operate their regulated marketization reforms. The present chapter suggests that popularized versions of leader-centric, normative, and change-oriented academic theories of visionary leadership were harnessed towards the material and ideal interests of elites within the Labour government. The discourse of visionary, transformational leadership offered a means of acculturating staff in public service organizations towards, first, accepting the government's entitlement to determine the overall vision for service-wide reform framing their service organization visions; and second, committing themselves towards acting as conduits for the government's present (and possible future) reform agendas.

From the context of our extreme case, we will turn in Part II to our empirical investigation of the complex change process embodied in mounting and implementing three interventions for different public service sectors from the suite introduced in Chapter 1, their impact on senior staff from public service organizations, and the immediate outcomes by the time the research concluded.

PART II
'BRITISH EXCEPTIONALISM' IN ACTION

LARGE-SCALE INVESTMENT IN DEVELOPING PUBLIC SERVICE LEADERS

5

Investigating an extreme case: national interventions to develop public service leaders

Part I concentrated on contextual reasons explaining why the United Kingdom (UK) Labour government invested in mounting or financially supporting a suite of national leadership development interventions for different public service sectors in England. Part II concerns three of these interventions, examining how strategic and intermediate-level elite groupings, supported by elite associates, orchestrated each intervention across, and also within, administrative system levels; how the target population of local elites and elite associates received each intervention, and why; how the training and development provision impacted on the thinking and practice of senior public service organization staff who experienced it; and how far the interventions did operate as an elite policy meta-lever, acculturating senior staff as leaders committed to implementing and operating public service reforms, or generated outcomes that were neither intended nor appreciated by the architects of the interventions.

We first introduce our research, conducted in the period 2006–9. The findings will be reported in Chapters 6–8. In the present chapter we summarize the rationale, scope, and methodology of the investigation, and outline the conceptual framework for the study within our theoretical orientation, highlighting the heuristic concept of 'leaderism'. Relevant elements of the administrative system are briefly described: central government; the three national leadership development bodies (NLDBs) we investigated; public service organizations for which they catered; and representative bodies for senior staff in these organizations. The main elite, elite associate, and non-elite groupings based at each administrative system level are listed.

Developing Public Service Leaders. Wallace et al., Oxford University Press. © Mike Wallace, Michael Reed, Dermot O'Reilly, Michael Tomlinson, Jonathan Morris, Rosemary Deem (2023). DOI: 10.1093/oso/9780199552108.003.0005

The research project: developing organization leaders as change agents in the public services

The critical realist ontology outlined in Chapter 3 and our explanatory purpose informed the research design and methods. Inferring causal mechanisms within the contexts we investigated from their empirically discernible effects necessitated grasping why and how the interventions constituting the suite were established or reconfigured, were implemented, and produced the results they did. While unique in its details, this phenomenon exhibited features of other phenomena at a moderate level of abstraction, constituting an instance of complex public service change processes (Wallace, Fertig, & Schneller, 2007). To explore 'whys' and 'hows', we opted for the 'science of the singular' (Simons, 1980), a 'three-in-one' case study: the 'in-depth exploration from multiple perspectives of the complexity and uniqueness of a particular project, policy, institution, program or system in a "real life" context' (Simons, 2009, p. 21). Our case was extreme (Yin, 2003) in that the entire suite of national leadership development interventions was of unprecedented scope. We investigated three of these interventions, each orchestrated by elites and associates across (and within) strategic and intermediate administrative system levels, variably received by targeted elites and elite associates from local-level public service organizations, generating intended and unintended outcomes. We also examined a strategic-level initiative to coordinate and encourage collaboration across the suite between NLDB chief executives responsible for each intervention.

Positioning ourselves to infer generative mechanisms causing what we found empirically required a contextualized understanding of perceptions, discourses, and motivations framing the actions of elites and their associates with a stake in national leadership development provision. We adopted a qualitative methodology to explore the diversity of meanings, including interpretations of actions, connected with the interventions for school education, healthcare, and higher education (HE). Data were generated from two sources. First, an archive of public documents and webpages from official websites was assembled (Table 5.1). Selected items were scrutinized through critical discourse analysis (CDA) informed by Fairclough's (2003, 2015) approach. Second, four rounds of confidential, semi-structured interviews were conducted in 2007–8 with individual informants from different administrative system levels. Following preliminary analysis of the first three rounds, more than half of the senior staff from public service organizations interviewed in Round 1 were re-interviewed in Round 4 to follow up on emergent themes. Informed by the approach to qualitative data analysis of

Table 5.1 Documentary sources for critical discourse analysis, interviews conducted in 2007–8

Documentary Sources (1997–2008)	No. Documents
Government documents (central government, health, and education departments)	48
Government documents addressed to NLDBs	7
NLDB documents	56
Sectoral representative body and other stakeholder documents	17
Total	**128**

Interviews (2007–8)

Type of interviewee	Round, No. Interviews			
	1	**2**	**3**	**4**
Secondary schools (5), headteachers, senior staff	25			11
Primary care trusts (5), chief executives, senior staff, Professional Executive Committee (PEC) chairs	21			15
Hospitals (4), chief executives, senior staff	20			10
Universities (6), vice-chancellors, senior staff	30			19
NLDB chief executives, senior staff, commissioned trainers		27		
Other HE leadership development providers		5		
Representative body senior staff		18		
Central government politicians, senior civil servants			17	
Total (218 interviews with 163 informants)	**96**	**50**	**17**	**55**

Huberman and Miles (2002), interviews were transcribed, coded, and analysed; matrices were constructed to display comparative findings, and the dataset was scanned thematically. We concentrated mainly on the hierarchical workings of power, while also considering horizontal relationships within government, amongst NLDBs, and between NLDBs and representative bodies for staff from public service organizations. The investigation explored:

- the elite orchestration of interventions within and between central government and the NLDBs, and interaction between NLDBs and representative bodies for senior staff in public service organizations;
- the balance within national leadership development programmes between training senior staff from these sectors as leaders of change for government-driven reforms and for locally derived change agendas;
- any influence of the relationship between each NLDB and the Labour government on this balance;
- impacts of the programmes, or of the government-promoted discourse of leadership more broadly, on the self-perceptions of senior service organization staff as leaders and change agents, and on their local-level change orchestration linked to reforms or alternative agendas.

We interviewed senior staff from secondary schools, primary care trusts (PCTs), hospitals, and universities. Foci included the extent to which informants perceived themselves as professionals with expertise in service provision or administration, or professional leaders and managers, or both; whether participation in external leadership development offered by NLDBs or other providers had affected these self-perceptions; and implications for their acculturation towards acting voluntarily as conduits for government-driven reforms. There was no clear-cut distinction between senior staff with a background or present responsibility as service professionals or administrators and those with a responsibility as leaders and managers. Roles typically combined service professional or administrative elements with leadership and management elements, affecting the self-perceptions of informants as professionals first and foremost, or else as administrators, leaders, or managers. Our informants had variable experience as professionals with responsibility for some aspect of service provision, administrators responsible for supporting professional staff, or private sector managers. Most informants with a service professional or administrative background did not report continuing to contribute directly to service provision or its operational-level support; exceptions included Professional Executive Committee chairs in PCTs who were practising general practitioners (GPs), and several senior secondary school staff. Causer and Exworthy (1999, p. 85) contend that senior staff with a service professional background are 'likely to retain a measure of identification with the professional group'. It was possible that informants with a service administrative background might also retain some identification with both their administrative group and the service professionals whose work they supported.

Variation in service professional experience reflected sectoral differences connected with organizational size, complexity, and degree of professional specialization. All the senior staff from secondary schools had a service professional background as classroom teachers. In the larger and occupationally multi-specialized organizations comprising PCTs and hospitals, only a few senior staff had a service professional background as nurses or doctors. Two thirds of PCT and hospital informants, including the eight chief executives interviewed, had an administrative or management and leadership background. Several had participated in the general management training scheme introduced by the past Conservative government; a few had worked in the private sector. In the universities, large organizations featuring diverse academic specialisms, four fifths of informants, including the five vice-chancellors interviewed, had a service professional background as academics; the rest had pursued a career in university administration. Overall, two thirds of our senior staff informants had experienced past professionalization within teaching, nursing, medicine, or academic subjects, where their socialization as professionals had begun long before the advent of the Labour government. Most informants who had not been professionalized in this way had spent most or all of their previous career in the same service sector, administering, managing, and leading the work of service professionals. They had been acculturated towards supporting service provision in the social and political context preceding the Labour government's public service reforms.

The conceptual framework guiding data generation and analysis

The focus for data generation was underpinned by our conceptual framework. Analysis was abductive, moving from findings (answering our theoretically informed research questions) to inferences about possible generative mechanisms explaining them, revisiting and adding to the findings as we refined our understanding of the mechanisms at play in this context. The conceptual framework operationalizes our structurally based elite perspective on shaping culture and change orchestration (Chapter 3).

The framework drew on results from our initial discourse analysis of Labour government policy documents, confirming that this strategic-level elite discourse linked leadership with regulated marketization reforms for public services.

Within the context outlined in Part I, we focused on two analytical levels and their interrelationship: the framing of perceptions, and their expression within interaction embodied in the change process (Figure 5.1). First, within the *domain of ideologies and discourses*, mutually supportive or incompatible ideologies underpin discourses, construed as socially conditioned patterns of meaning-making through written and spoken language. These discourses

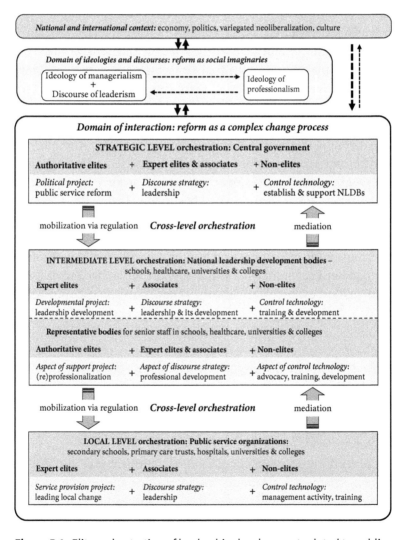

Figure 5.1 Elite orchestration of leadership development related to public service reforms

are articulated as part of the struggle to legitimate desired conceptions of leadership development provision, influencing perceptions of elite and non-elite groupings implicated in public service change. Each ideological discourse de-legitimates competitors, undermining their assumptive foundations and social practices aligned with them. Policy discourses generate powerful narratives to convince stakeholders that this way of seeing and doing is preferable (Fairclough, 2003). In supporting the economic ideology of neoliberalism (Chapter 2), the instrumental ideology of *managerialism* was ascendant. Its dominance marginalized the residual ideology of *professionalism*, once dominant within the Keynesian welfare state.

From our CDA early findings we identified an emergent adjunct of managerialism: the ideological discourse we term *leaderism*. We judged leaderism to differ significantly from other constituents of managerialism, warranting its categorization as a distinctive discourse, but not a new ideology. Leaderism and managerialism are equally instrumental as discourses, together serving the instrumental ideology of managerialism. So leaderism and managerialism serve the same ideological end of control over individual organizations and organizational systems, including those providing public services. Managers are valorized who act as visionary leaders to facilitate managerial control through nurturing and sustaining the commitment of followers. Consistent with managerialism as an ideology, generic leaderism is not intrinsically connected with promoting a view of the social world and how it should be. In our extreme case, authoritative elites within the Labour government firmly allied leaderism with furthering their public service reform agenda. But, in principle, leaderism could be associated with other projects, such as pursuing profit in business organizations.

Leaderism prioritizes 'leaders inspiring others in collaborative endeavours' (O'Reilly & Reed, 2011, p. 1083). It is relatively ambiguous about who count as leaders, and so whose interests are served. In its combination of transformational and distributed elements (Chapter 4), leaderism resonates with hierarchically distributed transmissional leadership, where the dominant social positioning of government elites accords them exclusive scope for choosing a vision. Leaderism may be defined as:

A belief in elite systemic direction-setting through a hierarchically distributed pattern of persuasive influence, nurturing cultural change necessary for dissolving incompatible interests by fostering the collective pursuit of goals to realize an elite vision for improvement that becomes accepted as in the interests of all, and subordinating any sectional interests-at-hand that are incompatible with this vision.

The discourse of leaderism extends beyond organizations to societal institutions, including government and administrative systems, notably those for public services. Here leaderism is equally instrumental in serving elite control of policy, as a foundation for legitimating the command situation where authoritative elite political leaders exercise their entitlement to set the course for reform and service organization leaders implement reforms and operate reformed services. Service organization leaders, in the process, engage with their staff and representatives of service user groups, who increasingly contribute to leading local provision. So, potentially, leaderism could be harnessed towards the expression of different political, economic, or social ideologies, whether across an administrative system or throughout society. In our extreme case, leaderism as an ideological discourse legitimated strategic-level elites in and around government acting as 'leaders of the system' within command situations, entitled to choose the vision for public service improvement according to their economic and political beliefs and values. Intermediate and local-level elites were subordinated as 'leaders within the system', expected to generate a jurisdictional vision consistent with the governmental vision.

The hierarchical distinction between leaders of and within the system, implicit in the quotation in Chapter 2 taken from a government pamphlet (OPSR, 2002), is made explicit in another government source: 'Political, not public service, leaders establish values. Official leaders then interpret underlying values in the context of their organizations—and in the light of long-standing public service values based around the desire to serve' (Performance and Innovation Unit, 2001, p. 30). Leaderism legitimates the instrumental promotion of visionary discourses associated with economic and political ideologies to convince stakeholders that a particular way of seeing and doing is preferable. They include new *social imaginaries*, 'representations of how things are or might or could be' (Fairclough, 2003, p. 207) that 'set the common-sense "background" of lived social experience' (Taylor, 2004, p. 23). Social imaginaries come to be taken as self-evident. They eventually become subliminal, no longer reflexively defended in the way that the ideology underlying a social imaginary might be.

Second, within the *domain of interaction*, three interrelated concepts capture the complexities of generating system-wide change through developing leadership capacity to promote or mediate government-driven reform (Deem, Hillyard, & Reed, 2007; Reed, 2002). At the strategic level, the Labour government's engagement in public service reform is construed as a *political project* informed by managerialism, leaderism, related technocratic New Public Management (NPM) policies, and, latterly, a reworked and co-optative form of professionalism. It is coupled with a *discourse strategy* to shape thinking and values about leadership through persuasive spoken language and written texts, and a loose configuration of *control technologies* for translating political aspiration and discursive intent into practice. They include interventions incorporating an NLDB, operating mainly through the 'culture management' form of managerialism. They promote one-way, co-optative *acculturation*: manipulating organizational and professional cultures of participants so they assimilate beliefs and values favouring their commitment to the goals of acculturators. Yet this is merely formal co-optation (Chapter 3): senior staff in public service organizations are contingently empowered to spread the government determined vision and associated or otherwise compatible practices (not to influence the content of that vision or the parameters for its implementation and operation, as informal co-optation would imply).

At the intermediate level, officials from NLDBs and representative bodies for senior staff from public service organizations are each construed as pursuing their own project, supported by their discourse strategy and associated control technology. The NLDB brief frames the project of officials as *developmental*: building leadership capacity by acculturating participants as leaders; articulating a discourse strategy focused on leadership and ways of developing this capacity for leading activity; and operationalizing the project through the control technology of NLDB training and complementary development activities.

The representative bodies relevant to our focus serve the material interests of their members: senior staff from different expert professional and administrative groups in public service organizations. The project of representative bodies is to *support* members; it includes promoting their interest in being treated as professionals. This support project entails the reprofessionalization, as leaders, of members who are already trained and experienced public service professionals (teachers, doctors, and academics who aspire to become headteachers, clinical managers, and vice chancellors respectively). It also encompasses the professionalization, as public service leaders, of members without a frontline service professional background (school business managers, general managers in healthcare, university and college administrators). For simplicity, we refer generically to 'professionalization as leaders', embracing both reprofessionalization and first-time professionalization. Support relates to conditions of work and remuneration; political and public recognition; the entitlement to professional development support relating to responsibilities and aspirations as leaders; and the accreditation of learning and the achievement of performance standards advantageous for individual career enhancement, contributing to the accrual of more cultural capital. Professionalization requires its articulation within the discourse strategy employed by representative bodies, promoting the professional development of members as leaders. It is operationalized through advocacy as a control technology, including attempts to influence the appropriate NLDB and, sometimes, a representative body's own leadership development provision for its members.

At the local level, senior public service organization staff participating in NLDB programmes are construed as pursuing a project linked to their role in *service provision* within their organizational jurisdiction. Their project variably employs a discourse strategy legitimating their actions as leaders of or within this jurisdiction, and a control technology comprising their own leading and management activity (whether linked to government-driven reforms or to other change agendas). They may also enable their colleague staff to access training opportunities.

Mounting national interventions to build leadership capacity for facilitating public service reform is framed as a complex, administrative system-wide change process. Strategic-level elite orchestration of this change within government and its agencies shapes the form each national leadership development intervention takes for a public service sector, and its relationship with other interventions in the suite. Complementary cross-level orchestration *mobilizes* the efforts of staff in NLDBs based at the intermediate level through regulation, variably spanning their brief, staffing, resource allocation, and evaluation.

Intermediate-level elite orchestration within NLDBs entails planning and implementing leadership development provision, plus engaging with representative bodies for senior staff in public service organizations. Orchestration activity between individual NLDBs contributes to their evolving interrelationship, and so to the suite of interventions. Elites in and around NLDBs may have some capacity for orchestration activity that *mediates* the practices and beliefs envisaged by strategic-level elites for developing the capacity for leading reform by modifying or subverting them (Chapter 3). Orchestration of this change within the intermediate level is complemented by cross-level orchestration to *mobilize* senior public service organization staff and 'middle managers' through their co-optative acculturation as local-level leaders acting as change agents for reform, and maybe also for local agendas.

Local-level orchestration of related change activity is the province of senior staff from public service organizations, who *mobilize* the efforts of other staff, and maybe community members, within their jurisdiction. They may also have variable capacity for orchestration activity that *mediates* the sort of leading activity that they are encouraged by intermediate-level NLDB staff and trainers to implement in their workplace.

Elites and their associates based at different system levels make distinct contributions to orchestrating the change embodied in building leadership capacity for public service reform. They broker its cultural acceptance and implementation, while possibly promoting change agency for local agendas. They steer the brokering process and mediate the change as it interacts with ideologically framed discourses and institutionalized practices, reflecting their professional and organizational cultures. The arrows in Figure 5.1 highlight the main directions of influence we investigated:

- The largely one-way impact of contextual factors on the domain of ideologies and discourses, comprising the prevailing ideology of managerialism and emergent discourse of leaderism, and their coexistence in competitive contradiction with the residual ideology of professionalism, eventually bringing its partial reformulation.
- Elite orchestration of the reform process within the domain of interaction: across administrative system levels from central government; through NLDBs in liaison with representative bodies of senior staff in public service organizations within the selected services; to senior staff who did or did not participate in NLDB provision. The flow of elite and elite associate influence was potentially reciprocal: 'top-down' mobilization of change through governmental regulation and the attempted acculturation of senior public service organization staff through NLDBs; 'bottom-up' mediation of this change, both by NLDB senior staff within the parameters set by regulation and by senior staff in public service organizations experiencing this provision who might not become acculturated as change agents for government-driven reforms.
- The flow of influence between the domain of ideologies and discourses and the domain of interaction connected with the promotion and enactment of leaderism, and its impact on the perceptions of those targeted and on their allegiance to some form of professionalism.

Mounting the national leadership development interventions: organizations, interactions, elites

Figure 5.2 depicts the organizations and flows of interaction involved in mounting and operating the national leadership development interventions. Each NLDB was located at the intermediate level within the hierarchically ordered structure of political and economic domination (Chapter 3), coincident with the three administrative system levels. The National College for School Leadership (NCSL) and National Health Service Institute for Innovation and Improvement (NHSIII) were wholly dependent on, respectively, the strategic-level government education and health departments responsible for their creation and funding. The most senior government ministers for these departments were members of the Prime Minister's Cabinet, involved in articulating their departmental priorities with the overall government strategy. The Cabinet Office was responsible for supporting the Prime Minister and the Cabinet with inter-departmental priorities, including public service improvement. Various specialist units supported Cabinet committees responsible for coordinating work in other departments contributing to the achievement of the government's objectives. The Leadership Foundation for Higher Education (LFHE) dependencies were more complex.

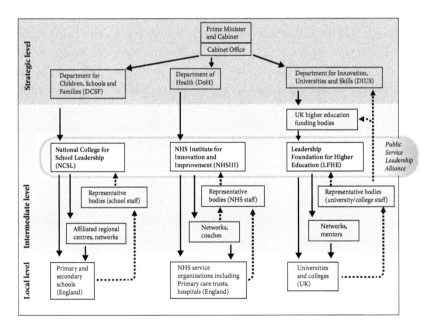

Figure 5.2 Administrative system and flows of interaction related to NLDBs for schools, healthcare, universities and colleges (2007)

They comprised the two representative bodies for universities and colleges responsible for conceiving the LFHE and retaining oversight Universities UK (UUK) and the successor to the Standing Conference of Principals (SCOP), GuildHE; the government department responsible for universities, initially the Department for Education and Science (DfES) and, from 2007, the newly created Department for Innovation, Universities and Skills (DIUS); and the HE funding bodies comprising the Higher Education Funding Council for England (HEFCE) and its equivalents for Wales, Scotland, and Northern Ireland, with each contributing to the allocation of this funding via HEFCE.

All three NLDBs fostered the development of senior staff networks, thereby contributing to the social capital of participants. Contracted trainers in nine regional centres provided NCSL training programmes, while the NHSIII and LFHE had established a cadre of coaches or mentors whom senior staff could consult. The NLDBs depended on attracting enough senior staff from public service organizations to take up the provision on offer. Representative bodies for senior staff in each public service sector liaised with NLDB officials to ensure that provision aligned with the expectations and perceived needs of their members. While establishing or reconfiguring each NLDB involved the relevant government department, an informal networking forum for NLDB chief executives was inaugurated by the government's Cabinet Office to share good practice, promote collaboration, and explore possibilities for greater efficiencies and avoidance of duplicated provision. Figure 5.2 highlights how this forum was formalized as the Public Service Leadership Alliance (PSLA). Responsibility for PSLA facilitation was delegated to senior staff from the National School of Government, the NLDB for the government civil service.

The main elite groupings relevant to our research focus were based in the organizations described. Table 5.2 categorizes individuals in these organizations according to three hierarchical orders of authority accompanying their formal position within the organization (based on the typology introduced in Chapter 3). Uppermost are members of authoritative or expert elites, occupying a top executive role. In each case, the role intrinsically entails responsibility for making major decisions affecting the whole jurisdiction or organization, including resource allocation. These elite members are supported by their most senior staff, next in the hierarchy, conceived as elite associates, and, below them hierarchically, by non-elite staff. The shaded elite, elite associate, or non-elite groups indicate the elite-linked status of individuals whom we were able to interview within each rung of the hierarchy. In line with our elite perspective, we interviewed occupants of top and senior formal positions in their organizations, plus non-elite trainers contracted by NLDBs to provide leadership development programmes or other activities.

Table 5.2 Elite groups relevant to national leadership development body operation, status of informants interviewed [*]

Administrative system level, organizations, and groups	Authoritative elites	Expert elites	Expert elite associates	Non-elites
STRATEGIC				
Prime Minister, Cabinet Office	**Prime Minister, Cabinet Office Minister**	**Top civil servants, political advisers**	Senior civil servants	Civil servants
DfEE (1995–2001) DfES (2001–7) DCSF (2007–10) DoH (1988–) DIUS (2007–10)	**Secretary of State and other departmental ministers**	**Top civil servants, political advisers**	Senior civil servants	Civil servants
Leader of the Opposition and shadow ministers	*(Elite aspirants)*			

Administrative system level, organizations, and groups	**Expert elites**	Expert elite associates	Non-elites
INTERMEDIATE			
Higher education funding bodies, including HEFCE	**Chief executive**	Senior administrators	Administrators
NCSL NHSIII LFHE	**Chief executive**	Senior staff	Associated trainers
Representative bodies for public service organization senior staff	**General secretary**	Senior officials	Officials
LOCAL			
Secondary schools	**Headteacher**	Deputy heads, assistant deputies	Teaching staff
Primary Care Trusts	**Chief executive**	Executive and clinical directors	Other PCT staff
Hospitals	**Chief executive**	Executive and clinical directors	Other hospital staff
Universities	**Vice chancellor**	Deputy VCs, pro-VCs, senior administrators	Academics, administrators

[*] Shaded groups = one or more informants interviewed either was, or had been, within the group

Next, we begin our account of findings from our research evidencing the Labour government's rationale for its novel investment in national leadership development interventions for each public service, and specifically for school education, healthcare, and HE. We then examine how elites and their associates in and around government, and their counterparts from representative bodies for senior staff in HE, orchestrated the establishment or reconfiguration of the NLDBs operating in 2007. These results are the starting-point for our abductive explanation of why and how the unprecedented suite of national leadership development interventions was mounted, setting the stage for reporting further findings on the orchestration of leadership development provision within the three NLDBs and the response of senior staff from public service organizations.

Keeping track of contextual factors, generative mechanisms, and direct and indirect outcomes

A reminder of our 'spoiler alert' (Chapter 1) introducing Appendix 1: the schematic summary provides a visual reference point to aid in following our cumulative explanatory account of our empirical findings in the next chapter and the rest of Part II, and in exploring their more diffuse and speculative impact on contemporary leadership development interventions and contribution to wider social change in Part III.

6

Elite orchestration of national leadership development interventions for public services

Why, and how, did the United Kingdom (UK) Labour government mount interventions for different public service sectors, or otherwise financially support representative bodies for senior staff in public service organizations in mounting their own intervention? A major economic factor (Chapter 2) was the ideological commitment of authoritative elites within the Labour government to a social democratic form of variegated neoliberalization, supported by managerialism, that framed the political project of public service reform entailing new regulated marketization policies. Indicative documentary sources suggest that the interventions were motivated by a quest to mitigate governmental dependence on senior staff in public service organizations to put its reform policies into practice. In our terms, these interventions constituted a control technology capable of acculturating senior staff as local-level leaders committed to acting as government 'change agents', spearheading the reforms within their organization and local community. Chapter 4 traced the emergence of a conceptual factor: a visionary, explicitly transformational but implicitly transmissional, leader-centric conception of leadership. Our empirical research sought a fuller answer to 'why' through a critical analysis of relevant discourse expressed in government documents; and to 'how', focusing on the strategic-level orchestration of the interventions, through interviews with members of authoritative and expert elites and their associates.

We concentrate on the linkage between two components of our conceptual framework (Chapter 5, Figure 5.1): the domain of ideologies and discourses and the domain of interaction at the strategic level within central government (plus cross-level orchestration between the intermediate and strategic levels with the intervention for higher education (HE)). First, we examine how central government elites and associates construed their political project

Developing Public Service Leaders. Wallace et al., Oxford University Press. © Mike Wallace, Michael Reed, Dermot O'Reilly, Michael Tomlinson, Jonathan Morris, Rosemary Deem (2023). DOI: 10.1093/oso/9780199552108.003.0006

of public service reform by analysing the discourse expressed in high-level government documents to synthesize key reform elements and themes. We review their alignment with the Labour government's endeavour to further its social democratic variant of neoliberalization through extending the regulated marketization of public service provision. Second, we consider how central government elites and associates construed leadership and its contribution, within their discourse strategy, to the change process embodied in the implementation of reform and other changes entailed in operating reformed public services. Third, we examine how they construed the role of leadership development provision to be offered by national leadership development bodies (NLDBs) as a control technology, fostering the desired contribution of leadership to public service reform. We briefly consider the consistency between this construal and the possibility that the leadership development interventions might have potential as an elite policy meta-lever for orchestrating future changes. Fourth, we show why a national intervention was launched or reconfigured for each public service by 2006, how government elites and associates orchestrated the national leadership development intervention for schools and for healthcare (including its reconfiguration in 2005), and how they supported the instigators of the intervention for HE. Finally, we begin our abductive explanation of why the elite orchestration activity entailed in establishing these interventions occurred as it did, by highlighting key contextual factors and inferring generative mechanisms accounting for the findings.

Government discourses of public service reform, its leadership, and leadership development

The general election manifesto of the Labour Party (1997) constitutes a social imaginary, representing how things might be better, including a summary construal of the public service reform project contingent on being elected to office. It was subsequently elaborated in government documentation as a programme of elements, evolving throughout the period of Labour government. The manifesto is characterized by lexical proliferation and undefined terms. 'Reform' features alongside other terms drawing attention to three aspects of the political project of public service reform within the overall 'vision . . . of national renewal', through promises to:

- 'save', 'restore', and 'rebuild' service provision, reinvigorating what the Conservative government had failed to maintain;

- 'change', 'improve', and 'modernise' this provision, rendering it 'modern', in order to develop and sustain a workforce capable of responding to the externally imposed demands of 'the modern world' with its 'new world economy';
- develop 'customised, personalised' services, offering a bespoke mix of services in response to the needs of individual service users.

Explicit reference is made to updating school education (entailing 'change', 'improvement', and 'modernisation') and to reinvigorating (entailing 'save', 'restore', 'rebuild') and updating healthcare (entailing 'change', 'improvement', 'modernisation'). By 2005, after seven years in government, the articulation of public service reform in the Labour Party (2005) manifesto shifted further towards the individualization of specific services, with references to the promotion of 'personalised learning' for school education and 'personalised healthcare for all of us'.

Public documents produced within government elaborate the Labour Party's social imaginary through their formulation of Labour government policies. The texts express a 'nodal' discourse (Fairclough, 2006, p. 18), articulating with related discourses through representations of the political project components, including the discourses of standards, accountability, or user choice between providers. The 'order' of this discourse (Fairclough, 2003, p. 220) conceptualizes the structuring of constituent discourses (here, a hierarchical ordering of the discourse of public service reform and discourses of reform for different services). The term also refers to enactments of the discourse within one or more conventional, so institutionalized, types or 'genres' of text, written and spoken. Genres are characterized by regularities in purpose, form, and content (say, 'white papers' published by government departments, setting out policy proposals). The government nodal discourse of public service reform is enacted through genres long established within the institution of government, forming a 'genre chain' beginning with high-level agenda-setting publications from government departments that coordinate the work and expenditure of 'spending' departments, including education and healthcare. Spending departments may publish 'green papers', policy consultation documents informing the publication of their 'white papers' containing final proposals, commonly after winning a general election. Our analysis of the government's project of public service reform is concerned with these genres. However, the genre chain also contains lower-level links, spanning written instructions to public service organizations connected with implementation, media releases, and spoken genres including political speeches or media interviews.

To identify major characteristics of public service reform as a nodal discourse, twenty-two government agenda-setting documents published between 1997 and 2008 were selected. Each incorporates 'headline elements of reform' within a summary account. Assumptions, phrases, and story-lines expressed in these texts were analysed inductively with reference to academic commentaries and research to identify key elements, their aggregation into heuristic themes, and shifting emphases over time. The documents included seven white papers (marked * below) and a green paper (marked **). They were published by the Treasury (1998a, 1998b, 2000); the Cabinet Office (1999, 2008) and units within it—the Office of Public Services Reform (OPSR) (2002, 2005), succeeded by the Strategy Unit (2006, 2007); the Department for Education and Employment (DfEE) (1997*; 1998**), subsequently the Department for Education and Skills (DfES) (2001*; 2003a; 2004b*; 2005*); and the DoH (1997*; 2000*; 2002a, 2004a, 2005a, 2006).

Four heuristic themes were identified. First, *management technocracy* encapsulates the emphasis on introducing technocratic management procedures and processes, especially when the Labour government took up office. Terms signifying this theme include 'standards', 'accountability', 'incentives', 'intervention', 'commissioning', 'technology', 'value for money', 'delivery', 'inspection', and 'regulation', as in the statement: 'Clear accountability for delivering national standards has been fundamental in helping to drive up the performance of services' (OPSR, 2005, p. 16). Private sector practices, such as objective-setting, quantified accountability measures, and performance management, were applied to public services. Government politicians employed such procedures and processes as means for coordination and control, imposing their implementation on senior staff in public service organizations.

Second, *populist individualism* refers to reorientating public services so the starting-point for single or multi-service provision becomes the wants, needs, and preferences of each service user, signified by such terms as 'choice', 'contestability', 'needs', 'consumer', 'customer', 'citizen', 'taxpayer', 'access', 'voice', 'empower', 'responsive', and 'personalisation', illustrated by the statement: 'Bottom up pressures of choice, personalisation, voice and user engagement are means of ensuring that public service users' needs, preferences and aspirations are transmitted directly to and acted upon by commissioners and providers of public services' (Strategy Unit, 2006, p. 61). While heralded in the 1997 election manifesto, this theme was elaborated from the build-up to the 2005 general election, evidenced in the manifesto slogan: 'Our NHS: free to all, personal to each' (Labour Party, 2005, p. 56).

Third, in contrast, *communitarianism* encapsulates the valorization of collectivities, 'localities', and regions as possessing intrinsic moral worth, making it imperative for public service organizations to engage with their community and to co-operate with each other for mutual benefit. Signifying terms span 'partnership', 'public', 'local', 'devolution', 'collaboration', 'national', 'principles', 'values', and 'responsibility', exemplified by the claim: 'A school's main priority is to serve its pupils, their families and their community, but we also want schools to contribute to the family of schools and to the development of the education system' (DfES, 2001, p. 38). Documents from 2005 increasingly articulate the devolution of power to public service organizations.

Fourth, *system efficacy* encompasses the government's focus on means for systemic improvement of public service provision, including private sector involvement, and on supporting the drive for economic prosperity. Signifying terms include 'capacity', 'system', 'vision', 'technology', 'funding', 'regulation', 'sector', 'workforce', 'skills', 'professional', 'freedom', 'choice', 'flexibility', 'innovation', 'delivery', 'productivity', and 'efficiency', exemplified by the Treasury (1998b, p. 1) statement: 'A central priority . . . is to implement policies which will create the right environment for growth and opportunity in the economy and improve the productivity of the public sector itself, so that every pound of taxpayer's money is spent efficiently and effectively on delivering the Government's objectives.' Initially, the political project of public service reform was represented in terms of individual services, shifting towards a systemic approach, adapted for each service sector. Retrospectively, Blair (2010, pp. 480–481) claimed to have established 'a template of the reform: changing the monolithic nature of the service; introducing competition; blurring distinctions between the public and private sector; taking on traditional professional and union demarcations of work and vested interests; and in general trying to free the system up, letting it innovate, differentiate'.

Headline elements of reform could embrace more than one heuristic theme. Thus, populist individualism and communitarianism are combined in the statement: 'ensuring individual citizens and communities have **a greater say in local services**, including through greater use of customer satisfaction measures to judge the success of services and strengthening local accountability over services' (Cabinet Office, 2008, p. 18) [original bold].

The four heuristic themes summarizing the Labour government's discursive representation of its political project resonate with our modelling (Chapter 2) of public service neoliberalization through regulated marketization (Figure 2.1), and the Labour government's regulated marketization policies (Table 2.3). Management technocracy relates to market regulation through organizational control: imposing government-specified standards, targets, surveillance arrangements, and negative sanctions for underperformance or non-compliance. Senior staff in public service organizations are incentivized to operate within externally set parameters or risk public vilification, losing 'customers' who have been informed of substandard service performance, or even losing their jobs. Populist individualism promotes marketization, first, through the commodification of provision, encouraging citizens (including students accessing HE) to construe themselves as customers entitled to choose between providers; second, by regulating to expand the range of providers, and requiring them to be responsive towards user preferences. Communitarianism supports marketization more obliquely through collaboration between providers and engagement with other local community stakeholders in developing networks, so each collaborative grouping is positioned to compete with neighbouring groups for customers. System efficacy embraces the central design and implementation of a national system, balancing multiple-service marketization and regulation to spread the benefit of public services to all citizens while maximizing the potential for public services to support the market economy. Means include maintaining the health of the present workforce and educating the workforce of tomorrow.

Discourse of persuasion: leaderism and public service reform

We noted in Chapter 4 how, before the 1997 election, senior Labour politicians and advisers adopted leader-centric, visionary ideas centred on transformational leadership theory originating in the United States of America (USA). In Chapter 5 we argued that commitment to such ideas was expressed through the ideological discourse of leaderism, an extension of managerialism driven by a material interest in coordination and control. The government documents analysed indicate that this commitment to leaderism was elaborated, once in office, through a discourse strategy promoting 'hierarchically distributed transmissional leadership'. In relation to headline elements of reform, leadership receives mention in eighteen of the twenty-two agenda-setting government documents. The construal of leadership within the discourse of leaderism has characteristics favouring its deployment within the Labour government's discourse strategy to acculturate senior staff in public service organizations towards accepting and implementing government-driven reforms and operating the reformed services, entailing ongoing improvement activity. So generic leaderism is allied here to regulated marketization reforms within the Labour government's political project.

First, leadership is reserved for leaders engaging in change, including reform, and is sharply distinguished from management. The potential contribution of leaders to reform is valorized, and deemed to need government intervention for its realization (OPSR, 2002, p. 21): '**Inspirational leadership and management:** Public services reform requires support for and development of excellent leaders capable of tackling poor management and inspiring ambitious performance. The government needs to invest in high quality training and development to help fulfil the potential of all public servants, and in particular current and future leaders and managers' [original bold].

Second, leadership is represented as part of the solution for reforming public services and as part of the problem, requiring rectification through government investment in leadership development. The extract illustrates how leader-centric the government discourse of leaderism is: concerned solely with leaders and leading and construed in terms of influencing the led by 'inspiring' their 'ambitious performance'. The leader's inspirational direction-giving or encouragement to work on shared tasks is represented as garnering the commitment of the led to collective 'performance beyond expectations' (Bass, 1985). Leadership (more accurately, leader) development interventions constitute a non-headline element of public service reform, since present and future public service 'leaders and managers' require government support to be 'excellent leaders', and training and development to become so. It is implied that managers should become (excellent) leaders, and so influencers of change; but whether leaders are expected also to become managers is unclear.

Third, this quotation contains the beginnings of a promotional narrative for elaborating the social imaginary expressed within the political project of public service reform in the 1997 general election manifesto: public service provision becomes radically improved through reform; excellent leading activity by leaders enables its achievement; and government investment in their training and development enables them to become excellent leaders. Central to this imaginary is responsibilizing public service leaders for improving services (as defined by government politicians) through reform, to benefit service users and the government. Implicitly, leaders are to act as 'change agents' on behalf of government and service users (Wallace, O'Reilly, Morris, & Deem, 2011), deploying their corporate agency to implement reform, operate reformed services, and seek ongoing improvement. The agenda-setting documents do not use the term 'change agent'. Yet the expectation to act accordingly is discernible. Indicatively: 'The leadership of top managers is critical in bringing performance management to life and setting a prevailing culture in which it can operate effectively' (Treasury, 2000, p. 9).

The phrase 'leadership of top managers' apparently means, leader-centrically, top managers leading others by 'providing leadership'. 'Top managers' are responsibilized for leading the change needed to acculturate public service organization staff towards accepting and participating in the performance management regime introduced by the Labour government.

Fourth, leadership is represented as aligning groups involved with public services through articulating a unifying vision for reform and the operation of reformed services. The government, service providers, citizens as service users, and their representatives all have a significant, if unequal, contribution to make. Blair's foreword for one agenda-setting document (OPSR, 2002, p. 2) highlights the part of government politicians in forging

> a genuine partnership between the Government and people in the front line like yourselves. It needs us to play our part by providing an overall vision of where we must go and backing that with a real commitment to deliver that vision.
>
> But it also needs us to listen and learn from your experience, to give you the recognition, resources and support needed to bring about the changes we all want to see, and to work together to see how these changes can best be achieved.

Unification is on the government's terms. Its role is represented as a 'genuine partnership' with senior public service organization staff, a primary target audience for the document, though a partnership of unequals. The government's unificatory role starts with 'providing an overall vision of where we must go'. ('Providing an overall vision' positions the government as exclusive overall vision provider. The reference to 'we' embraces both the government and senior public service organization staff, but 'must go' pre-empts senior public service organization staff contributing towards choosing the direction for reform.) However, the government still 'needs to listen and learn from your experience' (though no commitment is made to act on what is learned). The government also needs to provide 'support' to 'bring about the changes we all want to see' ('we all' implies that public service organization staff want changes that the government wants). While 'we' (implicit in the text are government and senior public service organization staff) need to 'work together', it is only to 'see how best these changes can be achieved' (not to collaborate on their implementation). And 'you' (senior public service organization staff) are solely responsibilized to 'deliver' what the government has envisioned. The visionary emphasis resonates with Burns' (1978) formulation of 'transforming leadership', but it is transmissional: the government alone is legitimated (implicitly, as leader of the public service administrative system) in determining the vision and the shared moral purpose that is to transcend any incompatible sectional interests; the led (including senior public service organization staff as leaders within the system) are expected to unite in their allegiance to this vision, and compelled to work towards its fulfilment.

This quotation concerns government influencing public service providers. The agenda-setting documents also represent the government as promoting multiple directions of influence between itself, the public, and service providers, enabling representatives of each group to act as leaders in seeking to influence the others. Illustratively, a school education white paper (DfES, 2005, pp. 89–90) heralds a new arrangement connected with the national leadership development intervention enabling selected headteachers to advise the government. It was to:

> ask the College [National College for School Leadership (NCSL)] to identify, with the help of a range of partners, a new group of national leaders of education, drawn from those who are succeeding in our most challenging leadership roles. These top headteachers will work closely with the College to influence the direction and targeting of leadership [development] provision across the system. They will also be able to advise [government education] Ministers on the future direction of education policy on the basis of their expert experience.

In a healthcare example, the collective 'leadership' of various local community service provision organizations is urged to influence public service-professional staff and members of the public to accept and support the government's service reforms. (The leadership group implicitly encompasses senior staff and others appointed to contribute towards the governance of each provider organization, some representing the public, including patients.) According to the government: 'It is the responsibility of the NHS [National Health Service] community leadership (in PCTs [primary care trusts], practices, NHS trusts, foundation trusts) to engage fully with clinicians, staff, patients and the wider public to communicate and explain the need for change and the potential of the reforms locally to improve services and people's lives' (DoH, 2006, p. 7). In HE, the white paper (DfES, 2003a, p. 40) reifies universities and colleges by representing them as influential corporate leaders within their regional community:

> They have a key leadership role, are often engaged in community capacity building and regeneration and make an important contribution to civil society. Higher education's contribution to regional development very much depends on forging partnerships between institutions in each region . . . as well as with other partners involved in regional skills, business, and economic development.

The pattern of influencing by leaders based at different system levels is construed as combining relations that are hierarchical (e.g. senior staff–other professional staff within a service organization; government–service provider; service provider–public), bottom-up (e.g. service provider–government), and horizontal (e.g. service provider–service provider, service provider–business organizations). The discourse of leaderism legitimates all groups taking a leading role and seeking to influence other groups; everyone is apparently construed as a leader. Yet conspicuously absent within this imaginary is any specification of the relative influencing entitlement each group should be accorded in respect of the others, or articulation of how influence should be received (not just given), or even facilitated by receivers, within or between groups.

Fifth, a corollary of casting senior public service organization staff as leaders and according them sufficient agency to make devolved decisions about service provision is to hold them accountable for the outcomes: 'standards can only be delivered effectively by devolution and delegation to the front line, giving local leaders responsibility and accountability for delivery, and the opportunity to design and develop services around the needs of local people' (OPSR, 2002, p. 10). In Chapter 2 we noted how the expanded standards, targets, surveillance, and sanctions regime enabled the assessed performance of different public service organizations (and administrative organizations in healthcare) to be compared. This regime formed a basis for applying incentives and conferring bounded empowerment through 'earned autonomy' (DfES, 2003b). Instances included reducing the frequency of inspections for schools judged as performing well, and punishments—most starkly the vilification, through public 'naming and shaming' (Baker, 2008), of eighteen schools deemed to be failing. The government responsibilized leaders for devolved decision-making on service provision, holding them accountable for service outcomes. 'Steering not rowing' shielded the government from direct accountability. To extend this metaphor, the rowers stand to be blamed first, not the boat-builders and steerers. In consequence, the reformed public services are represented in later government documents to operate as an inspirationally led, self-incentivizing, and publicly accountable system of regulated marketization. Witness the statement: 'Contestability between providers, user choice and/or inspirational leadership are all powerful ways of driving performance without the need for so much top down control and bureaucracy' (Strategy Unit, 2006, p. 41).

Finally, the discourse of leaderism is linked obliquely with the residual ideology of professionalism through the advocacy of public service professionals being led by more senior colleagues from the same profession, if not the same area of expertise. The autonomy historically accorded to service professionals within their specialist knowledge domain (Chapter 2) had been curtailed through managerialism introduced by the predecessor Conservative government. It was now complemented by the Labour government's discursive move of construing senior professionals as leaders, managing professional work within their organization.

The government documents contained multiple references to senior professionals leading professionals. In school education, the term 'headteacher' (literally, head teacher) has long acknowledged the prior classroom teaching experience of incumbents. Academic theorization after the advent of large comprehensive secondary schools construed their headteachers as combining the roles of 'leading professional' and 'chief executive' (Hughes, 1976). However, the previous Conservative government's 'local management of schools' marketization policy required headteachers and senior colleagues to administer their school's operating budget, a task for which they were untrained. The Labour government intervened to reduce time spent on this task through the introduction of trained bursars, playing 'an important role in helping with school administration, freeing school leaders to concentrate on quality of learning and teaching in the school' (DfES, 2001, p. 58). In healthcare, with more than 100 applied knowledge specialties and sub-specialties (General Medical Council Intelligence Unit, 2011) and with multiple clinician roles, the government was concerned to promote clinical leadership, with 'more clinicians in health service management positions' (Cabinet Office, 2008, p. 27). Such positions ranged from senior consultants involved in organization-wide management to 'modern matrons', introduced in 2001, who 'lead by example in driving up standards of clinical care and empowering nurses to take on a greater range of clinical tasks to help improve patient care' (p. 29). In HE, characterized by diverse and highly specialized academic and applied knowledge, a service sector requirement was represented as the 'ability to recruit, retain and reward the best researchers who provide the essential research leadership' (DfES, 2003a, p. 14). Expert researchers are construed as leaders of academic colleagues within their specialist domain.

An emergent narrative was 'new professionalism' (Cabinet Office, 2008, pp. 26–34), expanding the compass of leaderism by co-opting professionalism to serve managerialist ends. It constitutes another form of bounded empowerment allied to 'earned autonomy'. 'Greater freedoms for high performers' (p. 29) implies that service professionals and their leaders will be accorded more latitude to make decisions about service provision, contingent on achieving standards set by government and its agencies. The entitlement to individual autonomy characterizing professionalism as an ideology is replaced by the professional *group* earning *relative* autonomy, bounded by the requirement that provision must lie within parameters set by externally imposed standards and surveillance, with the implicit threat that relative autonomy may be forfeited if these standards are not reached. 'New professionalism' legitimates senior professionals leading professionals, creating favourable discursive conditions for interventions to develop senior professionals as 'leaders within their profession', so for their cultural allegiance as professionals to tip towards membership of an emergent leadership profession, distanced from their prior socialization as service professionals.

Key tenets of the Labour government's discourse strategy, embodying the discourse of leaderism allied to public service regulated marketization reforms, are that:

- Leadership concerns leaders leading change.
- The capability of leaders in public service organizations to do so on behalf of government requires enhancement through development activity.
- Enhancement will result in leaders contributing more effectively to the achievement of reforms, so to the radical improvement of public service provision.
- Leadership can unify all groups involved in provision through participation in an unequal partnership where the government provides the vision for reform and all partners contribute to its realization by leading necessary change within and between their organizational jurisdictions.
- They may choose how (not whether) they lead the prescribed change conditional on their organizations reaching service standards set by government, or face sanctions.
- Senior professional staff are encouraged to lead their colleague service professionals within a 'new professionalism', replacing individual autonomy over public service provision with collective, hierarchically ordered relative autonomy, contingent on reaching externally set service standards.

Discourse of incremental intervention: leadership development to build the capacity to lead reform

Agenda-setting documents evidence the element of the government's discourse strategy publicizing its investment in the capacity-building policy lever of (leader-centric) leadership development, to expand leading activity of the kind the discourse of leaderism embodies in spearheading reforms. The rationale for this investment is represented as enhancing system-wide leading activity to facilitate the implementation of reforms and operation of reformed services in public service organizations, supported through their local, regional, or national administration. Significantly, this investment includes the serial announcement of national interventions for different public service sectors in our investigation. Each intervention centres on an NLDB, which we construe as an acculturative control technology for ensuring the implementation of the leadership development policy.

The earlier quotation from the OPSR (2002, p. 21) represents, in condensed form, four key characteristics of the government's engagement in public service leadership development. First, a direct causal link is inferred between leadership development provision and the proximal outcome of increasing desired leading activity by public service leaders, then between this leading activity and the ultimate outcome of achieving the government's public service reform programme. The government's goal for leadership development is to facilitate reform. Second, a distinction is made between 'training' and 'development', implying that they are distinct forms of support offering complementary means of fostering desired leading activity. Third, priority is accorded to both current and future leaders and managers, implying a time horizon reaching beyond the present round of reforms. It allows for the possibility of in-service provision for present incumbents of senior staff positions and preparatory provision for more junior colleagues, potentially creating a pool of staff from which recruitment may be made to senior positions in future. Fourth, the government is responsibilized for investing in this provision and, implicitly, ensuring that it is of 'high quality', so capable of achieving the government's investment goal.

Subsequently, responsibilization for ongoing investment is represented as shared with the public service professions whose members are, or may become, leaders: 'In every service, the Government and professions collectively have a responsibility to grow the next generation of leaders ... to ensure the highest quality leadership development and support is available to all our future and current public service leaders' (Cabinet Office, 2008, p. 31). Notably, the horticultural metaphor employed—to 'grow' future leaders—implies that trainers and developers can develop participants, rather as people cultivate plants, stimulating and controlling their growth. This metaphor underplays the individual agency of participants, its expression in their responses to provision offered, and such scope as they are accorded, as leaders, to exercise agency through choice of action consistent with their professional values within their area of jurisdiction, and maybe across jurisdictional boundaries.

Government documents produced within the education and healthcare departments heralded the national leadership development interventions for our focal service sectors. The documentary sources evidence a department-by-department commitment to interventions designed for different public service contexts. The accruing suite of interventions for these and other public services (Chapter 1, Table 1.1) did not demonstrably constitute more than the sum of the incrementally introduced parts.

School education. The first intervention was for the school education sector, proposed in a green paper (DfEE, 1998). The genre of a consultation document suggests that before finalizing their proposal education ministers sought feedback from other groups, including representative bodies for headteachers and teachers, on whose positive engagement the intervention would depend. The case argued for this intervention expresses the promotional narrative connected with part of the Labour government's elaborated social imaginary framing its political project of public service reform. Leader-centric leadership development improves leading activity, especially that of staff in the most senior formal positions, but their empowerment is bounded. Enhanced scope for corporate agency as leaders is circumscribed by enhanced accountability (p. 21): '**Better leadership: pay, performance and development:** Good heads are crucial to the success of schools. We need to develop strong leaders, reward them well and give them the freedom to manage, without losing accountability. We want to offer schools freedom to recognise leadership by other teachers who help the head give strategic direction in schools' [original bold]. Proposals for achieving 'better leadership' included, first, taking forward the training schemes for headteachers inaugurated by the previous Conservative government (Chapter 4) within a 'national framework for headship training for aspiring, new and existing heads'. The intention was announced that 'the National Professional Qualification for Headship [NPQH] should be mandatory by 2000 for all those coming new to headship' (p. 28), contrasting with the voluntary status of other provision offered by our focal NLDBs. Compulsion would reduce the government's dependence on voluntary take-up by enough applicants for the provision to reach a significant proportion of the target group. Second was investment in an NLDB (p. 28):

> To underline our commitment to improving the quality of school leadership, we will establish a prestigious new National College for School Leadership. The college will combine high quality educational content with the best in public and

private sector management . . . It will have a prestigious site commensurate with its importance, with the highest quality ICT [information and communication technology] facilities.

This representation of the proposed national body features several positive adjectives, including 'prestigious new' connected with the organization and 'prestigious' connected with its material manifestation on a site 'commensurate with its importance', plus superlatives: 'the best' content of provision, 'highest quality' ICT. It also draws attention to this NLDB's symbolic status in signifying the government's commitment to enhancing (leader-centric) leadership capacity in schools. The investment is couched as an offer of value to headteachers and other senior staff, and implicitly to their representative bodies, whose endorsement was sought during the consultation process. This consultation was bounded (asking 'what do you think of our proposals?' and not, more openly, 'what needs doing?'), reflecting the government's superordinate social positioning and dependence, nevertheless, on senior staff in public service organizations to act as a conduit for reforms.

Healthcare. The original NLDB (predecessor to the National Health Service Institute for Innovation and Improvement (NHSIII)) was the NHS Leadership Centre (NHSLC), announced in the NHS Plan white paper setting out the government's intentions for implementing reform. The genre of a white paper signalled the government's firm commitment to this investment (DoH, 2000, p. 87):

To deliver a step change in the calibre of NHS leadership, the Government will establish a new Leadership Centre for Health. Operating through the NHS Modernisation Agency the Leadership Centre will be in place by 2001. The Centre will promote leadership development closely tied to the Modernisation Agency's work to deliver improved patient services. It will benefit all staff by widening access to work based development programmes, delivered online as well as face to face. It will provide tailored support for clinicians and managers with leadership potential at different stages in their careers and for those already in leadership roles.

The NHSLC was to be located within the NHS Modernisation Agency, a newly established executive agency within the Department of Health (DoH) driving implementation of the government's healthcare reform agenda. The NHSLC is represented as contributing to the systematization of leadership development provision through an NLDB, facilitating healthcare reform as an integral component of the national agency with responsibility to 'deliver improved patient services'. Systematization of programmes is construed in terms of diversifying the sites of provision, including virtual, to extend accessibility to participants across the country. The focus is on improvement within a present role that entails leading activity or preparation for an aspirational future promoted role, linked to a construal of individual careers in terms of sequential, cumulative stages.

Higher education. The government's funding support was announced in an education department white paper (DfES, 2003a, p. 76) for a proposal by the representative bodies Universities UK (UUK) and the Standing Conference of Principals (SCOP) (Chapter 2) to establish the national leadership development intervention for the HE sector. The reform of this sector was based, in part, on the assumption that

> universities must be free to take responsibility for their own strategic and financial future. Strong leadership and management, freed from excessive red tape, will help them not just to respond to change, but to drive it . . . Because leadership and management are key to the challenges ahead, we will help to fund HEFCE's [Higher Education Funding Council for England] and Universities UK's proposal for a new Leadership Foundation to support the sector to improve leadership and management.

The purpose of the Leadership Foundation for Higher Education (LFHE) is represented as being to 'identify and meet key leadership and management needs across the sector, and build a cadre of professional leaders and managers'. It is to 'draw on the best international expertise', to develop 'models of good practice' and encourage leaders and managers to 'support links between higher education and business' (p. 78).

Announcing these NLDBs contributed to the government's discourse strategy, each reflecting the same assumptive causal logic: (leader-centric) leadership development provision enhances the capacity for leading public service organizations, creating conditions for sustaining this capacity into the future; enhanced leading activity is instrumental for implementing the government's political project of public service reform. Elements of provision offered variously by NLDBs contribute to their potential as an acculturative control technology. They cover the formal programme format; different sites of provision to maximize access; the preparatory and in-post focus; the possibility of compulsory participation as a preparation for promotion; and exposure to valorized models of leadership and lists of skills or competencies offered by private sector practice. While the discourse strategy reflected in these government documents links leadership development to leadership facilitating the implementation of extant reforms, it stops there. It does not extend to creating a cadre of senior public service organization staff acculturated as leaders responsible for service improvement, acting as change agents for any future government public service reform agenda. So the potential of national leadership development interventions as an elite policy meta-lever is not explicit, but the possibility that they might have such potential is not ruled out either.

Emergence and accretion of national leadership development interventions

The idea for the first national leadership development intervention goes back to the mid-1990s with the activities of authoritative elite-aspirant politicians and their elite associate advisers in the Labour Party, then the political party with the second largest number of MPs, constituting 'Her Majesty's Most Loyal Opposition'. Senior Labour Party politicians had increasingly adopted the metaphorical concept of leadership during that period (Chapter 4). Blair was reportedly influential in prioritizing the promotion of leadership within public services, especially school education. He topped the hierarchy of relational social positions and so held authoritative elite status within the Labour Party as its formal leader and aspiring prime minister, entitled to select and dismiss members of his 'shadow' cabinet. Shadow cabinet members each monitored a government department, in preparation for office if the Labour Party won the next general election, and Blair subsequently confirmed their appointment as department ministers. They and their advisers also met with senior civil servants in the relevant department before the general election as part of the preparation. Leadership figured prominently in Blair's personal discourse style (Chapter 4), with references to political leadership in his autobiography (Blair, 2010) and to school leadership in a speech (Blair, 1996a) in which his construal of leadership imagined himself as leader of a future government (implicitly, corporate leader of the education system), and headteachers as local leaders of their schools (implicitly, leaders within the education system). He asserted the normative importance of their leading activity: 'we know the qualities that make a successful school—clear leadership from the head …' In his Labour Party conference speech earlier that year, he had proclaimed: 'Ask me my three main priorities for Government, and I tell you: education, education, and education' (Blair, 1996b).

Elites and their associates in the newly formed government immediately embarked on realizing the Labour Party's social democratic variant of neoliberalization through regulated marketization reforms for public services. The form of managerialism supporting the regulatory side of this agenda was neo-Taylorism, with entrepreneurialism promoting efforts to attract service user 'customers' (Chapter 2) on the marketization side. Regulatory reforms, including those for schools and healthcare, introduced an unprecedented regime of 'targets and terror' (Bevan & Hood, 2006): performance against stipulated targets was assessed, ranked, and publicized, generating resentment amongst staff in public service organizations, relayed to government by their representative bodies. A National Association of Headteachers (NAHT, 2007, p. 1) policy statement called on 'the Government radically to alter its target obsessed and test driven agenda; to allow schools to cherish their children and produce happy and emotionally balanced adults who contribute to the well being of society and are not just the fodder for statistical bean counting'.

Awareness within government of this 'hard power' impact on staff included its unintended contribution to perpetuating the shortage of applicants for headteacher posts inherited from the previous Conservative government (Select Committee on Education and Employment, 1998). A mitigatory 'soft power' form of intervention might help to soften this impact. A senior civil servant we interviewed, with a cross-departmental role, acknowledged that there was a 'worry about targets ... mainly their reception by professionals ... we were spending fifty million [pounds] on inspection. What are we spending on capacity building? So, leadership capability ... that argument was beginning ... it became a legitimate form of investment. It became a recognized bit of reform'. Momentum built incrementally amongst departments for developing leadership capacity, illustrative of the horizontal workings of power amongst strategic-level elites and associates:

> I don't think anyone sat down and said, let's have fifteen leadership bodies, but ... there were discussions across departments, and people were all moving in this direction, there was a real belief that this was ... a really important capacity building initiative. And there were arguments about whether it could be a unified one or a differentiated one, but I don't think that argument was won ... mostly the [departments for the] sectors felt that there was ... more distinctively separate about them than there was homogeneity ... in terms of generating a single one, we argued for greater integration, but there wasn't the political appetite for it.

This response is consistent with the documentary discourse, confirming that separate sectoral innovations had accreted incrementally, each adding precedent for the next. One informant hinted at how elites and associates across government had contributed:

> Leadership becomes a big deal, in a few departments it's getting a lot of funding and attention, a lot of hope is being invested in it in policy terms, and there's even some evidence to suggest that's a well-founded hope. Then the sectors that are sometimes running behind, like FE [further education], it gets one too, HE kind of came along after … ministers get hold of these ideas, policy ideas are percolating around different officials, they then get generated. The Treasury has begun to accept them as a reasonable form of investment; particular outputs are attached to them so that everyone begins to be a little more comfortable about investing public money, and it's more of a networked influencing process.

Our interviews with senior politicians, advisers, and senior civil servants concerned with schools, healthcare, and HE concurred with this portrayal of the horizontal diffusion of ideas within the Labour government, but also emphasized the overarching impact of hierarchical power relations. Authoritative elites directed and authorized investment: one adviser acknowledged Blair's foundational role and engagement in maintaining momentum, noting how he 'always did emphasize the importance of frontline leadership'. Table 6.1 summarizes characteristics of the interventions we studied, following their establishment (and reconfiguration for healthcare). All three focused leader-centrically on developing individual senior staff as leaders. The LFHE offered most additional support activities, reflecting greater scope for manoeuvre afforded by its relatively distanced formal relationship with government. The scale of interventions contrasted starkly, the funding base and target 'market' for the LFHE's provision being smallest and the engagement of its officials in programme design and provision being largest. These characteristics were the outcome of extensive elite orchestration activity to establish or reconfigure interventions. Strategic-level senior politicians with responsibility for different government departments separately established the NCSL and reconfigured NHSLC to create the NHSIII, resourced via their departmental budgets. These NLDBs were accorded formal status, legitimating close government oversight of their operation. The LFHE was orchestrated by intermediate-level elites from representative bodies for senior staff who persuaded senior government politicians at the strategic level to support for their proposed intervention financially. Next, we detail how the interventions whose formal relationship with government was close became established (school education) or were reconfigured (healthcare).

Table 6.1 Initial characteristics of established or reconfigured national leadership development interventions for schools, healthcare, and higher education

Characteristic	School education (England)	Healthcare (England)	Higher education (UK)
NLDB, year of inception	National College for School Leadership (NCSL), 2000	NHS Institute for Innovation and Improvement (NHSIII), 2005	Leadership Foundation for Higher Education (LFHE), 2004
Primary leadership focus	Developing individual leaders at senior career stages	Developing individuals at different career stages as leaders of innovation within one programme contributing to the development of innovations for improving healthcare	Developing individual leaders at senior career stages, also executive teams
Main initial areas of activity	Leadership development programmes NPQH, HEAD-LAMP, LPSH (Chapter 4), commissioning research, developing online and networking opportunities, e.g. 'Talking Heads' confidential network	Leadership development programmes, e.g. black, Asian, and minority ethnic heritage (BAME) 'Breaking Through' programme, 'Gateway to Leadership' scheme for attracting talented 'middle managers' from inside and outside the NHS	Top Management Programme for senior staff, diverse programmes, e.g. mentoring between senior staff in HE and the private sector, commissioning research, events to inform governors
Target group for leadership development	25,000 headteachers, 70,000 deputy heads, senior teachers, 'middle managers' (Bolam, 2004)	37,000 staff with senior management and management positions, senior staff within a total of 700,000 clinical staff (NHS Information Centre, 2008)	11,000 senior staff and 'middle managers', 4,000 governors (UUK/SCOP, 2003)
Budget (£ millions)	£28m for the first year (NCSL, 2003)	£70m for the first year (NHSIII, 2006a)	£10m for the first three years (Blue Alumni, 2010)
Designing and commissioning	Commissioning programme provision in nine regional centres within universities, developing new programmes, e.g. 'Leading from the Middle' for 'middle leader' staff	Commissioning leadership development	Designing programmes and activities provided by associates

Elite orchestration of acculturative control technologies for school education and healthcare reform

The National College for School Leadership. No informants could recall where the idea of the foundational national leadership development intervention for schools originated. However, the discourse of leaderism had been widely internalized. A senior civil servant involved in launching the NCSL perceived the importance of leadership to be self-evident, echoing the slogan of the Clinton presidential campaign (Chapter 2): 'It's like, if it's "the economy, stupid", it's "leadership, stupid" . . . You've just got to address that issue.' A politician described an opportunistic process where the perennial quest for new policy ideas was complemented by power to enact them, reflecting the corporate agency possessed by strategic-level authoritative elites in government:

> Plagiarism is one of the greatest gifts that we have in politics. . .you meet at a seminar, you meet at a conference . . . you may just have met in conversation in the lift. There's something that sparks. Very few things in life are entirely invented by a single person; they're usually a synergy of putting together things that have just touched you. And I loved doing that, just listening to people, and thinking: 'There's something in that; why don't we do it?'

Informants confirmed the proposal for the NSCL in the green paper (DfEE, 1998) to be uninformed by established development interventions involving a central body, including the Police College (Chapter 1), or those of the previous Conservative government such as the National Development Centre for School Management Training (Chapter 4). One senior civil servant stated that such precedents were ignored because they were not 'focused on the thing that we thought was most important, which was leadership'. The long-institutionalized structural arrangement of siloed government departments favoured the incremental approach that ensued. In consequence, the NCSL (and subsequent interventions centred on an NLDB) strongly emphasized unique, service sectoral aspects of leading activity—here leading learning and teaching—alongside reference to generic aspects like 'giving direction'.

Our informants concurred with Blair's (2010, p. 211) claim that the NCSL was one of the 'new national agencies to drive improvement' in public services, so headteachers were, implicitly, change agents for the government's reform programme. One politician stated: 'They've sold their soul, so that if they really want to be in that arena then they have to play by the rules; and the rules are that . . . when the policy has been decided it's their job to inspirationally implement it.' Inspirational leadership was key to making reform happen. A senior civil servant pointed, counterfactually, to the normative association Blair had made between the quality of leadership and that of educational provision: 'I've never yet been in a school which was badly led which was providing decent standards . . . nor did the prime minister and nor did the secretary of state.' An adviser linked leadership with establishing the NCSL to develop capacity:

> If your basic model of reform is to devolve responsibility to the frontline and hold people to account, then public service leadership becomes absolutely fundamental . . . unless the headteachers are really good, it's not going to work, or it's not going to realize its full benefit . . . we knew that having great school leaders was important and that's why the College [NCSL] was set up.

The NCSL proposal was influenced by the inheritance of a teacher and headteacher shortage and leadership training programmes for aspiring and serving headteachers established by the previous Conservative government (noted earlier). Reportedly, political priorities were to resolve the recruitment shortfall and build leadership capacity through the NPQH and other leadership development programmes commissioned or provided by the NCSL.

NPQH's title, the National Professional Qualification for Headship, enshrines an implicit Labour government aspiration to professionalize experienced teachers (often shouldering significant management responsibility) as professional 'headteachers-in-waiting'. Professionalization entailed a preparatory accredited training course and assessment linked to the inherited national standards for headship (TTA, 1998). Successful completion brought the formal credential of a professional qualification, signifying a threshold level of competence in achieving these national standards, rendering NPQH-holders eligible to be considered for appointment to their first headteacher post. Possession of the NPQH qualification eventually became mandatory (DfES, 2004c) for aspiring headteachers to be appointed; all other provision would be voluntary. A senior civil servant pointed to the symbolic value of the government demonstrating support for senior school staff by investing in their development: '[The NCSL] should have a positive impact on the quality of leadership. The symbolism of it, however, is almost as important as anything else. I mean, we are saying that leadership of schools is absolutely critical to their success, and how do we convince them of that when you haven't even got an institution which is dedicated to it?'

The NCSL was commissioned through a prospectus (DfEE, 1999) announced by Blair, inviting responses and culminating in the NCSL's establishment in 2000, occupying a new building in Nottingham. The assumption that 'business knows best' was reflected in the range of strategic-level elite members from the private sector appointed to formal advisory positions. The governing council (NCSL, 2003, pp. 25–26) was chaired by the non-executive chair of a multinational company; members included several company directors and a former executive of the Hay Group consultancy company. Amongst the 'leadership patrons' who were 'working with NCSL to share best leadership practice across the private and public sectors' was the chief executive of a multinational company. These appointments legitimated private sector practices as being worthy of emulation within public services, empowering strategic-level elite members to express a significant collective voice within the oversight of this intervention.

The NCSL's status as an executive non-departmental public body signifies an 'arm's length' relationship with government: separated from the education department, employing its own staff, and with an allocated budget. Nevertheless, this status legitimated close government oversight through an annual remit letter linked to corporate planning and reporting, with departmental representation on the NCSL's governing council. The first remit letter articulated the NCSL's envisaged role in contributing to the government's reform agenda (Blunkett, 2000, p. 2): 'I intend to involve the College fully in the development and delivery of Government policy on all relevant aspects of school improvement.' Subsequently, the NCSL's operation was monitored closely, and after four years the DfES (2004d, p. 1) commissioned a formal review 'to examine the policy to delivery chain'. The resultant streamlining of the NCSL's remit and appointment of a new director evidences the tight regulatory control ministers were prepared to exert.

The NHS Leadership Centre, then NHS Institute for Innovation and Improvement. After instigating the NCSL, Blair (2010, p. 266) engaged with the healthcare minister and advisers in developing the NHS Plan. A politician reported how leadership development was construed as a policy lever, integral to the reform programme: 'an important element of a quite wide-ranging set of public service reforms ... You have to have lots of different levers to pull, all at the same time, of which the leadership of local organizations is obviously an important part.' The proposal for the NHSLC as a unit within the NHS Modernisation Agency legitimated a very close relationship with government. An executive agency is a tightly controlled form of 'arm's-length' public body: inside a government department, but with its own management structure and budget. The Modernisation Agency and NHSLC were subject to ministerial directives and required to implement departmental policy. The Modernisation Agency was established to 'spread best practice' (DoH, 2000, p. 11). The NHSLC was to facilitate the implementation of NHS reform through 'leadership development closely tied to the Modernisation Agency's work to deliver improved patient services' (NHSLC, 2003). An informant involved with the NHSLC alluded to a government expectation that leaders in healthcare organizations should act, implicitly, as its change agents for reforms: 'The task really is taking all of those various strands of national policy and making sense of them in terms of the services that you are responsible for providing.' Accordingly, the NHSLC pursued multiple tasks (DoH, 2002b). They included reviewing existing leadership development provision within the NHS; developing national programmes, some provided through Strategic Health Authorities (SHAs), which administered the NHS in each region; and developing a leadership 'qualities' framework.

NHS arm's length bodies were reviewed three years later within a government-wide efficiency drive, bringing terminations, mergers, and the reallocation of functions (DoH, 2004b). The NHS Modernisation Agency, and therefore the NHSLC, were replaced by a new arm's length body with an innovation focus: 'the introduction into practice of new ideas to improve services and patients' experiences.' Its mission would be to 'support the NHS and its workforce in accelerating the delivery of world-class health and healthcare for patients and public by encouraging innovation and developing capability at the frontline' (DoH, 2005b, p. 5). The new NHSIII incorporated a reduced range of NHSLC leadership development programmes. Responsibility for several programmes was transferred to SHAs (p. 33). According to one senior civil servant, the NHSIII would develop and promote the implementation of healthcare innovations to address government-set targets by producing 'national frameworks based on "What is best practice? What's the best technology use? How do you match it? What are the leadership requirements to deliver this?", to be handed over to organizations to interpret and take forward in their local context'. So the NHSIII focused on the identification of leading activity needed for implementing innovations, and promotion of its development. Appointments to the NHSIII governing board included the chief executive of a multinational company who had also founded a consultancy specializing in innovation, legitimating the input of private sector expertise in shaping the thrust of NHSIII's provision.

The NHSLC's exclusive leadership focus was diluted. It had been constructed as a national centre of expertise in leadership development provision working with SHAs, to which much of that provision was now devolved. The NHSIII was an umbrella organization for developing and implementing innovations flowing from government-set targets. It included a leadership 'priority programme' dedicated to promoting leading activity needed to put innovations into practice throughout the English NHS. Leadership was one of four priority programmes, all potentially time-limited, so continuing commitment was not guaranteed: 'Work on each priority programme will continue for an agreed time to deliver a set of agreed outputs and will then end. This will enable resources to be freed to focus on the next set of priorities' (NHSIII, 2005, p. 6). The leadership programme included elements retained from the NHSLC, alongside continuing responsibility for the framework of leadership qualities. Situated on the University of Warwick campus, the NHSIII's status as a Special Health Authority (arm's length) afforded the government tight departmental control over its activities.

Elite orchestration of an acculturative control technology facilitating higher education reform

The Leadership Foundation for Higher Education. The idea for an NLDB for universities and colleges did not originate with government. The proposal was generated by intermediate-level expert elites and their associates connected with representative bodies for senior staff in universities and colleges, endorsed by the representative body for governors. Two factors flowing from the sectoral context of this partly public-funded service were especially salient. First, older universities had been autonomous organizations from their inception, and the previous Conservative government had enabled polytechnics and colleges, hitherto under local government control, to apply for this status from 1992 (Chapter 2). Since then, the government 'command situation' in respect of universities and colleges had been founded on resource allocation through distributing grants for teaching and research, and on legislation in 1998 to introduce student payment of tuition fees within the regulated marketization reforms. Consequently, the government's material interest in what became construed as university and college leadership reflected its dependence on the international reputation of UK universities for high quality teaching and research, coupled with their economic contribution to the supply of highly skilled 'knowledge-workers' and to technological and commercial innovation. A senior civil servant informant noted how government attention to the way universities and colleges were led arose between 1992 and the accession of the Labour government, coinciding with the conceptual shift distinguishing (leader-centric) leadership from management:

> There was sort of general angst about where was leadership going within the universities . . . underpinned by the importance of the vice chancellor or the university leaders in setting the strategy for their organizations at a time of turbulence . . . we

don't control universities from Whitehall, never have done and don't plan to; therefore, what is the success of the sector built on? . . . autonomy [of universities and
colleges] and the fact that they can decide to go and do things in whatever way
they please, and we rely on them having leaders that can do that.

Since the government's jurisdiction did not encompass the internal workings of universities and colleges, concern within the government education
department over the development of leadership capacity was simply 'to assure
ourselves it was happening'.

Second, at this time the UK government devolved the allocation of funds
for the sector through three funding councils responsible for distribution
to individual universities and colleges within, respectively, England (the
responsibility of the UK government), Scotland (the Scottish government),
plus Wales (the Welsh government), alongside a government body in Northern Ireland (the Northern Ireland Executive). HEFCE, the funding council
for HE in England, often administered combined allocations for the entire
UK, primarily for research contributions that were agreed with the other
funding councils and their devolved government body. The formal status
of funding councils was that of 'non-departmental public bodies', relatively
autonomous from the UK or their devolved government, delimited by its policy and overall funding decisions, and free from directive political control.
A senior civil servant described HEFCE as an intermediary body that 'translates ministers' strategic policies into policies on the ground . . . a body that
translates government's strategy into objectives for the sector . . . you've got
that sort of arm's length principle'. The funding councils were instrumental
in promoting and financially supporting applied research and, subsequently,
allocating government funds for establishing and sustaining the NLDB
for HE.

Senior civil servant informants from the education department and
HEFCE reported 'a generic worry about leadership' within the UK government, sharing a leader-centric view of leadership with their counterparts
concerned with school education and healthcare. HEFCE's corporate construal of leadership was 'agreeing strategic direction in discussion with others
and communicating this within the organisation; ensuring that there is the
capability, capacity and resources to deliver planned strategic outcomes; and
supporting and monitoring delivery. As such this embraces elements of governance and elements of management' (HEFCE, 2004, p. 35). However, there
was less emphasis on leaders acting as change agents for the government's
sectoral reforms than with school education or healthcare because student
payment of tuition fees, the main policy lever employed for marketization
reform, constituted an inducement for each student to act as a customer.

HEFCE operated as a buffer between universities and government, rather than a regulator. In the words of an education department senior civil servant: 'What did you need to do in order to get the government's reform programme working in HE? Not much, because it was already there . . . the introduction of the fixed tuition fee suddenly made students realize that they were paying money . . . it has made them consumers. It's made students much more demanding of the service they should get.'

The drive for a national intervention centring on an NLDB came from the representative bodies for senior staff, supported by the Committee of University Chairs (CUC) representing chairs of governing bodies for universities and colleges, together forming an advocacy coalition that engaged with HEFCE and government ministers. The confluence of material and ideal interests between all these groups illustrates how a mix of intermediate- and strategic-level elites could exert collective horizontally and hierarchically ordered power by working in tandem across their jurisdictional boundaries. Government ministers were assured that a national leadership development intervention for the sector was happening, without them having to instigate it.

The primary instigator was UUK, representing vice chancellors and principals. UUK is the name adopted in 2000 by what was the Committee of Vice Chancellors and Principals (CVCP) (Chapter 4), whose agency, the Universities and Colleges Staff Development Agency (UCoSDA), conducted research in the early 1990s recommending a national framework for management and leadership development. UCoSDA was also renamed, becoming the Higher Education Staff Development Agency (HESDA). A steering group from UUK was convened in 2001, with support from SCOP, CUC, HEFCE and the other funding councils, and expert inputs from others (UUK/SCOP, 2003). Applied research commissioned by HEFCE and conducted by HESDA (HEFCE, 2002) showed that 'up to 70% of [HE] institutions had no systematic institutional approach to senior management development' (UUK/SCOP, 2003, p. 2). An international comparison with seven other Anglophone countries suggested that provision was more extensive elsewhere.

These findings reportedly prompted the Chief Executive of HEFCE 'to float the concept of an international Leadership Academy for Higher Education', on which the UUK steering group and SCOP built in developing their business case for a Leadership Foundation for Higher Education. It received public government endorsements, as already mentioned (DfES, 2003a). The LFHE was designed as a membership body, launched in 2004, and projected eventually to become self-funding. To offset costs, members were charged from the outset for taking up provision. The new NLDB incorporated

HESDA, whose activities were transferred, including the flagship Top Management Programme (TMP) inaugurated in 2001 for senior staff aspiring to top management positions (LFHE, 2004a). A senior civil servant from HEFCE implied that the 'pump-priming' approach to government funding for the LFHE was routine for government-approved organizations whose status was 'at arm's length'. The NLDB's survival would depend on 'customers' valuing its provision enough to pay all its costs: 'All organizations like that move from initially a large measure of public support through us, and then that would probably slide downwards where the customers . . . universities are interested in buying from them; will they pay for it?'

The LFHE was established as a limited company, then additionally registered as a charity. Representation on its governing board came largely from the HE sector, including key figures from UUK and SCOP, plus one public service representative from healthcare, and the chair from the private sector. There was no government or funding council representation, consistent with the more distanced relationship obtaining between the LFHE and government than with the NLDBs for the two public-funded services in our study. The LFHE's mission embraced 'developing and equipping today's and tomorrow's leaders in higher education—as individuals and as teams in their institutions' (LFHE, 2004a, p. 7). Including teams as groups of leaders within their organizations implies a slightly more inclusive construal of leading activity than for our other two NLDBs. The LFHE's role was also to stimulate debate and to advise member organizations so that they 'can make informed choices about how best to develop their leaders and their own organisations'.

The government's funding contribution legitimated HEFCE commissioning an external evaluation of the LFHE, on behalf of all four funding councils, after two years. The consultants recommended continuing financial support because 'the work of the LFHE is of such importance to the ongoing development of the UK HE sector that further (limited) financial support beyond 2008/09 is strongly merited. Accordingly we are recommending that the Funding Councils consider further limited financial support for the three years beyond 2008/09' (Oakleigh Consulting Ltd, 2006, p. 6). Further funding was duly provided. A second evaluation in 2010 reported that the LFHE still received financial support from the funding councils (Blue Alumni, 2010), so the government retained a measure of control over LFHE provision. The first evaluation also commented on the insularity of the LFHE from its inception (Oakleigh Consulting Ltd, 2006, p. 18): 'The consensus of consultees is that HE must do more to listen to and share the experiences of other sectors both nationally and overseas and not approach its own future with the narrow view that learning can only come from within.' Its operation, apparently, was as siloed as that of the other two NLDBs.

Explaining how the elite orchestration of national leadership development interventions began

We now attempt to explain the UK Labour government's foundational engagement in the first part of the complex change process that our empirical extreme case embodied. Our abductive approach (Chapter 3) entails theoretically informed conjecture about the causal powers and generative mechanisms plausibly explaining why, within this context, the inauguration phase of the change process came about as it did. We begin with contextual factors identified in Part I and their impact on orchestration activity. These contextual factors collectively shaped the emergence of the interacting generative mechanisms we infer from the documentary and interview evidence reported here. Appendix 1 summarizes the contextual factors and generative mechanisms underlying the inauguration of the NLDBs. The arrows signify the direct causal impact of the context on the first generative mechanism in the causal network, then the causal impact of that generative mechanism on one or more of the others, and so on.

Context. First, 'British exceptionalism' explains why the UK Labour government had scope to express such extensive corporate agency in pursuing its political project of public service reform and experimenting with national leadership development interventions involving an NLDB. The counterfactual bears witness: we found no evidence of significant political opposition. Second, room for unilateral manoeuvre empowered elites in and around the government to express their ideological commitment to neoliberalism, supported by managerialism (and incorporating leaderism). They sought to further the neoliberalization of public services begun by the predecessor Conservative government along a new trajectory for the workfare state, embodying a social democratic motivation and an expanded emphasis on the regulatory end of regulated marketization. Third, institutionalized public service regulated marketization reforms introduced by the outgoing Conservative government formed the starting-point for this shift. Fourth, the Labour Party capitalized on 'blowback'—expressions of resistance to the economic regime shift brought about during that era—to achieve office and then pursue further public service reforms along the social democratic trajectory of regulated marketization. The ensuing political project of public service reform brought a new, continually evolving agenda for service-specific reforms

(Chapter 2). Fifth, pursuing this agenda generated a governmental dependence on senior staff within each public service organization to implement and operate reforms, in the face of any lasting allegiance to the residual ideology of professionalism from the bygone era of the Keynesian welfare state.

The discourse strategy focused on the reform agenda at the point when documents were published, but senior staff were responsibilized for leading the implementation, operation, and, on occasion, readjustment of an unceasing stream of additional reforms throughout the period of Labour government. Once NLDBs were established, a continuing flow of new participants experienced their provision. Contextual conditions were thus created for the national leadership development interventions to constitute an elite policy meta-lever insofar as they were designed to acculturate participants as leaders of service improvement, shouldering responsibility for leading the implementation and operation of whatever reforms the central government of the day might require.

Generative mechanisms

Leader-centric construal of leadership plus remote containment. Two contrasting but integrally linked aspects of this mechanism had a combined causal impact. Together, they channelled the deployment of corporate agency by strategic-level and intermediate-level elites, as leaders, while delimiting their scope for directing their corporate agency toward ends that might be unacceptable to the government. Both aspects affected the nature of the leadership development interventions and responses of participants. First, evidence cited in Part I about the construal of leadership within central government, alongside evidence cited here about its expression within the discourse of leaderism, indicates that it was thoroughly leader-centric. The dominant denotative meaning of leadership (Chapter 1) was that of an individual quality, the skilled activity of one-way influencing embodied in leading others, legitimated by a hierarchically superordinate social position as a designated leader. The *leader-centric construal of leadership* impacted on decisions of elites in and around government, and those from representative bodies for HE, to promote leadership development interventions involving an NLDB. Each focused primarily on individuals occupying senior formal positions and, to a lesser extent, 'middle managers', as leaders, and on their leading activity—thus promoting *leader* development in the name of leade*rship* development.

The obverse of the leader-centric construal of leadership and its impact on the national leadership development interventions was central government regulatory *remote containment* of the scope for expressing corporate agency amongst intermediate and local-level elites. Leader-centric promotion of leading activity emphasizing visionary and inspirational direction-setting channelled the way leaders deployed their agency. The visionary emphasis legitimated actions expressing their moral and service-professional values and reflecting their own ideological commitments, contingent on their acceptability to authoritative elites in government. These values and ideological commitments underpinned a vision for transforming service provision in their organization. They generated this vision alone, or else these commitments informed their efforts at influencing other staff, and maybe service users, to engage collectively in articulating a shared vision consistent with the values of leaders, to which all might become committed. The Labour government sought public service transformation—but of a restricted kind. Hence the bounding (Chapter 4) that rendered the government's promotion of implicitly or explicitly 'transformational' leadership merely transmissional of the governmental vision for public service reform. Transmissional bounding was legitimated by the superordinate social position of government ministers as democratically elected 'leaders of the system'.

We earlier (Chapter 2) documented the remote containment of public service reform through strengthened regulation, including centrally imposed standards, targets, surveillance, assessment of performance against targets, and threat of sanctions. The leader-centric construal of leadership underpinning the national interventions included the 'devolved responsibility', or responsibilization, of senior staff in public service organizations, as leaders, for indirect outcomes of their leading activity including standards met, targets reached, inspections passed. The causal impact of this responsibilization was to legitimate government ministers holding senior staff accountable for achieving stipulated outcomes. However, our informants connected with government were agreed that the radically tightened regulation of public service provision did not inhibit senior staff in service organizations from leading local improvement activity independent of the reform agenda. One adviser commented approvingly: 'If you look at what the great headteachers are doing . . . they're just tearing away, they're reinventing the curriculum . . . changing their relationships with other schools, they're building relationships with business, with universities, whatever. So, they're entrepreneurial headteachers . . . there's nothing in what the government does that really prevents you doing that.' Our interviews with senior staff (to be reported in Chapter 8) suggest that those deemed to be leaders experienced the centralized regulatory regime as a serious constraint on their scope for agency. This regime, ironically, undermined their efforts to promote further marketization, the obverse of the regulatory reforms. The report of a government-sponsored conference fostering collaboration between NLDBs on promoting 'customer-focused leadership' in public service organizations illustrates this ironic unintended consequence. It stated: 'A commonly recurring theme . . . was the oppressive climate of targets and assessment imposed by the government (many of which are in direct opposition to improved customer focus) and a concern that "customer focus" would simply add to the range of metrics against which they were expected to deliver' (Bolden, 2006).

Remote containment also applied to the leadership development interventions involving NLDBs, insofar as they might operate as an elite policy meta-lever for influencing senior staff in public service organizations to accept their responsibilization and accountability as leaders. The accompanying expectation that senior staff would lead the implementation and operation of government-driven reforms compounded the causal impact of remote containment through strengthened regulation. It delimited their corporate agency as leaders, so their actions and the consequences for service provision would remain within bounds acceptable to government ministers, service users, or both. This two-sided generative mechanism precipitated two different, but associated, generative mechanisms: one concerning the content and impacts of the leadership development interventions; the other, their remote containment.

The leader-centric construal of leadership causally impacted on the *attempted acculturative formal co-optation* by elites in and around central government of senior staff (and middle managers), implicitly acting as change agents for the government and, voluntarily, leading the implementation and operation of reforms for their organization. Consistent with our conception of an elite policy meta-lever was the widespread construal, amongst these elites, of leadership development interventions incorporating an NLDB as a means for acculturating senior staff as leaders committed to government-driven reforms and ongoing improvement; it was to be implemented by the NLDB staff, any regional partners, and trainers working for NLDBs. This type of acculturative co-optation was *formal* (Chapter 3): acculturated leaders gained the semblance of enhanced corporate agency, here as leaders of and within their organizational jurisdiction. Yet it was contingent on leaders choosing to deploy their agency in pursuing a trajectory within the limits of acceptability to government, or risk facing sanctions. They stood to gain 'bounded empowerment', not freedom to choose whatever actions might best express their service-professional values—let alone contribute to policy development (as their informal co-optation would have implied). Of the three service sectors we investigated, senior staff in universities and colleges had greatest scope for corporate agency since their organizations are, formally, autonomous from government. Yet their dependence on government funding, and latterly on students paying tuition fees—a government reform of HE—still enabled government ministers to delimit the corporate agency (within wider parameters) exercised by senior staff, governors, and representative bodies acting on their behalf.

The central government *specification* of national leadership development interventions (or, for the LFHE, approval by the government agency HEFCE) variously included NLDB design, remit, funding, location, reporting, and review arrangements. It constituted remote containment in respect of leadership development provision. The causal impact was to set parameters for each intervention and its establishment, operation, further innovation, and redirection in response to reviews. The power retained by central government to enforce a directional shift was most starkly evident in actions imposed after reviews, whether connected with staffing, provision, funding, or reconfiguration.

In summary, the Labour government initiated the national leadership development intervention for schools, reconfigured its counterpart for healthcare, and financially supported representative bodies for senior staff in universities and colleges in mounting theirs. The government made this move because interventions stood to contribute toward the acculturative formal co-optation of senior public service organization staff as conduits for the regulated marketization agenda. Government departments serially orchestrated the siloed establishment, remodelling, or financing of each NLDB. Little effort was made to inform each endeavour by reference to past interventions or other current interventions connected with service-specific NLDBs, on the grounds that provision must be sensitive to service-specific contexts and development needs. The form, focus, and funding of each NLDB was specified in line with the central government aspiration to acculturate senior staff in public service organizations as leaders who would operate as change agents for the implementation and operation of central government's public service reforms. NLDB staff were recruited accordingly. In what follows we report on what transpired next, and its implications for the government's acculturative aspiration.

7

Elite orchestration and mediation of national leadership development provision

This chapter portrays the second part of the complex change process embodied in mounting these interventions: their implementation, orchestrated by elites and their associates within the national leadership development bodies (NLDBs). How, and why, did NLDB senior officials respond to their remit and develop their range of provision within parameters set and variably monitored by government? We are principally concerned with the horizontal workings of power inside the intermediate-level component of our conceptual framework, within the domain of interaction (Chapter 5, Figure 5.1), attending also to the cross-level flows of influence between the intermediate and strategic levels connected with the continuing endeavour of government elites and their associates to orchestrate NLDB provision:

- Intermediate-level orchestration of NLDB provision in response to their remit and financing, facilitated by a supportive relationship with representative bodies for senior staff in public service organizations.
- NLDB mediation, from intermediate to strategic level, of the national interventions as orchestrated by government; and, for the LFHE, within the intermediate level in respect of the representative bodies instigating this NLDB.
- Cross-level orchestration from strategic to intermediate level, entailing a government intervention to promote greater coordination between all NLDBs through what became the Public Service Leadership Alliance (PSLA) (Chapter 5, Figure 5.2).
- NLDB mediation, from intermediate to strategic level, of the government intervention through their response in engaging with the PSLA and changing their practice.

Developing Public Service Leaders. Wallace et al., Oxford University Press. © Mike Wallace, Michael Reed, Dermot O'Reilly, Michael Tomlinson, Jonathan Morris, Rosemary Deem (2023). DOI: 10.1093/oso/9780199552108.003.0007

- Cross-level orchestration from intermediate to local level through the direction of NLDB provision towards mobilizing participants by co-optatively acculturating them as leaders acting as change agents for government-driven reforms and other agendas.

Tracking the course of mobilization from strategic through to local level and mediation from intermediate to strategic level indicates how faithful the intermediate-level implementation of the interventions was. First, we explore how intermediate-level expert elites and their associates connected with NLDBs orchestrated provision: pursuing a *developmental project* to coordinate and, in part, offer leader-centric forms of leadership development provision, nationwide; enacting a *discourse strategy* centred on a valorized construal of leadership and individual learning; and employing a *control technology* comprising training and development activities to inculcate desired leading activity, attitudes, and values.

Second, we examine how intermediate-level expert elites and associates from representative bodies pursued their *support project*, on behalf of their members within the target groups for NLDB provision, by seeking to influence and support the NLDB for their public service sector. One aspect was the further professionalization of senior staff with a background as professionals providing a service, including teachers, doctors, or academics, or the professionalization of hitherto senior administrative staff, primarily general managers, as *professional leaders* through their participation in NLDB provision. The relevant element of their *discourse strategy* couched leadership development in terms of professional development, connected with the element of their *control technology* combining advocacy and, often, a contribution to NLDB leadership development provision directed towards the professionalization of their members as professional leaders of, or within, their organization.

Third, we consider the government-initiated cross-level intervention of sponsoring the PSLA (Chapter 5, Figure 5.2), an informal networking forum fostering mutual exchange and collaboration amongst NLDBs. Finally, we extend the abductive explanation begun in the previous chapter to encompass intermediate elite orchestration entailed in implementing and refining NLDB provision, and the delimitation of its mediatory scope by government regulation.

Elite orchestration of NLDB leadership development provision

Interviews were conducted in 2007, after the National College for School Leadership (NCSL) had existed for seven years, the National Health Service Institute for Innovation and Improvement (NHSIII) for two (though its leadership development provision had been transferred from the predecessor NHS Leadership Centre (NHSLC) after four years), and the Leadership Foundation for Higher Education (LFHE) for three. Strategic-level (and, for the LFHE, intermediate-level) orchestration of the NLDBs had established their location, organizational structure, staffing, governance, and network of relationships with partners or trainers. Commissioning and provision had been consolidated. The NCSL and LFHE had been externally reviewed (Chapter 6), as had the NHSLC, resulting in the successor NHSIII. The two NLDBs with a close formal relationship to government were remodelled, reflecting government elite concerns. The NCSL was judged to have engaged in activities that were insufficiently focused on government priorities (Barber, 2007; DfES, 2004d), implying mediation of its brief that government elites found unacceptable. Hence the CEO's replacement and the move to narrow the range of provision and terminate several activities. The NHSLC was reconfigured and downsized within the move to promote NHS-wide innovation. The LFHE review result was congratulatory, prompting the government to extend its financial support.

Table 7.1 summarizes characteristics of the three interventions in 2007. All concentrated on development programmes that comprised training for individuals at different career stages, mostly focused on preparation for a more senior position, rather than supporting incumbents in their present role. There were also contrasts. The school education sector features many more, and smaller, organizations than do the healthcare or HE sectors. NCSL senior officials gained government approval for creating a novel consultant role (Chapter 6). Experienced headteachers, judged effective according to national student assessment results and Office for Standards in Education (Ofsted) inspections, were invited to apply for status as 'national leaders of education'. Successful applicants would inform policymakers and receive training to support other local schools deemed ineffective, alongside retaining responsibility for their school (NCSL, 2006b). This was also the only NLDB with formally accredited training: the National Professional Qualification for Headship (NPQH) programme (DfES, 2004c). NCSL and NHSIII training featured programmes for people of colour and other ethnic groups who were under-represented in senior roles, then termed black,

Table 7.1 Characteristics of the national leadership development interventions for schools, healthcare, and higher education by 2007

Characteristic	School education (England)	Healthcare (England)	Higher education (United Kingdom (UK))
National body	National College for School Leadership (NCSL)	NHS Institute for Innovation and Improvement (NHSIII)	Leadership Foundation for Higher Education (LFHE)
Main leadership development focus	Developing individual staff at different career stages as leaders, mainly preparing for more senior roles Identifying and developing experienced headteachers as 'national leaders of education' or 'consultant leaders', supporting other schools	Developing individual NHS staff at different career stages as leaders, mainly preparing for more senior roles, including chief executives and senior medical staff, and black, Asian and minority ethnic (BAME) staff, aiming to build capacity for leading innovation and improvement	Developing senior staff as leaders, individually and as teams, mainly preparing for more senior roles Stimulating debate about leadership, governance, and management Advising universities and colleges on their leadership development provision
Expectations framework (including leadership)	Advisory DfES national standards for headteachers, revised following consultation 'within the profession' NCSL leadership development framework of 'leadership stages', informing the suite of national training programmes	NHS Leadership Qualities Framework, linked to 360° feedback protocol, informing leadership development programmes Development of a medical management and leadership competency framework informing medical training	-
Link with other HR processes	Aspiring headteachers must be supported by their school (implying needs identification) Standards inform compulsory annual headteacher and teacher appraisal	Programmes contribute to developing the NHS 'leadership talent pipeline' in association with the Department of Health (DoH)	No formal link: LFHE commissions practice-oriented research and reviews on HR processes, e.g. workload allocation models, continuing professional development framework for service management professionals

	NCSL	NHSIII	LFHE
Commissioning leadership development	NCSL commissions national programmes that trainers design and provide	NHSIII commissions national programmes that trainers design and provide	LFHE staff develop and manage delivery of programmes, university and college staff commission programmes delivered in-house
Main forms of leadership development provision	National training programmes for individuals as leaders at different career stages, e.g. Fast Track programme for teachers with potential for leadership positions, accredited training for 'school business managers', Leadership Pathways, for senior teachers, including BAME staff, considering headship, NPQH qualification for aspiring headteachers, administered through regional centres Learning Gateway online collaboration and e-learning resources Commissioned practice-oriented research e.g. literature reviews, empirical studies	National training programmes for individuals as leaders, e.g. Graduate management programmes for general management, HR, and finance trainees, Breaking Through programme for BAME staff, induction for staff externally recruited into management positions, programmes for chief executives and directors, coaching for newly appointed executives, medical leaders programme Suite of commissioned programmes, e.g. future focused leadership, personal impact Development needs diagnostic tools, healthcare commissioning tools	National training programmes for individuals as leaders, e.g. Future Leaders for staff aspiring to management roles, Senior Strategic Leadership for senior staff, e.g. deans, TMP for senior staff preparing for top management roles Governor Development programme Events, e.g. Leadership Summit Short courses and seminars, e.g. Research Team Leadership, leadership seminars Phone and email helplines for member organizations, online resources Funding for small development projects Coaching and mentoring for senior staff

Asian and minority ethnic group (BAME) staff. The NHSIII inherited a major programme initiated by the NHSLC to empower BAME staff to achieve promotion within the NHS. Reflecting the extensive range of administrative roles in large healthcare organizations, NHSIII provision, uniquely, catered for career administrators with no grounding in a service profession, including those recruited directly into management positions.

Government-approved frameworks articulating expectations for leading activity informed the design and evaluation of NCSL (DfES, 2004a; Ofsted,

2003) and NHSIII provision (NHSLC, 2002). The Department for Education and Skills (DfES) had revised the original 'standards' for headteachers (Chapter 4). Headteachers were responsibilized for implementing government policy (and implicitly its school reforms): 'The Standards recognise the key role that headteachers play in engaging in the development and delivery of government policy and in raising and maintaining levels of attainment in schools in order to meet the needs of every child' (DfES, 2004a, p. 1). The NHS framework made brief and less directive reference to government healthcare policy: one feature of the leadership quality 'political astuteness' was 'being attuned to health strategy and policy at a national and local level and being able to plan a way ahead that takes account of these strategies' (NHSLC, 2002, p. 7). The government white paper announcing the LFHE asserted it would be 'charged with developing models of good practice in leadership and management' (DfES, 2003a, p. 78). The LFHE's more distanced relationship with government empowered LFHE senior officials to frame its provision as promoting reflective self-development through engagement with the HE context, rather than prescribing: 'Leadership is recognised by everyone but difficult to define precisely. It is diverse and multi-faceted. We are less concerned with seeking the perfect definition. Our focus is on the landscape or context in which leadership, management and governance are practised' (LFHE, 2005, p. 4).

Contextual factors were reflected in the degree of linkage between leadership development provision and other managerialism-inspired 'human resource' (HR) processes. The NCSL (2006a) was implicated in government efforts to address the national shortage of headteachers, in a context of governmental measures for increasing their accountability, while the national standards for headteachers contributed to the focus for the compulsory annual appraisal of headteachers and other senior staff. The NHSIII leadership development programmes were construed as part of the government health department's strategy to establish an NHS-wide 'leadership talent pipeline' within a long-term strategy for building leadership capacity across the NHS. The formally more autonomous HE sector offered little scope for government intervention to build leadership capacity beyond financially supporting the LFHE, precluding strategic-level initiatives to foster talent management practices; consequently, the LFHE's role was confined to informing member organizations about such possibilities through its desk-based research publications.

NLDB orchestration of provision centred on specifying priority programmes and commissioning or contracting specialist expertise. The LFHE alone, the smallest NLDB, relied on developing and managing training provision, including the contracting of trainers, rather than commissioning training organizations to provide courses. Accompanying the shared dominant focus on training programmes for individuals as leaders, a minor emphasis for the NCSL and LFHE was collective leading in teams. Training courses were complemented by online support, especially in the NCSL: e-learning and a network for confidential exchange between headteachers and other senior staff radically extended its reach (NCSL, 2005a). Variable forms of additional support complemented the development programme suites, spanning practice-oriented research (NCSL and LFHE), diagnostic tools (NHSIII), and coaching and mentoring (NHSIII and LFHE). Notably, the titles of all NLDB development programmes headlined generic leadership; none mentioned government reforms. NLDB responses to the government's concern with developing senior staff, especially in schools and healthcare, as government change agents for its reforms were couched within the overarching construal of provision as generic.

Differentiation of NLDB discourse strategies for government and potential participants

The NLDB discourse of leadership and its development lay towards the periphery of the government's nodal discourse of public service reform. The discourse strategy of the NCSL and NHSIII most markedly differentiated messages for specific audiences, reflecting their close formal relationship with government and remits that encompassed building leadership capacity to facilitate the implementation of reforms (Chapter 6). The formally more distanced LFHE was still dependent on government funding, so subject to the government expectation of developing leadership capacity that would enable universities and colleges to thrive within the competitive student recruitment environment fostered by the reform of introducing student tuition fees. NLDB public documentation directed towards a government audience employed formal genres connected with each NLDB's accountability, including strategic plans and annual reports. Reference to government reforms for the service sector typically received mention: directly, as in 'The National College for School Leadership is a key player in bringing about education reform' (NCSL, 2003, p. 9); or by implication, as where NHSIII leadership programmes benefit 'both NHS as a system, and the individuals involved' ... by 'ensuring that leaders in the NHS are equipped with the capabilities to drive through and sustain both incremental and transformational change' that implementing healthcare reforms entails (NHSIII, 2006b, p. 101). The LFHE (2004b, p. 3) referred more obliquely to 'equipping current and future leaders in higher education with the skills and awareness of good practice to help them deliver continuous improvement and respond to future challenges', alongside current challenges (including those flowing from the reform requiring students to pay tuition fees) that include 'encountering an increasingly competitive market for higher education, nationally and internationally, needing to offer a market focused and entrepreneurial response' (p. 9).

Such documents did more than contribute to the nodal discourse of public service reform, especially when each NLDB was being established. They emphasized the structural position of senior staff in public service organizations as experienced professionals, legitimately influencing others within their jurisdiction, and motivated by professional service values underlying their orchestration of local service provision. Illustratively, the NCSL's leadership development framework relayed the results of extensive consultation within the profession, including the message that 'leaders who are capable of transforming their schools are driven by a passionate commitment to a set of educational and moral values; they need time and opportunity to explore and test their values so that they can act consistently and with confidence in the school workplace' (NCSL, 2001, p. 3). The leadership qualities framework inherited by the NHSIII asserts: 'Outstanding leaders bring a sense of integrity to what they do that helps them to deliver to the best of their abilities. Features of this quality include: believing in a set of key values borne out of broad experience of, and commitment to, the service which stands them in good stead, especially when they are under pressure' (NHSLC, 2002, pp. 5–6). The values that matter for HE are construed differently as an organizational property that leaders should model through their behaviour, expressed in the role expectation that 'those in leadership roles will work with others to shape a vision, provide a sense of direction, act as a role model for the institution's [university or college] values, and ensure that the organisation delivers its missions' (LFHE, 2005, p. 4).

Documents targeting potential participants in NLDB provision via marketing genres, including prospectuses or brochures, occasionally referred to reforms as part of the context for leadership, rather than a specific leadership task or focus for developmental activities. Illustratively, an NCSL prospectus heralded a benefit of participation in a programme for 'middle leaders' as 'an increased ability to lead innovation and change in the context of their own school and the national agenda for reform' (NCSL, 2005b, p. 8); an NHSIII programme for chief executives and medical directors included 'international health leadership forum visits where you can explore specific health policy and reform issues with international colleagues' (NHSIII, 2006c, p. 22); and an LFHE brochure for its Top Management Programme (TMP) claimed that 'learning and networking with other higher education professionals of a similar calibre and very different experiences … enables good practice, continuous improvement and responsive leadership to be enjoyed across the sector' (LFHE, undated, p. 6). Also noteworthy is the contrast between the leadership frameworks for NCSL and NHSIII, both leader-centrically focused on leading activity to influence others. The national standards for headteachers were produced by government. They link leadership, so, by implication, NCSL's provision, directly with leading the 'delivery' of reforms. The NHS Leadership Qualities, produced by the original NHSLC for healthcare, make only minor reference, couched less directively in terms of leaders' political astuteness in 'taking account' of reforms within their leading activity. LFHE provision is similarly leader-centric in designing the large bulk of its programmes for individuals as leaders, concentrating on their leading activity.

Mildly subversive NLDB control technologies for training and developing public service leaders

Our interviews with NLDB senior officials and their commissioned trainers further evidenced the very moderate mediation inherent in the differentiation of the NLDBs' discourse strategies. Table 7.2 indicates that all our NLDB senior official, and most trainer, interviewees had some past experience as service professionals within their present or another public service sector, involving management responsibility. Several mentioned how aspects of that experience informed their current practice, with one NCSL senior official speaking of personal values as an education professional driving the decision to apply for this position:

> I was actually very passionate about working with an organization that had a clear vision, and had clear goals that were about improving outcomes for young people … one of the things that I've always been passionate about, whether or not as an English teacher, or a deputy head, or a head, or working in a local authority, is actually that none of this matters if it doesn't mean that things are going to be better for young people.

Table 7.2 Past experience as public service professionals of senior officials from national leadership development bodies and trainers interviewed

NLDB	NCSL	NHSIII	LFHE
Senior officials interviewed	3 headteachers	1 NHS doctor and chief executive 1 NHS general manager and chief executive 1 local government manager and NHS trainer 1 further education (FE) lecturer	2 academics and trainers 1 deputy head-teacher and academic 1 senior civil servant
Trainers interviewed	1 headteacher 2 headteachers and LEA advisers 1 teacher, trainer, and LEA chief inspector 1 teacher, vice-principal (FE), trainer, and LEA adviser 1 teacher, head of department, and LEA adviser (1 Ofsted lay inspector)	1 NHS general manager 1 ward sister, academic, and NHS chief executive 1 academic and trainer (2 had no public service professional experience)	2 academics 1 NHS manager and trainer (1 had no public service professional experience)

This senior official had adopted a distanced stance when informing participants about the NCSL's duty to support them with implementing reforms for schools: 'I am very clear that the College has a role to provide support for leaders and managers to enable them to effectively implement the curriculum reforms, but at the same time . . . making it clear to our clients that we are not necessarily the people that are promoting these.' However, several trainers did not have prior public service professional experience.

The approaches adopted within each NLDB's control technology of training and development were based on acculturating participants to view themselves as leaders, but they stopped short of fostering the formal co-optation of participants by encouraging them to perceive themselves as leaders acting as change agents for government-driven reforms or future agendas. Instead, NLDB trainers reportedly 'challenged' participants to take reforms into account as a contextual factor affecting their leading activity. The approach of the intermediate-level elite and associate NLDB senior officials and their commissioned trainers was mildly subversive, most markedly in the NCSL and NHSIII, despite close government oversight. Leadership development activities did promote the acculturation of participants as leaders committed to orchestrating service provision and its ongoing improvement, though guided by their values as public service professionals. So the values of participants acknowledged and supported through the provision included those that might be contradictory to the political and economic values of strategic-level authoritative elites in government, ideologically underpinned by neoliberalism and backed by managerialism. Participants were encouraged to act, implicitly, as local-level corporate agents, empowered to decide whether and, if so, how to address reforms; to consider the degree of alignment between the values and ideology underpinning reforms and their professional service values; and to weigh up the risks and opportunities associated with alternative responses to reform requirements.

NCSL senior officials and two associated trainers implied that provision was supporting the development of senior school staff as change agents for reform by encouraging them to interpret and respond to government policy in the light of local needs. While attention was given to the implications of reforms for participants, provision was cast in terms of generic leadership. Participants were encouraged to decide whether to apply leadership concepts and practical strategies discussed to address reforms, alongside any other change agenda. An NCSL senior official commented:

> I don't think there are too many headteachers that say that their role is actually just about managing the change process on behalf of the government . . . the most effective headteachers . . . are passionate about wanting the best for their youngsters, and sometimes they find the government agenda almost an irrelevance to that, or potentially worse, working against it . . . the challenge for the College is . . . providing opportunities that are generic enough to enable people to respond to their own circumstances as they see fit.

A colleague senior official indicated how provision was designed to assist participants in doing so: 'How do you get people to enact . . . autonomy in a highly accountable working environment, and how do you get them to do it with confidence? . . . Their job is to interpret policy. What we try to give them . . . is the confidence and the competence to do that, whatever context they're working in.'

Scope for mediation rested with NCSL senior officials, who tightly delimited the contribution of trainers offering NCSL programmes regionally, requiring them to use NCSL materials; standardized assessment arrangements for NPQH were regionally and nationally moderated. NCSL staff trained, assessed, and updated 'lead facilitators' from each training provider for this programme. They employed a cascade 'training trainers' model: the lead facilitator trained other facilitators, and was responsible for regional quality assurance procedures. One trainer claimed to have only a '10 per cent opportunity' for personalizing the prescribed materials and training approach, consistent with this statement:

> We've had diktats down from National College saying, this has to change, this is what needs to be included in this programme, and we respond. I feel now that actually that is shifting, that we have a little bit more flexibility to amend things, as long as we don't amend the frame, and to meet the needs of the candidates as we see them when we're working with them.

The NHSIII's leadership development contribution was also mildly subversive in casting provision as generic. Reflecting the NHSIII's innovation remit, this control technology focused more exclusively on leading the development and implementation of planned change: innovation for healthcare improvement. Scope for innovation was, nevertheless, delimited by the thrust of NHS healthcare reforms to create an increasingly marketized national system. One NHSIII senior official explained that 'a core part of leadership development has got to be around change capability, and formal, disciplined tools and techniques for change; and I believe that every senior leader in the NHS needs to have those skills'. A colleague elaborated on the process being developed for improving work productivity, encompassing senior staff as leaders and team members:

> It is a methodology which is iterative, which includes a heavy emphasis on co-production, and a very heavy emphasis on observation of whatever it is that we are trying to change . . . this work methodology we've refined a lot, has gateways in it which mean one can't move on to the next stage without a sign-off . . . it has proved pretty good.

Trainers described how they operationalized the developmental approach, one referring to sequential pedagogical moves for raising awareness and stimulating reflection about improvement:

> challenge them . . . why are they doing things in the way they're doing . . . their view of the world . . . the level of performance that they're achieving now . . . how

> they spend their time . . . where they're taking their career . . . Secondly . . . broaden their perspective, being able to get them to see how things might be done a little differently . . . Next, it is giving them new ideas . . . a framework or a model within which they can place their ideas . . . Fourth, there is a transfer of knowledge aspect . . . how this is done in other industries . . . to broaden their perspective.

There was less potential for mediation within LFHE provision since government reforms for the sector concerned strengthening conditions for operating in a marketplace with students from diversifying social backgrounds as 'paying customers'. Broadly paralleling the control technologies of the other two NLDBs, the LFHE cast its provision in terms of generic leadership, with an emphasis on leading change, and reflecting leaders' professional service values. LFHE senior officials and two trainers implied that one focus for leading change was developing individual self-awareness and emotional intelligence. An LFHE senior official elaborated:

> Emotional intelligence is raising an awareness of what they truly are capable of, what they think, what they believe, where the assumptions come from, things that they may have never asked themselves previously . . . The second part . . . is awareness of others and recognition of diversity within groups that might even have similar subject areas but actually have a very different take on life. Therefore, the leadership agenda is driven partly by understanding what others need from a particular engagement. And if you try to engage them in change, and that change is actually either counter-cultural for them or is not perceived to being of their interest, then don't be surprised if they dig their heels in.

One trainer noted a complementary focus of programmes offered to an individual university or college: harnessing generic leadership development to support diagnosing and implementing an organization-wide change, such as 'the delivery of a significant new paradigm for the institution [university or college], to be more internationally aware, to become more commercially aware, to work in partnership with other people more actively'.

The LFHE had eschewed using a leadership framework, but a senior official drew attention to

> transformational leadership as being one of the approaches that seems to fit most comfortably the environment of higher education . . . this is very much about values-based leadership, values that are held very deeply, very passionately by a lot of people, and a set of shared values; it is about dealing with people as people.

Though scarcely subversive, given the formal autonomy of universities and colleges from government, the LFHE legitimated senior staff basing activity for leading change on their service professional values. To this extent, leadership development provision in all three NLDBs did not align with the government's responsibilization of senior staff in public service organizations as leaders acting as change agents for reform, captured in the comment (Chapter 6): 'when the policy has been decided it's their job to inspirationally implement it.' Our evidence of mild subversion did not extend to overt resistance. It seems feasible that the scope for manoeuvre exploited in all the NLDBs enabled staff and trainers to express their professional values, mostly born of experience as public service professionals.

Significance for NLDBs of representative bodies for senior staff in public service organizations

Representative bodies supported staff in all three public service sectors. We report on the representative bodies our interviews suggested were most concerned with building the leadership capacity of their members. Table 7.3 summarizes their details, reflecting the instigation of the LFHE by Universities UK (UUK) and the Standing Conference of Principals (SCOP) (Chapter 6). Their counterparts for schools and healthcare were less central to the establishment of the NSCL and NHSLC or its successor, NHSIII, since the relevant government departments had launched them. Nevertheless, representative bodies from different sectors did engage with their NLDB or advise their members about its provision. We interpret this endeavour as the part of their *support project* directed towards furthering the material and ideal interests of members in their further professionalization as leaders, including professional development opportunities and credentials, working conditions, remuneration, and formal recognition.

The representative bodies were of diverse types, some hybrid. They included trade unions in the school education sector, entitled to engage in national negotiations over pay and conditions of service, and profession-oriented bodies in healthcare and HE, more focused on continuing professional development (CPD) for members and advocacy connected with government policy. Their membership comprised individuals or organizations from different sectoral subgroups, mostly benefiting staff in top and senior management positions within public service organizations. The representative bodies shared an advocacy role targeted towards government and the public; in healthcare, NHS staff in top management positions within central

Table 7.3 Representative bodies for senior staff in schools, healthcare, and higher education engaged with building leadership capacity, 2007

Service sector	Characteristics of representative bodies relevant to NLDB provision in 2007			
	Type of representation	Membership	Advocacy on behalf of members	Leadership development provision for members
Schools				
Association of School and College Leaders (ASCL)	Professional association and trade union	Secondary school head-teachers and other senior staff	Lobbies government, publicizes position on policies, contributes to consultations	ASCL professional development company provides leadership development programmes and consultancy, including NCSL's headteacher induction, organizes conferences and events
National Association of Headteachers (NAHT)	Professional association and trade union	Primary and secondary school headteachers and other senior staff	Lobbies government, publicizes position on policies, contributes to consultations	Provides professional development incorporating leadership development programmes and consultancy, includes NPQH, organizes conferences and events

Continued

Table 7.3 *Continued*

Service sector	Characteristics of representative bodies relevant to NLDB provision in 2007			
	Type of representation	Membership	Advocacy on behalf of members	Leadership development provision for members
Healthcare				
British Association of Medical Managers (BAMM)	Professional association for advocacy, registered charity	Doctors with management responsibility	Lobbies government, publicizes position on policies, contributes to consultations, publishes reports, e.g. proposed career structure, leadership development syllabus, medical leadership standards	Provides a professional development programme on becoming a clinical leader, promotes networks
Institute of Health Management (IHM)	Independent professional body, limited company	NHS and private health and social care managers, consultants	Lobbies government and NHS administration, publicizes position on policies, contributes to consultations, publishes management standards, code of conduct	Provides professional development including leadership development programmes, accreditation scheme, promotes networks, organizes conferences and events, piloting a scheme for members to record their participation in CPD

NHS Alliance	Pressure group representing providers of primary care	General practitioners (GPs), community health-care staff, organizations including primary care trusts (PCTs), health boards, local authorities	Lobbies government and NHS administration, publicizes position on policies, contributes to consultations, publishes reports, e.g. on PCT management (commissioned by DoH), advises primary care organizations	Organizes events, promotes networks
NHS Confederation	Advocacy body for healthcare organizations, registered charitable company	All organizations providing NHS-funded services (NHS, charity, private sector), benefiting all staff	Lobbies government and NHS administration, publicizes position on policies, contributes to consultations, publishes reports to inform public debate, e.g. on leadership challenges in the NHS	Promotes networks, the subsidiary trading company organizes conferences and events to inform senior health professionals
Higher education				
1994 Group	Mission group for small research-intensive universities	Universities in the association, benefiting vice-chancellors and other senior staff	Lobbies government, funding bodies, publicizes position on policies, publishes research reports	University of Essex provides a leadership development programme for senior staff from member organizations, and one for heads of department

Continued

Table 7.3 Continued

| Service sector | Characteristics of representative bodies relevant to NLDB provision in 2007 | | | |
	Type of representation	Membership	Advocacy on behalf of members	Leadership development provision for members
Association of Business Schools (ABS)	Professional association, registered charity	Business schools, benefiting their staff	Lobbies government and business organizations, publicizes position on policies, contributes to consultations, publishes research and policy analysis reports	Provides leadership development programmes for deans and other senior staff in member business schools, using graduates of programmes as trainers, organizes conferences, promotes networks
GuildHE (previously SCOP)	Representative body for HE	Principals of small universities and colleges	Lobbies government, publicizes position on policies, contributes to consultations, publishes reports, contributes to oversight of LFHE	Forum for vice chancellors and principals (observer status on the board of LFHE), promotes network for senior staff of small universities and colleges funded by LFHE
Universities UK (UUK)	Representative body for HE	Vice-chancellors or principals of universities	Lobbies government, publicizes position on policies, e.g. parliamentary briefings, contributes to consultations, publishes research and policy analysis, contributes to oversight of LFHE	Promotes networks, organizes events (observer status on the board of LFHE), considering UUK leadership development provision for target groups that LFHE does not address

NHS administrative organizations were also targeted. Where a representative body embodied a formal association between different groupings (as with diverse types of primary care provider within the NHS Alliance), it conferred increased agency on members from all constituent groupings by engaging in collective advocacy to further their shared interests. Half the representative bodies across all three services provided leadership development programmes for members, creating the potential for competition with NLDB provision. UUK and GuildHE (successor to SCOP) did not provide programmes but retained close oversight of the LFHE's provision they had instigated.

The support projects of these representative bodies varied with the service sector and membership grouping. One mutual, though differently weighted, area of concern lay with the professionalization of members through their development as *professional leaders*, occasionally 'leaders and managers', or simply 'managers'. The phrase 'professional leaders' connotes the capability for leading activity resting on the acquisition of specialist knowledge and influencing skills, and experience with applying them in different settings (Chapter 2). So professional leaders could potentially become construed as members of a putative leadership profession, more 'chief executives' than 'leading professionals' providing the public service itself (Hughes, 1976).

Our documentary sources did not couch professionalization as leaders in such terms; however, evidence from each sector suggests that the aim to serve their members did include this aspiration. Illustratively, the ASCL identified itself on its website homepage as 'the professional association for leaders of secondary schools and colleges', implying that senior staff stood to benefit from the support of a bespoke professional association for leaders. In healthcare, the professionalization of general managers (without experience as a clinical professional) featured in the IHM chief executive officer's account of its role: 'As a professional body the Institute of Healthcare Managers aspires to take on the role of enabling healthcare managers to become a profession, by working towards professional registration' (Hodgetts, 2007). The introduction of general managers in the 1980s (Chapter 2) had resulted in a perception amongst healthcare professionals that these managers lacked the credibility of senior clinicians shouldering management responsibility (Exworthy, 1994). Regarding HE, the stated aims of the UUK and SCOP business case for the LFHE (UUK/SCOP, 2003, p. 1) included to 'contribute to the further development of professional leaders and managers'. The UUK and SCOP thereby adopted the terminology of the white paper (Chapter 6), consistent with the professionalization of senior staff in universities and colleges as members of a leadership and management profession.

Our interviews and documentary evidence confirmed that visionary and leader-centric discourse had been adopted within all the representative bodies. They primarily emphasized individual leading activity, as in the claim that the UUK (undated) 'brings together the leaders of UK universities to discuss and debate current and future higher education issues'. It was complemented by a minor focus on collective leading and more mutual influencing, as where 'Schools and colleges are led by teams of leaders with a variety of backgrounds and a variety of expertise and focus. School improvement is brought about by teams of leaders, teachers and other professionals working together' (ASCL, 2006a). This quotation illustrates how leadership was associated with valued change (here, 'school improvement'), whether connected with reforms or with other agendas.

Professionalization as leaders within the support projects of representative bodies was implicit in the element of their *discourse strategies* promoting leadership development as a form of continuing *professional* development, to which members were entitled in seeking to advance their individual learning and career as leaders. Indicatively, the IHM was committed to specifying and designing CPD provision to professionalize healthcare managers: 'Management competencies including . . . leadership . . . would also be implicit within the CPD requirements maximizing the scope for reflection upon experience' (Hodgetts, 2007). Advocacy included responsibilizing government to support such development within its political project of public service reform, exemplified by the NHS Confederation (2007, p. 14):

> Increasingly, NHS organisations are finding it difficult to recruit people to the top jobs because of the pressure and exposed position people find themselves in. From politicians to the NHS itself, we all need to take collective action to ensure that our senior managers are supported in their important roles, that turnover is reduced and that the NHS rebuilds its leadership capacity.

Representative body training courses focused on individual career development. The ASCL's professional development company supplemented the preparatory training introduced by government to give participants an advantage in seeking a first headship. Its brochure asserted: 'Being ready for headship is one thing, getting a job is another. This course aims to teach the skills that NPQH does not reach and thereby improve the chances of achieving a first headship' (ASCL, 2006b).

Subversive assistance: representative body control technologies for developing professional leaders

Control technologies enacting representative body support projects served the interests of members and represented them to others. Aspects of most relevance (Table 7.3) were, first, advocacy to inform and persuade government policymakers, their agencies, and NLDB senior officials about the development needs of members as leaders; second, training or other developmental activities, including conferences, networking opportunities, or leadership development provision. Table 7.4 summarizes those aspects of the control technologies of advocacy and CPD for members most directly impacted by the three national leadership development interventions. All but one of the representative bodies that invested in their own leadership development provision, and the two that established their NLDB (the LFHE) to provide it for them, also sought and capitalized on diverse opportunities for formal or informal advocacy, evidencing the horizontal workings of power within the intermediate level between NLDBs and representative bodies. Such opportunities included contributing to NLDB governance, responding to NLDB consultations, holding regular meetings with NLDB senior officials and inviting them to speak at conferences, and collaborating on activities serving NLDB and representative body interests.

Two representative bodies did not pursue advocacy to influence their NLDB: senior officials from the NHS Alliance noted that leadership development was just one component of the NHSIII's brief, so there was little prospect of its provision being expanded; senior ABS staff perceived there was no overlap between their leadership development offering for business school members and LFHE provision, so no conflict of interests prompting them to engage. The focus for advocacy in the other representative bodies was either to extend opportunities for their members to realize their material and ideal interest in furthering their professional and career development as leaders, or to protect members from possible threats to this interest.

The mutual dependency relationship between each NLDB and any representative body reflected a complex set of other relationships affecting their dominant or subordinate relational social positions, spanning:

- the formal relationship between each NLDB and government (NCSL and NHSIII tightly regulated; LFHE steered by representative bodies responsible for establishing it within the bounds of acceptability to government funding bodies providing financial support);

Table 7.4 Aspects of control technologies employed by representative bodies related to leadership development provision of the NCSL, NHSIII, and LFHE

Service sector and NLDB	Aspects of representative body control technologies related to NLDB provision		
	Relationship with NLDB (as perceived by senior staff from representative bodies)	Advocacy on behalf of members connected with NLDBs	Impact of NLDB provision on professional and career development for members
Schools—NCSL			
Association of School and College Leaders (ASCL)	**Moderately influential:** regular engagement, supportive but sometimes critical, ASCL contributes to NCSL provision	Member representative on NCSL board, entitled to be consulted on provision (e.g. prompted NCSL programme for aspiring leaders), NCSL CEO invited to speak at ASCL conference	ASCL bids to become commissioned trainer for NCSL programmes, avoids overlap with ASCL's other provision, ASCL members participate in NCSL provision
National Association of Headteachers (NAHT')	**Moderately influential:** regular engagement, supportive but sometimes critical, NAHT contributes to NCSL provision	Member representative on NCSL board, entitled to be consulted on provision (e.g. influenced NPQH programme), NCSL CEO invited to speak at NAHT conference, senior NAHT officials attend NSCL conference	NAHT bid to become commissioned trainer for NPQH, collaborating on development of NCSL mentoring for new headteachers, NAHT members participate in NCSL provision

Healthcare—NHSIII

British Association of Medical Managers (BAMM)	**Moderately influential** (for clinical leaders): regular engagement, supportive of relevant NHSIII work, avoids overlap with NHSIII provision	Regular meetings with NHSIII staff, invited to BAMM activities	BAMM leadership development programme designed to complement NHSIII provision for medical managers by catering for more senior staff than NHSIII
Institute of Health Management (IHM)	**Moderately influential** (for healthcare managers): regular engagement, NHSIII staff contribute to IHM provision	Regular dialogue with several NHS staff includes giving them feedback, encourage NHSIII to join networks that IHM promotes	IHM accreditation scheme and pilot for monitoring individual engagement in CPD include participation in NHSIII provision, use NHSIII staff as trainers for IHM provision
NHS Alliance	**Relatively uninfluential** (for senior primary care staff, as little NHSIII leadership development provision for them): infrequent engagement	Little advocacy directed towards NHSIII as its leadership development provision is only a small part of NHSIII's remit	NHSIII has low impact as little leadership development provision for senior primary care staff
NHS Confederation	**Very moderately influential** (for specific improvements, not leadership development provision): regular engagement	Representation on NHSIII sounding board, collaborating with NHSIII to develop leadership and management competencies for doctors	NHSIII caters for individuals from member organizations participating in its leadership development provision

Higher education—LFHE

1994 Group	**Moderately influential** (for 1994 Group senior staff): regular engagement	Regular meetings with LFHE senior officials and responses to consultations, engaged with LFHE about potential overlap between 1994 Group and LFHE leadership development provision	LFHE reviewed 1994 Group provision outcome that it was judged complementary to LFHE provision, some 1994 Group universities are LFHE members so senior staff participate in LFHE provision

Continued

Table 7.4 *Continued*

Service sector and NLDB	Aspects of representative body control technologies related to NLDB provision		
	Relationship with NLDB (as perceived by senior staff from representative bodies)	Advocacy on behalf of members connected with NLDBs	Impact of NLDB provision on professional and career development for members
Association of Business Schools (ABS)	**Relatively uninfluential** (for senior business school staff): no overlap between ABS and LFHE leadership development provision, little engagement	Little advocacy directed towards LFHE as LFHE leadership development provision complementary to that of ABS	LFHE caters for ABS members from LFHE member universities participating in LFHE provision
GuildHE (previously SCOP)	**Very influential:** frequent engagement as 'critical friend', very supportive, LFHE responsive in funding support for small universities and colleges	Senior representative on LFHE board (observer status), regular informal meetings with LFHE senior officials, focus on leadership development needs of senior staff in small universities and colleges	LFHE funds the GuildHE promoted management network for small universities and colleges, GuildHE encourages its members to participate in LFHE provision, e.g. TMP programme, LFHE provides conference facilitators
Universities UK (UUK)	**Very influential:** frequent formal and informal engagement, very supportive	Representative on LFHE board (observer status), LFHE representative on UUK sub-board, also attends UUK seminars, UUK relies on LFHE to identify leadership development needs in member organizations	Many UUK members participate in LFHE programmes, e.g. TMP, UUK considering whether to complement LFHE provision through UUK provision for any groups that LFHE does not cater for

- the scope of the NLDB remit (NSCL and LFHE concerned exclusively with leadership development; NHSIII concerned mainly with improvement with leadership development as one priority programme);
- the degree of influence that the representative body was legitimated in wielding over an NLDB (some representative bodies had no formal entitlement to be consulted; others did but senior NLDB staff were not obliged to comply with any course of action advocated; still others could contribute to steering NLDB practice);
- the extent of representative body engagement in leadership development provision and its overlap with that offered by the NLDB (some representative bodies did not make such provision; others did but sought to avoid overlap with that of the NLDB; yet others acted as commissioned trainers for NLDB programmes).

Overall, the social position of the representative bodies for school education and healthcare was subordinated to that of the NSCL and NHSIII in respect of their leadership development provision. The brief of these NLDBs, plus priorities and expectations about achieving them, were set and monitored by strategic-level elites within the relevant government departments, restricting scope for NLDB senior officials to alter course. While representative bodies could express views, offer ideas, request changes and, for the NCSL, tender to become commissioned trainers for its programmes, power to decide the NLDB response rested with NLDB senior officials. This extract from a statement of NAHT (2007, p. 19) policy illustrates how some representative bodies did publicly voice criticisms of the relevant NLDB, though we found no evidence of an NCSL response:

> The National College must realise that it does not have a monopoly on quality school leadership and professional development; neither does it have the right to deny school leaders access to other quality providers. [The NAHT] Conference calls upon National Council to continue to engage in dialogue with the NCSL to move away from a 'one size fits all' model for school leadership.

The issue concerns the interest of NAHT members in protecting the NAHT's longstanding investment in its own leadership development opportunities, and their instruction to representative body senior officials and members serving on its governing National Council, urging them to continue with advocacy.

However, representative body senior officials tended to be positive towards their NLDB where provision served the professional and career development interests of members; thus an NAHT informant noted how 'we have actually been involved and been supportive, insofar as you can be with an organization [NCSL] that has its own way of doing things'. In this way the representative bodies assisted the NLDBs in mildly subverting the acculturative co-optation of senior staff from public service organizations participating in this provision as government change agents for public service reforms. They helped to promote NLDB provision as generic, mirroring the representative body provision offered by half of their number. Their advocacy and, where offered, their leadership development provision promoted developing the capability of members, as professional leaders, to lead any change consistent with their professional values, in most cases founded on experience as public service professionals.

The social position of the representative bodies for HE evidenced a sharp contrast between the UUK and GuildHE and others. UUK and GuildHE occupied a relatively dominant position, reflected in the comment of a UUK informant: 'We're active components of the Leadership Foundation, both in terms of sitting on the board ... but also in promoting and supporting its activities ... we meet at a number of levels throughout the year, we keep each other informed of developments, we offer advice and guidance to help steer the Leadership Foundation.' A focus for GuildHE successful advocacy was sustaining the LFHE's funding of the Management of Small Higher Education Institutions Network (MASHEIN), originally funded by the Higher Education Funding Council for England (HEFCE) and transferred to the LFHE. MASHEIN activities included management training, work shadow placements, and an annual conference for senior management teams of small universities and colleges (LFHE, 2005). However, the corporate agency of these representative bodies was delimited by their dependence on the funding councils providing financial support. LFHE provision must be deemed acceptable by both senior officials from these two representative bodies and senior funding council staff, themselves in a subordinate social position to their government education department.

The 1994 Group also engaged with the LFHE, despite occupying a relatively subordinate social position in respect of it. Advocacy had been to protect the 1994 Group's leadership development provision for its member universities. With the creation of the LFHE, these organizations might subscribe to membership of the LFHE instead. An informant from the 1994 Group pointed to the threat that duplicated provision would pose to the sustainability of their leadership development programmes: 'Why on earth would our members be paying a subscription fee to the Leadership Foundation to provide a certain set of resources or courses . . . [while] having to pay a separate fee to us for us to provide something . . . why weren't the Leadership Foundation including it within their own portfolio of activities?' The response of LFHE senior officials reflected their relative dependence on widespread acceptance amongst the universities and colleges the LFHE was to serve, despite its dominant social position that legitimated providing whatever would fulfil its purpose. They offered to review the 1994 Group's provision, reporting that 'the leadership course was . . . "a jewel in the crown of activities", that it did provide something which was a niche product which our members would find useful, but which complemented the work that the Leadership Foundation were doing'. Accordingly, the 1994 Group vice chancellors retained this course for members as complementary to LFHE provision. The upshot was to realize the interest of LFHE senior officials in gaining the acceptance of the 1994 Group, several of whose senior staff subsequently attended the LFHE's flagship TMP programme. This resolution was possible because the LFHE's loose relationship with government gave senior officials flexibility in compromising to meet a sectional interest.

We have seen how strategic-level elites in and around government were motivated to mount the suite of national leadership development interventions as a means of facilitating public service reforms. This motivation stems from a dominant social position founded on legitimation minimally requiring the acquiescence—though, better, the endorsement and active support—of those through whom a change desired by the dominant group is to be implemented. Similarly, intermediate-level elites within NLDBs, on whom the government depended for the implementation of each intervention, were in a dominant social position in respect of elites from representative bodies. Yet the legitimation of these NLDBs was dependent on being accepted and supported by representative body senior officials bent, in turn, on serving the sectional interest of individual members in their professional and career development. Domination resting on legitimation is never absolute, and all three NLDBs were vulnerable to losing their legitimacy. They were externally evaluated after several years in operation, involving consultation with representative bodies and measures of NLDB reach, take-up, and satisfaction with the target group of senior staff in public service organizations. These evaluations had consequences for NLDB senior officials (Chapter 6).

Overall, representative bodies assisted the moderate mediation by NLDBs of the government's intended link between building leadership capacity and facilitating its public service reforms. Senior officials from these representative bodies achieved their influence through advocacy, and often their own leadership development provision, pushing NLDB provision towards serving professional and career development interests through its generic focus. The emphasis on leading change took account of current reforms alongside other change agendas, but participants were apparently encouraged, as professional leaders, to refer to their values in framing their leading activity, which, for most, was grounded in experience as public service professionals.

Attempting to make the parts add up to a whole: promoting cross-NLDB coordination

The proliferation of separate national leadership development interventions prompted concern amongst strategic-level elites from the government's Cabinet Office regarding their combined efficiency and quality, and their limited ability to cater for senior staff from public service organizations moving between services. One senior politician had reportedly asked: 'Why have we got fifteen public sector leadership bodies? Let's just have one, we can save lots of money, because surely leading a hospital is just the same as leading a university', reflecting the assumption that leading activity is generic. A senior civil servant allowed for some organizational context-sensitivity, also noting how departmental budgets for leadership development were coming under increasing pressure because the return on investment in the interventions was unclear. Greater coordination between them would reap efficiency and quality gains, while opening up the prospect of providing credentials to encourage cross-sector careers:

> Each sector was developing and funding its own particular leadership requirements in a way which seemed both duplicative and not good value for money . . . there might have been a need for customizing maybe about 20 percent of the leadership development products. I would argue that 75–80 percent was common to each, and there was much to be gained from joining up forces in terms of procurement and delivery . . . if there were good practices in one sector, to help to spread that over into other sectors . . . We should be encouraging greater mobility across public sectors in terms of leaders . . . potentially through giving them more portable qualifications and leadership development.

In 2005 this concern prompted the construction of a business case within the Cabinet Office for creating a Public Service Leadership Consortium (PSLC), in consultation with NLDB senior officials. It was positively received by ministers of the relevant departments. The PSLC was a forum for NLDB senior officials, chaired by the Cabinet Office, aiming 'to add value above service specific leadership initiatives by delivering a programme of joint action on leadership development, procurement and the sharing of best practice between the public services' (OPM, 2006, p. 35). Conversations reportedly enabled officials from new NLDBs to learn from their counterparts in established ones. A senior civil servant highlighted the unintended impact of different financial incentives built into arrangements imposed on NLDBs, governing payment for participation:

> Some [NLDBs] had to fully recover their costs, some didn't. Some of them were to have an element of members' fees to support the business, some weren't. Those make a huge difference in how you structure the business, and how you can do leadership; whether it's going to be a commodity that can be just consumed by an individual, or whether it's something that is far more organizational.

This funding factor may have compounded leader-centric construals of leadership in contributing to the commodification of leadership development provision in our focal NLDBs. All three charged for provision, targeted largely at individuals, whose own organizations typically funded their participation through a CPD budget. Participation was voluntary. Part of its attraction, promoted by representative bodies for senior staff, was as a form of professional and career development.

The incremental process of mounting national leadership development interventions had favoured each service sector having its bespoke intervention, justified on the grounds that leadership is context-dependent, so its development must be context-sensitive. If participation was to be voluntary, provision stood to attract more target senior staff if they perceived it to be directly relevant to their own service context. Our interviews confirmed that the contextuality of provision had become part of the justification for each NLDB's sectoral jurisdiction, its provision, and marketing. An NCSL senior official stated:

> In terms of leadership, context matters, and in terms of school leadership, which is our remit, the education or the school system environment is critical. So what you

would do in that system may not be the same as you might do in the justice or the
police system, or in the health system.

A senior civil servant reported some reticence to engage with other NLDBs:
'Historically there's been, perhaps, less collaboration than one might have
expected because of the fear that if it was demonstrable that by combining
forces into, not necessarily a single organization, but a smaller number of
organizations, it might threaten their organizational integrity.' The potential
for NLDB mergers had reportedly prompted NLDB senior officials to 'protect your turf, argued largely on the basis that there was a certain uniqueness
and importance [of contextualized provision] . . . making it very geared to
the needs of the specific sectors'.

Sunk investment by different government departments in service sectoral
NLDBs meant that Cabinet Office orchestration of NLDB coordination must
rely on acculturation and voluntary participation. Initiatives were undertaken to generate PSLC activities relevant to all NLDBs that would further
government priorities, including regulated marketization reforms: 'The tension between the specialist versus the generic . . . one way that we sought
to resolve that was focusing in, initially, on a specific area which I think
most would accept was cross-cutting, which was around customer focus;
what did customer-focused leadership look like?' The Cabinet Office commissioned a set of learning resources for the NLDBs, providing a curriculum for customer-focused leadership development that included 'analysing
your customers', 're-designing your organisation around the customer' and
'entrepreneurial skills' (PSLC, 2006). Another initiative to inform NLDB
practice was a report on the 'market' for public service leadership development, recommending ways in which the PSLC could contribute to improving
it (OPM, 2006). Yet another, with a regulatory emphasis on accountability
for NLDB provision, was a PSLC-sponsored evaluation framework devised
by members whose foci included 'key performance outcomes—did the
organisation's performance improve?', 'community impact', and 'return on
investment' (Cabinet Office, 2006, p. 1).

Strategic-level elite engagement in orchestrating cross-NLDB coordination ceased in 2007 when the cross-NLDB coordination responsibility of
the Cabinet Office was delegated to intermediate-level elite senior officials
within one NLDB: the National School of Government, serving the government civil service (Table 1.1). The PSLC was rebranded as the Public Service

Leadership Alliance (PSLA), with a continuing emphasis on cross-NLDB initiatives, exemplified by a commissioned academic review of NLDB practices for evaluating their provision. The authors (Riley & Stoll, 2007, p. 1) noted how 'evaluation varies and few evaluation frameworks have been developed', suggesting limited implementation of the earlier PSLC framework. Further, 'tracking the impact of leadership on change to the organisation, locality or system is a desirable but frequently elusive outcome', implying that evidence was still lacking of any return on the government investment in terms of the full putative chain of influence, whereby leading activity impacts serially on the behaviour of the led, public service provision, the service experience of users, and, ultimately, its outcomes.

Our interviews with NLDB senior officials confirmed the limited impact of cross-NLDB initiatives. However, there was now more facilitative activity, encouraging exchange to identify areas where senior officials from two or more NLDBs perceived that collaboration would be mutually beneficial. An NHSIII senior official testified to the favourable conditions this forum created: 'We know each other well enough to be able to collaborate, but it is a question of finding the right things on which to collaborate.' A colleague described one area of bilateral interest: 'I'm about to attend the senior command programme that the Defence Academy runs . . . to road test it from a health perspective, because we don't have an equivalent of that in terms of a foundation core programme for senior leaders.' Another NHSIII bilateral collaboration was to support senior officials with establishing the National Police Improvement Agency. NCSL interviewees mentioned working with the Centre for Excellence in Leadership (the NLDB for FE) on measuring the impact of its provision, and with the NHSIII on succession planning. In contrast, the LFHE senior officials simply reported attending PSLA meetings. Any cross-NLDB collaboration seems marginal compared with the extent of siloed NLDB operation.

The horizontal and vertical workings of power here were complex. Scope for cross-level orchestration by elites and their associates based in the Cabinet Office, the government department responsible for departmental coordination, was, ironically, constrained by the prior actions of their colleagues from departments already investing in a national leadership development intervention for one or more service sectors. The opportunity had passed for within-government strategic-level orchestration of the interventions as a suite, based on the contrary assumption that leadership and its development are more generic than contextualized. Since the case for mounting each intervention had emphasized its context-sensitivity, reflected in each NLDB's brief, the appointment of its senior officials, and its provision, the developmental project pursued by senior officials in each NLDB remained wedded to context-sensitive provision for that service sector. Every NLDB was accountable to the department overseeing and resourcing it (including the LFHE, alongside accountability to its founding representative bodies). Consequently, they appear to have moderately mediated the cross-level orchestration effort by combining compliance in attending PSLC meetings with relatively superficial engagement, at most, in cross-NLDB initiatives. Intermediate-level orchestration of the successor PSLA by senior officials from the National School of Government was subject to less mediation because the concern with cross-NLDB coordination to fulfil the strategic-level elite agenda was diluted. NLDB senior officials were accorded sufficient corporate agency to decide whether to engage in modest areas of collaborative work, either where one NLDB was sharing expertise with another, or where a confluence of NLDB interests promised mutual benefit. The separate parts of the national leadership development interventions, therefore, remained greater than the suite as a whole.

Counterfactual possibilities underline how government elites and associates did possess sufficient corporate agency to consider alternative intervention approaches, initially and along the way. Means existed for the UK government to mount a single, centrally funded, cross-public service intervention offering generic provision, or to adopt a 'hub and nodes' structure with the hub setting parameters for a national sub-intervention for each service sector offering contextualized provision. The Cabinet Office reviewed public service leadership development provision after our research ended, its recommendations revisiting issues of quality and efficiency linked to the separate establishment and practice of the NLDBs. One recommendation advocated 'encouraging joint provision of cross-sector interventions', highlighting the option 'to explore the idea of a top-sliced **Challenge Fund**, which could be held centrally or by one of the academies ... on behalf of the PSLA, to incentivise joint provision and stronger collaboration' [original bold] (Cabinet Office, 2009, p. 4). This proposal came long after the NLDBs had been established with departmental funding or funding council financial support. It was difficult to persuade senior civil servants and ministers to commit more than a small proportion of their departmental budget to cross-departmental initiatives, as a senior civil servant whom we quoted earlier confirmed. We found no evidence of this recommendation being enacted before the Labour Party lost the general election of 2010, ending its term of office. The incremental approach to mounting interventions apparently created conditions within government that militated against emergent efforts to promote greater coherence, efficiency, and synergy.

Explaining how the implementation of the interventions was orchestrated and mediated

Implementing our three national leadership development interventions was the province of intermediate-level elites and associates: principally NLDB senior officials, with variable engagement (and, for the LFHE, oversight) of senior officials from representative bodies for different groupings of senior staff in public service organizations. Strategic-level senior civil servants within the sponsoring departments and the Cabinet Office continued their engagement, shaping NLDB provision and its uptake as implementation proceeded. Appendix 1 summarizes the additional generative mechanisms inferred from the evidence presented in this chapter. Next, we briefly recap the generative mechanisms identified in Chapter 6, since they are precursors for those connected with implementation.

Within the relevant *context*, a foundational two-fold generative mechanism reinforced the dominant social position of strategic-level elites and associates within central government, legitimating their establishment and occasional reconfiguration of, or financial support for, national leadership development interventions serving each public service sector. This generative mechanism combined channelling and delimiting the corporate agency of local-level elites: staff in top management positions within public service organizations, supported by their senior staff associates. Subscribing, on the one hand, to a *leader-centric construal of leadership* legitimated strategic-level elites within government in deploying their corporate agency as leaders of the national system for administering the public services, and so leaders of the government's public service reform programme. It also legitimated them in deploying this corporate agency to promote the corporate agency of local-level elites in public service organizations, on whom central government depended for implementing its public service reforms, as leaders within this national system. Pursuing, on the other hand, *remote containment* of the corporate agency conferred on local-level elites in public service organizations legitimated strategic-level elites in keeping the diversity of local-level elite responses to government-driven reforms within acceptable limits to government, favouring the faithful transmission of these reforms into public service practice.

This foundational generative mechanism produced a dual flow of additional mechanisms, each channelling or delimiting agency, including the corporate agency of intermediate-level or local-level elites. Thus, the government's *attempted acculturative formal co-optation* of senior staff in public service organizations as leaders within their organizational jurisdiction was directed towards channelling their agency, as local-level elite and associate leaders of reform, through participating in national leadership development interventions centring on NLDBs. Simultaneously, remote containment delimiting the scope for that agency took a more detailed form: *specification* of parameters for each NLDB implementing the intervention for a particular service sector, dictated by government elites alone or reflected in their approval of a proposal from representative bodies for senior staff in public service organizations.

Generative mechanisms

Mediatory subversion by NLDB senior officials blunted the central government endeavour formally to co-opt senior staff in public service organizations by acculturating them as leaders within their organizational jurisdictions, who would subscribe to present government-driven reforms for their service sector and act voluntarily as its change agents by leading the implementation of reforms and operation of the reformed service. This mediation reduced the potential of the interventions to operate as an elite policy meta-lever through responsibilizing senior staff for implementing and operating any reforms of the present or a future government.

Yet the degree of subversion was mild; we found no evidence of subversive intent, nor any challenge to the leader-centric construal of leadership adopted by government elites. On the contrary, NLDB senior officials, their commissioned trainers, and senior staff from the relevant representative bodies shared a similar focus on individual leading activity, with minor emphasis on collective leading of others by, say, leadership teams. The subversion was subtle, possibly subliminal. Central government expectations were moderately frustrated in that leadership development provision focused on leading activity as a generic professional practice, founded on the expression by leaders of their professional values, whether drawn from their experience as public service professionals, as leaders, or as aspiring future leaders. Current reforms were presented as constituting a significant contextual factor, with no evidence of responsibilizing public service providers to respond to future reforms introduced by this or a future government. NLDB senior officials thereby diluted the government elite association between leadership and leading its reforms, empowering participants to focus, implicitly, on acting as change agents for local change agendas they wished to pursue as organizational leaders.

Senior officials from most of the relevant representative bodies were supportive of NLDB senior officials. Representative body advocacy served the material interest of their members amongst senior staff from public service organizations in furthering their individual professional development or career prospects by participating in NLDB provision. Though not expressed in such terms, this advocacy pursued the further professionalization of senior staff, with a service professional background or not, as professional public service leaders, based on their acquisition and application of expert leadership-related knowledge and skills. NLDB provision offered a high-profile route for their acquisition.

Delimitation of mediatory subversion sharply bounded the corporate agency of NLDB senior officials. Our evidence is partly counterfactual. Delimitation appeared to pre-empt any actions on their part that might encourage senior staff from public service organizations to ignore or resist government-driven reforms or, more radically, to form some local alliance that might coalesce as a counter-elite to challenge regulated marketization reform and the legitimacy of government elites to pursue it. We did find evidence of NLDB practice being bounded by the combination of expectations, targets, incentives, surveillance, and potential sanctions built into administrative arrangements for the NCSL and NHSIII, and those governing the provision of financial support for the LFHE. The formal reviews of each NLDB demonstrated how government elites were empowered to initiate and enforce any desired shift of direction or to reward valued compliance with their expectations.

Equally telling, also in part for counterfactual reasons, was the emergence of a lasting endeavour, initiated by government elites within the Cabinet Office, to increase cross-NLDB coordination and control of all the NLDBs that central government elites based in different departments had incrementally introduced. This move was prompted by mounting evidence that the incremental approach had caused some inefficiency in the administration of provision and gaps of procedure, raising a question over the quality of leadership development across the public services. Given governmental reliance on measurable impact and return on investment as means for evaluating policy success, a conspicuous absence was conclusive evidence from evaluations of NLDB provision that the government's sunk investment in the interventions *was* generating significant improvement in public service provision undergoing reform. Such evidence would have to be capable of demonstrating that NLDB provision was increasing leadership capacity, and that leading activity was making a significant contribution to improving service provision, and so to valued service outcomes. The PSLC coordination initiative addressing the evaluation of provision was prompted by disparities in NLDB approaches and the limited attention paid to service outcome assessment. Department-level responsibility for establishing or reconfiguring each NLDB, and recruiting NLDB senior staff, rested on the assumption that leading activity and its development were more context-specific than generic. Unsurprisingly, NLDB senior officials also subscribed to this assumption. Their accountability was to their sponsoring department, not the government as a whole. Since engagement in coordination activities was voluntary, NLDB senior officials were empowered moderately to mediate PSLC initiatives through limited follow-up within their NLDB. Yet these initiatives did highlight Cabinet Office concerns, broadly complementing the much more directive departmental delimitation arrangements. Once coordination was delegated to senior officials from the NLDB for the government civil service, the ambition of the successor PSLA was confined to promoting collaboration between individual NLDBs on agendas of mutual concern. It is unclear whether this purely facilitative exercise made any further contribution to delimiting NLDB provision, and so to its mildly subversive dilution of the linkage between leadership development and reform.

We conclude that moderate NLDB subversion resulted in provision that did not faithfully reflect the reform-linked expectations of UK Labour government ministers and their senior advisers who inaugurated the first NLDB seven years before. Nevertheless, the remote containment of this provision through delimitation, from NLDB administrative arrangements and review to the promotion of cross-NLDB coordination and collaboration between individual NLDBs, created conditions favouring leadership development provision that was broadly compatible with expectations of ministers and advisers, and certainly did not challenge them.

The next chapter will begin by shifting focus to the senior staff from public service organizations who were the targets for NLDB provision, and for the government's discourse strategy promoting leadership to facilitate the implementation of its political project of public service reform. The extent of national target groups and the scale of provision were such that, at any time, only a small proportion of target group members could participate. Yet non-participants were equally subject to the government's discourse strategy and responsibilized to contribute towards the implementation and operation of government-driven reforms. We will examine the extent to which senior staff who had, or had not, experienced this provision were formally co-opted through their acculturation as leaders within their organizational jurisdiction, committed to acting as change agents for government-driven reforms and for local change agendas.

8

Elite mediation of acculturation

change agents for reform or professionalized leaders?

The elites and their associates responsible for instigating the National College for School Leadership (NCSL), for school education, reconfiguring what became the National Health Service Institute for Innovation and Improvement, (NHSIII) for healthcare, and financing the Leadership Foundation for Higher Education (LFHE), for higher education (HE), envisaged their role in terms of building leadership capacity. It amounted to soft power, operationalized as an acculturative control technology for formally co-opting senior staff in public service organizations as leaders who would act voluntarily as change agents for the implementation and operation of government-driven reforms. National leadership development body (NLDB) provision had potential for perpetrating symbolic violence on participants if they misrecognized it and were persuaded to perceive this provision as serving their material and ideal interest in professional development and career advancement. Participants stood to gain empowerment as local-level leaders if they complied with government reform expectations, whether fully acculturated to act as government change agents or not. Alongside this priority, senior staff were encouraged to pursue local change agendas that were compatible with the reforms. To what extent did senior staff who had, or had not, experienced NLDB provision perceive themselves as leaders who were government change agents or, as leaders of and within their organizations, entitled to initiate and support local agendas? How did these perceptions impact on their practice, and why?

For senior staff, the significance of participating in NLDB or alternative leadership development provision might range from profound to negligible. It represented one of many possible experiences with potential to influence the perceptions and practices of senior staff targeted through the remit of each NLDB. Targeting might fail to reach, let alone influence, the target group nationwide. Engagement of those participating would be affected by their motivation; and provision would be experienced within the context of their socialization, mainly as service professionals, now with some responsibility

Developing Public Service Leaders. Wallace et al., Oxford University Press. © Mike Wallace, Michael Reed, Dermot O'Reilly, Michael Tomlinson, Jonathan Morris, Rosemary Deem (2023). DOI: 10.1093/oso/9780199552108.003.0008

for the work of other staff. Therefore, our research focused on relevant experiences, perceptions, and reported practices of the most senior staff from a small number of secondary schools, primary care trusts (PCTs), hospitals, and universities. All those interviewed were members of the relevant NLDB's target group. The majority had experienced NLDB provision, other forms of external leadership development, or both; a minority had experienced neither. All had long exposure to the government's discourse strategy promoting leaderism through official publications, directives, and inspection reports, or as refracted through mass media output.

This chapter explores the contribution of NLDB provision and other external leadership development to shaping the perceptions and practices of informants in ways that elites in government both did and did not intend. We examine the third part of the complex change process embodied in the focal interventions implemented by NLDB officials and commissioned trainers: perceptions of the contribution made by these interventions to the mobilization of senior staff as leaders. The chapter concentrates on the local-level component of our conceptual framework within the domain of interaction (Figure 5.1), tracking:

- the cross-level orchestration of NLDB provision from intermediate to local level through leadership development activities, and any acculturative influence of this provision on senior staff in public service organizations who participated;
- any mediation of NLDB provision from local to intermediate level by senior staff in public service organizations, attending to their motivation for engaging in NLDB provision or rejecting it, and the extent of their acculturative formal co-optation as leaders acting as change agents for government-driven reforms or other agendas.

We draw on findings from our interviews with senior staff in secondary schools (in respect of NCSL), primary care trusts and hospitals (NHSIII), and universities (LFHE). Senior staff related their experiences of leadership development (from the NLDB or other sources) to their change orchestration activity by pursuing, implicitly, a *service provision project* of leading change, whether related to reforms or other agendas; almost universally adopting a leader-centric construal of leadership underpinning their associated *discourse strategy*; and employing their own *control technology* to bring about organizational or local change comprising their management practice, any engagement in their own leadership development, and support for training other staff as leaders. We assess whether their responses further mediated the governmental endeavour formally to co-opt them as local-level leaders.

First, we report the extent to which informants who had experienced NLDB provision perceived the control technology of NLDB training and development activities to be directed towards acculturating them as change agents, responsibilized to bring about government-driven reforms. The findings cross-check our evidence (Chapter 7) that NLDB senior officials diluted the linkage between leading and reforms intended or otherwise assumed by government elites. Second, we explore the association informants made between leading activity and change, and the balance of their change agency within their service provision project between engaging with reforms and initiating other local changes. Third, we discuss how informants construed leadership itself. The combined influence is considered of central government and NLDB discourse strategies on the discourse strategy adopted by informants, as leaders of and within their organizational jurisdictions, and their control technology for enacting change through management and developmental activity. Fourth, we examine whether informants who had participated in NLDB and other leadership development provision were motivated to improve their present practice as leaders or to fulfil an aspiration to further their career advancement. Fifth, we consider immediate outcomes for the formal co-optative goal of mitigating government dependence on senior staff to implement and operate public service reforms. Finally, we extend our abductive explanation, incorporating responses of local-level elites and associates to the national leadership development interventions, and their contribution towards the further professionalization of senior staff from public service organizations as professional leaders.

National interventions to develop public service leaders of reform? The testimony of senior staff

Roughly two-thirds of informants had sought (and most had also experienced) NLDB provision; around four-fifths of informants had sought or experienced external leadership development from other providers (Table 8.1). The NLDBs alerted them to what was available and attracted a significant proportion to participate in one or more NLDB offerings. Sometimes informants did so alongside participation in other external leadership development provision. A minority of informants were aware of NLDB provision but not motivated to engage, primarily because they accorded it low credibility. Most

Table 8.1 External leadership development sought or experienced by public service senior staff

Public service sector	School education		Healthcare				Higher education		Total
			Primary		Hospital				
	Secondary		care						
Type of organization	school		trust		trust		University		
No. informants	25		21		20		30		96
Service sector NLDB or other external leadership development providers	*NCSL*	*Other*	*NHSIII*	*Other*	*NHSIII*	*Other*	*LFHE*	*Other*	
Category of provider No. informants seeking or experiencing provision:									
from sectoral **NLDB**	20		13		8		18		59
and/or from other providers		18		18		16		25	77
Type of external provision No. informants seeking or experiencing:									
Substantial leadership development programmes	16		9		6		15		46
		3		9		15		13	40
Short courses, other support (e.g. mentoring)	9		7		5		13		34
		20		22		19		29	90

Note: Individuals may have sought or experienced provision from their sectoral NLDB and/or other providers. The account of an informant may appear in one or two cells for the category of provider and type of external provision.

informants experiencing NLDB provision had participated in a substantial training programme spanning more than five days, a short course, mentoring, or coaching. Around half the secondary school informants with experience of NCSL provision had completed the National Professional Qualification for Headship (NPQH) qualification, while about a third of their counterparts in universities had sought or experienced the LFHE's Top Management Programme (TMP).

About half the informants from each public service sector who had experienced NLDB provision noted how it focused on developing generic change agency. This provision typically encompassed activity entailed in leading or managing change, with occasional references to self-reflection during the change process, radical change or transformation, or changing organizational cultures. Informants reported that provision did not emphasize government reforms, yet aspects did relate implicitly to this agenda. One school senior teacher stressed learning through the NPQH programme that 'you've got to be an entrepreneur; you've got to take some calculated risks', consistent with the marketization reform thrust. A primary care trust (PCT) chief executive reported a focus on joining-up local services, aligned with the government's move towards personalized provision:

> You're a change agent and you need to think about a bit more than just your own backyard if you're going to effect change that impacts on the way the population access public services. People don't live in a health bubble, or an education bubble, or community safety bubble; they live in a community where all those things are happening.

Merely a fifth of secondary school informants, a tenth of PCT and hospital informants, and a fifth of HE informants stated that leading reforms had been emphasized when discussing a particular reform or reform-related themes. A hospital chief executive referred to addressing reform themes linked to marketization and regulation: 'It was around choice … meeting the public's expectations … improving accountability, accepting that contestability in public services was a thing that was going to continue … I guess one of the reasons why they run it from central government [is] in order to get, and keep, people thinking about it.' The opportunity to inform themselves was valued, one deputy headteacher commenting that 'part of it is about keeping people updated on new ideas and new reforms … if you're in education and you're in a leadership team you need … to know about what's going on … making sure that we're up-to-date with what's going on in other institutions, in the borough or in the country … [and] working towards a common focus'.

A few secondary school and university informants viewed leadership development itself as a government-driven reform rather than a reform facilitator. Thus, the NPQH programme for schools was construed as a reform to reduce the chronic headteacher shortage. Conversely, just a tenth of hospital and university informants and a single secondary school informant referred to NLDB provision that emphasized leading local change, unrelated to reforms, when focusing on a participant's current work. A university pro vice chancellor (PVC) recalled participating in 'action learning sets as a way of reflecting on a particular project that one had at the time'. These informants' accounts corroborated our interpretation of the NLDB evidence (Chapter 7) that provision was largely generic. Reforms were presented as an important contextual factor that participants should consider in enhancing their change agency as local-level leaders with scope to improve practice according to their service professional beliefs and values, not as the focus for their leading activity as government change agents.

Senior staff self-perceptions as change agents: for government, their community, themselves?

Informants almost unanimously perceived themselves as change agents, whether they had experienced NLDB provision or not, though far fewer felt responsibilized to act as conduits for government-driven reforms. Their self-perceptions fell into three categories, with most informants covering more than one (Table 8.2). Roughly two-thirds viewed their change agent role as including faithfully implementing reforms (consistent with government expectations); two-thirds perceived it to include legitimating them, as local-level leaders, to adapt reforms; two-thirds regarded it as legitimating them in undertaking local initiatives unconnected with reforms. The spread of self-perceptions across categories suggests that senior staff saw themselves as neither reform conduits nor independent initiative-takers alone. NLDB provision had not turned participants into government change agents. Neither

Table 8.2 Public service senior staff perceptions of their change agent role

Public service sector	School education	Healthcare		Higher education	
Type of organization	Secondary school	Primary care trust	Hospital trust	University	
					Total
No. informants	25	21	20	30	96
Perceived change agent role:					
Faithfully implementing reforms	13	16	12	26	67
Adapting reforms to local circumstances	19	11	15	14	59
Taking independent initiatives	14	16	15	27	72

Note: Individuals may have mentioned one or more categories. The account of an informant may appear in more than one cell within the column for the public service sector concerned.

had informants ignored reforms and acted solely on behalf of their community or themselves; the reforms had demanded their response. Informants across the public service sectors spoke of harnessing reforms towards their service improvement priorities within parameters that their compliance with regulatory pressures allowed. One secondary school headteacher stated: 'This school is in a process of deep change, but we've had to do a few quick fixes to keep Ofsted [Office for Standards in Education inspectors] off our backs while we bring about the deep change, so that our exam results don't dip.' A hospital chief executive echoed this point:

> You take the compliance piece into account . . . there's no point in arguing about it. But I've also got to push on from there to develop a service portfolio which is strong enough, both in service model terms and service quality terms to be the best in the United Kingdom, Europe and, wherever possible, the world.

University informants reported most emphasis on faithfully implementing reforms where remote forms of regulation were especially salient. Governmental regulation did not dictate a response, but acquiescence was widely deemed advisable. Universities remained dependent on securing public funding sources; research and teaching quality were also signalled by performing well in related comparative measures, enabling universities to attract students and impress employers. A deputy vice chancellor exemplified how reconnaissance informed efforts to maximize the university's performance in the next research assessment exercise: 'I sat on one of the bodies set up by the HEFCE [Higher Education Funding Council for Education] and HRC [Humanities Research Council] to look at how research should be assessed in the humanities, as part of the process to look-over this last year. Clearly, we . . . are aware of the changes that are coming, are getting ourselves set up . . . to work within those new set-ups.' Most PCT informants also reported a commitment to faithfully implementing reforms, possibly since PCTs themselves constituted a structural healthcare reform, operating as a conduit for other reforms affecting primary healthcare. One PCT chief executive observed: 'The Health Service is nothing if not a top-down organization, so I directly regard myself as the agent with responsibility for [implementing reforms]. And that's what my objectives would say in every given year: implement the next wave . . . that's my job.'

Most informants implied that their position as leaders entitled them to choose whether to adapt reforms while also pursuing an unconnected local

change agenda; the reforms had not pre-empted initiative-taking. The prevalence of adaptative change agency appeared to flow from senior staff pursuing their service provision project, expressing their service professional
or service-related administrative and managerial values. They endorsed and
actively engaged with reforms aligned with these values, downplaying, or
offering minimal compliance with, those that did not. A secondary school
assistant deputy headteacher commented: 'It's about finding a balance and
making sure that the learner in the classroom is getting the best possible experience, even if reforms don't always match the way things happen practically.'
Senior staff in universities had greatest scope to choose which reforms and
other change agendas to address, according to their priorities, exemplified
by one vice chancellor: 'As an organization, if you rush around after every
new development, that's fatal. So you have to make a judgement about which
initiatives are for you, and which initiatives are not.' This mildly mediatory
orientation combined acting as a change agent for government, the local
community, and themselves. A hospital director of strategic development
commented:

> It's a pretty uninspiring vision to say, 'Our vision is we're going to implement gov-
> ernment policy'. So, if you're wanting people to go with you on the journey, then
> having a broader vision which makes sense locally, and is articulated in a way
> which has meaning locally, is a much better way to make progress.

This informant implied that scope for change agency as a local-level leader
could be maximized by articulating a local vision endorsed and supported by
those who were led. Yet scope was delimited: pursuing the informant's service provision project entailed balancing concerns of the informant, the local
community, and government. Conversely, senior staff whose administrative
and managerial values aligned with a particular reform were accorded extensive corporate agency to promote its faithful implementation, reflected in the
endeavour of a hospital director of strategic development (previously a management consultant and entrepreneur) 'to turn this into a hospital that's also
an efficient business'. Scope for change agency was conditional on compliance
with requirements of the government's reform agenda.

This evidence suggests an answer to our first question addressed in this
chapter: although perceptions varied, most informants saw themselves as
leaders acting, in part, as government change agents (whether endorsing this
responsibility, accepting it, or else feeling pressured to do so); but as leaders
they also acted, voluntarily, as change agents on behalf of their community

and themselves. NLDB provision was not, reportedly, key to shaping their perceptions.

Senior staff construals of leadership and their leanings toward leaderism

Informants almost universally viewed themselves as a leader within their organizational jurisdiction, whether positioned as elites occupying formally designated 'top' executive positions or as elite-associates occupying subordinate senior roles as leaders and managers. Most had previous experience as public service professionals or administrators. All employed leadership discourse in some degree, mostly subscribing to a leader-centric construal focused on individual leading activity to influence others, legitimated by their formal management role. Nearly two-thirds of informants expressed discourse either resonant with, or referring to, the metaphor of transformational leadership (Chapter 4, Table 4.2): from vision-building; through subscribing to a personal framework of moral values, decision-making, and direction-setting; to inspiring and developing colleagues. The 'vision thing' was centre-stage. One headteacher encapsulated the hierarchical process of assembling contributions to a collective organizational vision:

> I have a clarity about 'What is our vision?', 'What is our purpose as a school?' That is something that has come from my own experience . . . from the governors, and it's something that's coalesced as well from staff . . . I both become the giver of the vision, but also the crystallizer of the vision so that it is . . . jointly owned and shared by every person in the organization.

Other senior staff in top formal positions adopted a more transmissional orientation as the exclusive source of a vision, a hospital informant asserting that 'the job of the chief executive is actually to set a vision and to lead people towards that vision, in part by empowering them, and in part by giving them the tools to do the job'. Resonating more with inspirational and charismatic characteristics of transformational leadership was a PCT chief executive's self-depiction as a 'strategic thinker and analytical, but I've also got a lot of enthusiasm, personal enthusiasm which can be very motivating for people . . . my style tends to be about enthusing, involving, and having fun with people'. Nearly half used discourse associating leadership with their agency as leaders, legitimated by their formal position. One university vice chancellor prioritized direction-setting: 'I'm not going to have democracy, and I think people do understand what that means ... they need to say something, not just whinge when they haven't been listened to ... I will listen, but then I'll decide.'

In contrast, about a quarter of informants expressed discourse related implicitly or explicitly to the less individualistic metaphor of distributed leadership, emphasizing hierarchically shared leading activity. A hospital medical director perceived that 'leadership at the top is effectively a sum of the little leaderships that take place everywhere in the organization'. A horticultural metaphor captured how a PCT chief executive empowered senior colleagues to lead synergistically: 'Water the passion and the energy and the enthusiasm of people ... and direct it into things that are productive and beneficial; as far as possible not to constrain them with inappropriate systems and processes'. Yet this collectivity-oriented discourse was still confined to leading activity: influencing others. There was no reference to complementary constituents of leadership as a goal-oriented group phenomenon, say, receptivity to the influence of others, or facilitating influencing activity.

The prevalence of such leadership discourse, irrespective of whether informants had experienced NLDB or alternative external leadership development provision, suggests that the government's discourse strategy had aligned with the developmentally focused discourse strategy of NLDBs, and with diverse media sources in furthering the discursive shift towards leader-centric construals of leadership within public services. Just one informant, a hospital medical director, reported rejecting this dominant discourse: 'I don't talk about leadership in the way a lot of people talk about leadership; I talk about how you set about making a hospital better.'

A partial parallel obtained between the leadership discourse of informants and the governmental discourse of leaderism, allied with the instrumental, control-oriented ideology of managerialism. We previously noted (Chapter 5) how central government politicians construed themselves as democratically elected leaders of the public service system, legitimating their articulation of a vision for public service reform; they regarded senior staff in public service organizations as leaders within this system, responsibilized to 'deliver' the central government vision by putting it into public service practice. Senior staff in top executive positions had come to construe themselves as leaders of their organization; senior colleagues construed themselves as leaders within it. Being leader of the organization legitimated local-level elites in these top positions engaging in vision-building, alone or more invitationally, and pursuing a public service project, associated discourse strategy, and control technology to ensure this vision was implemented, with support from elite associate senior staff. One deputy headteacher's depiction of leading a school bears witness: 'What are the changes worth taking on that are tailor-made for your establishment? And it's then a period of consultation, a period of training, professional development, taking people on board, steps in change, revisiting change and taking time to embed change.'

The longstanding public service professional or administrative values of informants appear to have influenced their change agency more than any recent acculturation as leaders responsible for implementing the present government's public service reform project. Overall, they evidenced commitment to faithful implementation of reforms aligned with their values, readiness to implement less compatible reforms selectively and adaptively, and the desire to pursue independent change agendas. The corporate agency that senior staff in top executive positions were empowered to deploy in furthering their service professional or administrative and managerial values aligned with the government's rhetoric: 'earned autonomy' (Strategy Unit, 2006) for compliant public service organizations; reformed organizational governance extending local community representation in direction-setting; and public services reconfigured as a 'self-improving system', bounded by regulatory mechanisms circumscribing local innovation. So informants were empowered to act according to the governmental discourse of leaderism, seeking local-level managerial control by promoting transmission of the central government vision, guided by their service professional or administrative and managerial values, with more or less input from colleagues and local community representatives. Ironically, this 'bounded empowerment', delimited by regulation, left most senior staff informants somewhat distanced from, rather than acculturated conduits for, government-driven reforms.

Symbols of capability: acquiring credentials as a professional leader through leadership development?

We analysed the reasons our informants gave for seeking and experiencing external leadership development in terms of their aspiration to gain from doing so, applying Bourdieu's (1986) metaphor comprising symbolic forms of 'capital' (Chapter 3). These forms of capital offer their possessors a representation of their capability as a leader in a present role, or an indication of their prospective capability should they seek promotion:

- *Cultural capital*, the accumulated and valued expert knowledge and abilities connected with leading activity, augmenting the social positioning of participants relative to non-participants;

- *Social capital*, the membership of networks comprising senior service professionals and others who can provide support;
- *Symbolic capital*, the conferral by others of characteristics contributing to a good reputation, including perceived competence and moral integrity as a leader, and maybe also kudos for being selected to participate in a prestigious form of leadership development.

Forms of symbolic capital were implicit in reasons informants gave for engaging with external leadership development, and so unwitting collusion, through their participation, in sustaining domination by strategic-level elites in government. Primary reasons varied along two dimensions: whether informants or other senior colleagues initiated the decision to apply; and the balance of aspiration between improving present practice as a leader and preparing for career advancement. Table 8.3 shows that several informants gave more than one reason. A significant minority of senior staff who were not in top formal positions were prompted by colleagues to apply for an external leadership development opportunity. One PCT deputy chief executive was advised to apply for a specific opportunity: 'My chief exec was pretty clear that she thought I needed to do that, because that was missing out of my tool-bag.' In Bourdieusian terms, a shortfall was diagnosed in the informant's cultural capital, which participating in external leadership development could supply. Symbolic capital could also be signified—a university dean of faculty perceived being selected to apply for external leadership development as an acknowledgement of the informant's potential for further development as a leader: 'I felt flattered by the attention, and I felt that people were taking care of my career.'

Most informants implied that they had initiated seeking external leadership development to meet their perceived learning needs and aspirations as leaders, notifying or consulting senior colleagues in the process. Along the 'balance of aspiration' dimension, the most common motivation across the three service sectors for seeking external leadership development was for individuals to improve their current practice as leaders and the thinking that informed it. Most wanted to know more about aspects of leading activity, especially ways of influencing those they were responsible for leading, amounting to cultural capital. One assistant headteacher hinted at a practice knowledge deficit, having worked in only three schools, so sought to broaden this knowledge-base: 'Being on those leadership teams with people more experienced than myself and listening and contributing . . . and I'd never seen it done any other way . . . it would benefit me to have a wider perspective.' The cultural capital sought was knowledge of alternative approaches to individual and collective leading activity. Social capital could be acquired

Table 8.3 Why senior staff sought external leadership development from NLDBs and other providers

Public service sector	School education	Healthcare		Higher education	
Type of organization	Secondary school	Primary care trust	Hospital trust	University	Total
No. informants	25	21	20	30	96
Reasons for seeking external leadership development:					
Response to being selected or recommended to apply	6	9	3	11	29
Improve thinking and practice as a leader	14	7	9	20	50
Opportunity for professional development as a leader	4	2	4	3	13
Career enhancement through preparatory training	10	5	1	11	27
Other motivations	8	8	7	10	33

Note: Individuals may have mentioned more than one reason. The account of an informant may appear in more than one cell within the column for the public service sector concerned.

alongside cultural capital by engaging with senior staff from other organizations and trainers during external leadership development activities, as a secondary school head of business studies noted: 'There are certain issues that you don't feel confident dealing with, so you go on a course. There's no right answer often, is there? But actually talking to other people, and it's a good time to network and look at how [other] schools do things.' This account illustrates how participants contributed towards each other's acculturation and stock of resources as leaders: passing on practice knowledge of leading activity and forging relational ties from which they might benefit in future. Participants' contribution towards their own acculturation as local-level leaders operating within a context of government-driven reforms, if not as government change agents, still served the material interest of strategic-level elites in sustaining their domination through widespread acceptance of this context and of operating within its parameters.

One hospital executive director of nursing voiced an intrinsic motivation in positive emotional terms to improve practice: 'It's natural curiosity ... you always think that you can do things a bit better, you can learn some tools and techniques.' Such means of leading activity represent another aspect of cultural capital: knowledge of techniques for leading and how to deploy them effectively. A few informants construed external leadership development as continuing professional development (CPD): updating or gaining new knowledge and skills to fit the changing parameters of service provision framing their work. A hospital director of strategic development observed: 'It was a good while since I did my MBA [masters degree in business administration] ... some of the academic theory has developed since then, but it's also particularly thinking about how to apply that in a current NHS environment, which is quite different.' Cultural capital was implicitly to be gained here by revisiting old knowledge to inform leading activity in a changing context.

Almost a third of informants reported a career motivation, often alongside other reasons for seeking external leadership development, to enhance their promotion prospects. Their balance of aspirations leaned firmly towards the future. One secondary school deputy headteacher had applied to participate in the NPQH programme as a credential operating, in our terms, as symbolic capital from the point of application, since an NPQH qualification was compulsory for appointment to a first-time headship: 'I was applying for headships ... You needed to be able to tick the box to say that you had either applied for it, or were on the course, or had got it, whichever'. Having participated, the informant found that 'it made me think long and hard, particularly about teamwork, how you identify which members of staff maybe in the school are isolated and not involved, and which people are overused because they're the willing horses . . . I suppose it was largely pragmatic, but it was of value.' The forms of capital gained were part-symbolic: a prospective credential acknowledging that the cultural capital of new knowledge would be acquired through participation and, after completion, that it had been acquired. They were also part-cultural: new knowledge, including insights about teamwork learned during the programme. Yet the 'pragmatic' motivation to obtain the credential simply by applying for a place had been more crucial for progressing the informant's career advancement aspiration at that time.

However, several informants expressed a more evenly balanced aspiration, leaning towards both present and future. Another deputy headteacher voiced equivocation: 'When I first applied for NPQH . . . I remember thinking distinctly at the time, "I don't know whether I want to become a head, but I do know I want to become better at my job and be more informed about what I do on a day-to-day basis".' For this informant, acquiring cultural capital connected with improving present practice as a leader was more salient than acquiring symbolic capital indexing the eligibility to apply for a first headship. Acquiring social capital through networking was also important for individuals seeking career advancement, reflected in the comment of a hospital chief operating officer that 'I thought there would be advantage in getting to know a network of other new chief executives'. Social capital could also be acquired after appointment, as a university pro vice chancellor did though participation in the LFHE's TMP programme: 'The PVC job is quite difficult actually, when you first arrive . . . there's no other PVC with that portfolio in the university . . . you need to build up some sort of networks, so the TMP was useful for that.'

Whether or not senior staff were motivated by career considerations when seeking external leadership development, the record of participation could constitute lasting symbolic capital investment, to be 'cashed in' whenever individuals might seek another post. A record of investment in developing capability, here as a leader, had long been accepted in job selection processes to index the capability itself (e.g. Morgan, Hall, & Mackay, 1983). So participating in any substantial leadership development provision from an NLDB or other provider constituted a source of symbolic capital. It could be augmented where assessment resulted in a formal credential that a standard of competence or preparedness had been reached (as with the NPQH programme coordinated by the NSCL), or where selectors viewed the record of participation to index such preparedness (as with the LFHE's TMP programme). One university pro vice chancellor stated: 'I was interviewed for a vice chancellor position recently, and the first question that I was asked was why I hadn't been on the TMP.' This comment indicates how symbolic violence operates in shaping expectations of local-level elites and associates positioned as selectors for this 'top leader' role. Completion of the TMP had become normalized as a source of credentials indexing the readiness of candidates for appointment to the role and their capability to perform competently in it. So aspirants had a material and ideal interest in participation to facilitate their accession to local-level elite status and enhancement of their corporate agency as leader of their organization.

Seemingly, the habitus, or pre-reflexive thinking and actions, of such informants reflected the institutionalization of external leadership development as a means of acquiring cultural, social, and symbolic forms of capital. They were motivated by the aspiration to advance their careers, alongside their self-perception, and that of virtually all other informants, as leaders. The active endeavour of a significant minority to develop their capital according to this habitus suggests that emergent *professionalization* as leaders was beginning to occur amongst those with or without a public service professional background, as most representative bodies advocated (Chapter 7).

An external evaluation of the LFHE supports our HE sector findings. A web-based survey of senior staff with LFHE experience covered motivations for participating in nationally available provision (Blue Alumni, 2010, p. 17):

> the most cited objective (34% of respondents) for attending the open programmes was to develop personal leadership skills and confidence in a leadership role. The next most cited reason (21%) was career and personal development. Many people felt that having the open programme on their CV [curriculum vitae] would improve their chances of selection.

Informants may have linked their career advancement aspiration with the benefit of acquiring a record of participation as a credential signifying their potential competence to selectors. Their assumption was corroborated by other respondents, confirming that participation represented potent symbolic capital for selectors (p. 9):

> Having formal leadership and management development programmes on an applicant's curriculum vitae is also seen as increasingly desirable. Whilst senior staff and governors first look for previous job-related performance when recruiting managers, about half of the leaders and governors we interviewed (52%) also looked for formal leadership and management development in applicants' CVs.

We interpret strategic-level government elites as having perpetrated symbolic violence on senior staff in public service organizations, reinforcing the dominant social position of government elites by mitigating their dependence on senior staff for the local-level implementation and operation of regulated marketization reforms. We earlier reported (Chapter 6) how government elites represented NLDBs as a means of developing leadership capacity in each public service sector, and an acknowledgement of the importance and contribution of senior staff. Our interviews suggested that the interventions were envisaged as an acculturative control technology for the formal co-optation of senior staff as leaders, willing to act as change agents for government-driven reforms. This attempt had not succeeded as its instigators intended (Chapters 6 and 7). The longstanding service professional culture to which senior NLDB officials, commissioned trainers, and representative bodies subscribed had influenced them to dilute the linkage envisaged by government elites between developing leaders and implementing their public service reforms.

Further, most of our senior staff informants had experience as public service professionals (secondary school teachers, healthcare clinicians, university academics); a few were career service administrators or private sector general managers. Neither group became acculturated as government change agents committed to the faithful implementation of reforms that ran counter to their service professional or service-related administrative and managerial values. But they (and senior officials from their representative bodies) had misrecognized the soft power-play of government elites. Individual senior staff colluded by participating in NLDB provision (with representative body encouragement) to pursue a material and ideal interest in improving their practice or promotion prospects as leaders. An unintended consequence was their incipient further professionalization as leaders: acquiring forms of capital from participation bolstered their agency within the present role and created potential to enhance it through promotion to a post carrying greater management responsibility. This professionalization altered their habitus as professionals, overlaying their service professional or service-related administrative and managerial culture with expertise in leading activity—but without wholly replacing that prior cultural allegiance. We have already noted how most informants sought to advance their values underpinning that extant culture as local-level leaders, rather than identifying themselves as professional leaders of change, irrespective of its content. Yet they also acknowledged how their scope for agency as leaders was delimited by regulatory measures introduced or supported by government elites.

Developing public service leaders: acculturation for mitigation, intimidation via regulation?

NLDBs' accountability to their sponsors necessitated senior officials providing regular updates on their activity and its impact through the publication of their annual reports, plus the occasional review or commissioned external evaluation. Annual reports represent a genre of NLDB discourse designed to demonstrate that an NLDB's performance matches or surpasses expectations set by sponsors and other backers, alongside demonstrating propriety in funding expenditure. Consequently, the discourse of this genre tends to emphasize achieving performance expectations while downplaying, or remaining silent, on any shortfall; reliance is placed on the audience assuming that performance claims are supported by adequate evidence, without necessarily providing it. External evaluation reports are a genre designed to present judgements founded on evidence generated to fulfil the commissioning sponsor's brief, and to offer recommendations flowing from these judgements. They equally rely on audiences assuming that evaluatory claims can be substantiated, without necessarily supplying the evidence. Consequently, the annual reports and external evaluation report discussed here provide only partial accounts of NLDB activity and impact.

When the Labour government's time in office ended in 2010, the NCSL's remit had been extended (in 2009) to include directors of children's centres; its new name was the National College for Leadership of Schools and Children's Services (NCLSCS) (NCSL, 2009). Some indication could be gained by then of the proportion of the target group each NLDB had reached since its inception, its annual participation in provision, and its impact on leading activity in the workplace. However, coordination between the independently mounted and governed national leadership development interventions remained very limited, as the Cabinet Office (2009) review (Chapter 7) had confirmed. Disparity between interventions included their arrangement for reporting and placing results in the public domain. NLDBs provided variable detail, employing different metrics: the sponsoring government department monitored the performance of the NCLSCS and NHSIII using a balanced scorecard with thirty-four and eighty-nine performance indicators respectively (NCLSCS, 2010; NHSIII, 2010), but few NCLSCS results and no NHSIII results were made public; only the LFHE was externally evaluated during the Labour government's final year. Table 8.4 summarizes evidence provided in annual reports and the LFHE evaluation indicating the extent of provision and its impact.

Table 8.4 Outcomes of national leadership development interventions for schools, healthcare, and higher education reported in official documents, 2010

Outcomes	School education (England)	Healthcare (England)	Higher education (UK)
NLDB, year of inception	National College for School Leadership (NCSL) *, 2000	NHS Institute for Innovation and Improvement (NHSIII), 2005	Leadership Foundation for Higher Education (LFHE), 2004
Provision for target group since inception, or in 2019–10	135,000 participants from 93% of primary schools and 99% of secondary schools in England since 2000, including 29,000 NPQH graduates; 16,000 participants during 2009–10 (NCLSCS, 2010)	29 trusts and 3,000 'NHS leaders' used the instrument for identifying NHS trust board development needs (NHSIII, 2009); 280 participants in the Graduate Management Training Scheme in 2009–10; more than 180 participants on the 'Gateway to Leadership' programme since 2002; the Medical Leadership Competency Framework included in postgraduate training; 150 senior staff received executive coaching in 2009–10 (NHSIII, 2010)	95% of UK universities and colleges (152 in total) are LFHE members; more than 2750 participants in provision (from 10 countries), including 63 participants in TMP, in 2009–10; more than 75% of target leaders, managers and governors participated in provision since 2004 (LFHE, 2010)

Continued

Table 8.4 *Continued*

Outcomes	School education (England)	Healthcare (England)	Higher education (UK)
Impact of provision	A survey found that 84% of participants in 2008–9 believed NCSL was raising standards, 81% believed it had made a positive effect on their school (NCSL, 2009); participants from 86% of schools engaging in 2009–10 reported a positive impact; Ofsted inspections judged leadership and management to be 'outstanding' in an increasing proportion of schools (NCLSCS, 2010)	Four participants in the black, Asian, and minority ethnic heritage (BAME) 'Breaking Through' programme had been appointed to substantial trust board-level roles (No other evidence was reported in public documents we accessed)	90% of participants in 2009–10 indicated that provision was extremely or very valuable (LFHE, 2010); 82% of participants surveyed reported developing and applying new skills benefiting their organizations; LFHE influenced the increase in systematic leadership development within universities and colleges from 30% in 2000 to 70% in 2010; 44 TMP alumni appointed as heads of universities or colleges since 2001 (Blue Alumni, 2010)

* NCSL was renamed the National College for Leadership of Schools and Children's Services (NCLSCS) in 2009.

The NCLSCS (previously NCSL) and the LFHE had reached a high proportion of the target group (Chapter 6, Table 6.1), who had participated in some aspect of provision. Such evidence as the NHSIII offered suggests that its commissioned leadership development and the development of a competency framework for medical leadership, representing a fraction of NHSIII activity, reached only a minority of the target group. However, establishing the NHSIII in 2005 entailed Strategic Health Authorities taking over responsibility for some provision of the predecessor NHS Leadership Centre (NHSLC) (Chapter 6) and catering for members of this target group since. The Darzi review (DoH, 2008, p. 67) had proposed a national council 'responsible for overseeing all matters of leadership across healthcare', with the ability 'to commission development programmes'. The result was to create the NHS National Leadership Council (DoH, 2009). So momentum for developing new provision had shifted away from the NHSIII by 2010.

Accounts of the impact achieved by the interventions were equally variable: the NCLSCS and LFHE referred to internally collated participant evaluations and external sources of impact information; the NHSIII incorporated minimal evidence of impact in its annual reports. Much impact evidence cited comprised opinions expressed by participants in response to internal evaluation or external survey questions, or to NLDB evaluation interview questions. Further evidence was not offered to substantiate these opinions or the assumed causal effect of provision on wider valorized changes. What exactly *was* the positive effect on their school that 81 per cent of participants in NCSL provision believed it had achieved, and how did they know? How did NCLSCS provision generate whatever leading activity Ofsted inspectors judged 'outstanding' in quality and effectiveness within inspected schools? What proportion of all participants in the NHSIII Breaking Through programme did the four who gained promotion represent? How did the LFHE influence the asserted increase in systematic leadership development amongst universities and colleges? Assuming that the claimed impacts were achieved, what counted as resultant improvements in service provision or outcomes was founded on the judgements of participants, not those of central government ministers responsible for each public service sector.

While there was a clear focus in these documents on the impact of leadership development on service improvement, government-driven reforms received little mention. We have seen how NLDB provision was largely generic and senior staff we interviewed were acculturated as leaders, but less so as co-opted change agents for reform, whether they had experienced NLDB provision or not. They continued to be guided by their service professional or administrative culture in seeking improvements, affecting their response to reforms and pursuit of local change agendas. So NLDB reporting and these external evaluations appear not to have unpacked the cited indicators of service improvement; no accounts refer explicitly to any impact of NLDB provision on the practice of participants related to reforms.

Our interviews with senior staff investigated the perceived impacts of any external leadership development experiences on them as leaders of, or within, their organizations. Table 8.5 synthesizes the spread of responses into three categories. An individual response might cover more than one category, and reported impacts ranged from impressionistic to specific. Around two-thirds of informants, all of whom had experienced external leadership development, referred to one or more impacts on themselves as leaders acting as change agents, irrespective of the change agenda.

The first category, mentioned by a third of informants, was a perceived direct impact on their *practice* as a change agent. One deputy headteacher noted giving colleagues more scope to express their views in meetings:

> I probably contribute less directly in meetings, listen more, and then … sum up and try and move us on … when I first started in the deputy role, I wanted to get my point across, and … maybe I wasn't listening to other people's point of view. That sort of self-reflection I think, more than anything else, I've picked up from the NPQH.

Whereas a hospital medical director had established a productive working relationship with a key stakeholder group:

> I'm much more aware of public health issues, and I'm much more prepared to go to the city council now. Whereas before I would have gone to the PCT, because I wouldn't have been able to get to the city council. Now I know I've got a route to the city council, where actually public health issues are probably dealt with in lots of ways, better ways.

The second category was mentioned by a slightly higher proportion of informants. Two-fifths reported some perceived impact on the *thinking* that informed their practice as a change agent, primarily by giving them a broader perspective on change. A PCT director of planning commented on how attending an NHSIII training course had prompted a more purposive consideration of papers for hospital board meetings:

> When I've been doing things like pulling together papers, I think I've more consciously been asking myself, why am I doing this? Why am I giving it to the board?

Table 8.5 Perceived impact of external leadership development on public service senior staff

Public service sector	School education	Healthcare		Higher education	Total
Type of organization	Secondary school	Primary care trust	Hospital trust	University	
No. informants	25	21	20	30	96
Total no. informants perceiving one or more impacts	15	12	13	21	61
Perceived impacts of external leadership development:					
Practice as a change agent	7	7	5	14	33
Informing thinking about practice as a change agent	14	8	10	9	41
Other (e.g. informing preparation for inspection)	4	4	3	5	16

Note: Individuals may have mentioned more than one impact category, so the view of an informant may appear in two or more cells in the column for the sector concerned.

What am I asking the board to do? . . . I definitely feel less obliged to just churn out
a paper, and probably think more about an intelligent paper.

A university pro vice chancellor pointed to an enhanced capability for thinking through how to initiate change through others: 'I'm much better at
remembering, "Actually I've got make sure that this person, who's really going
to be the change agent, is motivated and clear about what they've got to do"
. . . The Top Management Programme helped me better understand that.'
The residual category covered diverse impacts mentioned by a few informants. Indicatively, one school deputy headteacher, who had participated
in the NCSL's NPQH programme, harnessed the personal portfolio of evidence about practice created in the programme towards a school inspection:
'When Ofsted [Office for Standards in Education] came to measure the leadership and management of the sixth form, the work I'd done with the NPQH
was very, very helpful.' Two senior hospital staff extended their networking
activity to include staff from other hospitals who were also bringing about
changes.

The findings suggest that a significant minority of our interviewees did
perceive some positive impact from external leadership development on
their efficacy as change agents, through confined to specific aspects of their
change agency or the thinking that informed it. External leadership development provided by NLDBs and others seems mainly to have reinforced
the existing culture of participants as service professionals and, for a significant minority, further professionalized them as leaders of, or within, their
organizational jurisdictions. This cultural reinforcement legitimated acting
as their own change agents, pursuing the variably adaptive implementation
of government reforms according to their service professional or administrative values. Leadership development interventions involving an NLDB had
scarcely mitigated central government dependence on senior staff in public
service organizations through their transformational acculturation as willing
conduits for recent, current, or future reforms.

Yet participation had prompted the greater reflexivity associated with professionalization by stimulating participants to reflect on their practice, the
assumptions underlying it, the social and political context in which their
service was located, and possibilities for service improvement. Interviewees
indicated how participating in external leadership development had influenced their thinking, increasing their awareness of current reforms and
relevant contextual factors. It had empowered them in developing their adaptive change strategies. One primary care trust (PCT) director of primary care
commented: 'The thing I would take from [the programme] would be greater

confidence in questioning because of the recognition that the system is very much faulted, and that's enabling in a lot of ways.'

Conversely, evidence from the follow-up interviews with more than half of our informants from public service organizations suggests that their empowerment was still bounded by central government regulation, tightly delimiting the adaptative implementation of reforms. An emergent theme for these follow-up interviews was to examine how the government's use of 'policy levers' (Chapter 1) to promote the implementation of its public service reforms had affected senior staff responses to reforms for their sector. Table 8.6 reveals that the most impactful policy lever comprised *mandates*: formulating and imposing rules about desired practices and expected outcomes, then enforcing them. Mandates prompted the implementation of reforms (Chapter 2, Table 2.3) mentioned frequently by informants from all four types of public service organization. These reforms extended service regulation through specifying aspects of service content and expected standards, outcome measures, targets for their achievement (in school education and healthcare) and means for assessing performance in achieving required outcomes. They also supported marketization through the publication of performance outcomes, compiling and publishing (or, for HE, encouraging commercial publication of) comparative league tables, informing potential 'customers', whether as parents and pupils, patients, or students, as one basis for choosing their preferred provider. Additionally, managerialism was deployed in support of marketization through the mandatory introduction of performance management (widely practised in the private sector) into schools. The reforms most often mentioned by informants from secondary schools, PCTs, and hospitals, and second most often by informants from universities, were mandatory.

Our informants expressed mixed attitudes towards mandated reforms, despite the year-on-year increase in government expenditure on public services. A few signalled full commitment behind their readiness to respond. One secondary school deputy headteacher spoke approvingly of the inspection system: 'I have found the Ofsted process, all the times I've gone through it, quite fair … focus down continually on pedagogy and what's happening in the classroom … that's where improvement comes.' A PCT director of strategy noted how the recent launch of 'World Class Commissioning' (of services from healthcare providers) 'has made us realize that none of us have the skills, capability or ability to achieve world class commissioning, so we've got to change. So, I think the setting the bar thing, and going out and benchmarking everybody against each other, is quite a good lever.' One hospital chief executive declared: 'I'm not one of those people who thinks

Table 8.6 Responses of senior staff in 2008 to policy levers associated with public service regulated marketization reforms

Policy levers, contribution of reform to neoliberalization of public services	School education	Healthcare		Higher education
Type of organization	Secondary school	Primary care trust	Hospital trust	University
No. informants re-interviewed (total 55)	11	15	10	19
Informants reporting response to reforms	9	13	7	18
Reforms mentioned by 2+ informants (no. informants, reform)				
Mandates a) Specify service content and standards **(regulation)** Monitor and publicize providers' standard of service **(marketization and regulation)**	3: League tables of national tests and examination results 3: Ofsted inspections 2: Targets for mini-mizing pupil exclusion rates	8: Public Service Agreements, improvement targets, league tables, Quality and Outcomes Framework for general practice services 5: World Class Commissioning competencies and their assessment	5: Public Service Agreements, improvement targets, league tables	5: Publication of Quality Assurance Agency (QAA) teaching reviews, Research Assessment Exercise (RAE) results published, commercial league tables publicized 4: National Student Survey

b) Promote private sector management practice (managerialism in support of marketization)	2: Performance management			
Inducements Construe service recipients as customers, or as purchasers on behalf of customers (**marketization**)		4: Practice-based commissioning and payment by results for secondary healthcare	2: Practice-based commissioning and payment by results for secondary healthcare	9: Financial incentives linked to performance ir teaching (Teaching Quality Enhancement Fund), research (RAE)
Capacity-building Promote private sector management practice in service provider organizations (**managerialism in support of marketization**)	6: Strengthen leadership (little reference to leadership development)	1: Leadership development (weaker than other levers)	1: Strengthen leadership 1: Leadership development	2: Culture change extending scope of leadership to organization-wide management tasks

Note: Individuals may have mentioned more than one reform. The view of an informant may appear in two or more cells in the column for the sector concerned.

targets have been a waste of time, because I think they have focused attention in really key areas, and therefore generated step change.' A university dean referred to the Research Assessment Exercise (RAE) as

an overwhelmingly powerful lever . . . there's a very, very close correlation between the introduction of the RAE and the rise of the quality of research, and I don't think that's accidental at all, as people are adept in organizations like these at looking at the rules and seeing how they can use those to their advantage.

More commonly, informants indicated their acceptance of mandated reforms and measured approval of their impact, suggesting that additional regulation was becoming institutionalized as normal practice. A secondary school deputy headteacher reflected: 'I haven't got a problem with performance management, with league tables . . . We play the games that we're asked to play really, when it comes to GCSE results and things like that, we work within the boundaries we're kind-of given. But I don't think anyone really moans . . . it probably has raised standards.' A PCT chair commented on how the Quality and Outcomes Framework (QOF) for GP practices 'has been a significant driver in terms of concentrating on the quality-of-care agenda . . . and the contractual arrangements around enhanced services have been good in terms of drive, improving quality and certainly tackling the patient safety angle'. A hospital director of finance reported that 'what is driven is performance. You have to hit the performance targets . . . but to be fair most of the performance targets are things that you'd want to hit anyway.' A university finance director implied that feedback from imposed performance assessment had productively informed responses aligned to the university's interests: 'On a positive, the Student Satisfaction Survey, because you can see where that is actually making a difference to the student experience, and look at where we can prioritize some expenditures to help.'

A few informants from school education and healthcare found either a mandated reform or its use by central government to be unacceptable. A deputy headteacher in a secondary school commented on national targets, assessment of student learning, and publication of results: 'We've always set our own targets about attainment and I don't think any good school wouldn't do that. What people find a bit insidious is this comparison with all other schools when you have completely different make-ups [local contextual factors affecting the student profile].' Nevertheless, the universal response was to avoid sanctions by complying with the letter, if not the spirit, of the mandated reform. One PCT director of commissioning acknowledged: 'Our organization's priorities and organizational effort and attention is undoubtedly directed by the government performance framework; that is still very high priority and it's sort of the thing that gets PCTs on and off the government's radar.' A hospital medical director criticized the low trust in hospital staff implied by imposed improvement targets:

> What I would be advising a minister is: 'Let's identify the five or six key performance indicators that would give you the confidence that everything else is ok.' . . . those key temperature gauges that would tell the centre that this organization was working well and effectively for patients, and then they could trust us to get on with it . . . There is too much telling us how, not just managing us on the 'what'.

No university informants claimed to have rejected aspects of mandated reforms to which they had responded. HE was subject to fewer mandates than the other sectors, and they were less tied to formal sanctions. However, allying the policy lever of *inducements* to specific mandates reportedly prompted a strong response. Inducements comprising financial rewards or comparative reputational advantage created favourable conditions for attracting students internationally, or for securing research funding, in return for high performance in mandated teaching and research review exercises. While senior staff in universities and colleges possessed sufficient corporate agency to choose whether to respond to performance-related incentives by engaging in these exercises, the financial and reputational rewards associated with them could only be obtained through participation. HE had already been sufficiently marketized to render major inducements 'an offer you dare not refuse' so, effectively, mandating a response. Teaching income increasingly depended on choices made by potential students (or their parents), as consumers.

An increasing proportion of research income was coming from competitive bidding for research grants, those allocated by government-sponsored research councils often being directed towards ministerial priorities. The annual government 'block grant' to individual organizations for conducting research was based on the outcome of its assessment within the most recent RAE; only the most research-intensive universities were allocated significant income. One university director of planning reflected: 'If we're not able to attract research students, if we're not able to convince research councils to pay us to do research, then . . . the writing is on the wall for us as a research-intensive institution . . . that's the key lever that we're dealing with . . . we can see the direction of travel, and that's what we are trying to prepare people for.' But the commercial publication of league tables meant that other universities and colleges could also gain reputational value, with potential for attracting students and winning research grants, by performing well in comparison to competitors. Tactics included using modest funding from the RAE to underwrite doctoral studentships, especially in newer universities. A pro vice chancellor noted: 'We're not a very research-active university, but our research income is around twelve million [pounds] or so and it would hurt if it went; and it's a very good recruiting tool.'

Verdict on leadership development: a relatively weak policy lever, scarcely an elite policy meta-lever

Compared with the frequent reference to enforced mandates (and mandate-related inducements for HE) impacting on informants' response to reforms, leadership development was little mentioned. One PCT chief executive, who had participated in a substantial NHSLC leadership development programme, pointed to its lack of impact: 'What policy levers have had the most influence on me? . . . It hasn't been leadership development, clearly. I think in terms of implementing change, I think partnership working arrangements, all that set of things around partnership working is really important in the wider sphere of health improvement for the city.' The rationale behind the government instigation of, or financial support for, national leadership development interventions linked developing greater leadership capacity with enhanced leading activity for promoting the implementation of reforms across the country (Chapter 6). These interventions amounted to *capacity-building*, a policy lever based on investment in developing a desired capability; here, leading the reform implementation process as government change agents. The symbolic violence perpetrated by elites in central government through the interventions had shifted the habitus of senior staff, raising their profile as leaders and acculturating them towards engaging proactively in change for service improvement within their jurisdiction. We noted how the unprecedented national leadership development interventions might have even greater potential as a facilitative elite policy *meta-lever* if they were, further, to acculturate senior staff in public service organizations as leaders committed to implementing current government-driven reforms for their service sector and the reform agenda of any future government.

The final row in Table 8.6 summarizes the few relevant responses from informants, focused more on 'strengthening leadership' than on leadership development as the means to this end. Illustratively, a deputy headteacher reported that 'We're all focused on what's happening in the classroom along with looking at the quality of leadership and how you can strengthen leadership, because they [leaders] need to pull it [classroom practice] along'.

A university vice chancellor spoke approvingly about the extent of external leadership development provision for senior staff, while pointing to its limited organizational reach: 'The top down, training people in leadership, that's all going fine. I don't have any problem with that, but nobody below is listening. So the managed are who you need, and the led; the followers I would want to reach.'

Our sample is small. Yet such evidence as the NLDB annual reports and external evaluation of the LFHE mentioned does not challenge the very modest reported impact of leadership development on senior staff responses to government-driven reforms. The findings suggest an answer to our second question posed at the beginning of the chapter: the self-perceptions of informants as agents of change, and on whose behalf, were far less affected by potentially acculturative leadership development experiences offered by an NLDB or other providers than by the threat of punitive sanctions or financial loss imposed by radically increased regulation. Whatever the attitude of informants towards mandated reforms (or inducements judged imperative to pursue), the overwhelming response was to comply with these strengthened forms of regulation, and so to contribute measurements of performance that could be publicized to service 'consumers' in furthering public service marketization. Even informants who accepted neither the means of measurement nor their deployment reported a concern to minimize the avoidable risk of public vilification or financial sanction. Our evidence suggests that the government's use of enforced mandates as a major policy lever was enough to achieve compliance amongst senior staff, despite not being fully acculturated as leaders committed to acting as government change agents. Little of the potential was realized that these acculturative leadership development interventions may have possessed. Intimidation through the enforcement regime provided mitigation enough for implementing mandated reforms, or those reforms employing financial inducements on which public service organizations partly depended. The national leadership development interventions were a 'soft power' acculturative adjunct to mitigation through intimidation. They may have reinforced the wider acculturation of senior staff as leaders, if not government change agents, and they do appear to have encouraged some emergent professionalization of senior staff as *leaders*, rather than as service professionals or administrators. If they had failed, thus far, to achieve the acculturative impact government ministers had envisaged, the 'hard power' regulatory regime ensured compliance anyway. Neoliberalization was empowered to proceed apace, facilitated by the compliant actions of senior staff in public service organizations, increasingly as professional leaders.

Explaining immediate outcomes of implementing the interventions

The interventions and central government or NLDB public discourses of leadership and its development affected the responses of local-level expert elites and their associates, especially those who had participated in NLDB provision. To understand why they made these responses, and the immediate outcome, we further extend our abductive explanation of the findings from our documentary sources and interviews, summarized in Appendix 1. We identified four linked mechanisms and their immediate outcomes by the time our research ended.

The cumulative causal impact of the precursor mechanisms is briefly recapped first, framing our account of the focal mechanisms they triggered and the immediate outcomes. Within the context discussed previously, the foundational generative mechanism combined a *leader-centric construal of leadership* with *remote containment* of the implementation and operation of the Labour government's public service reform agenda. Central government elites and associates harnessed their construal of leadership towards influencing local-level elites and elite-associates (senior staff in public service organizations), upon whom the government depended for putting reform policies into practice, nationwide. This generative mechanism channelled and delimited the corporate agency of elites based at other administrative system levels, supported by their associates: intermediate-level elites and associates (NLDB senior officials) who implemented and operated the national development interventions for each public service sector (supported by senior officials from representative bodies for senior staff in public service organizations); and local-level elites and associates (senior staff in public service organizations) on whom NLDB provision was targeted.

From this dual mechanism flowed a series of unitary mechanisms, each either channelling corporate agency, as leaders, or delimiting its scope to contain its deployment. The government's *attempted acculturative formal co-optation* of senior staff through the leadership development interventions involving NLDBs was contained through the *specification* of their parameters and surveillance arrangements. Senior NLDB officials were empowered to engage in mild *mediatory subversion* of the acculturative attempt, loosening the focus of provision on leaders acting as change agents for government-driven reforms envisaged by government elites and elite-associates. Most informants from public service organizations who had participated in NLDB provision confirmed that it had linked leading with change agency in general, rather than with implementing government-driven reforms. Senior officials from representative bodies supported this move, insofar as it furthered the professionalization of their members as leaders. *Delimitation of this mediatory subversion* through the implementation of government regulatory or financial arrangements within the NLDB specifications, and contingent corrective action, kept subversion within very modest limits.

Subversion created favourable conditions for legitimating senior staff from public service organizations who participated in NLDB provision engaging in their own mild *mediatory subversion* of their acculturative formal co-optation as change agents for reforms. Most senior staff we interviewed (whether or not they had experienced NLDB provision) appeared not to have been acculturated, and so formally co-opted, as leaders committed to acting as change agents for government-driven reforms. All had been subject to diffuse advocacy through the government's discourse strategy linking leadership with reform. They subscribed to a leader-centric construal of leadership, regarding themselves as leaders who were change agents on behalf of themselves and the community their organization served. Our senior staff informants continued to express their professional service values connected with provision or administration through faithfully implementing reforms that were aligned with their values, and more adaptively implementing reforms that were misaligned to make them fit these values as far as possible; they also pursued local agendas that were not inimical to regulated marketization reform.

Senior staff valued NLDB provision as a leadership development opportunity, motivated to improve their present practice as leaders or enhance their prospects for becoming a more senior leader within, or of, a service organization or multi-organizational jurisdiction. The availability of this provision caused *leader capital indexation* amongst senior staff. The record of participation provided a credential, signifying the acquisition of various forms of capital as a leader, indexing either an individual's capability as a leader who had been 'developed' in the present role, the potential to perform a future role competently, or even 'acting professionally' (Chapter 2) by expressing a professional attitude towards improving their practice as a leader. Forms of capital acquired through participation might be cultural (leadership knowledge and skills) and social (membership of networks including senior staff from diverse public service organizations who could, in principle, provide mutual support). Where colleague senior staff or job selectors accepted that participation had yielded cultural and social forms of capital, they constituted symbolic capital. Symbolic violence operated through the national leadership development interventions providing resources for senior staff that served their material and ideal interest as individuals. Possessing forms of capital as a leader helped to bolster mild mediatory subversion by senior staff from public service organizations who had experienced NLDB provision, reinforcing the legitimacy of deploying their agency to express their service professional or administrative values as leaders, but also pre-empting any collective resistance to their continuing domination by government elites.

A regulatory generative mechanism prompting leader capital indexation within school education was the *accreditation* of preparatory training for aspiring headteachers through the NPQH, introduced by the previous Conservative government. Labour government engagement with the remote containment end of the foundational generative mechanism delimiting the corporate agency of local-level elites and associates resulted in the NPQH programme being harnessed towards this end. The regulatory potential of NPQH was strengthened and the NCSL was made responsible for its oversight. Aspiring headteachers undertook training followed by formal assessment, so here leader capital indexation was additionally evidenced by the NPQH qualification based on assessed performance. Once the NPQH qualification was made mandatory in 2004 for aspiring headteachers to become eligible for appointment to their first headteacher post, it became a form of accreditation signifying readiness and the capability to become the formal leader of a school.

NPQH was the sole instance of this generative mechanism in our investigation. Possessing the mandated accreditation became institutionalized as a necessary threshold indicator of capital acquired as a leader for selectors to consider an applicant eligible for appointment to a first headship. Yet our interviewees from universities pointed to the symbolic capital benefits accruing from participation in the LFHE's TMP, non-accredited but widely promoted by LFHE senior officials who would refer to the number of TMP alumni among current vice chancellors. A record of participation alone seemingly indexed leader capital sufficiently for many selectors to accept it as symbolizing the potential to perform competently as a vice chancellor, socially positioned as leader of the university or college. The NHSIII did not feature an equivalent preparatory training programme for aspiring chief executives in healthcare. However, NLDBs were not the only potential source of accreditation as a generative mechanism. Several representative bodies for senior staff provided informal accreditation (Chapter 7). The Institute of Healthcare Management was engaged in specifying competencies for healthcare managers and embedding them in its CPD provision for members. In principle, a record of participation in this CPD could index acquisition of the specified competencies when seeking a post.

The final generative mechanism was consequent on the acculturation of senior staff from public service organizations towards a leader-centric construal of leadership and themselves as leaders, and on their contribution to mild mediatory subversion of the central government attempt at acculturative formal co-optation as conduits for reform. Most held hard to their service professional or administrative values and continued expressing them within parameters circumscribed by the remote containment measures. The *restricted professionalization of senior staff as leaders* entailed senior staff gaining expertise in leading activity. Professionalization embodies two components (Chapter 2): institutional (where an occupation increasingly reflects characteristics of professions as a social institution, including specialist training) and service (acting professionally in serving the material interests of clients through an ethical commitment to service quality and improvement). The main institutional component comprised the radical increase in opportunities for specialized training, as leaders of or within public service organizations, through the substantial leadership development programmes offered or commissioned by NLDBs and other providers. The government's discourse strategy frequently associated the term 'professional' with leading activity. Witness NPQH: participants were required to undergo this extensive form of training, an institutional component of professionalization associated with occupational status as a profession, to acquire their 'professional qualification' to be a headteacher, and even required to meet 'national standards' (DfES, 2004a, pp. 4, 10) resting on the principles that 'the work of headteachers should be: learning-centred, focused on leadership and reflect the highest possible professional standards', implying that they should express approved 'values at the heart of their leadership'. Commitment to 'professional standards' resonates with the service component of professionalization, an ethical commitment to acting professionally in the interests of clients (here, school students and their parents).

The counterfactual is also instructive: other institutional components of professionalization were conspicuously absent. Autonomy as a public service leader was bounded by the remote containment end of the foundational generative mechanism, the obverse of the leader-centric construal of leadership adopted within government. In school education and healthcare, senior staff could at most 'earn' a relative degree of autonomy—ironically, through their compliance in leading the implementation of reforms and meeting service performance expectations. Autonomy as a leader was less circumscribed in HE. Yet it was still bounded by the imperatives to secure funding from government sources and avoid reputational and consequent student recruitment damage by performing well in performance assessments. Other institutional components of professionalization were lacking: a code of ethics, restricted entry to the profession, occupational self-regulation. Professionalization was very restricted. Central government allowed senior staff in top executive positions scope for corporate agency as local-level leaders, influencing other staff or partners within their organizational jurisdiction to transmit reforms into practice, undertake local change agendas compatible with reforms, and ensure that government-set expectations for service performance were achieved. Agency as a leader was confined, most directly in the school education and healthcare sectors, to choosing how government requirements were to be achieved within their local context.

Immediate outcomes of the leadership development interventions involving the NLDBs for school education, healthcare, and HE had become apparent by 2009, when our study concluded. First, these interventions did not operate as an elite policy meta-lever, since so few of our local-level informants, whether having experienced NLDB provision or not, appear to have been acculturated towards perceiving themselves as leaders committed to acting as change agents for whatever reforms central government might pursue. Acculturation is not a reliably manipulable process (Chapter 3); for senior staff in public service organizations, this process would require the well-established professional culture of those targeted to become replaced by an alternative, partially incompatible, set of beliefs, values, and norms. If leadership development were ever to operate as an elite policy meta-lever, it might take longer than a generation, when an increasing proportion of those eligible to participate had begun their professional career after the reforms with which our study was concerned had become institutionalized as normal public service practice. Acculturative co-optation as leaders acting as conduits for any future government's reforms would require much more radical overlaying of the existing professional culture. In our investigation, the senior staff who came closest to expressing such acculturation were from PCTs, a structural reform whose implementation was ongoing, tasked with facilitating other primary healthcare reforms. Most senior staff from our three public service sectors worked in deeply institutionalized organizations, whose origins reached back over a hundred or more years (schools, hospitals, universities). They would have much prior socialization to unlearn and devalue if they were to embrace the cultural alternative being promoted formally by government.

Second, some acculturative formal co-optation of senior staff had occurred, nevertheless. NLDB and other leadership development provision had contributed to reinforcing the self-perceptions of senior staff as leaders. An increasing proportion were now acquiring expert leadership-related knowledge and skills backed by credentials, characteristic of established professions, and were exhorted to commit themselves towards acting professionally in their leadership role. However, this professionalization was restricted, and not accompanied by any expansion of the corporate agency of the most senior staff to choose courses of action as leaders acting as change agents on behalf of their local community or themselves. Any autonomy to lead had to be earned through demonstrated compliance.

Third, despite the empowerment accompanying their social position as local-level elites, the corporate agency of senior staff in top executive positions within their organizational jurisdiction was constrained by the imperative to operate within bounds set by strategic-level elites in government. Self-styled 'leaders of the public service system', these elites had deployed their far greater corporate agency towards augmenting regulatory means for the remote containment of scope for local-level corporate agency (by 'leaders within the public service system'). Thus, the central government political project of public service reform, aimed at bringing about the radical 'transformation' of public service provision, enforced the transmission of reforms into practice within bounds acceptable to government ministers. The upshot was further to restrict any expression of the residual public service professional ideology to which senior staff might subscribe as school educators, healthcare providers, or academic educators and researchers. Being a public service leader meant finding what restricted local-level room to manoeuvre might exist within the imperative to comply with public service reforms, imposed by the Labour government in pursuing its social democratic variant of neoliberalization through ever more tightly regulated marketization, supported by managerialism.

That was then. What happened next? The suite of interventions had been unprecedented, but it made a foundational contribution to a growing international movement embodying engagement amongst policymakers in leadership and its development as a means of improving public services (Chapter 1). We will open Part III by examining the increasingly remote legacy of the interventions we studied for more contemporary public service leadership development provision in England. We will subsequently compare this provision with the nearest equivalent in four other countries at the forefront of the international movement, institutionalizing the 'vision thing' and providing variably favourable conditions for leadership development to offer some potential, in principle, as an elite policy meta-lever.

PART III

DEVELOPING PROFESSIONALIZED LEADERS FOR NEOLIBERALIZED PUBLIC SERVICES

9

Institutionalizing national leadership development interventions for English public services

We saw in Part II how the attempted acculturative co-optation of senior staff in public service organizations via our extreme case of investment in national leadership development interventions may have done less to ensure the local-level implementation and operation of government-driven reforms than formally to co-opt senior staff into accepting responsibility for organizational performance, and so the imperative to play safe by complying with tightened regulation. When our study ended in 2009, it was plausible that the interventions could yet become yesterday's 'management fad', vulnerable to termination if United Kingdom (UK) government elites were to conclude that sunk investment in regulation alone was sufficient to achieve their public service reform agenda. This possibility raised the question: how much future might large-scale leadership development interventions have in England and beyond, in the face of competing demands for government spending?

Given what has happened since, the short answer to this question is 'a lot'. But why? Part III works towards an explanation. In the present chapter, we consider how pervasive the subsequent proliferation of large-scale leadership development interventions for public services had become in England and beyond by 2020, when the COVID-19 pandemic curtailed face-to-face activity, temporarily at least. Our analysis draws on three main sources: publicly available webpages and policy and practical guidance documents of key stakeholder groups, from government departments to trainers; Organisation for Economic Cooperation and Development (OECD) publications comparing different government approaches; and academic publications, including literature reviews and reports of research on public service leadership development.

We begin by reviewing the legacy in England (UK-wide for Higher Education (HE)) of the UK Labour government's engagement with national leadership development interventions for each public service sector during

Developing Public Service Leaders. Wallace et al., Oxford University Press. © Mike Wallace, Michael Reed, Dermot O'Reilly, Michael Tomlinson, Jonathan Morris, Rosemary Deem (2023). DOI: 10.1093/oso/9780199552108.003.0009

the 2000s (Chapter 1, Table 1.1). We consider how the unfolding political and economic context has affected the profile of national leadership development interventions, associated with a change in the political complexion of government and the consequent trajectory of neoliberalization underpinning public service reform. This political project was more emphatically directed towards the further marketization of public services, alongside stringent austerity measures triggered by the global financial crisis, while retaining much of the regulatory regime that the Labour government had established (Jones et al., 2020). The national leadership development interventions for school education, healthcare, and HE were reconfigured at least once; the national leadership development body (NLDB) for school education was closed and its role fully centralized within the Department for Education (DfE).

Our empirical research findings were restricted to the early days of national leadership development interventions covering England. Many senior staff we interviewed will have retired or moved on. Each subsequent generation has less experience of provision and its administration within their public service prior to the Labour government reforms. They have less pre-reform experience as the foundation for their service professional or administrative culture to be overlaid through their acculturation as change agents for recent reform agendas. So are senior staff becoming more acculturated as leaders, acting as UK government change agents for continually accruing regulated marketization reforms, or becoming otherwise acculturated to comply? In the absence of research addressing this question directly, we seek some sense of an answer by considering pertinent findings from a substantial investigation in each of our three focal services. Together, they confirm that in terms of leading activity and service provision, times certainly *have* changed—in ways that partly belie the generic discourse of leaderism and its alliance with regulated marketization reforms, and hence the likelihood of national leadership development interventions realizing their potential, in practice, as an acculturative elite policy meta-lever.

Chapter 10 locates national leadership development interventions in England within the contemporary international spread of large-scale interventions through an illustrative comparison between the English interventions for our three public service sectors and a broadly parallel intervention in four other Anglophone industrialized countries: the United States of America (USA), Canada, Australia, and New Zealand. We chose these countries since they were also at the forefront of investment in public service leadership development; all had engaged systematically in variants of neoliberalization extending to public services (Clark, 2002; Harvey, 2007; Jessop, 2016; Redden, Phelan, & Baker, 2020); and there are many *partial* parallels between the major institutions through which neoliberalization was being pursued, including systems of government, and between their individualistic and performance-oriented societal cultures. The four countries have historical connections with the British Empire and associated diaspora (Halligan, 2010; House, Hanges, Javidan, Dorfman, & Gupta, 2004); one legacy is their common national language. Yet there are also significant differences with historic origins. Structural contrasts include the hierarchical complexity of government tiers, the division of responsibility between tiers for particular service sectors, the comprehensiveness of the welfare state prior to neoliberalization, and private sector dominance, most starkly in the USA (Domhoff, 2013).

Differences between Anglophone countries, including England, generated varying points of departure and parameters for public service neoliberalization from the 1970s, influencing each subsequent trajectory, and so the context for major leadership development interventions. We list contextual factors shaping our selected interventions in each country, summarizing their main characteristics as a basis for estimating the relative potential of each indicative intervention to operate as an elite policy meta-lever. Any intervention, however generic the leadership development provision, was likely to support senior staff in operating *within* the existing neoliberalized policy regime. However, only those interventions with potential to act as an elite policy meta-lever might be capable of operating as an acculturative control technology for *further* neoliberalization.

What we found informs the account developed in Chapter 11 of how subsequent versions of the interventions investigated in Part II are implicated in wider societal change connected with ongoing neoliberalization of English public services. We also consider how they and interventions in other Anglophone countries are located within an international movement that has institutionalized leadership discourse and public service leadership development in support of further neoliberalization, despite its limitations as an elite policy meta-lever; promoted the restricted professionalization of senior staff from public service organizations as leaders; and, ironically, perpetuated a deeply institutionalized technology for training that research on practical learning support has long questioned.

The contemporary context of public service leadership development interventions in England

Most contextual factors shaping the pre-pandemic legacy of the Labour government's suite of interventions are an evolution of those discussed in Parts I and II. First, despite constitutional conditions for 'British exceptionalism' remaining, a divided electorate serially inhibited the scope for unilateral action that elites from the political party forming the central government could typically employ. The 2010 general election produced a 'hung' parliament. The Conservative Party had most Members of Parliament (MPs), but not a majority of all MPs elected. A coalition government (hereafter 'the coalition') was formed with another political party, the Liberal Democrats; the Conservative Party contributed most government ministers, including those responsible for school education and healthcare. The coalition ended when the Conservative Party achieved a small majority of twelve MPs in the 2015 general election. However, the prime minister soon bowed to pressure from a substantial minority of Conservative MPs to hold a national referendum on whether the UK should terminate its membership of the European Union (popularized as 'Brexit'). A narrow majority of citizens choosing to vote in the 2016 referendum opted to leave. This axis of political division continued to preoccupy the Conservative government. It lost the Conservative Party's overall majority of MPs in the 2017 general election and so formed a minority government with support from the Democratic Unionist Party of Northern Ireland, with an overall majority of just two MPs. A Conservative Party internal election to choose a new leader in 2019 returned a prime minister who championed Brexit. The Conservative Party subsequently gained a large majority of eighty MPs in the 2019 general election, the UK formally departing the European Union at the beginning of 2020. Throughout this decade, compromise to the customary scope for unilateral government action did not stop authoritative elites from the Conservative Party exerting most influence on central government policies affecting public service provision.

Second, the incoming coalition government of 2010 replaced the Labour government's social democratic variant of neoliberalization by reverting to the intensively pro-market orientation of the past Conservative government. The coalition extended public service marketization through multiple reforms, expanding user choice amongst alternative service providers and facilitating 'market entry' by those from the private and voluntary sectors. This variant was also supported by managerialism: the retention of neo-Taylorist regulatory arrangements and private sector-based management practices introduced by the previous government; reforms creating enhanced conditions for entrepreneurship amongst existing and potential providers from the public, private, and voluntary sectors (especially in healthcare and HE); and continuing to responsibilize senior staff for managing the staff culture within their organizations.

Third, a novel factor shaping the Conservative neoliberalization trajectory was an unprecedented focus on extending economic austerity measures to eliminate a ballooning deficit in government expenditure following the 2008 financial crisis. Amongst the most deeply affected western economies were those of the USA and the United Kingdom (UK). Previously, the Labour government had taken advantage of sustained economic growth and low interest rates to fund major investment in improving public services, especially healthcare (Vizard & Obolenskaya, 2013), by extending its borrowing and so the spending deficit: the difference between government revenue from taxation and expenditure, primarily on public services. The financial crisis radically increased this deficit.

The periodization offered by Jessop (2019) encompasses how austerity has contributed to neoliberalization through depressing public expenditure. The first five stages were introduced in Chapter 2. We located the Labour government's public service reforms and its associated national leadership development interventions within Jessop's stage 5, which we labeled as blowback and adjustment to maintain neoliberal momentum. We now apply Jessop's final two stages to the impact of the financial crisis and consequential austerity policies on public service provision in the UK, with implications for ongoing governmental investment in national leadership development interventions. Our labels for these stages are informed by Jessop's account:

- *Stage 6: shoring up the neoliberal economic regime* at public expense. Senior Labour government politicians endeavoured to halt the financial crisis by ramping up the spending deficit through emergency public expenditure, alongside mitigatory tax increases. Elites from other UK political parties challenged the principle of 'big government' through discourse vilifying large-scale expenditure on social welfare, demanding further austerity measures to curb state spending.
- *Stage 7: retrenchment and the normalization of permanent austerity* brought on by the failure of government efforts to hold to account business elites whose risky investment behaviour had prompted the financial crisis, beyond imposing fines and modest re-regulation. The emergent government priority to reduce the massive deficit by cutting expenditure on public services was pursued through what became an enduring austerity agenda.

Stage 6 covers the immediate impacts of the financial crisis in the UK, including Labour government expenditure on bailouts to rescue failing banks (Kickert, 2012), followed by an economic recession, which lowered tax revenues and increased the burden of social welfare support as unemployment rose (Office for National Statistics, 2018). The resultant increase in the spending deficit exacerbated a chronic pressure on governments to delimit expenditure on citizen welfare reaching back to the collapse of Keynesian economics, the rise of neoliberalization, and the shift towards workfare. The financial crisis piled on further pressure to expand what Pierson (1998, p. 554) had dubbed a 'context of permanent austerity' in the UK and other western countries a decade earlier, resulting from successive government responses to the burgeoning health and care needs of ageing populations.

Stage 7 relates to the subsequent translation of the 'context of permanent austerity' into an integral component of the public service reform project pursued by authoritative elites from the Conservative Party and allied political parties within their variant of neoliberalization. Indicatively, the spending deficit was reduced by four-fifths between 2010 and 2019 (Freeguard, Shepheard, Guerin, Pope, & Zodgekar, 2020); and differential cuts in government departmental budgets flowed from policies restricting public service expenditure (Emmerson, Johnson, & Joyce, 2015).

Government departments responsible for school education and healthcare in England were relatively protected. Even so, spending per pupil fell by 8 per cent in real terms by 2019 (Farquharson & Sibieta, 2019); National Health Service (NHS) spending increases averaged only 1.1 per cent per year in real terms from 2010 to 2015 (Harker, 2019), despite rising demand. After five years of financial pressure on the English NHS to 'do more with less' by making year-on-year efficiency gains, the limit was reached: in 2015–16 two-thirds of NHS provider organizations overspent their annual budgets (King's Fund, 2016, p. 8). In 2010, government ministers imposed a two-year pay freeze for staff in school education, healthcare and other service sectors, followed by five years of 1 per cent capped pay rises (Ferguson & Francis-Devine, 2021). Cuts variably affected the number and working conditions of service providers, the quality and quantity of service provision, and updating of the service infrastructure itself. Notably, an ongoing schools rebuilding programme was cancelled (Hansard, 2010). Yet the contribution of government spending to partly public-funded HE varied little in real terms (Bolton, 2019). The austerity programme and many of its impacts continued (Emmerson, Farquharson, & Johnson, 2019) until (temporarily) overtaken by the Conservative government's emergency response to the pandemic.

The fourth contextual factor was near-universal subscription to the generic discourse of leaderism amongst strategic and intermediate-level elites and their associates, with central government ministers allying leadership with their regulated marketization reforms. They, alongside senior staff from representative bodies and senior officials from NLDBs, promoted 'leaders inspiring others in collaborative endeavours' within public service organizations through leadership development for the different sectors. The title of the Conservative Party (2015) general election manifesto reiterated the longstanding construal of politicians as leaders of the nation: 'Strong leadership, a clear economic plan, a brighter, more secure future.' Belief in organizational leadership as key to public service effectiveness was reflected in the manifesto claim that 'We know what works in education: great teachers; brilliant leadership' (p. 33), and in a DoH (2016, p. 3) mandate to the agency Health Education England that 'The NHS needs high quality leaders at every level and in every area to ensure that it is able to deliver high quality compassionate care to the people it serves'. The 2016 HE white paper published by the Department of Business, Innovation and Skills (DBIS) referred to senior staff in universities and colleges simply as 'leaders' (DBIS, 2016, p. 10). The representative body UUK (2017) echoed this usage through repeated references to 'university', 'institutional', and 'agency' leaders in its review of HE sector-owned agencies.

Senior staff in public service organizations were directed, urged, or induced to implement more reforms for their sector and operate the reformed services with fewer resources. Table 9.1 summarizes the main elements of further neoliberalization for our service sectors in England, highlighting how the shared emphasis on extending marketization took bespoke form in each sector, as government elites built on or departed from past Labour government-driven reforms.

School education diversified rapidly, with more schools funded directly by central government. Hollowing out of the state (Clarke & Newman, 1997) continued, furthering the reduction in local government control over schools begun by the past Conservative government decades before. The number of academy schools was greatly extended, each overseen by a board of trustees whose members might include senior executives from the private sector. A minority of academies became part of an 'academy chain' comprising several schools administered by a multi-academy trust. Hitherto, these academy schools had been administered by local government through their local education authorities (LEAs). Additionally, local groups of parents and other stakeholders were encouraged to apply for approval to establish a new type of academy: 'free schools', also central government-funded and outside local authority jurisdiction.

Healthcare experienced yet another 're-disorganization' (Pollitt, 2007) to adjust the purchaser–provider split (previously reformed by the Labour government) and encourage greater competition, incorporating private and voluntary sector providers. In this organizational reconfiguration, local Care Commissioning Groups (CCGs), including general practitioner (GP)

Table 9.1 Further neoliberalization of school education, healthcare, and higher education by coalition and Conservative governments, 2010–19[*]

Elements of neoliberalization introduced by UK coalition and Conservative government, impact on marketization and/or regulation	Regulated marketization reforms and year of implementation		
	School education (England)	Healthcare (England)	Higher education (England)
Construe service recipients as customers, or as purchasers on behalf of customers (**marketization**)		Primary care trusts (PCTs) and Strategic Health Authorities (SHAs) abolished, Care Commissioning Groups (CCGs), including general practitioners (GPs), created to commission local community healthcare (2013) NHS England created with oversight of commissioning (2013)	Universities and colleges allowed to charge higher tuition fees and recruit more students, maintenance grants for poorest students raised (2012) then abolished (2016), cap on student recruitment removed (2015)
Inform customer choice about service providers and their quality of service (**marketization**)			Research assessment by the Higher Education Funding Council for England (HEFCE), commercial league tables of results (2014) Voluntary participation in assessment against the Teaching Excellence and Student Outcomes Framework (TEF) (2016–2018), Office for Students (OfS) established as HE regulator (for England), provided information on HE providers and provision (2018)

Create alternative forms of service provider (**marketization**)	More academy schools replaced failing schools, other schools invited to apply, multiple school academies encouraged, funded directly by central government, many with business sponsorship, governed by an academy trust, a not-for-profit company (2010) Free schools set up by local groups including parents, businesses, funded directly by central government (2010)	Encourage different types of 'challenger' provider, including private universities offering UK degrees, overseas universities with a UK base, private universities partnering with a UK university
Promote market entry for private sector organizations as service provider sponsors, providers, financers (**marketization**)	Abolition of 'building schools for the future' programme part-funded by the Private Finance Initiative (PFI) Business corporations encouraged to sponsor academy schools	Commissioning of healthcare providers includes those from the private sector
Remove administrative market barriers (**marketization and regulation**)	Teaching School Alliances where 'lead' schools judged by the Office for Standards in Education (Ofsted) to be 'outstanding' provide support to other local schools, some 'lead' schools charge for membership and activities	Reduced administrative tiers: SHAs replaced by NHS England, includes local branches (2013) Single registration system for new providers in England authorized to award degree- and use 'university' in their title (2018)

Continued

Table 9.1 *Continued*

Elements of neoliberalization introduced by UK coalition and Conservative government, impact on marketization and/or regulation	Regulated marketization reforms and year of implementation		
	School education (England)	Healthcare (England)	Higher education (England)
Specify service content (**regulation**)	Revised national curriculum, academy schools and free schools exempt		
Specify service standards (**regulation**)			
Monitor and publicize providers' standard of service (**marketization and regulation**)		Monitor (NHS) to prevent NHS provider anti-competitive behaviour (2013), included in NHS Improvement (2015)	The Offfice for Students (OfS) operated TEF (2018)

* Main sources as for Table 2.2

representatives, replaced PCTs. CCGs now purchased local community health services and secondary care, with varying potential to choose amongst NHS and private sector providers. NHS England, a new central commissioning body, oversaw the CCGs through regional offices and local teams. Strategic Health Authorities, hitherto responsible for planning regional provision, were abolished (further hollowing out the NHS). The remit of the regulatory body Monitor (NHS) included preventing anti-competitive behaviour amongst purchasers and providers.

Past Labour government reforms were extended to marketize HE and commodify provision through the introduction of student loans. The coalition government shifted the balance of funding for student tuition between the state and students, cast as customers. University and college fee regulation was eased, enabling universities and colleges to charge higher tuition fees and recruit more students, while increasing the size of student loans and subsequently removing maintenance grants for the poorest students. A complementary move was to encourage more universities and colleges, including those from the private sector, to enter the HE market. Conditions were created for expanding student choice and fostering increased competition between HE providers, including those identified as 'challenger universities' (Firetail Ltd, 2016, p. 2), engaging in innovation to establish or consolidate an advantageous market niche such as specializing in technology. An incremental HE sector-wide response to the additional administrative burden in universities and colleges brought by marketization was to increase the number of academic and non-academic staff with management roles and non-academic professional service roles. A survey (Wolf & Jenkins, 2021, pp. 26–27) reported a 60 per cent increase between 2005–6 and 2017–18 in the number of staff classified as 'managers and non-academic professionals'. The proportion of the total staff complement they represented rose from 18 to some 25 per cent.

Leading public service marketization and operation under conditions of permanent austerity

The altered trajectory of public service neoliberalization and the austerity measures framed the political project of public service reform pursued by the coalition and subsequent Conservative government. Senior staff from public service organizations in these and other sectors were tasked with implementing and operating further marketization and associated regulatory reforms in a context of diminishing resources. The governmental discourse strategy featured leaderism, as the examples already cited illustrate, though less prominently than that of the Labour government. Leaderism had been integrated into a social imaginary for public services resonant of the Labour government's 'earned autonomy'. The Conservative parallel notion of 'supported autonomy' was articulated for schools, but government policy for other public services aligned with its core tenets. Supported autonomy was geared to an even more hollowed out and marketized administrative system than 'earned autonomy', comprising central government and individual provider organizations. There was little role for local and regional governance or for formally constituted horizontal networks where senior staff from any one organization had no formal jurisdiction over the others. Central government set parameters for service provision, including accountability arrangements. Senior staff from individual provider organizations were responsibilized, as leaders, to use their autonomy. Yet it was significantly constrained by the imperative of achieving centrally set service standards to avoid negative sanctions. This imaginary was articulated in the 2016 school education white paper (DfE, 2016, p. 4):

> We believe in supported autonomy: aligning funding, control, responsibility and accountability in one place, as close to the front line as possible, and ensuring that institutions [provider organizations] can collaborate and access the support they need to set them up for success. And we will work to build a system which is responsive to need and performance, ensuring that institutions respond to changing needs. Autonomy will be both earned and lost, with our most successful leaders extending their influence, and weaker ones doing the opposite.

Speculatively, the contribution of leaderism to the discourse strategy may have been more assumptive than expressed because the metaphor of leadership had become so naturalized within government and throughout the public services since the mid-1990s. Its usage, connoting legitimate forms of influencing behaviour, may have become largely pre-reflexive, shared, self-evident. We outlined in Chapter 5 how generic leaderism, as a discourse within the instrumental ideology of managerialism, may be allied with discourses linked to economic and political ideologies, including social imaginaries that become widely accepted, and so gradually backgrounded as taken-for-granted ways of construing how the social world is or should be. Leadership may have acquired the status of 'common-sense' (Hall & O'Shea, 2013, pp. 9–10):

> a form of 'everyday thinking' which offers us frameworks of meaning with which to make sense of the world . . . It works intuitively, without forethought or reflection

. . . Its virtue is that it is obvious. Its watchword is, 'Of course!'. It seems to be outside time. Indeed, it may be persuasive precisely because we think of it as a product of Nature rather than of history.

To the extent that leadership of and within public services had become 'common-sense', senior staff in public service organizations might no longer need persuading within the new imaginary that they were leaders and should act accordingly in seeking to gain (and avoid losing) 'supported autonomy'. Being leaders legitimated their influencing activity and, for many, a career-oriented motivation to further their development and associated credentials as leaders. The government's discourse strategy could harness assumptive leaderism as 'common-sense' background for persuading senior staff to accept their part in earning and deploying their supported autonomy, complying with arrangements holding them accountable for service outcomes, and accepting direction by authoritative elites within government. Nevertheless, this discourse strategy still responsibilized senior staff to implement and operate public service reforms for their sector, since their active engagement was deemed essential to achieve the service outcomes for which they would be accountable. Continuing government investment in national leadership development interventions provided a forum for articulating leadership, reinforcing the acculturation of participants as leaders, and acculturating career-oriented newcomers to a particular public service.

Leadership development as an enduring control technology

For the coalition and Conservative government, the past Labour government's investment in national leadership development interventions for each public service sector constituted yesterday's reform, today's resource. Leadership development remained as prominent a control technology for realizing the political project of public service reform pursued by the coalition and successor Conservative government as it had been for the Labour government. Table 9.2 shows that the range of public service sectors covered by the suite of national leadership development interventions was undiminished. For most interventions, the formal relationship between the NLDB and the government was unchanged. A minority were reconfigured in line with evolving government marketization policies for the sector, and government sole or contributory funding of several interventions was reduced or terminated, reflecting the drive to reduce the spending deficit through austerity measures. The intervention for local government had been independent since its inception (Chapter 1), but the coalition government sold the Fire Service

Table 9.2 Legacy by 2019 of national leadership development interventions that the UK Labour government had established or reconfigured by 2010

National leadership development body	Public service sector	National jurisdiction	Formal relationship with a department of the UK government, reflecting the extent of central regulation
Local Government Association	Local government	England, Wales	**Distanced:** a representative body of local authorities. Academy for Executive Leadership and Leadership Centre for Local Government leadership development programmes were absorbed into Local Government Association provision, including Society of Local Authority Chief Executives and Senior Managers (SOLACE) programmes. In receipt of contributory government funding
Civil Service Leadership Academy	Civil service	UK	**Close:** a unit within the UK Government's Cabinet Office. Following a review, the National School of Government and Centre for Management and Policy Studies were closed. Civil Service Learning was established in the Cabinet Office, offering leadership development for civil servants, followed by the Civil Service Leadership Academy in 2017 for senior civil servants
National body closed * Replaced by national professional qualifications and accredited providers	School education	England, international	**Close:** following a review, the National College for Leadership of Schools and Children's Services was reconfigured in 2013 by the UK government's Department for Education (DfE) as the National College for Teaching and Leadership, an executive agency. It was closed in 2018. Its leadership development programmes leading to national qualifications were marketized and offered commercially by providers selected by the DfE. Providers included private companies and schools that inspectors judged 'outstanding'. Government funding for some places. Programmes offered online were available internationally

NHS Leadership Academy*	Health	England	Close: NHS Institute for Innovation and Improvement was closed in 2013 following a review in 2010. The NHS Leadership Academy was launched by the UK Government's Department of Health in 2012 and incorporated into NHS England and NHS Improvement in 2019. University and business consultants commissioned to assist the creation of leadership development, offered nationally, supported regional provision offered by NHS Local Leadership Academies
Social Care Institute for Excellence	Social services	England, Wales, Northern Ireland	Distanced: continued to be an independent charitable company, received contributory government funding, also provided paid-for leadership development activities
Defence Leadership Centre	Defence	UK, international	Close: The Defence Leadership Centre continued, with leadership development offered internationally. Some provision involved HE and commercial partners. A unit within the UK Government's Defence Academy, part of the Ministry of Defence. An executive agency
College of Policing	Police	England and Wales	Moderately close: following a review in 2011, the National Policing Improvement Agency was closed in 2012 when the College of Policing was established as a not-for-profit company and arm's length body of the UK Government's Home Office, becoming operationally independent. It established a national policing curriculum, and provided leadership development programmes
Education and Training Foundation	Further education	England	Moderately close: following a review, the Learning and Skills Improvement Service was closed in 2013 when the Education and Training Foundation was established by representative bodies as a charity. It was supported by the UK Government's DfE. The Foundation established a membership body and professional standards, provided leadership development, some involving an HE partner, and received contributory government funding

Continued

Table 9.2 *Continued*

National leadership development body	Public service sector	National jurisdiction	Formal relationship with a department of the UK government, reflecting the extent of central regulation
Advance HE*	Higher education	UK, international	**Distanced**: the Leadership Foundation for Higher Education was merged with other developmental change-oriented agencies in 2018 to form Advance HE, which continued providing leadership development programmes. Received contributory government funding from national funding councils and from the Office for Students in England. A charity and non-profit company
Fire Service College	Fire and rescue service	England, international	**Distanced**: following a review, the Centre for Leadership was terminated when the Fire Service College was sold by the UK Government's Department of Communities and Local Government in 2013 to the private sector Capita Group. The Fire Service College continued to provide leadership development. A private for-profit company
National Leadership Centre	Cross-public service	England	**Close**: in response to the report of the Public Services Leadership Taskforce, the National Leadership Centre was established in 2018. It provided a collaborative leadership development programme for recently appointed chief executives of public service organizations, including the government civil service, schools, healthcare, HE, promoted networking for all senior staff in public service organizations, and conducted research on public service leadership and its impact on service productivity. Part of the Cabinet Office

* Previous versions of the shaded NLDBs were investigated during 2006–8 in our empirical research (Part II).

College to a private company in 2013. It continued to provide leadership development on a commercial basis.

An innovation was to augment the sector-specific coverage by establishing a cross-public service intervention. The National Leadership Centre (NLC) was established in response to the Conservative government's Public Services Leadership Taskforce (2018) report. The authors advocated promoting collaboration amongst staff in top executive positions from different public service sectors, since improving public services 'means finding new ways to solve problems and work across traditional organizational boundaries' (p. 27). The new intervention's purpose was 'to support cross sector leadership, facilitating and supporting people to work together on the toughest challenges we face as a country' (NLC, 2020, p. 6). This intervention was untypical of the Conservative government: promoting collaboration amongst local and intermediate-level expert elites, across organizational and service boundaries, and for cross-public service benefit, ran counter to the marketization thrust founded on organizations competing for their own benefit within a service sector.

The interventions for our three service sectors were each reworked in line with the drift of government-driven reforms for their sector. In 2013, central government tightened control of the NLDB for school education, merging it with the Teaching Agency, previously responsible for teacher training. The new organization's remit was broadened accordingly. Whereas the predecessor NLDBs (National College for School Leadership, National College for Leadership of Schools and Children's Services) had been set up as a company and non-departmental public body, with a modicum of independence from the government's education department, the National College for Teaching and Leadership (NCTL) was an executive agency of the DfE, responsible for carrying out its policies. Extending governmental control reflected the 'steering' side of structural reforms, where government set public service system parameters—here, for national leadership development provision, already initiated by establishing an expanding network of 'Teaching Schools' inspired by the model of teaching hospitals (DfE, 2010). Teaching Schools had previously been judged as 'outstanding' by Office for Standards in Education (Ofsted) inspectors. Staff (alongside professional trainers and university staff) could offer NCTL-designed national leadership development programmes, for which they were remunerated, with the NCTL responsible for quality assurance. This aspect of the shift reflected the 'rowing' side of structural reforms, creating a national marketplace for provision, and providing an opportunity and financial inducement for senior staff from eligible schools to engage in entrepreneurialism by seeking market entry. In 2018 the NCTL was closed, and central steering became even more directive in consolidating the leadership development marketplace. The DfE specified learning outcomes for an expanded suite of programmes, each culminating in a national qualification (e.g. DfE, 2020), inviting tenders from private companies or teaching schools, and selecting a set of regional providers across England.

Reconfiguration of the NLDB for healthcare was driven more by austerity than by marketization. Yet this shift also reflected a concern to hollow out the National Health Service (NHS) as an administrative system by reducing the intermediate layer of organizations interposed between the 'steering' central government department and the 'rowing' service commissioning and provider organizations. The NHS reform white paper (DoH, 2010a), was followed by a review of NHS 'arm's length bodies' associated with the commitment to 'reducing NHS administrative costs by more than 45%' (DoH, 2010b, p. 4). Such bodies are relatively independent of the government's sponsoring department. This review proposed to abolish the NHS Institute for Innovation and Improvement (NHSIII) and consider the future of its leadership development provision. Since NHS reforms included removing SHAs, another intermediate organizational layer, their contribution to regional leadership development provision ceased. The emergent national leadership development intervention was the NHS Leadership Academy, established within the Department of Health (DoH). The Leadership Academy commissioned university and management consultants (reflecting the assumption that 'business knows best') to help create national leadership development programmes, while supporting regional provision by NHS Local Leadership Academies. Centralization of provision accorded with the 'steering' side of the NHS structural reforms, enhanced by incorporating the NHS Leadership Academy into the DoH and eliminating the less steerable intermediate-level NHSIII. The focus on leadership development provision was intensified by reverting to an exclusive focus on leadership development (resonant of the original NHS Leadership Centre (NHSLC)) established by the Labour government), but on an unprecedented scale.

The NLDB for HE had operated within the marketplace for senior staff training since its inception in 2004, with government funding support (Chapter 6). Prior to the election of the coalition government, the Leadership Foundation for Higher Education (LFHE) had earned almost 80 per cent of its income through university or college membership payments and participation in activities (Blue Alumni, 2010, p. 1). The declining contribution from central government grants was expected to cease in 2012. Subsequently, the LFHE continued earning income from national funding councils, but solely for specified activities. Its continuing financial viability rested on willingness amongst universities and colleges to pay increasing fees for membership and provision. Concerns over subscription rates for the LFHE and other agencies established by Universities UK (UUK) and GuildHE, as representative bodies for senior staff in HE, prompted a UUK review. It determined that 'a lack of effective coordination of the land-scape at the sector level, allied to the need for some agencies to diversify income streams, has led to a degree of mission-creep and duplication of services' (UUK, 2017, p. 4). A proposal to merge the LFHE with other agencies was implemented, creating AdvanceHE, funded through university and college membership subscription and payment for activities. UUK and GuildHE retained some oversight through their nominated members of the AdvanceHE Board. The theme of 'transformative leadership' formed one strand of its provision (AdvanceHE, 2019, p. 8), operationalized through leadership development programmes inherited from the LFHE. This strand included national funding council-commissioned activity, exemplified by the 'Wales Higher Education Executive Leaders Programme' (p. 19) for the Higher Education Funding Council for Wales. Central government 'steer-ing' of the NLDB, already 'at a distance' (Kickert, 1995), had now been disengaged.

The survival of these national leadership development interventions sug-gests that their future was assured, alongside that of others in England (Table 9.2). They had outlived management fad status. Despite serial gov-ernment reconfiguration of the interventions for school education and healthcare, the eventual demise of the NLDB for school education, and full marketization of the intervention for HE, a substantial range of leadership development provision was sustained throughout. When the coalition and Conservative governments shifted the trajectory of public service neoliber-alization towards marketization underwritten by austerity measures, they retained national leadership development interventions. These interven-tions continued to constitute an acculturative means of formally co-opting senior staff towards leading the implementation and entrepreneurial oper-ation of structural reforms for public-funded service sectors. Strategic-level elites within these successor governments broadly echoed the foundational generative mechanism inferred in Part II, explaining why and how the previous Labour government had launched and sustained its suite of inter-ventions. The discourse strategy perpetuated an assumptive leader-centric construal of leadership, tallying leading activity with seniority of position carrying management responsibility. National leadership development inter-ventions for different public-funded service sectors constituted a collective control technology, enhancing central capacity for the remote containment of local responses amongst senior staff in deploying 'supported autonomy', as obtained for school education and healthcare. Senior staff in HE had formal autonomy to operate in their partly public-funded service marketplace, bounded by their dependence on securing income from central government funding sources and by regulatory mechanisms to ensure that 'trading' practices stayed within parameters acceptable to government ministers.

Relevant government and representative body documents evidence how leadership development was linked with the narrow conception of professionalization highlighted in Part II, underpinning the restricted professionalization of senior staff as local leaders. It was a legacy of the professionalization and accreditation trajectory of leadership stimulated or supported by the Labour government's investment, sustained since by elites within the successor governments and relevant representative bodies. Least distinction was made in school education between service professionals and professional leaders. The coalition government's white paper (DfE, 2010, p. 24) classified teachers and leaders as professionals, distinguishing the latter as 'professionals in leadership positions'; thus leading activity was associated with a formal management position. The National Professional Qualification for Headship (NPQH), the landmark qualification for headship, was made non-compulsory from 2012, enabling the appointment of headteachers with no teaching experience to academy or free schools. Yet NPQH remained within the expanding range of national 'professional' qualifications for senior staff (DfE, 2021a). The distinction was sharper in healthcare, with its multiplicity of service professions, legacy of past governmental and representative body endeavours to professionalize leadership, and, reportedly, consistent 'failure to engage clinicians—particularly, but not only doctors—in a sustained way in management and leadership' (King's Fund, 2011, p. ix). While government documents focused on health service professions, the aims of the NHS Leadership Academy (2014) included 'professionalising leadership to raise the profile, performance and impact of health system leaders, requiring and supporting them to demonstrate their fit and proper readiness to carry out their leadership role and defining what we expect from them'. The professionalization of senior staff in HE as leaders, though no longer a government concern, was championed by AdvanceHE (2019, p. 9), claiming to provide public benefit through charitable activities that included 'developing the professionalism and profile of leadership, management and governance' through its leadership development programmes.

'Supported autonomy' in action: regulated market leaders versus public service protectors

Leaderism is implicit in the social imaginary of 'supported autonomy' articulated by UK government elites. Recent research into aspects of practices entailed in governing and organizing provision offers clues about the extent to which leadership of, and within, public service organizations matches in practice the discursive construction of generic leaderism encapsulated in our characterization (Chapter 5). To what extent do these practices involve 'leaders inspiring others in collaborative endeavours' towards realizing some shared vision for improvement? Are these collaborative endeavours devoted to implementing and operating regulated and marketized services connected with the government's political project of public service reform? If the UK government was gaining traction by promoting 'supported autonomy' (implicitly incorporating leaderism) within its discourse strategy and leaderism allied to regulated marketization reform through its control technology of leadership development, then research into organizational practices might show that leaders were inspiring others, and that their collaborative endeavours were directed towards regulated and marketized service provision. Relevant findings from our three illustrative examples of substantial research challenge such an expectation.

First, in the school education sector, Greany and Higham (2018, pp. 10–18) investigated responses within schools to the UK government's 'self-improving school-led system' agenda reflected in the social imaginary of 'supported autonomy'. Data generation in 2015–17 included a telephone survey of almost 700 headteachers and other senior staff and 168 interviews with a range of staff, including headteachers, from academies and other schools. A key finding connected with leading activity was that the government pursuit of this agenda had 'intensified hierarchical governance and the state's powers of intervention, further constraining the professionalism of school staff and steering the system through a model we term "coercive autonomy"'. The imperative to demonstrate compliance within the accountability regime far outweighed the degree of autonomy at school level, with 77 per cent of survey respondents reporting that ensuring their school performed well in Ofsted inspections was amongst their top priorities. The published Ofsted inspection criteria constituted an important source of guidance. The authors note how the accountability framework had 'allowed the state to continue to steer the system from a distance *and* to increasingly intervene and coerce when and where it deems necessary' [original italics]. The research did not examine visions for improvement. Yet it implies direction-setting to be widely dominated by accountability requirements, especially the Ofsted inspection criteria, constraining local-level choice over the content for any vision on which senior staff might consult other staff and local stakeholders, including parents.

Around half of survey respondents did not support the trajectory of current government policy; only a fifth approved. Most schools had some collaborative arrangement with other schools for mutual benefit, with two-thirds of primary and two-fifths of secondary school respondents reporting that their strongest partnership was an informal 'local cluster', rather than a formal Teaching School Alliance or multi-academy trust connected with government policy. Overall, respondents perceived the regulated marketization reforms to be reducing school-level autonomy through the spread of multi-academy trusts. The 'hollow' within the state created by the academy schools policy was being filled by an emergent and less democratically accountable alternative to local authority governance. Most senior staff appear not to have been acculturated as government change agents. However, some did operate in this way: the reforms provided varied incentives for senior staff to act 'selfishly' within the regulated marketplace by competing against others. While only a third of primary school respondents agreed that 'schools in my locality compete with each other to recruit students', nine-tenths of their secondary school counterparts did so. This finding does not demonstrate that respondents were competitive, but it suggests competitive behaviour to be commonplace, especially in secondary schools. Marketized provision apparently generated a structural bias. Once one local school started competing against others for students, the rest were pressurized to respond. Otherwise, they risked losing students to the competitor and a consequent decline in their local reputation and operating budget, and eventually, perhaps, becoming unviable. The cumulative reach of the national leadership development intervention was very extensive: some 230,000 places on its programmes, accessed by staff from 96 per cent of secondary and 79 per cent of primary schools (Greany, 2018). Therefore, a significant proportion of respondents are likely to have experienced its provision. If so, it seems that most did not become acculturated as government change agents. Enthusiasm for government reforms may have more connection with the political views of senior staff as individual citizens than with leadership development.

Second, in healthcare the study relating to our concerns (Hyde, Granter, Hassard, & McCann, 2016) focuses more narrowly on the impact of New Public Management on the working lives of 250 'junior' and 'middle' managers in four NHS healthcare organizations: an acute hospital trust, an ambulance trust, a primary care trust, and a mental health trust. The clinical background of nurse and ward managers and clinical team leaders meant they had experienced prior socialization as frontline healthcare professionals; others had pursued an administrative career. The research team employed immersive ethnographic methods during the period 2010–12, conducting more than 400 hours of observations and 80 recorded and 39 unrecorded interviews (Hassard, Hyde, Cox, Granter, & McCann, 2017). In these settings (Hyde et al., 2016, pp. 176–177):

> the overall demotion of need for care as a determinant of resource allocation was a widespread finding—one that was deeply troubling for NHS managers, who are often clinical professionals with a deep belief in the NHS's *free at the point of need* ethos. Even when they didn't have clinical backgrounds, many were passionate supporters of this ethos. [original italics]

Pressure to compromise on patient care came from senior staff whose organization-wide managerial and budgetary priorities were distanced from the close engagement of junior and middle managers with service provision. Senior staff were subject to pressure from government-imposed budgetary constraints, coupled with expanding public demand for services. Informants reported that senior staff, including 'human resource managers', set financial and service provision targets to cope with stringent budgetary constraints, while simultaneously promoting entrepreneurialism: they encouraged junior and middle managers to generate departmental income through offering and charging other organizations for training or other services. The combination of targets and measures to reach them compromised, and distracted informants from engaging in, leading activity devoted to their fundamental priority: providing patient care. The researchers noted 'the challenges managers faced . . . as they were told to reimagine themselves as entrepreneurial, transformational leaders and effective business people whilst also administering and monitoring their public services' (p. 180). Middle managers quite widely perceived their role to include strategically focused and inspirational leading activity to make desirable change happen yet, reportedly, the relentless press of operational management demands largely frustrated the aspiration to fulfil this aspect of their role (Bresnen, Hyde, Hodgson, Bailey, & Hassard, 2015).

Ministers from the Labour and subsequent coalition governments had long heralded increased autonomy and entrepreneurial capacity for NHS organizations as NHS Trusts. Resonant of 'supported autonomy' for schools, autonomy for healthcare organizations translated, for junior and middle managers, into domination by imperatives handed down by senior staff to meet organizational targets. These hierarchically ordered 'demands from above' within the organizations undermined the agency of informants as 'leaders in the middle' to promote patient care through the twin imperatives to 'do more with less' and be more 'business-like' within the healthcare 'market'. Middle managers had become chronically overloaded (Hyde et al., 2016, p. 182):

> The first major shock for clinicians who had moved into managerial jobs was the sudden loss of fixed working hours . . . any new demands for immediate information . . . landed readily at their feet, and this was on top of an already teeming workload . . . our assessment was that most of these jobs were bordering on the impossible.

The UK government's NHS reorganization in 2012 had abolished PCTs—ironically, an innovation at the time of our own research just five years before (Chapter 6). Junior and middle managers in the PCT being studied were left to contribute towards leading the planning and implementation of the closure process while seeking to secure their own future employment.

To the extent that informants perceived themselves as leaders, these findings imply that they did not tie the generic discourse of leaderism with regulated marketization and were no more acculturated as change agents for government reforms than most senior staff in schools. By the time of this research, the NHSIII was due for replacement by the NHS Leadership Academy, as discussed earlier. If any of the informants had experienced NHSIII leadership development provision, it did not appear to have motivated or equipped them to become entrepreneurial leaders.

Third, in the HE sector a major survey, completed in 2017 by UK academic staff, evidences their experiences and perceptions of contemporary university governance (Erickson, Hanna, & Walker, 2020) and the expansion of entrepreneurialism. Respondents were not senior 'manager-academics', though they may have shouldered some departmental responsibility for the work of other staff. The results suggest the emergence of an enduring cultural divide and hierarchical distancing between academic staff and senior managers, consistent with a growing body of literature (Craig, Mernic, & Tourish, 2014; Deem, Hillyard, & Reed, 2007; Docherty, 2011; Gill, 2014). Academics remained committed to working within a collegial community of scholars; senior managers ('manager-academics' who had originally pursued an academic career and career administrators) were reportedly wedded to a very hierarchical form of managerialism, coupled with the instrumentalization of knowledge generation. They were perceived to be pursuing entrepreneurial operation, competing against other universities within the UK and internationally within an equally hierarchical HE marketplace; variable priority, according to their relative positioning within this marketplace, was given to attracting high-tariff students, particularly from overseas, and research income from prestigious funders. The survey was designed to mirror the annual National Student Survey (NSS), where students evaluate their HE experience. Academics were invited to evaluate their experience of senior managers. Respondents, numbering almost 6,000, were self-selected (as are students completing the NSS Survey).

Mirroring league tables produced for NSS results, the researchers constructed a league table of university senior management teams for the seventy-eight universities with at least twenty-five survey respondents, recording the percentage of staff who were satisfied with the way their university was being managed. Mean satisfaction was below 11 per cent, ranging from over 36 per cent (Oxford University) to 0 per cent (three universities), with no clear pattern in terms of geographical location or status indicators, such as membership of the Russell Group of research-intensive universities. Thus, the large majority of academic respondents, across the UK HE sector, were dissatisfied with the practice of senior staff, positioned as local-level elites and elite associates to act, collectively, as leaders of and within their organization. Perceived competence of senior managers appears to have been distributed randomly across the sector, suggesting that the corporate agency of vice chancellors and the agency their senior colleagues was sufficiently extensive for them to choose different practices, with different impacts on academic staff.

From qualitative comments, the researchers derived five interrelated themes, symptomatic of leading activity by senior staff and its consequences. The first theme concerned hierarchically asymmetrical accountability: senior staff evaluated the performance of academics through an extensive range of measures, while denying academics formal means of evaluating the performance and impacts of senior managers. So this survey represented an exceptional opportunity for academics, yet their senior managers were not the primary audience, nor were they directly held to account. A respondent commented on the distancing of senior managers (p. 9):

> Academic staff ultimately do not run the university. It is run by a small group of senior administrators with little idea about running a university. This leads to a lot of 'initiatives' that detract from the day job of teaching, revising curricula, and doing research ... they ought to know more about what they are purporting to manage, and not rely on performance indicators and the quasi-anonymous process of cascading down information. They might manage, but don't lead. As a consequence, they assume their right to lead, rather than earning it.

Initiatives added a burden on top of the day job, associated with the second theme of perpetual change, that was perceived to make little positive impact on teaching or research. It was linked to a third theme—expansion programmes, often involving 'vanity' capital projects entailing new buildings (the province of vice chancellors, especially). They were subsidized through student fees, staffing cutbacks (resulting in widespread workload increases), and a fourth theme: a concomitant increase in precarious and insecure academic staff contracts that inhibited them from expressing their individual and collective voice. The upshot, captured by the final theme, was a cumulatively negative impact on staff wellbeing and mental health. The researchers concluded that the survey had revealed 'an acute situation of endemic bullying and harassment, chronic overwork, high levels of mental health problems, general health and wellbeing problems, and catastrophically high levels of demoralisation and dissatisfaction across the UK HE sector' (p. 15).

In tandem with school education and healthcare, insofar as senior staff were cast by strategic-level and intermediate-level elites as 'leaders', and perceived themselves to be leaders, their reported practice did not square well with the generic discourse of leaderism. There is little evidence of 'inspiring others in collaborative endeavours', or of academic staff being acculturated towards entrepreneurialism. However, many reported practices of senior staff were consistent with the alliance between leaderism and the implementation and operation of regulated marketization reforms and austerity measures: from asymmetrical accountability regimes within universities; through 'vanity' projects to attract students within a competitive marketplace; the incorporation of managerialist practices originating in the private sector, including precarious and insecure contracts; to a reduction in expenditure on staff responsible for achieving the core purposes of universities. To this end, senior staff appeared to be acting voluntarily as change agents facilitating UK government reforms, despite their formal autonomy from government. The cumulative reach of leadership development provision offered by the LFHE suggests that at least some of the sixty current vice chancellors who were alumni of the Top Management Programme, and other senior staff who had experienced LFHE provision, were amongst those whom survey respondents held responsible for their dissatisfaction. If so, the LFHE experience may have assisted the co-optative acculturation of senior management team members (or reinforced it, depending on their political views as citizens) towards being leaders within the reformed HE sector.

The practices of senior staff reported or reflected in the findings from these studies do not align with generic leaderism. Yet they are consistent with the deployment of corporate agency towards implementing and operating regulated and marketized public services in a context of permanent austerity through forms of managerialism resonating with two ideal types: neo-Taylorism and entrepreneurialism. Whatever contribution the national leadership development interventions may have made in acculturating senior staff in these three service sectors, it had not been to stimulate organization-wide subscription to a shared vision for improvement, let alone commitment to its achievement. Leading activity here seems more transmissional of government policy than transformational of public service provision.

Briefly revisiting the explanation developed in Part II of the origins, operation, and immediate outcomes of the three leadership development interventions we investigated (Appendix 1), it appears that the drift of the contextual factors and linked generative mechanisms continued to apply, although many details had changed in the period since. In terms of *context*, scope for unilateral action by central government was retained during an unusual period of political division through engineering an overall parliamentary majority. The trajectory of public service neoliberalization had shifted; regulated marketization was still being pursued but with a renewed emphasis on marketization reforms. What was new was the integration of 'permanent austerity' measures. However, the long-beleaguered residual public service professional ideology had survived amongst staff in public service organizations, as our examples of recent research illustrate.

The overarching pattern of *generative mechanisms* that we inferred also appears to have been sustained, causing similar *immediate outcomes*. At the centre of the causal network was the content of provision offered by a national leadership development intervention, each reconfigured, for the three focal public service sectors. This provision continued to be more generic than concerned with reforms of the day. One mechanism no longer obtained for remote containment to promote the transmission of reforms into practice:

the formal accreditation by central government of the NPQH as a requirement for a first school headship. Compulsion had been removed to enable headteachers with no service professional background to be appointed to academy and free schools. However, the record of participation in any leadership development provision still held currency in all three focal service sectors as a credential conferring symbolic capital when seeking career advancement. It contributed to the ongoing restricted professionalization of senior staff from public service organizations who were formally co-opted more as professional leaders than as government change agents. So the leadership development interventions did not appear to have achieved significantly greater impact as an elite policy meta-lever in the years since the demise of the Labour government. Meanwhile, remote containment through direct and indirect regulatory arrangements continued to delimit the practice of senior staff in line with government-set or supported expectations. The institutionalization of leader-centric leadership development interventions as a route to professionalization and the delimitation of leading activity via regulation had proceeded apace since the time of our research.

Given the prevalence of 'policy tourism and policy borrowing' (Whitty, 2012, p. 354) amongst authoritative elites and their elite-associate advisers (including consultants and academics) from different national and regional jurisdictions, a diffuse *legacy* of the Labour government's investment in national leadership development interventions may have been to offer one source, amongst others, of ideas or examples of practice informing interventions in other countries. Certainly, large-scale leadership development interventions for senior staff in public service organizations have proliferated since the early 2000s. In the next chapter we compare the 'legacy' interventions for school education, healthcare, and HE in England with others of national or regional scope in four other Anglophone countries.

10

The 'new normal'

International investment in public service leadership
development

We saw in Chapter 1 how international engagement in leadership development interventions for senior staff in government civil services and other
public service organizations pre-dated the suite of national interventions we
investigated, and how they have proliferated since. Here we extend our consideration of the diffuse legacy of this extreme case through an international
comparison between the subsequent incarnations of national interventions
for our three focal public services in England and a national or regional intervention for each of these public services in the United States of America
(USA), Canada, Australia, and New Zealand.

First, to complement our account for England (Chapter 9), we outline
relevant contextual details for these four countries indicating that their governments are also pursuing some variant of neoliberalization encompassing
public services. The factors identified provide a basis for examining the
potential of our chosen interventions within each country to act, in principle, as an elite policy meta-lever, and so whether they might be capable
of supporting public service neoliberalization as an acculturative control
technology. Second, we compare a major intervention in each of the four
countries with that already discussed for England within school education,
healthcare, and then higher education (HE). Finally, we review the varying
potential of these interventions to support the professionalization of senior
staff as local-level leaders within parameters set by authoritative elites in government or other elite groupings, and to operate as an elite policy meta-lever
for further neoliberalization.

Major leadership development interventions in context

Table 10.1 draws on 'country files' compiled by Pollitt and Bouckaert
(2017), outlining relevant contextual features of the five countries: the governance of school education, healthcare, and HE, plus recent regulated

Developing Public Service Leaders. Wallace et al., Oxford University Press. © Mike Wallace, Michael Reed, Dermot O'Reilly,
Michael Tomlinson, Jonathan Morris, Rosemary Deem (2023). DOI: 10.1093/oso/9780199552108.003.0010

Table 10.1 Governance and recent regulated marketization reforms and austerity measures for school education, healthcare, and higher education

Contextual factor	USA	Canada	Australia	New Zealand	England
Structure of national government	Federal republic, 50 states	Confederation of 10 provinces, 3 territories	Confederation of 6 states, 3 mainland territories, 7 others (mainly islands)	Unitary state, 78 regional and unitary councils	Unitary state, UK government, devolved government Scotland, Wales, Northern Ireland

Government tiers responsible for school education, healthcare, HE

	USA	Canada	Australia	New Zealand	England
Public-funded schools	State government, devolution to local government school districts, federal government funding contribution including incentives	Provincial government	State government, federal funding contribution (subsidies for private, non-profit, and for-profit schools)	National government	UK government, devolution to local government for most schools
Public-funded healthcare	Not universal public access to healthcare, federal and state funded government health insurance and welfare schemes, private sector (for-profit, non-profit) contribution to public healthcare	Provincial government funded insurance scheme with federal government support, private sector (mostly non-profit) contribution to public healthcare	State government, federal funded insurance scheme and contribution to funding providers, private sector (for-profit, non-profit) contribution to public healthcare	National government overall, district health boards with operational responsibility	UK government, private (mostly for-profit) sector moderate contribution to National Health Service (NHS) provision

Partly public-funded higher education	State government for public universities and colleges, state and federal government student grant schemes, federal student loan schemes, competitive research funding	Provincial government for public universities and colleges (also federal government for aboriginal peoples), federal competitive research funding	State government for public universities, federal government contribution to tuition fees via grant and loan schemes, competitive research funding	National government for universities and colleges (all public), teaching grants, student tuition grants and loans, performance-based and competitive research funding	Most universities and colleges are independent charities, UK government student loan scheme and competitive research funding

Indicative recent government regulated marketization reforms, austerity measures

Schools	Variable state promotion of school choice through charter schools, magnet specialist schools, vouchers for private schools, funding cuts	Variable provincial promotion of school choice through charter schools or equivalent schools, specialist curricula, federal government direction of provinces to cut funding, varying responses	Ongoing promotion of school choice, including private school subsidies; cut in federal funding contribution	National standards for primary schools, charter schools (both reversed 2017), national curriculum, international pupil recruitment strategy, funding cuts	Promotion of school choice via academies, free schools, local provision of national leadership development, cancelled school building programme, staff pay freeze
Healthcare	Compulsory health insurance (reversed 2019) with federal subsidy for those on low incomes, federal cut in discretionary public health spending	Variable centralization of provincial healthcare administration, little marketization of public healthcare, varied provincial funding cuts	Promotion of private sector involvement in public healthcare provision, federal cut in state funding for hospitals, staff job losses	Proposed centralization creating a national health agency and abolishing district health boards, funding cuts	Reorganization of providers and purchasers, national leadership development, imposed efficiency savings, staff pay freeze
Higher education	State funding cuts	Provincial funding cuts	Federal removal of student number controls, cut in student grants, increase in maximum tuition fees allowed	International student recruitment strategy, increase in maximum tuition fees allowed	Increase in student loans and maximum tuition fees allowed, removal of student number controls

marketization reforms and austerity measures. The degree of central government involvement in steering provision, including engagement with national leadership development interventions for school education and healthcare, was most extreme in England. The five countries had each developed elements of a Keynesian welfare state, though only partially so in the USA, before governments embarked on neoliberalization (stage 3 of the periodization discussed in Chapter 2). The extent of reform required to create a regulated market incorporating the private and voluntary sectors was least here, where the ideologies of private sector-based managerialism and neoliberalism and the ideological discourse of leaderism all originated. So the USA, without universal public access to healthcare but with integral involvement of the private sector in public service provision, became a key exporter of ideologies applied to public services in other Anglophone countries, and elsewhere.

Within the two-tier federal and regional (state or provincial) strategic-level governments in the USA, Canada, and Australia, responsibility for administering school education, healthcare, and HE spans both tiers (except for Canadian school education, which is solely a provincial matter). Administrative responsibility rests exclusively with central government in the unitary states of New Zealand and the United Kingdom (UK), creating more favourable conditions for unilateral nationwide intervention. The British first-past-the-post and five-year-cycle electoral system (Chapter 1) gives the UK government more scope than the New Zealand government, whose electoral system features proportional representation—making coalition governments more common—and a four-year cycle. Table 10.1 suggests that British exceptionalism did play out through the recent UK government engagement in regulated marketization reforms and austerity measures for our three focal public services in England (Chapter 9), compared with governments in the other countries.

We focus next on leadership development interventions, pre-pandemic, for public service organization staff in public funded schools, healthcare, and HE. While substantial, these interventions represented a fraction of provision overall. Our review of interventions for each public service sector focuses on five aspects to provide evidence for an associated analytical purpose:

- scope, in terms of: (a) geographical remit, whether national or regional; (b) the longevity of the present intervention and any precursor; (c) strategic-level government, intermediate-level representative bodies of senior staff in public service organizations, or voluntary sector organizations responsible for undertaking or sponsoring it; and so (d) the degree of association, if any, between the intervention and government (for considering how an intervention might be harnessed towards government, representative body, or voluntary sector organization agendas);

- linkages between the interventions and other practices for managing people in public service organizations (for analysing the integration of leadership with management practices from the private sector);
- the commissioning and main content of leadership development provision, including target groups and forms of learning support (for considering any contribution to individual professionalization as leaders and the link between learning through participation in provision and present or aspirational future practice in the workplace);
- any expectations or standards for leading activity framing provision (for analysing how the ideological discourse of leaderism may be perpetuated through the normative construal and metaphorical entailments of leadership being promoted);
- the potential of the intervention to operate as an elite policy meta-lever according to, as appropriate, the relative social position of authoritative elites within strategic-level government and expert elites from intermediate-level bodies representing senior staff in public service organizations, or from voluntary sector organizations (for identifying the countries and service sectors where this potential appears greatest).

Leadership development for public-funded school services

Table 10.2 summarizes characteristics of one major intervention for each country. All had operated for more than a decade, evidencing a common longstanding commitment to leadership development provision. The varying association between each intervention and strategic-level government reflects the division of responsibility for public-funded school education between national, state or province, and more local tiers. The greatest complexity is reflected in the US example. We judged the district government to be strategic-level, given its span of authority over public-funded education. New York City is the largest US school district, under mayoral jurisdiction, with more pupils enrolled here than in all school districts combined within most states (National Center for Educational Statistics, 2020). The New York City (NYC) Leadership Academy, a local-level non-profit organization based there, offered leadership training and consultancy within the school district and also nationwide. Alongside its flagship preparatory 'Aspiring Principals Program', connected with state certification of those eligible to apply for a

Table 10.2 Strategic-level leadership development intervention connected with public-funded school education in the five Anglophone countries

Intervention, characteristic	USA	Canada	Australia	New Zealand	England
			SCHOOL EDUCATION		
Intervention	New York City (NYC) Leadership Academy	Ontario Leadership Strategy	Bastow Institute of Educational Leadership	Leadership Strategy	National Professional Qualifications
Scope	New York, national	Provincial (Ontario)	State (Victoria)	National	National (England)
Year of launch/reconfiguration	2003	2008	2009	2018 (past interventions from 2002)	2017 (NCSL launched 2000, NPQH 1997)
Responsibility for intervention	NYC Leadership Academy, a non-profit organization	Ontario Ministry of Education (OME)	State of Victoria Department of Education and Training (VDET)	Ministry of Education (NZMoE)	Department for Education (DfE)
Degree of linkage with strategic-level government	**Moderate:** awarded US Department of Education grants (e.g. 'School Leadership') Applicants included school districts, non-profit organizations Partnered with states, districts, schools providing leadership development	**Moderate:** the Ontario Leadership Strategy, an OME initiative, included developing principals Compulsory principal qualification regulated by Ontario College of Teachers (OCT) representing teachers and principals	**High:** Bastow Institute of Educational Leadership (BIEL) within VDET, commissioned and provided leadership development programmes supporting the VDET 'education state' school improvement agenda	**High:** NZMoE policy contracting providers to offer leadership development programmes	**High:** DfE created national professional qualifications for different career stages, specified learning outcomes, selected private companies and schools as providers

Link with practices for managing people, including practices from private sector	State and district-level processes variable, e.g. may require aspiring principals to complete university-delivered preparatory training to gain principal certification Annual principal performance evaluation	Research-informed advice for school boards on succession planning, included attracting 'aspiring leaders' Five-yearly performance appraisal for principals and vice principals	Potential link to aspiring principal certification (using advisory national standards), BIEL talent management framework Annual performance and development review for principals and assistant principals	Annual performance agreement, appraisal of principals and teachers, required for renewal of certification	Performance management incorporating annual headteacher and teacher appraisal, informed by national standards for headteachers and teachers
Responsibility for commissioning leadership development	State or district-level, e.g. NYC Department of Education commissioned NYC Leadership Academy programmes	OCT approved proposals from providers to deliver compulsory Principal's Qualification Programme (PQP), other qualifications	BIEL invited tenders from private sector, non-profit sector, universities for provision Delivered some programmes	NZMoE contracted private sector, non-profit sector, universities to design and provide leadership development programmes	DfE selected providers through a procurement process
Main leadership development provision	'Aspiring Principals Program', standards-based accredited preparatory training for state-compulsory certification of principals	Providers of PQP for aspiring principals included professional associations, universities, other qualification programmes OME funded mentoring for new principals	Programmes for different career stages including principal, aspiring principal assessment	Programmes for different career stages including aspiring principals, first-time principals Support from leadership advisers, principal learning groups	National professional qualification programmes for different career stages including aspiring senior leadership, headship, executive leadership

Continued

Table 10.2 *Continued*

Intervention, characteristic	USA	Canada	Australia	New Zealand	England
			SCHOOL EDUCATION		
Expectations framework (including leadership)	Professional Standards for School Leaders informed state education departments Standards revised by National Policy Board for Educational Administration (2015, pp. 9, 18), representing principals, district administrators, universities	Ontario Leadership Framework specified organizational practices and personal resources, developed by Ontario Institute for Educational Leadership (2013, p. 12) representing principals, board administrators, ministry civil servants	State of Victoria Department of Education and Training (2007, pp. 3, 9) Developmental Learning Framework for School Leaders specified capabilities at increasing levels of proficiency, developed by VDET with academic and Hay Group input	NZMoE leadership model for principals informed the Education Council New Zealand (2018, pp. 5, 6) Educational Leadership Capability Framework Reflected in professional standards within employment agreements	National Standards for Headteachers (DfE, 2015, pp. 5, 7), and for teachers
a) Inspirational motivation: *Leaders communicate high expectations, engage followers in developing commitment to a shared vision* (Bass, 1985)	**Mission, vision and core values:** Effective educational leaders develop, advocate, and enact a shared mission, vision, and core values of high-quality education and academic success and well-being of *each student* . . . articulate, advocate, and cultivate core values that define the school's culture and stress . . . child-centered education	**Building a shared vision:** School leaders establish, in collaboration with staff, students, and other stakeholders, an overall sense of vision or purpose for work in their schools to which they are all strongly committed . . . Encourage . . . openness to change in the direction of the school's vision	**Cultural leadership:** An effective leader demonstrates . . . capacity to lead the school community in promoting a vision of the future, underpinned by common purposes and values that will secure the commitment and alignment of all stakeholders to realise the potential of all students	**Strategically thinking and planning:** Leaders ensure that the organisational vision, goals and expectations . . . are shaped in ways that engage the organisational community . . . motivate, and will keep the organisation improving in line with a strong moral purpose	**Excellent headteachers: qualities and knowledge:** Communicate compellingly the school's vision and drive the strategic leadership, empowering all pupils and staff to excel

b) Distributed leadership: *Mutual influencing activity* (Bolden, 2011)	Potential of intervention as an elite policy meta-lever
Effective educational leaders: ... develop and promote leadership among teachers and staff for inquiry, experimentation and innovation, and initiating and implementing improvement	**Moderate:** authoritative elites in federal government controlled grants, state or district governments controlled commissioned provision (within state or federal control over school education)
Structuring the organization to facilitate collaboration: School leaders ... distribute leadership on selected tasks	**Moderately high:** authoritative elites in provincial government controlled school education, expert elites from representative body OCT mediated acculturation through the intervention
Rationale: Effective leaders recognise that ... staff expertise needs to be maximised by distributing authority and responsibility throughout the school	**High:** authoritative elites in state government controlled BIEL, as its training branch, and controlled school education (authoritative elites in federal government controlled some funding)
Building and sustaining collective leadership: ... attends to the conditions and practices that are needed for [teachers to share knowledge, enquire into practice]	**High:** authoritative elites in national government controlled the commissioning of provision, controlled school education
Excellent headteachers: systems and processes: headteachers ... distribute leadership throughout the organisation, forging teams of colleagues who have distinct roles	**High:** authoritative elites in UK government controlled specification of national professional qualifications and providers, controlled school education

principalship, were diverse initiatives. They included a 'school leadership teaming model' where aspiring principals and assistant principals participating in different training programmes were paired, anticipating the possibility of both being appointed to the same school. Funded through a federal 'Investing in Innovation' grant (US Department of Education, 2016), the aim was to 'yield leadership best practices for turnaround schools nationally' (NYC Leadership Academy, 2015, p. 3). The strategic-level federal Department of Education exerted influence on state governments and, in this case, the largest school district in the country through the policy lever of inducements: competitive funding for federal government priorities, enabling information to be gathered on 'leadership best practices' for national dissemination. The linkage with strategic-level government was diffuse, with the federal government funding its own priority and the government of this exceptionally large district as a beneficiary of the voluntary sector organization's leadership development provision for senior staff in the district's schools.

Our Canadian provincial case featured more extensive, though still diffused, government involvement. Funding from the strategic-level Ontario Ministry of Education (2021) within its Leadership Strategy included compulsory accredited training and certification of aspiring principals, mediated by the Ontario College of Teachers (2017). This intermediate-level representative body for teachers and principals regulated the qualification by specifying the curriculum and approving providers. Strategic-level government control of the intervention was closest in the other three countries: the state or national government department, or its closely monitored agency, shaped the content of leadership development, its commissioning, and provision (Bastow Institute of Educational Leadership, 2021; DfE, 2021b; New Zealand Ministry of Education, 2021).

Leadership development in all five countries was linked to compulsory appraisal for senior school staff, incorporating their work as leaders. The discourse of 'performance' was embedded either in the name of this management practice or with associated employment practices (the annual performance agreement in New Zealand; inclusion of appraisal within performance management in England). The underlying orientation of appraisal was apparently regulative, with the potential to apply sanctions for 'underperformance' alongside supporting professional development through the identification of leadership development needs. Common to all countries except England was a formal accreditation process, involving assessment of aspirants' potential and licence to assume the top management role as principal. In 2012 the UK government had withdrawn the requirement for new, first-time headteachers to possess the National Professional Qualification for

Headership (NPQH) qualification (Chapter 9). These management practices were the institutionalized legacy of past reforms, reflecting the managerialist assumption that 'business knows best', insofar as authoritative elites in past governments had translated appraisal systems from their private sector origins.

Responsibility for commissioning and specifying leadership development provision rested with strategic-level government everywhere except Canada. Here the Ontario Teachers College (OTC) approved applications from various organizational groupings to provide leadership development programmes (funded by the provincial government) for the certification of aspiring principals and in-post support of those appointed to a principalship. Provision was uniformly leader-centric: training individual leaders. The shared priority to invest in substantial preparatory programmes for aspiring principals suggests that political elites in strategic-level governments wished to shape the supply of appointable candidates for first-time principalships who could be acculturated towards government-endorsed beliefs, values, and capabilities, and would demonstrate potential for further development. The interventions varied in scope and specificity, with training extended to senior school staff carrying responsibility for the work of colleague teachers in Victoria and England, and to district board superintendents in Ontario. Provision incorporated online elements within all the interventions, extending their reach beyond face-to-face training, and engaged participants in authentic tasks with colleagues in their schools, providing conditions for contextualized learning needed to integrate ideas introduced during training into their practice.

Frameworks of expectations, couched in terms of 'competencies', 'standards', or 'capabilities', specified the behaviour and attitudes expected of principals or headteachers and other senior staff, informing appraisals, certification, and leadership development provision. The frameworks variably reflected views of stakeholders beyond government: some were compiled by representative bodies for principals and other stakeholders and endorsed by strategic-level governments (USA, Ontario, New Zealand); others were compiled within government education departments, alone (England) or with input from academics and consultants (Victoria). The discourse of the frameworks included a specification of what participants were expected to learn to do as leaders, in terms of their behaviour in achieving tasks; and also of how they should be as leaders, in terms of personal characteristics, such as being contingently empathetic or directive. These frameworks incorporated in their construals not only metaphorical concepts covering leadership and leading activity, but also values and beliefs about good practice in leading. They were informed by diverse evidence, from reflection on practitioner experience to insights from selected academic research and normative theory. The State of Victoria Department of Education and Training (2007, p. 23) framework cited the standards for headteachers in England (DfES, 2004a) revised by the NSCL, evidencing the diffuse international legacy of this UK leadership development intervention.

Values underlying the frameworks concerned social relationships serving formal positions with management responsibility that were construed to embody leading activity (here, promoting student education by influencing school staff colleagues, other adults, and students). The value orientations prescribed how effective leading practice should be pictured, legitimating evaluation against the stipulated expectations as a basis for subsequent sanction, reward, or developmental support to address shortcomings or enhance capability. The frameworks constituted a social imaginary within leadership development provision: a normative representation of how leaders should aspire to be; a reference-point for acculturating participants towards a normative conception of leading practice; and a grounding for judgements made by their evaluators.

Assemblages of concepts and prescriptions within the frameworks shared many parallels. A striking commonality of discourse was the prevalence of phrases resonating with all four leader behaviours embodied in the academic theory of transformational leadership (Chapter 4, Table 4.2), though no frameworks were explicitly based on it. Testimony to the enduring attraction of metaphorical entailments such as 'vision' or 'moral purpose' within these strategic-level governments or intermediate-level representative bodies was the re-contextualized use of such entailments in all the frameworks. Illustratively, Table 10.2 cites a phrase from each framework resonating with the transformational leadership element 'inspirational motivation' through its embodiment of vision-building.

Far less prominent was reference to mutual influencing activity consistent with the metaphorical concept of distributed leadership (where collective influence is the source and mutual influencing activity is the metaphorical entailment). This construal was less leader-centric than transformational leadership, but still hierarchical in advocating that staff in top management positions (principals or headteachers) should encourage the distribution of influencing activity, as leaders, amongst their more junior colleagues. An illustrative phrase resonating with distributed leadership is also cited in Table 10.2. The individualistic, hierarchical emphasis of entailments resonating with the inspirational motivation component of transformational leadership sits uneasily alongside the more collective and less hierarchical entailment resonant of distributed leadership. However, their co-existence implies a joint concern amongst framework authors and endorsers with placing expectations on principals and other senior school staff to combine leading 'from the top' with enabling a delimited form of 'leading from within'. Seemingly, the aim was to benefit from the potential for contributions based on diverse staff professional expertise and experience, while bounding their scope. All the frameworks aligned with the ideological discourse of leaderism featuring in our research (Part II). The social imaginary promoted by the frameworks envisaged principals or headteachers (as members of local-level elites) positioned at the top of the school staff hierarchy engaging in 'elite systemic direction-setting' and fostering 'a hierarchically distributed pattern of persuasive influence' designed 'to realize an elite vision for improvement'.

Finally, we estimate the potential of each indicative intervention to operate as an elite policy meta-lever, dependent on the main elite groupings involved, judging it to be high where one or more tiers of strategic-level government held direct responsibility for mounting and steering the operation of the intervention, as in Victoria, New Zealand, and England. By contrast, the intervention in Ontario entailed a partnership between strategic-level government elites and expert elites in the intermediate-level representative body OCT, legitimating the OCT's mediatory role in protecting the interests of teachers and principals within bounds acceptable to authoritative elites in government. It was structurally less amenable to operation as an elite policy meta-lever in offering a vehicle both for government-driven educational reforms and for promoting the cognate concerns of school staff, whose beliefs and values about school improvement might not coincide with those of governments. The intervention in the even more devolved public-funded school education system within the USA was still less structurally conducive to operation as an elite policy meta-lever. All three government tiers were involved, though primarily as commissioners and funders of leadership provision aligned with the mission of the NYC Leadership Academy. We did not find any examples of a statewide leadership development intervention, and the federal role was confined to promoting federal government priorities through competitive funding schemes where participation was voluntary.

Leadership development for public-funded healthcare services

Table 10.3 summarizes a strategic-level intervention or, where we found none, an intermediate-level intervention in each country. Several interventions were quite recent, but commitment to leadership

Table 10.3 Strategic or intermediate-level leadership development intervention connected with public-funded healthcare in the five Anglophone countries

Intervention, characteristic	USA	Canada	Australia	New Zealand	England
			HEALTHCARE		
Intervention	National Center for Healthcare Leadership	Canadian College of Health Leaders LEADS Canada	Safer Care Victoria (SCV) Leadership and Learning	Public Health Leadership Programme (PHLP)	NHS Leadership Academy
Scope	National	National	State (Victoria)	National	National (England)
Year of launch/ reconfiguration	2001	2012 (LEADS Canada launched 2006)	2017 (previous interventions from 2009)	2009	2012 (NHS Leadership Centre (NHSLC) launched 2001)
Responsibility for intervention	National Center for Healthcare Leadership (NCHL)	Canadian College of Health Leaders (CCHL)	SCV, within Department of Healthcare and Human Services (VDHHS)	New Zealand Ministry of Health (NZMoH)	UK government DoH oversaw NHS in England
Degree of linkage with strategic-level government	**Low (intermediate-level intervention):** a non-profit membership organization promoting leadership development in healthcare systems (No government representation in NCHL's governance or alliances with other organizations)	**Relatively low (intermediate-level intervention):** a non-profit membership (and advocacy) organization for healthcare senior staff, partnering with other stakeholder groups including the federal and provincial government health departments	**High:** as part of VDHHS, SCV developed and provided leadership development programmes supporting the VDHHS 'better, safer care' improvement agenda	**High:** responsibility of a national government ministry that initiated, commissioned, and funded PHLP	**High:** NHS Leadership Academy and its ten Local Leadership Academies were part of NHS England and NHS Improvement, a DoH sponsored non-executive departmental public body, from 2019

Link with practices for managing people, including practices from the private sector	No direct link. Staff in healthcare organizations might use the NCHL competency model to inform needs identification	No direct link. Staff in healthcare organizations might use CCHL's LEAD capability framework to inform needs identification, certification to inform appointments	No direct link. Potential for the VDHHS CEO leadership capability framework to support talent management	NZMoH set and applied applicant selection criteria, included being in a leadership role, commitment to public health core values, and remaining in this service	NHS Leadership Academy contributed to development of a talent management support programme, established an appraisal hub with 360° feedback instrument
Responsibility for commissioning leadership development	Alliance members commissioned their own provision	CCHL delivered provision, certified coaches and facilitators, partner universities, professional and non-profit organizations offered provision with CCHL elements	SCV staff developed and delivered provision, partnered with health service organizations to support this provision and that of the Institute for Healthcare Improvement (a non-profit provider)	NZMoH commissioned two consultancy companies to design and deliver the PHLP programme	NHS Leadership Academy faculty and its regional partners delivered core programmes and other initiatives

Continued

Intervention, characteristic	USA	Canada	Australia	New Zealand	England
			HEALTHCARE		
Main leadership development provision	NCHL facilitated alliances between healthcare organizations, including Leadership Excellence Networks: collaboration to improve leadership development provision. National Council for Administrative Fellowships: recruiting for postgraduate fellowships in healthcare organizations, offering graduate leadership-focused management programmes	Programmes for individuals at different career stages including the Certified Health Executive Program. Individual and team assessments, coaching, online Community for Practice. All provision promoted development of capabilities within LEADS framework in healthcare organizations	Programmes included: Organizational support, e.g. for executive and senior teams, formal and informal leaders in areas of clinical practice. Individual support for future system leaders, e.g. fellowships for future clinical leaders, leadership development for mid-career, senior career stages. Individual support for current leaders, e.g. action learning, mentors	A training programme for individuals, as leaders. Aimed at developing specified leadership competencies. Comprised preparatory work, two blocks of three workshop days away from the workplace, case studies based on the consultants' experience, expectation to undertake projects applying programme insights in the workplace, individual coaching, alumni network	Provision included: Suite of national programmes for individual NHS staff at different career stages, and for staff from black, Asian and minority ethnic (BAME) groups. Graduate management training scheme. Talent management hub. Coaching and mentoring programmes and facilitation. Diagnostic tools. Facilitated networking

Expectations framework (including leadership)	NCHL (2018) Health Leadership Competency Model, originally developed with Hay Group input, revision by Rush University with stakeholder consultation	CCHL (2021a) LEADS in a Caring Environment leadership capabilities framework, revised after stakeholder consultation	State of Victoria Department of Health and Human Services (2019a, pp. 10–11) CEO leadership capability framework, informed by stakeholder engagement	New Zealand Ministry of Health (2021, p. 2) leadership competencies, identified following consultation with public health staff, developed via PHLP programme	Healthcare Leadership Model (NHS Leadership Academy, 2013, pp. 3, 9), developed with input from Hay Group and the Open University
a) Inspirational motivation: *Leaders communicate high expectations, engage followers in developing commitment to a shared vision*	**Execution:** Achievement orientation—a concern for surpassing standards of excellence **Relations:** Team leadership—the ability to lead groups of people towards shared visions and goals . . . setting [the team's] mission, values and norms, and holding team members accountable. . .for results	**Achieve results:** Goal-oriented leaders . . . inspire vision by identifying, establishing, and communicating clear and meaningful expectations and outcomes **Engage others:** Engaging leaders . . . Create . . . environments where others have meaningful opportunities to contribute	**Shaping the future:** Shapes, articulates, inspires and mobilises others around a shared vision of the future health system . . . encourages dialogue and engagement in decision making	**Setting direction—creating the future:** Relevant PHLP outcomes: have clarified . . . personal values and created an inspiring leadership vision, know how to create shared purpose, vision and goals for a public health issue	**Sharing the vision:** Communicating a compelling and credible vision of the future in a way that makes it feel achievable and exciting . . . inspire hope and help others see how their work fits in . . . encourage others to become 'ambassadors' for the vision

Continued

Table 10.3 Continued

Intervention, characteristic	USA	Canada	Australia	New Zealand	England
			HEALTHCARE		
b) Distributed leadership: *Mutual influencing activity*	–	–	Empowers others to make decisions	**Delivering results—collaborative working:** Relevant PHLP outcome: understand how to work collaboratively	It applies equally to the whole variety of roles and care settings that exist within health and care
Potential of intervention as an elite policy meta-lever	**Low:** intermediate-level expert elites facilitated leadership development provision in member organizations, minimal engagement with authoritative elites in federal or state government	**Low:** intermediate-level expert elites controlled the LEADS Canada programme, engaged in advocacy with authoritative elites in federal or provincial government	**Moderately high:** authoritative elites in state government controlled the SCV intervention, but not non-profit and private sector organizations contributing to public healthcare funded through federal insurance	**High:** authoritative elites in national government controlled the PHLP programme's design, funding and applications, controlled public-funded healthcare	**High:** authoritative elites in the UK government controlled the NHS Leadership Academy and NHS healthcare organizations across England

development provision was longstanding in all five countries. Variable association between interventions and strategic-level government reflects the pattern of jurisdictional responsibilities across government tiers and differing contributions of the non-profit and private sectors to the public-funded element of healthcare. In the USA, with no universal healthcare entitlement, all government tiers contribute towards health expenditure alongside personal or employer-funded insurance, with extensive private and non-profit involvement in provision. England lies at the other extreme. The UK government very largely funds NHS provision, mostly through public sector healthcare organizations but with moderate non-profit and private sector involvement.

Intermediate-level non-profit organizations mounted the interventions for the USA and Canada (we found no strategic-level interventions). Both representative bodies provided support services and advocacy on behalf of their members, including those from private sector, government agency, and non-profit organizations. The National Center for Healthcare Leadership (NCHL, 2016) was inaugurated as 'an industry catalyst to ensure the availability of accountable and transformational healthcare leadership for the 21st century', promoting leadership development with little formal linkage to relevant tiers of government. In line with Canada's more comprehensive public healthcare system, the Canadian College of Health Leaders (CCHL 2021b) expressed commitment to the value of 'Public Service. We value our contribution to the health of Canadians and to the health system through the leadership excellence of our members.' The CCHL offered leadership development provision and engaged with strategic-level government through partnering and advocacy. The interventions in Australia, New Zealand, and England were all mounted by strategic-level government health departments, and so closely linked to them (New Zealand Ministry of Health, 2021; NHS Leadership Academy, 2014; State of Victoria Department of Health and Human Services, 2019b).

A formal link between interventions, and with other management practices relating to leadership development, was apparent only in New Zealand and England where most organizations providing public funded healthcare are in the public sector. The NHS Leadership Academy's linkage was most extensive. Its talent management hub and leadership development programmes contributed towards the enactment of a national framework for 'people development' across the career span (NHS National Improvement and Development Board, 2016).

Operation of the interventions varied over the commissioning and provision of leadership development. Of the two intermediate-level interventions, the NCHL's role in the USA was confined to facilitation, whereas the CCHL's provision in Canada included a credential certifying achievement and ongoing commitment to career-long learning as a healthcare leader. Amongst the three government-orchestrated interventions, control over commissioning and provision either rested with the government department (Safer Care Victoria (SCV) in Victoria, the New Zealand Ministry of Health (NZMoH) in New Zealand), or was delegated within the department, subject to oversight (the Department of Health (DoH) in England). Provision was leader-centric throughout, though the dominant focus on individuals at different career stages, as leaders, was complemented by the SCV in Victoria, offering collective support for executive and senior teams. The emphasis on individual leaders amongst both intermediate-level representative bodies and strategic-level government interventions suggests a confluence of interests between expert elites in the representative bodies and authoritative elites in governments: acculturating senior staff towards the beliefs, values, and capabilities connected with setting direction and shaping healthcare organizational cultures that these elites deemed desirable. Paralleling the interventions for schools, methods combined online study with face-to-face training, supported practical reflection and planning through coaching, mentoring, action learning or alumni networks, and facilitated contextualized learning in the present workplace through projects or other authentic tasks.

In tandem also, the leadership development interventions for healthcare featured an expectations framework of 'competencies' or 'capabilities' articulating desired ways of and reasons for 'being a leader' and 'doing leading activity', construed as behaviours, values, or personal qualities. Compiling the current versions involved stakeholder consultation. The frameworks all reflected the managerialist assumption that 'business knows best': the Hay Group consultancy influenced the framework for school education in Victoria, also contributing to this government's interventions for healthcare and that of the UK government covering England. The State of Victoria Department of Health and Human Services (2019a, p. 12) referred to the NHS Leadership Academy (2013) framework as an example of 'global best practice'—another instance of intertextuality, here acknowledging the NHS Leadership Academy framework as a source of ideas.

The US intervention framework, designed for a substantially private sector membership, included 'business literacy' and 'financial skills'; while the initial LEADS capabilities framework (Lead self, Engage others, Achieve results, Develop coalitions, Systems transformation) was designed by a university research team, it had been honed through use with Canadian healthcare organizations—also mainly private sector-based. The NCHL alone headlined its role in terms of transformational leadership, but Table 10.3 evidences how all five frameworks employed discourse resonating with entailments of the 'leading is transforming' metaphor, including 'inspirational motivation' and other leader behaviours of transformational leadership theory. The frameworks differed over whether leaders were expected to articulate and then share their vision (Canada, New Zealand, England) or to engage others in developing a collective vision (USA, Victoria). Resonance with this entailment of transformational leadership or others was oblique, as each metaphorical concept became selectively reproduced and reconfigured in these contexts to create a new metaphorical blend. In contrast to the school education frameworks, there was little resonance with distributed leadership, except for the English example. Yet the relationship that should obtain between leaders occupying hierarchically ordered roles within and between organizations providing public-funded healthcare was not spelled out—which leaders might also be followers of more senior leaders? Differences in the metaphorical concepts that these frameworks reflect may not mean that patterns of influencing practice are necessarily different. But it does mean that the discourse embodied in the frameworks guiding the developmental focus of interventions may promote different patterns, depending on the metaphorical concepts and entailments each framework foregrounds or omits.

We judged the potential of interventions to operate as an elite policy meta-lever as being greatest where authoritative elites within strategic-level governments mounted and oversaw them: Victoria, tempered by the relative independence of non-profit and private sector organizations delivering public-funded healthcare; New Zealand, though for a single programme; and England, where the UK government controlled the NHS structure and funding as a national public service. Expert elites from the intermediate-level representative body mounting the US intervention had little association with government. Their counterparts in Canada engaged with government on solely an advocacy basis, so authoritative elites in federal or provincial governments could choose whether to respond.

Leadership development for higher education

We found no strategic-level interventions. Government engagement was largely confined to contributory resourcing of teaching and competitive bids for research funding, alongside system regulation. Even in the UK, as previously noted, national government resourcing of AdvanceHE had become restricted to commissioning specific research or training activity once Higher Education Funding Council for England (HEFCE) contributions towards core funding ceased. Table 10.4 summarizes characteristics of one intermediate-level intervention operating nationwide for each country. Leadership development provision was long established in the USA and Canada, and elsewhere had been sustained for more than a decade. The intermediate-level organizations responsible for the interventions ranged from a non-profit membership organization in the US (also engaging in advocacy, especially with the federal government) and another with a UK and international remit; through a national representative body with an advocacy role for all universities in New Zealand; to university centres of expertise in HE leadership development in Canada and Australia. Authoritative elites within strategic-level governments exercised no direct leverage over leadership development provision since the interventions had no formal government link. Eligibility to participate included applicants from public or private universities and colleges (apart from New Zealand, with no private universities). In contrast with the interventions for school education and healthcare, connection with other processes for managing people was not mentioned, other than participants being nominated by their organization for the American Council on Education (2021) fellowship programme and the Universities New Zealand (2021) programme for women senior staff. The interventions apparently left to HE organizations any surrounding people management processes for building and sustaining leadership capacity, such as appraisal, and performance and talent management.

In all cases, staff from the organization hosting the intervention or associated senior practitioners designed, delivered, or facilitated access to leadership development provision. The common leader-centric orientation focused exclusively on individuals at one or more career stages, developing them as leaders in their present role or preparing them for an aspirational future one. Formal certification was central to one programme for senior administrators offered by the Centre for Higher Education Research and Development (2021) in Canada. It was optional for the ACE Agile Administrators programme, where being assessed could earn participants a 'microcredential', and the Australian 'eLAMP' programme targeting 'emerging leaders and managers', offered by the L H Martin Institute (2021). We previously commented (Chapter 8) on the record of participation having long been recognized as a credential signifying promotion potential for the Top Management Programme (TMP) of AdvanceHE (2021b) in the UK, exemplified by its marketing claim that 'Over 60 of the current UK Vice-Chancellors and Principals are TMP HE alumni, with many of the other past participants of TMP

Table 10.4 Intermediate-level leadership development intervention connected with partly public-funded higher education in the five Anglophone countries

Intervention, characteristic	USA	Canada	Australia	New Zealand	England (UK-wide)
			HIGHER EDUCATION		
Intervention	ACE Leadership	Centre for Higher Education Research and Development (CHERD)	L H Martin Institute (LHMI)	New Zealand Universities Women in Leadership Programme (NZUWiL)	AdvanceHE Development Programmes
Scope	National	National	National	National	National, international
Year of launch/ reconfiguration	2018 (Fellowships programme since 1965)	1987	2007	2006	2018 (LFHE launched 2004)
Responsibility for intervention	American Council on Education (ACE)	CHERD, University of Manitoba	LHMI, University of Melbourne	Universities New Zealand (UNZ)	AdvanceHE

Continued

Table 10.4 *Continued*

	USA	Canada	Australia	New Zealand	England (UK-wide)
			HIGHER EDUCATION		
Degree of linkage with strategic-level government	**Relatively low (intermediate-level intervention):** a non-profit membership (and advocacy) organization for senior staff in universities and colleges promoting leadership development	**Low (intermediate-level intervention):** a university centre of research and training expertise, remit included leadership development provision for senior staff in universities and colleges	**Low (intermediate-level intervention):** a university centre of research and training expertise, remit included leadership development provision for senior staff in universities and colleges	**Low (intermediate-level intervention):** the leadership development programme of a national representative body for universities	**Low (intermediate-level intervention):** a non-profit membership organization for universities, colleges, research institutes, remit included leadership development provision for senior staff
Link with practices for managing people, including practices from private sector	No direct link, but participants for ACE's fellows programme were nominated by their university or college	No direct link	No direct link	No direct link, but participants were selected and funded as nominees of their university	No direct link
Responsibility for commissioning leadership development	ACE staff delivered programmes, partnered with a technology company to expand online provision	CHERD staff delivered programmes	LHMI staff and academics delivered programmes	UNZ steering group of women senior staff delivered programme	AdvanceHE staff and associates delivered programmes

Main leadership development provision	One-year fellowship programme for mid-career 'emerging leaders' seeking promotion, giving experience at another university or college Promoted advancement of women to senior posts, network for women in HE Convened summits on key topics e.g. inclusion Agile Administrators programme on leading innovation, assessed for 'microcredential' award	Residential or online leadership development programmes for administrators and academics at different career stages, including Certificate in University and College Administration programme, course for senior administrators, women in academic leadership programme, leading academic departments programme	Emerging leaders and managers programme for aspirant and newly appointed administrative and academic staff with management responsibility, online plus workshops, optional assessment and certification Suite of workshops on governance for senior staff and governors, option of delivery for universities and colleges regionally	Residential leadership training programme for women aspiring towards or in a post carrying management responsibility as academics or administrators	Suite of leadership development programmes for senior staff at different career stages along the 'AdvanceHE Development Pathway', including the Top Management Programme for aspiring vice chancellors and other senior staff (also offered in Australia and New Zealand) Coaching
(No expectations frameworks)					
Potential of intervention as an elite policy meta-lever	**Low:** intermediate-level expert elites controlled ACE programmes, engaged in advocacy with authoritative elites in federal or state government	**Low:** intermediate-level elite university staff offered programmes commercially, no engagement with authoritative elites in provincial governments	**Low:** intermediate-level elite university staff offered programmes commercially, no engagement with authoritative elites in state governments	**Low:** intermediate-level elite university staff associated with UNZ offered the programme, no engagement with authoritative elites in the national government	**Low:** intermediate-level expert elites offered programmes commercially, no engagement with authoritative elites in national governments

HE holding some of the most senior posts throughout higher education'. A commonly reported impact reported by past TMP participants was to stimulate reflection on their career development and progression (McCracken, McCrory, Farley, & McHugh, 2021). Overall, there was considerable emphasis on programmes designed to prepare participants for possible promotion to a more senior post carrying management responsibility. Internationally, the individual pursuit of credentials signifying potential for career advancement constituted a key feature of the HE marketplace for leadership development, rather than any government-driven endeavour to build HE leadership capability. Alongside traditional face-to-face training, online provision was being actively developed in all the interventions apart from the programme in New Zealand. This programme was designed to maximize opportunities for women senior staff to network by engaging with each other in depth through the residential component and biennial symposia and regional roadshow for alumni (NZWiL, 2015). AdvanceHE operated on the largest scale, offering training programmes, opportunities to receive one-to-one interactions with a professional coach, and online access to diverse sources of information.

We found no evidence of expectations frameworks being employed to focus provision, perhaps reflecting the minimal connection between these interventions and strategic-level governments, plus the structural autonomy accorded to individual universities and colleges. We judged all the interventions to have little potential for authoritative elites within strategic-level governments to deploy as an elite policy meta-lever because the basis for directive government control was largely absent. These interventions were more akin to commercial ventures: no instigators were for-profit organizations, yet all charged for their services through membership or participation fees; none received contributory governmental core funding.

Common scope for professionalization, divergent potential as an elite policy meta-lever

Extending our explanation summarized in Appendix 1 to consider what international *legacy* the suite of national leadership development interventions introduced in England by the UK Labour government may have left, the modest evidence from our comparative review confirms this legacy to have been diffuse, and increasingly so, amongst the five Anglophone countries. By the advent of the COVID-19 pandemic, it seems clear that this form of intervention had continued to proliferate and evolve, and had a relatively secure future within and beyond England that was likely to outlast the pandemic. Indeed, major leadership development interventions had become institutionalized as a facilitator of public service neoliberalization, whether through reforms and the operation of reformed services, or simply via the operation of services that had never been provided by public sector organizations alone. Most leadership development interventions featuring in our review were established in the 2000s, enduring since in the same or a reconfigured form. Where strategic-level governments did not engage, intermediate-level elites from representative bodies of senior staff or university training centres did so, as with all three public service sectors in the USA, and those for healthcare and HE in Canada. The extent of national or regional government, representative body, or university training centre commitment and engagement in orchestrating the interventions depended on the nature of the service sector itself and the configuration of providers within it, resulting in the widely variable linkage between interventions and strategic-level government.

We highlighted in Table 10.1 how elites in strategic-level governments were introducing reforms and austerity measures for our focal public service sectors associated with stage 7 of neoliberalization (retrenchment and permanent austerity), whose trajectory had been influenced by the differential economic impact and aftermath of the global financial crisis. Website accounts of leadership development provision offered by the interventions lacked detail, but information for potential applicants or participants does suggest that their content was largely generic, directed towards individual leading activity. The SCV programme in Victoria for executive and senior teams was exceptional in embracing collaboration within a group sharing collective responsibility for leading other staff. Content included generic change or improvement, but not specific regulated marketization reforms or coping with austerity. Most provision included workplace projects, where participants were likely to engage in leading activity relating to the current neoliberalized policy regime. Other connections were evident with the operation of managerialist control technologies originating in the private sector that combined neo-Taylorism and culture management, as with the management of performance appraisal mentioned in the school education interventions. Reference was made to talent management within two government-driven healthcare interventions: the CEO leadership capability framework (State of Victoria Department of Health and Human Services, 2019a) was advocated as a tool for supporting talent management, and the NHS Leadership Academy developed resources for an NHS talent management support programme. Least mention was made in HE, possibly influenced by the dominant emphasis on developing individuals as leaders and the minimal linkage between interventions and strategic-level governments.

Provision across the interventions offered extensive opportunities for restricted professionalization: gaining expertise as leaders via specialized training that typically drew from workplace experience and fostered application in the workplace. Each intervention encompassed one or more training programmes for individuals based in different public service organizations, targeting staff at a career stage associated with some position of management responsibility. Most programmes aimed to support participants in furthering their aspiration towards career advancement through preparatory training for leading activity within a more senior post. The commonest target group comprised elite-associate senior staff occupying a formal position immediately below the elite top management role, exemplified by the focus on assistant or vice principals or deputy headteachers in schools. The cultural capital acquired in terms of expert knowledge was often complemented by social capital gained through networking with other participants during the training, sometimes sustained through alumni events (as with the PHLP programme for healthcare in New Zealand). All provision enabled participants to harness their leadership development experience as an informal credential for their career advancement. A few interventions were directed towards formal certification, orchestrated by a government or representative body. Participants were required, or could opt, to complete an assessment. Success brought eligibility to apply for selection to a more senior post, or otherwise symbolized their 'good standing' as a leader. Overall, the interventions offered individual staff at some or all career stages from 'emerging leader' to 'CEO' or 'system leader' a chance to learn about leading at a more senior level and to demonstrate their readiness for such a role.

A significant component of that leader-centric learning, for the interventions in the school education and healthcare sectors, was attempted acculturation towards embracing the social imaginary embodied in expectations frameworks articulating what leading activity is and should be. All the frameworks shared significant resonance with the metaphorical concepts of transformational leadership, and most also with distributed leadership, reflective of the ideological discourse of leaderism—whether the framework was developed by strategic-level elites in government or by intermediate-level elites representing, or offering training to, senior staff in schools or healthcare organizations. Local-level expert elites were legitimated, as leaders of their organizations, in exerting control over service provision within parameters set by strategic-level governments, including those parameters relating to public service neoliberalization through regulation, marketization and austerity measures. Such leaders were responsibilized for empowering their elite-associate senior colleagues and other staff to contribute through hierarchically distributed activity, as leaders within their organization, towards the collective achievement of a vision for service provision, and maybe also its improvement. Whether or not they had been consulted during the articulation of this vision, they were in turn responsibilized for committing themselves to its realization. However, parameters delimiting the scope for choice of local-level vision varied widely. Where strategic-level governments mounted or sponsored both the expectations frameworks and leadership development interventions, they were well positioned to promote the acculturation of participants towards local-level vision-building and working to achieve that vision within parameters that government ministers had defined or would find acceptable. Here, conditions were most favourable for the expression of symbolic violence by strategic-level elites in governments acculturating senior staff, as leaders, towards willingly implementing and operating reforms and related austerity measures through the incentive to gain credentials for individual career advantage. Elsewhere the prospects were less favourable, since intermediate-level representative bodies or university training centres were not under directive governmental control.

Consequently, we judged the indicative interventions to *offer widely variable potential to operate as an elite policy meta-lever*. Only about half had moderately high or high potential to do so. Even then, the illustrative evidence from England cited previously (Chapter 9) suggests that the acculturation of senior staff towards acting as change agents for government-driven reforms was not necessarily shared amongst 'middle managers' or professional service staff, on whom senior staff depended for the implementation and operation of reforms within their organizational jurisdiction. This aspect of the diffuse legacy left by the suite of national leadership development interventions (acknowledged in Appendix 1) was not the intention of authoritative elites within the UK Labour government who were responsible for their introduction, reconfiguration, or financial support.

Our contemporary indicative interventions with some potential to operate as an elite policy meta-lever were all mounted by strategic-level governments, enabling authoritative elites to maintain directive control over the remit and funding of these interventions. They catered for public-funded services in school education or healthcare, where governments controlled most or all local-level organizations responsible for public service provision, either directly through funding or through remuneration for provision where public healthcare was funded through insurance; they also controlled intermediate-level organizations responsible for regional or national service system administration. No US interventions came into these categories, and, amongst our Canadian interventions, the sole instance was the provincial government's school leadership strategy in Ontario. The state government interventions in Victoria and national interventions in New Zealand and England for school education and healthcare did offer such potential, though the intervention in New Zealand for healthcare was confined to one programme for a single target group; those in Victoria and England were extensive for both public service sectors, providing for multiple target groups according to their career stage.

The Anglophone country comparison confirms that the English national leadership development interventions no longer represented quite such an extreme case. Amongst strategic-level governments in other Anglophone countries Victoria in Australia, Ontario in Canada, and New Zealand were also engaged in major interventions for one or more public services. Basic conditions for the possibility of national leadership development interventions operating as an elite meta-lever for public service reforms appeared to obtain in all these countries for school education, healthcare, or both. Politicians in each national or regional government met the basic condition of hierarchically dominant social positioning that gave the potential to become implicated in generative mechanisms, inferred in Part II, founded on legitimated authoritative elite command and control. These generative mechanisms embrace promoting a leader-centric construal of leadership, the attempted acculturative formal co-optation of senior staff through major leadership development interventions as leaders acting voluntarily as change agents for government-driven reforms, and remotely containing their corporate agency through a regulative accountability regime.

However, whether such interventions could achieve the potential, in principle, that an elevated social position might afford their instigators is another matter. We will return to this issue, focusing on England, in the next chapter. Our study of public service leadership development revealed this phenomenon to be deeply contextualized, complex, and evolutionary. It is also constitutive of a much larger social phenomenon. We turn now to the contribution of leadership development interventions towards wider societal change.

11

Developing public service leaders

An elite 'weapon of mass distraction'?

The final chapter concludes our explanatory account of national leadership development interventions in England. Part I examined the political, economic, and discursive context for our investigation of the United Kingdom (UK) Labour government's engagement in public service leadership development; outlined the theoretical framing of the study; and explored leadership as a metaphorical concept, documenting how senior politicians within the Labour Party adopted a visionary construal of leadership prior to the Labour government's term in office. Part II reported findings from our empirical research into the extreme case comprising a suite of national leadership development interventions, focusing on those for school education, healthcare, and higher education (HE). In Part III we have reviewed their direct legacy in England (UK-wide for HE) and compared contemporary provision with examples of cognate interventions in other Anglophone countries. Here we confine our focus mainly to England, considering how the leader-centric discourse of leaderism, and major leadership development interventions, together contribute to changing the nature of social reproduction through the provision of services for citizens. Our argument draws on evidence presented in earlier chapters, alongside theoretical and empirical literature on institutional and organizational change, system governance, and the transfer of learning from training into workplace practice.

We open with a review, related to our first aim for the book, examining indirect outcomes of the national leadership development interventions in England constituting our extreme case. Our review focuses on the diffuse contribution that contemporary incarnations of these interventions are making towards ongoing public service neoliberalization, within wider social change. We extrapolate from the abductive explanation advanced in Part II of why and how the interventions we investigated were initiated, orchestrated, and mediated by elites and their associates based at different administrative levels; how the instrumental discourse of leaderism, allied to regulated marketization reform for public services, underpinned an attempt to

Developing Public Service Leaders. Wallace et al., Oxford University Press. © Mike Wallace, Michael Reed, Dermot O'Reilly, Michael Tomlinson, Jonathan Morris, Rosemary Deem (2023). DOI: 10.1093/oso/9780199552108.003.0011

acculturate senior staff in public service organizations as leaders committed to acting as government change agents for reforms; why the interventions generated immediate outcomes falling short of the reform-linked aspirations of their instigators or financial supporters within central government, yet supporting the restricted professionalization of participants as leaders; and why participants, and other senior staff who had not experienced this provision, overwhelmingly complied with central government regulatory requirements. Evidence was conspicuously absent of local or intermediate-level elites gathering around any emancipatory counter-project challenging the legitimacy of the accountability regime imposed by government elites.

Since then, these interventions have become integral to pursuit of the contemporary English variant of public service neoliberalization. The leading activity they promote largely concerns change. Engagement of senior staff from public service organizations in orchestrating change embraces multiple innovations: planned changes in service provision connected with reforms or continuous improvement agendas that entail operating within parameters set, supported, or otherwise accepted by strategic-level political elites in government. These innovations, in turn, are changing each public service as a societal sub-institution within the ongoing transition from a large welfare towards a smaller workfare state, contributing to a shift in the relationship between the state, the market, and professions as societal institutions.

Consequently, public service organizations are changing too. Longstanding hierarchically ordered relationships between those involved in organizational governance, staff responsible for marketized service provision, and citizens who receive services contain myriad weaker, part-emergent, horizontal relationships amongst the expanding diversity of public, private, and voluntary sector organizations providing public services. Governance regimes mirror the balance of those relationships, helping to sustain central government domination of public service providers and users by enabling the main stakeholder groups to express varying degrees of corporate agency in shaping local service provision and its take-up. The national leadership development interventions foster local leading activity, encouraging the pluralistic expression of stakeholder voice while bounding parameters for decision-making to minimize the chances of service providers falling foul of the national accountability regime. The reach of the interventions, and so their potential for influencing senior staff to lead in this way, rests on their appeal for those eligible to participate. A key motivation for senior staff is to gain support for their restricted professionalization as trained expert leaders, alongside credentials facilitating any aspirational career advancement.

We conclude with three emergent themes, related to our second aim: locating these interventions and the legacy of past iterations as an influential contributor to the international movement that has institutionalized public service leadership development as an enduring component of variably neoliberalized, comprehensively led, public service administrative systems. These themes offer potential starting-points for any reimagining and reworking, with emancipatory intent, of developmental support for collective endeavours entailed in providing public services for the wellbeing of all citizens, as a public good. Social domination structures are as difficult to detect from within as associated institutions and their operational logics are to change. Yet they are the product of corporate agency; achieving any degree of emancipation from the constraints they impose can be achieved only through corporate and, ultimately, primary agency (Chapter 3). Informing those who might act as agents for emancipatory change is a necessary first step, however naïve and insufficient.

First, we consider how leader-centric construals of leadership embodied in generic leaderism discourse have become ever more culturally embedded, with structural consequences. Leaderism widely reflects significant conceptual omissions of such leadership construals (Chapter 1), affecting the design of major leadership development interventions and creating favourable structural conditions for individualistic and hierarchical enactment of public service leadership. Second, we question the implicit principle behind the possibility of leadership development operating as an elite meta-lever. National or regional government elite control of major interventions may be less centralized than in England. Even here, expressing soft power through acculturative control technologies of this kind may be an intrinsically unreliable means of replacing service professional beliefs and values, such that they may continue to underpin motivations and expressions of agency amongst those targeted. Manipulating culture through interventions may be an impossible dream, even when sustained for more than a generation. Third, we highlight limitations of the long-institutionalized form taken by major public service leadership development interventions in the five Anglophone countries, drawing on educational research and theory about training and adult learning to point towards more productive alternatives for social learning support.

Elite orchestration of societal change: developing and delimiting public service leadership

We confirmed (Chapter 9) how politicians within the UK coalition and Conservative governments, as strategic-level authoritative elites, have continued pursuing neoliberalization, supported by managerialism. The neoliberalization trajectory has superseded the Labour government's social democratic variant by reverting to the more entrepreneurial, pro-market variant originally pursued by the Conservative government of the 1980s–90s. One thrust continues the political project of public service reform through regulated marketization, now augmented by enduring austerity measures. This political project is legitimated by the hegemonic structure of dominancy. Government elites combine the authority of senior politicians to regulate through rule and law-making with the expertise of their policy advisers and senior civil servants, founded on esoteric knowledge and skills, to acculturate those involved in policy implementation and operation.

Support also comes from a complex network of other expert elite groupings with whom political elites may be closely linked. A likely contributor to social networking and career advancement for a high proportion of authoritative and expert elites in central government and expert elites from the private sector is the privileged educational background they share (Sutton Trust & Social Mobility Commission, 2019), having attended private schools, or studied at the Universities of Oxford or Cambridge, or both (Table 11.1). Speculatively, the ability of their parents to pay private school fees suggests that many of the previous generation were already placed at the upper end of hierarchically ordered social positions, with remuneration to match. So, in significant measure, elite status may be transferred between generations.

Particularly salient for public service leadership development are 'corporate professional elites' (Reed, 2018, p. 305) and their associates. Authoritative elite government politicians (many with a business background) widely assume that the practices and associated expertise of their corporate counterparts apply to increasingly marketized public services. We have seen how the 'business knows best' assumption has prompted UK governments to commission top executives to advise them (Chapter 2), and to appoint senior executives to positions within the governance of their agencies, including national leadership development interventions (Chapter 6). It has also prompted two government departments (England; Victoria in Australia) and a non-profit organization's NLDB (USA) to employ consultants from the global management consulting company Hay Group to assist with designing leadership frameworks (Chapter 10, Tables 10.2, 10.3). The engagement

Table 11.1 Privileged educational background within the UK government and private sector, 2019

Occupational role	Occupancy of senior position	Private school (%)	University of Oxford or Cambridge (%)
Government politician	Cabinet member	39	57
	Junior minister	52	36
Government civil servant	Permanent secretary	59	56
	CEO, public body	30	25
Private sector, FTSE 350 companies	Chair	34	27
	CEO	27	15
Private sector journalist	Newspaper columnist	44	44
UK population	-	*7*	*<1*

of such influencers resonates with that aspect of the role which Wedel (Chapter 3) ascribes to the socially networked 'shadow elite' that is both public and formal.

Strategic-level authoritative elites in government also have powers of coercion or inducement (Scott, 2008, p. 33) underpinning their domination through constraint where regulations are flouted, service standards missed, budgets overspent. The hard-power accountability regime has continued to forestall any concerted resistance since our research was completed: whether amongst politicians in local government, as intermediate-level authoritative elites and elite-associates; their executive officials, as expert elites and elite-associates, where local government has survived 'hollowing out' and still contributes to local public service provision; or local-level expert elites and elite-associates from public service organizations. The potential of government elites to impose punitive sanctions generates a 'culture of threat' (Clegg, Courpasson, & Phillips, 2006, p. 336), encouraging compliant behaviour. Yet acculturation of those under threat may merely inculcate an attitude of 'resigned compliance' (Farrell & Morris, 2004), as our investigation suggested (Chapter 8): acknowledging this threat and the need to play safe, but without accepting the validity of the accountability regime, stipulated standards, or financial requirements.

Strategic-level elites in government are far from all-powerful. We highlighted (Chapter 2) how the prime minister of the Labour government acknowledged governmental dependence on senior staff from public service organizations across England as conduits for its regulated marketization reform programme (so, implicitly, furthering public service neoliberalization). Hence the motivation to capitalize on the discourse of visionary leadership emerging from the USA (Chapter 4): first articulating the ideological discourse of leaderism allied to public service reforms; then deploying it as a discourse strategy for persuading senior staff to accept responsibility for implementing reforms and operating reformed services. The incrementally established or reconfigured national leadership development interventions constituted an acculturative control technology, putting leaderism to work in formally co-opting senior staff as leaders committed to acting as government change agents.

This co-optation was merely formal, since the transfer of power was contingent on compliance in respect of reforms and adequate performance in achieving required service outcomes. Informal co-optation (Chapter 3) would have required government elites to transfer power to senior staff by enabling them to contribute towards decisions *shaping* policy, not just to implement it. The closest that evidence from our investigation came to constituting informal co-optation was the government's announcement (Chapter 6) that 'top' headteachers would be appointed as 'national leaders of education' who could 'advise' ministers within the government's education department on the 'future direction of education policy'. Seeking advice entails no obligation to take it. So power was not transferred to participate in education policy decision-making.

Further mitigation of government dependence was achieved by strengthening regulation. The initial generative mechanism we inferred to be driving the national leadership development interventions (Chapter 6) combined the promotional channelling of agency through leaderism, linked to regulated marketization reforms, with its pre-emptive bounding through the accountability regime to secure the transmission of these reforms into practice.

This regime deployed regulation as the basis for a classic 'divide-and-rule' (Xypolia, 2016) pre-emptive control technology: first, fostering a culture of threat encouraging all staff in public service organizations to play safe and minimize the risk of being held to account for performance failure; second, identifying and publicizing 'underperforming' service organizations, placing significant blame on senior staff as leaders; third, providing a potential starting-point for sections of the mass media to mount an 'elite-engineered' moral panic (Hall, Critcher, Jefferson, Clarke, & Roberts, 1978; Hunt, 1997) that might garner public support for the failure verdict; and fourth, relying on local and more diffuse nationwide public acceptance or endorsement of the regime—on the assumption that what was measured and found wanting was what mattered to members of the public, now cast as service consumers. Sanctions penalizing individual organizations, alongside marketization enabling local service consumers to seek better service provision elsewhere, militated against the emergence of local-level counter-elites that might reject top priority being given to centrally prescribed standards. We have seen (Chapter 9) how subsequent coalition and Conservative governments have retained the entire accountability regime while adding austerity measures that tighten budgetary constraints and render endeavouring to reach these standards an even greater challenge.

Strategic-level government elites are also relatively dependent on intermediate-level elites from representative bodies who mount national leadership development interventions for their members endorsing, or minimally not resisting, the governmental acculturation of local elites and elite-associates as government change agents for regulated marketization reforms. For HE, the ongoing enactment of the governmental political project of public service reform interacts with the support project of restricted professionalization pursued by intermediate-level expert elites from the representative bodies Universities UK (UUK) and GuildHE. AdvanceHE has succeeded the Leadership Foundation for Higher Education (LFHE) in offering leadership development provision for local elites and elite-associates working in extensively neoliberalized universities and colleges.

Bounded institutional innovation: structural and cultural conditions prompting chronic morphogenesis

The UK government's pursuit of neoliberalization is shaping the ongoing transformation of societal institutions connected with the economic system. For public services, this process entails the cumulative institutionalization of regulated marketization reforms as normal practice, alongside locally initiated improvement efforts within reformed service provision. Accreting innovations embrace organizational practices and growing private and voluntary sector involvement as service providers. They are altering public services as societal-level sub-institutions constitutive of the workfare state, itself a sub-institution of the state overall. Shifting regulations, norms, and conventions comprising institutional 'rules of the game' frame changes in associated operational logics, altering the structural conditions shaping parameters for the expression of agency. These shifts reflect changes in perceptions, expectations, and underlying values of authoritative elite government politicians, public service providers, and citizens that simultaneously alter the cultural conditions shaping how agency is expressed through interaction.

The potential for further public service transformation lies with elites, as corporate agents based at different system levels. The changes they initiate encompass what public services are; who and what they are for; how they may be accessed and provided; what comprise the limits of acceptability for the process and outcomes of provision; and what legitimate sanctions should be incurred for overstepping these bounds. Thus, institutional logics, as the ways of thinking that draw on rules and norms from relevant institutions in guiding action, are becoming hybridized. Marketized public service provision mixes organizational practices derived from the contributory sub-institutions, often spanning public, private, and voluntary sectors. It embodies an uneasy compromise between partially incompatible rules and norms framing service provision as both a public and private good, to benefit users as both citizens and consumers. Consequently, public services have become institutional 'fields of adaptation, interpretation and translation' (Clarke, Newman, Smith, Vidler, & Westmarland, 2007, p. 50): interacting and evolving sub-institutions in continual flux, with little prospect of a neoliberalized workfare state settlement. Social stability is sustained not through any lasting accommodation between the partially incompatible institutional logics, but through the pre-emptive accountability regime. Arguably, this potentially punitive regime ensures the normalization of chronically shifting compromises that hybrid logics entail.

The structural balance of relational social positions iteratively adjusts within and between elite and non-elite groupings connected with the emergent institutional configuration of 'contingent incompatibilities' (Chapter 3). Rules and norms surrounding the old order of the welfare state are incompatible with those surrounding practices and organizations connected with the societal institutions of the market and corporations characterizing the new order. The parallel relationship of 'competitive contradictions' within the associated cultural system plays out in tandem. Adherence to the instrumental ideology of managerialism, supporting further neoliberalization and conditions of permanent austerity, is incrementally encroaching on adherence to the residual ideology of professionalism. It is fuelling a growing belief in the professionalization of senior staff as leaders, achieved through specialist training that includes provision offered by national leadership development interventions. Yet adherence to the ideology of professionalism remains widespread in respect of public service provision itself, coexisting in tension with managerialism, and leaderism within it, as our examples of recent UK research depicted (Chapter 9). The governmental discourse of leaderism, as an offshoot of managerialism, responsibilizes senior staff in public service organizations for acculturating other staff and local citizens towards the government elite-driven vision for service improvement accommodating the hybrid mix of institutional rules and norms.

The Labour government's alliance of leaderism with regulated marketization reforms constituted a social imaginary for public services (Chapter 9): leading activity was linked with responsibility for reform implementation and operation. This social imaginary has become more muted within successor coalition and Conservative government documentation, suggesting that the discourse of leaderism has become deeply institutionalized as commonsense. Politicians in government are self-styled 'leaders of the country', so 'leaders of the system' for administering public services, entitled to specify the regulated marketization reform agenda. Staff in top and senior positions of management responsibility in public service organizations are 'leaders within the system', responsibilized for making public service reforms and reformed services work on the ground according to the partially incompatible, hybridized institutional logics emerging within their part-marketized service. Witness the normalized practice of marketing public-funded schools, NHS organizations, and especially universities and colleges—a UK HE staffing survey (Wolf & Jenkins, 2021, p. 27) reported that the proportion of non-academic professional staff working in marketing and related positions had doubled since 2005. Marketization may extend to entrepreneurial public sector organizations providing a 'marketizing service within a public service': NHS Elect (2021), an NHS organization hosted by an NHS hospital trust, supports other NHS organizations paying a membership fee for 'bespoke services'. They include marketing and design support.

The government elite social imaginary of 'supported autonomy' (Chapter 9) foregrounds scope for senior staff in provider organizations to exercise operational freedom. Yet autonomy is relative, contingent on outcomes senior staff achieve, according to the measurement of proxies for their 'performance' (noted earlier) set by government departments or by its agencies (as with HE). The accountability regime bounds scope for innovation, constraining divergence between practices, organizations, and institutional logics to those acceptable to government elites; they must also be accepted by citizens (on whom government elites ultimately depend for their re-election) as service users, recast as consumers. Any unacceptable transgression of boundaries attracts 'support' through corrective measures, whereby service providers forfeit most of whatever operational autonomy they hitherto enjoyed.

Choice over *how* senior staff respond in attempting to achieve required outcomes is similarly bounded, evidenced by publicized sanctions following occasional malpractice. An instance is the Al-Madinah School, established in 2012 as a free school for pupils aged 4–16 and designated as having a Muslim ethos. The report of its inspection a year later (Ofsted, 2013, p. 7), placed it in the punitive 'special measures' category, judging that 'failures in leadership and management are at the heart of the school's dysfunctional situation'. Months later, a government schools minister ordered part of the school to close due to 'the poor quality of secondary teaching and the lack of breadth in the secondary curriculum' (Malik, 2014).

Most notorious in healthcare is the staff failure to provide adequate care for patients in Stafford Hospital within the Mid-Staffordshire NHS Foundation Trust, late in the tenure of the Labour government. A review by the Healthcare Commission (2009, p. 6), then the healthcare regulator, found that 'the care of patients was unacceptable': the mortality rate for patients admitted as emergencies was consistently high; the accident and emergency department was understaffed; record keeping was poor. The trust's governance board had prioritized meeting national financial targets for cost improvement by reducing the number of beds available for patients and further reducing already low numbers of staff, and had 'focused on promoting itself as an organisation, with considerable attention given to marketing and public relations' (p. 10). Following remedial interventions and two independent enquiries, the trust was formally abolished in 2017.

Central government regulatory oversight of the formally more autonomous HE sector remains for research and teaching funded through public taxation or by individual students. However, formal autonomy in a sector with proliferating private sector providers may undermine student learning if such providers become financially unsustainable. The Greenwich School of Management, owned by a private equity company, was placed into administration (Jack & Hale, 2019) while still in the process of registering with the Office for Students, the independent regulator for HE teaching in England and a non-departmental public body of the DfE. The education of students was disrupted; they were eventually offered the option of transferring to other universities.

These diverse examples highlight how strategic-level elites within government and its agencies bound the scope for institutional innovation, even where subscribing, explicitly or by implication, to the social imaginary of 'supported autonomy' that implicitly confers licence to innovate. Yet autonomy over innovation is delimited by outcomes that innovations achieve and the process of their achievement. 'Support' may comprise directive steering through intervention involving negative sanctions by authoritative elites in government and authorized expert elites in government agencies.

The hybridization that the governmental pursuit of public service neoliberalization has brought across societal institutions, public services as sub-institutions, and their operational logics has created structural and cultural conditions prompting the expression of corporate agency amongst elites, from strategic to local levels, to produce chronic morphogenesis. Four decades of public service neoliberalization involving serial government-driven reform have resulted in a complex and still-evolving configuration of hybridized sub-institutions, characterized by tensions and uncomfortable compromises. The relative stability of this sub-institutional configuration rests on regulation—the accountability regime—bounding the licence to innovate that marketization and 'supported autonomy' promise. Our account bears out the observation of Peck (2010, p. 6) that neoliberalization political projects tend, sooner or later, to 'fail forward'. The emergence of unintended outcomes that undermine the goals of the project trigger ameliorative action, giving rise to more policy change and maybe a shift in trajectory. The national leadership development interventions in England have now featured within public service neoliberalization projects of several governments that have serially failed forward, prompting ever more reform, even 're-disorganization'. Structural and cultural conditions favouring the emergence of a workfare state settlement and a return to lasting morphostasis seem unlikely anytime soon.

Asymmetrical hybridization of public service organizations and their polyarchic governance

The promotion of bounded institutional innovation through government policies connected with the political project of public service reform has encouraged business elites to colonize local provision. The coalition and Conservative governments have eschewed the Labour government's policy of fostering formal collaborative networks between providers, where no organization or individual is socially positioned to exercise hierarchical control over other organizations in the network. But neither have such networks been prohibited. Regulated marketization reforms have created scope for horizontal relationships between service provider organizations (Chapter 9). Such relationships may entail organizations competing against each other for market share (as between universities); creating formal groupings to corner the local market in competition against other local providers (as within academy chains in school education), collaborating within informal groupings to pre-empt imposed competition (where local authority schools provide mutual support to reduce the likelihood of any being pressured into becoming an academy school); or collaborating within informal networks for the mutual benefit of providers and citizens receiving services (as some hospitals have developed with care homes).

An unintended consequence is the extensive reordering of power relationships within and between organizations involved in public service provision. The system of hierarchical relationships once characterizing the bureaucratic organizational form within the nationally and locally administered welfare state remains, principally between central government and local providers within the public sector. Exploitation of the creative space that a regulated marketplace offers for developing competitive or collaborative horizontal relationships between provider organizations is generating a complex hierarchical-horizontal mix within and, occasionally, between public services. Yet distanced or directive steering by political elites within the UK government, whether through the allocation of funding or the accountability regime, keeps hierarchical relationships in the ascendant, overall, across the national public service administrative system. Here, hybridization of the bureaucratic form is structurally asymmetrical: the hierarchical-horizontal balance of power is weighted towards the hierarchical. Strategic-level elites are empowered remotely to contain the array of horizontal power relationships within, and to a lesser extent between, administrative systems for each public service; in short, to regulate the public service market. The result is an emergent 'neo-bureaucratic' form of organization (Courpasson, 2011; Farrell & Morris, 2003; Morris, Farrell, & Reed, 2017; Reed, 2011), an ideal type of novel entity-in-itself.

Neo-bureaucratic organization is intrinsically hybridized, combining structural elements of bureaucracy exerting hierarchical control through hard power—top-down direction through 'command and control' involving targets, performance measurement, and the threat of sanctions—with acculturative soft power built on nurturing shared beliefs and values. In principle, hybridization between hierarchical control and horizontal relationships may be symmetrical, reflecting a fine balance between these two contributory factors. Or it may be asymmetrical, as with public service reform in England, where hierarchical control trumps horizontal relationships, extensive as they are. UK government elites have recourse to hard power but depend on intermediate and local-level elites to implement and operate reforms. That is where soft power comes in.

Generic leaderism offers an acculturative form of soft power, complementing uses of hard power by 'persuading others to want the outcomes you want'. We have mentioned (Chapter 5) how leaderism may be allied with different change agendas. Leadership development, underpinned by a leader-centric construal of leadership and focused on individual leading activity, offers potential for building the capability of elites and non-elites to harness leaderism towards the change agendas that government elites wish to pursue. Thus leader-centric leadership and its development, consistent with our loose definition of leaderism, promote 'elite systemic direction-setting through a hierarchically distributed pattern of persuasive influence by fostering the collective pursuit of shared goals'. The direction set is contingent on the ideological ends pursued.

While leaderism and leadership development may be generically applicable within the neo-bureaucratic form of organization, we are principally concerned with their application to public service reform in England. Strategic-level elite political 'leaders of the system' promote reform and mount or support national leadership development interventions; intermediate-level elites orchestrate these interventions for local-level elite and elite associate senior staff 'leaders within the system', themselves 'leaders of' or 'leaders within' public service organizations. The interventions concentrate on provision for senior staff occupying or seeking promotion to such positions. We have portrayed how a priority for strategic-level authoritative elites within central government, in allying leaderism as an acculturative form of persuasive influence with their regulated marketization reform agenda, is to acculturate senior staff as their change agents for present and possible future reforms. This leadership development provision also offers senior staff support with developing their capability to deploy soft power in acculturating other staff towards achieving service outcomes measured through the accountability regime, a necessity for senior staff to retain their local elite and associate positions.

Characteristic of neo-bureaucratic organization is a hard power–soft power control regime. Hard power is tempered by elite dependence on the co-operation of other elite groupings with the capability to resist, and on their willing support if optimal outcomes are to be achieved. Hence the recourse to soft power. A further unintended consequence of the shift in power relationships giving rise to neo-bureaucratic organization is the emergence of an associated governance system: the rules, norms, and practices determining who is empowered to contribute towards the steering and coordination of organizational activity, how, and within what limits. Governance legitimates the deployment of hard and soft power within a neo-bureaucratic control regime as elites engage with, and respond to, the non-elites and, maybe, other elites on whose acquiescence or support they depend to maintain their elevated social position in the structure of dominancy. Governance, too, is hybridized, symmetrically or asymmetrically, in line with the balance between hierarchical control and horizontal relationships characterizing the neo-bureaucratic form of organization to which it relates.

Governance performs a legitimation 'balancing act', however asymmetrical the hybridization of a neo-bureaucratic organization. With public services in England, where hierarchical control dominates over horizontal relationships, governance takes the form of a 'polyarchy': a political regime that is 'highly inclusive and extensively open to public contestation' (Dahl, 1971, p. 8). Polyarchic governance regimes combine elements of oligarchy (government by the few), technocracy (government by technical experts), and elements of democracy (pluralistic stakeholder participation). They may also incorporate plutocracy (government by the wealthy), especially within business corporations. Such regimes amount to an asymmetrically hybridized system of elite liberal democracy (Higley & Burton, 2006), giving elites (as leaders) overarching control over the other stakeholder groups involved by 'enabling both the official recognition of a plurality of members and political actors, the right to disagree with the leaders, and the simultaneous concentration of political power' (Clegg, Courpasson, & Phillips, 2006, p. 338).

Regarding English public services, strategic-level political elites in government constitute oligarchs with a democratic mandate noted earlier as 'leaders of the system', assisted by their special political advisers (SPADs). They are also supported by senior civil servants as technical experts in system administration. The most senior staff in organizations providing public services constitute local-level elite oligarchs, socially positioned as 'leaders within the system', and service professional staff constitute technical experts in service provision. Elite liberal democracy operates as an oligarchic divide-and-rule strategy: first, by partially decentralizing governance within rules that delegitimize challenge to the social positioning of elites and their associates; second, by advocating wide participation and allowing contestation that stops short of such challenge; while third, encouraging multiple subgroups to pursue diverse, often partially incompatible, sectional interests so that they remain fragmented and unlikely to coalesce around a shared agenda that could destabilize the established order.

The discourse of leaderism allied to public service reform and associated national leadership development interventions also serves the polyarchic governance regime that legitimates the asymmetrically hybridized form of neo-bureaucratic organization. Across public service administrative systems, the government social imaginary of 'supported autonomy' legitimates leading activity by senior staff in public service organizations to implement and operate reforms, pursue compatible local priorities, and forge collaborative networking arrangements with other providers within the regulated marketplace. Competition between provider organizations and collaborative groupings promote an uneven pattern of provision across the public service system, complementing the inhibitory effect of the divide-and-rule accountability regime on the emergence of any counter-elite grouping.

We have seen (Chapter 10) how expectations frameworks used by major leadership development interventions for school education and healthcare in England and other Anglophone countries reflected the generic discourse of leaderism, resonating with the theory of transformational leadership (Bass, 1985). We drew attention to the component 'inspirational motivation'. Another is 'intellectual stimulation' (Chapter 4, Table 4.2), where leaders encourage followers to be creative and innovative, to challenge their own assumptions and those of leaders, and to solve problems together. Indicatively, the UK government's expectations framework for headteachers, underpinning the National Professional Qualification for Headship (NPQH) within the national leadership development intervention for school education, implies central oligarchic control of the public-funded education system. Political elites in government may legitimately 'define high standards which are applicable to all headteacher roles within a self-improving school system' (DfE, 2015, p. 4). Yet headteachers are also expected to deploy their technical expertise, implying legitimation of their corporate agency as local-level expert elites. They are exhorted to 'Challenge educational orthodoxies in the best interests of achieving excellence, harnessing the findings of well evidenced research' (p. 7)—though, implicitly, within parameters that do not challenge government policy and do achieve centrally imposed standards and targets.

The status of government politicians as strategic-level authoritative elites reflects their legitimation in formulating policy and exerting 'command and control' to put it into practice. For implementation, they rely on expert elites across all administrative systems and at all levels and jurisdictions within them to exert varying degrees of complementary oligarchic and, especially, technocratic control (Reed, 2018; Savage & Williams, 2008). The location of expert elites within a complex matrix of hierarchical power structures and horizontal social relationships that are polyarchic and networked empowers them to negotiate and operationalize the faithful, or more adaptive, translation of policies into altered and novel practices. Senior staff in individual public service organizations, as local-level expert elites and associates, are especially significant for our focus: we have underlined how political elites in government depend on their support to 'make reform happen'. The individual and collective expertise of local-level elites and associates as public service professionals, their membership of overlapping expert and local community networks, and their consequent mediatory capacity empower them to interpret and realize policy directives in diverse local contexts. They are also equipped to cope with deleterious unintended consequences of policies connected with political projects promoting public service neoliberalization.

Senior staff legitimacy rests on their elevated local-level social positioning and expertise as leaders, often underpinned by their grounding as service professionals. The expectations framework guiding the leadership development provision of the NHS Leadership Academy (2013, p. 5) incorporates senior staff–colleague two-way challenge, but restricted to the pursuit of a shared purpose, resonant of 'inspirational motivation' within transformational leadership. Within this framework, the leadership behavioural dimension of 'inspiring shared purpose' includes 'staying true to NHS principles and values' and 'taking risks to stand up for the shared purpose'. Prompt questions include 'Do I have the resilience to keep challenging others in the face of opposition, or when I have suffered a setback?' and 'Do I support my team or colleagues when they challenge the way things are done?' Pluralistic participation is fostered, but delimited by the imperative to express 'NHS principles and values'. Challenging these principles is ruled out, and so, implicitly, is questioning the regulated marketization principles and values now embedded within the English NHS.

The national leadership development interventions in England are equally supportive of polyarchic 'supported autonomy', primarily in terms of technocratic control, offering participants a route to their restricted professionalization as leaders. The provision contributes to legitimating alumni engaging in leading activity within the workplace because they have gained expertise through specialist training, either government-funded or, for HE, in the legacy of what was once supported financially through past government 'pump-priming'. However, with rare exceptions, this training focuses on leaders as individuals. It caters for participants seeking to acquire informal credentials to serve their material interest in career advancement, encouraging compliant operation within the public service regulated marketplace. National leadership development interventions may help to discourage local experimentation that might push the boundaries of autonomy allowed by directive or distanced government-elite steering—yet another factor pre-empting emergent local counter-elite groupings that might form advocacy coalitions and challenge the structure of dominancy.

To sum up: a set of increasingly indirect outcomes, discussed at length here (and captured in Appendix 1), flow ever more diffusely from the national leadership development interventions constituting the extreme case we investigated empirically and their direct legacy. They encompass:

- The contribution being made by contemporary iterations of these interventions towards further variegated neoliberalization of public services along the trajectory pursued by central government;
- Their dominant concern with leading change encouraging perennial innovation within bounds imposed by governmental regulation;
- The consequent incremental change being brought about in the nature of public services as societal sub-institutions characterized by variable regulated marketization;
- The provision of these services by hybridized neo-bureaucratic organizations, where hierarchical relationships circumscribe weaker horizontal relationships within and between local service providers;
- The operation of public service provision within polyarchic governance regimes that bolster enduring government elite domination over public service providers, users, and other stakeholder groups.

Emancipation from metaphorical myopia, limited meta-leverage, a learning–practice gap?

This book has been devoted to developing a contextualized understanding, underpinned by a critical realist meta-theoretical position, of large-scale leadership development interventions and their contribution to public service neoliberalization. Critical realism embodies a core axiological commitment towards promoting emancipation from constraints evaluated negatively according to ethical values and social experience about the range of human flourishing (Chapter 3). Examining and explaining such constraints, as attempted here, provides a basis for raising awareness. The chances of informing, let alone persuading, the powerful may seem pessimistic, since the relations of domination and their impacts that we have studied are so deeply entrenched, and elites with vested material and ideal interests in sustaining them are so powerfully positioned. However, there is scope for cautious optimism, which we express in suggesting starting-points for practical reflection and action to emancipate public service leadership and its development from constraints that the investigation has highlighted. We briefly consider three themes emerging from our empirical research discussed in Part II and the update and Anglophone country comparison in Part III. Each has implications for understanding, policy, and practice within and beyond the contexts from which our evidence is drawn. We conclude by tempering this optimism with a note of caution.

Metaphorical myopia and why it matters

The assembled evidence reveals the dominant construal of leadership to be myopic, characterized by conceptual omissions that matter for investments in leadership development. We have repeatedly emphasized how this construal is highly leader-centric in foregrounding 'leader-ship', the quality of individual skill in performing leading activity to influence others, and in prioritizing designated leaders: senior staff who occupy positions carrying management responsibility. Yet some lip-service is also paid to leadership as a group phenomenon. Witness the advocacy of leadership spanning hierarchical levels and specialisms 'from the ward to the board' within the English NHS, and beyond NHS boundaries with other sectors such as social care, whose co-operation is needed to fulfil the NHS's remit (King's Fund, 2011, p. 21).

Leadership development across all the national or regional interventions in our cross-country comparison is equally leader-centric. Most provision focuses on developing the skills of individuals as leaders. We have highlighted (Chapter 1), following Day (2001, 2011), how individual *leader* development masquerades as (implicitly collective) leadership development. We found only rare exceptions, notably the intervention for healthcare in Victoria, Australia (Chapter 10), offering support for executive and senior teams. This limitation matters because it has implications for what can be learned through leader-centric leader-ship development (discussed later). Investment for those in designated positions associated with being a leader tends to increase with the hierarchical level of their formal position. AdvanceHE (2021a) offerings typify this investment hierarchy. We previously described how the long-established Top Management Programme (TMP) is widely regarded as an opportunity to prepare for career advancement, offering symbolic capital conferring competitive advantage in seeking promotion to a top management position. The programme entails three separate residential weeks, one comprising an international visit for the whole cohort, two 'impact days' complemented by an individual 360-degree feedback exercise and coaching, and a team diagnostic activity. By contrast, experienced academics moving to a first role carrying management responsibility are offered the Transition to Leadership Programme, confined to an introductory webinar and six three-hour online workshops. This limitation also matters because of the relationship between level of investment and potential scope for learning.

Why does metaphorical myopia miss what matters? First, leadership is a *relational* task-related group influencing phenomenon (Chapter 1). Leaders, designated or not, depend on the responses of other group members whom they attempt to influence. Leading activity alone is necessary but not sufficient for 'leadership success'. Support (often extending to initiative-taking), or at least compliance from others typically construed as 'followers', is also necessary but still not sufficient where achieving the group task is intended to benefit others, such as citizens using public services. The dominant leader-centric construal of leadership, and the 'leader-ship' development provision it frames, either ignore or underplay this dependency and its implications for developing the collective (relational) co-operation necessary for success in achieving group tasks that no individual group member could achieve alone.

Second, the dominant construal of leadership is seemingly generic, evidenced by the resonance with elements of transformational leadership in the competency frameworks (Chapter 10) associated with major leadership development interventions for school education and healthcare interventions in our comparator Anglophone countries. Yet leadership context matters too, as the empirical investigation of our extreme case and subsequent Anglophone country comparison confirm. The scope, in principle, for national or regional leadership development interventions to operate as an elite policy meta-lever differed starkly between interventions within the five countries.

Another contextual factor is the leader-centric priority that politicians and intervention designers give to leading activity associated with occupying, or preparing to assume, a formal position of authority within a hierarchical order. The aim of such leading activity is to influence the actions of others occupying a lower position, or else the actions of others across jurisdictional divides within horizontal networks. However, influence is multidirectional (Chapter 1), if often asymmetrically so: group members may enable and facilitate the leading activity of designated leaders; they, in turn, may facilitate contributory leading activity by other group members; leading activity circulates within the group according to complementary responsibilities or expertise that are, together, required to address the task at hand

(Buchanan, Addicot, Fitzgerald, Ferlie, & Baeza, 2007; Wallace & Huckman, 1999). Support provided by leadership development concentrating on individuals as formally positioned leaders, especially at or near the top of the formal management hierarchy, ignores the multiplicity of contributors to leading activity or its facilitation within and between different groupings in public service contexts. They may be inside the same organization or spread across administrative systems. Further, the significance of context extends to the group level. Most designated leaders in public service organizations larger than a small primary school are simultaneously positioned as followers. Staff occupying an intermediate position within the hierarchical ordering of posts carrying management responsibility are legitimated in influencing those lower down while being expected to accept being influenced by those higher up. Yet the dominant construal of leadership and leadership development focuses far more on their leading activity than on its delimitation by the expectation to 'follow orders from above'.

The associated hierarchical ordering of power to 'make decisions having major consequences' underlies our restrictive conferral of elite status, very largely, to those occupying top designated positions within a hierarchical order. They are legitimated in using authority to direct or delimit the actions of all those over whom they have jurisdiction as leader of the organization or administrative system. Within the contemporary neo-bureaucratic organizational form, the relationship between designated leaders and others is more hierarchical than horizontal; but horizontal leadership *across* jurisdictional boundaries remains significant—as the recent establishment of the National Leadership Centre reflects (Chapter 9). Its leadership development provision fosters cross-public service networking amongst local-level or intermediate-level elite chief executives, whose own jurisdictions lie within different English public service sectors.

Power differentials are integral to leadership as a relational group phenomenon characterized by attempts to influence and the responses they invoke. Conceptions of distributed leadership tend to downplay the workings of power in contexts where leading activity is shared across a group. Yet the concerted, often fluid contributions of different members to distributed leadership still focus on leading activity. Such conceptions tend to imply that everyone influences everyone, neglecting the corollary that everyone is also accepting the influence of everyone else and, in some sense, following their lead in doing the work entailed in pursuing the group task (Alvesson & Spicer, 2011). They also neglect the likelihood of differential access to sources of power within the group, whether based on authority, expertise, or even charisma, and expressions of power or the potential to express it being collaborative (exercising 'power with' others), conflictual (exercising 'power over' others), or both. Illustratively, all members of a surgery team may have unique and complementary expertise, yet surgeons are 'more equal' than, say, anaesthetists or theatre nurses in setting the direction of the medical operation. Conversely, there remains an asymmetry of accountability; if the operation is unsuccessful, surgeons are 'more equal' than other group members for the consequences of their direction-setting.

Third, the nature of leadership remains relatively ambiguous due to its inherently metaphorical nature. The notion of metaphorical 'myopia' (literally, short-sightedness) is itself metaphorical, the source for a more complex target: selective, and so 'one-sided', metaphorical representations of a phenomenon inferred through language. Reference to the 'myopia' of leader-centricity implies that something important is missing, but not that expanding the range of metaphorical entailments associated with leadership can generate a universalistic understanding of the phenomenon. The understanding that language makes possible is inherently limited. We have highlighted (Chapter 3) how the ontological stance embodied in critical realism assumes that social phenomena can be inferred, but not directly apprehended without the mediation of language. Inference is inherently subject to language's limitations and creative possibilities. Alvesson and Spicer (2011, pp. 22–23) cite their research experience of designated leaders being unsure how they did leadership, of followers construing leadership differently from leaders, and of the context promoting different understandings of leading and being led. Underlying the surface meanings for those involved is the shaping of perceptions through metaphors based on only a *partial* parallel between source and target. Small wonder that, after more than a century of leadership research and theorization, there is no consensus on how to characterize, model, or explain this phenomenon (Grint, 2011; Northouse, 2019), never mind measure it.

It may be impossible to avoid metaphor, yet the domination of transformational leadership discourse demonstrated the possibility of choosing which metaphor and its entailments draw attention to the aspects of leadership deemed most important. The metaphor may then inform and so potentially influence leadership practice. Hoyle and Wallace (2007, p. 436) advocate deliberative 'metaphoric re-description', either coining new metaphors or revisiting and reworking those in use. One possibility, offering modest emancipatory potential within a public service milieu dominated by neoliberalization, is 'temperate leadership' (Hoyle & Wallace, 2005, pp. 185–198). This neologism was construed as an explicitly value-laden (metaphorical) 'antidote' to what the authors judged to be *intemperate* leadership in school education promoted by the Labour government, and the national leadership development intervention centring on the National College for School Leadership (NCSL). The role of senior staff is re-described in terms of protecting teachers, as much as possible, from the inhibitory effects of government policy through 'a pattern of leadership that values teacher autonomy, displays trust—and accepts the associated risks, sponsors innovations that emerge from communities of practice and generally takes the strain, thereby minimising the stress experienced by teachers' (Hoyle & Wallace, 2007, p. 438). There is potential for further metaphoric re-description and associated developmental support for staff across the public services to help mitigate the cultural hegemony of leaderism, within managerialism, in the service of neoliberalization. One alternative starting-point might be to build metaphorical concepts and developmental support for groups and communities around 'collaboration' or 'teamworking', elaborated through entailments foregrounding complementary contributions towards the pursuit of some collective good.

Leadership development as an elite policy meta-lever: potential in principle, unachievable in practice?

We referred (Chapter 1) to the possibility that major public service leadership development interventions might offer potential to operate as a long-term elite policy meta-lever, facilitating the implementation of any relevant public policy agenda, whether of the present or some future government, through other policy levers. Such potential rests on twin assumptions: first, only groups whose members are powerful enough to mount large-scale interventions could deploy this meta-lever, restricting its use to elites in government; second, it is feasible to persuade senior staff trained as public service leaders that they should be ready to implement any government-driven reforms for their service sector. We elaborated (Chapter 3) how this readiness to act as change agents for *any* government of the day would require the 'bounded empowerment' of senior staff through acculturative formal co-optation, where they came to accept this expectation as integral to their role as leaders. Therefore, leadership development interventions must prove themselves capable of achieving such acculturative formal co-optation, overlaying the existing service professional culture to which senior staff already subscribed.

The first assumption was broadly confirmed by our empirical research, Anglophone country comparison, and illustrative examples of recent research on the impacts of regulated marketization reforms on staff in English schools, healthcare organizations, and universities. Major interventions are the province of elites, both within strategic-level governments and at the intermediate level. Elites representing senior staff are also positioned to mount interventions supporting the professional and career development of members. Insofar as the potential for major leadership development interventions to operate as an elite policy meta-lever rests on formal, positionally based elite power, our research suggested that those for public-funded school education and healthcare in England were at the extreme end of control by strategic-level elites within the UK government. We judged them to have high potential to operate as an elite policy meta-lever. They had become even more centralized since our research, extending to the demise of one NLDB, its role having been subsumed into the government's education department. Roughly equivalent interventions in Victoria, Australia, were similarly centralized, the province of strategic-level elites within the State of Victoria government. However, the interventions for these service sectors in the USA, Canada, and New Zealand, and the interventions for HE in all five countries, were less subject to government elite control, so we judged them to offer less potential as a meta-lever for national or regional government elites.

The second assumption was not confirmed: our research evidence from England (Chapter 8) suggests that the interventions mounted or otherwise financially supported by the Labour government had probably reinforced the acculturation of senior staff towards perceiving themselves as leaders, consistent with the government's discourse strategy, but not as government change agents. The perceptions of senior staff who had not experienced this provision were similar. Rather, senior staff may have become more acculturated towards 'resigned compliance' with the strictures of the accountability regime. A significant minority, apparently, were also acculturated towards their restricted professionalization as leaders, keen to gain cultural, social, and symbolic capital through their participation, or even formal accreditation (for senior staff in schools), to help them advance their own career.

The illustrative evidence offered by findings from a recent investigation for each of our three focal public services suggested that if senior staff had attempted to acculturate staff responsible for providing the service towards regulated marketization reforms, they had largely failed. Most senior staff in schools and staff in middle management positions in healthcare or universities did not seem to have been acculturated; senior staff in healthcare may have been more acculturated towards reforms or, possibly, towards compliance within the accountability regime. The outliers appeared to be senior staff in universities, including manager-academics and career administrators, though we could only infer this possibility from the impacts on academics, including those in middle management positions. But we do not know what proportion of staff featuring in these findings had participated in NLDB provision and, if so, whether they had been acculturated towards reforms as a result. More likely is *enculturation*, the incorporation of cultural elements within a person's early socialization into their first culture (Weinrich, 2009), through the socialization of staff who had started their career since the advent of the regulated marketization reforms, whose only professional experience lay within the neoliberalized service of the past two decades.

If our surmise is correct, it chimes with other research (Chapter 3) showing that professional and organizational cultures are not readily amenable to manipulation through culture management; they are far slower to change than the behaviour that can be controlled through neo-Taylorism, exemplified by the English accountability regime. If culture management does work, it needs a long timeframe—way beyond the year or so given to the most extensive leadership development programme. Our tentative verdict: however much potential leadership development interventions may have as an elite policy meta-lever since they are mounted by strategic or intermediate-level elites, this potential may be unrealizable because leadership development is underpowered to overlay extant professional service professional cultures through a re-socialization process. Only if provision remained on offer long enough to enculturate staff who had never experienced such cultures might leadership development work for the acculturative formal co-optation of senior staff as government change agents. There would be less of a gap between their cultural allegiances born of their original enculturation and the overlay that later acculturation would require. The leadership development interventions appear more potent as a source of credentials contributing to forms of capital that participants perceive to offer individual competitive advantage in seeking career advancement.

What has operated more like an elite policy meta-lever in England is the policy lever of mandates. Its institutionalization has enabled strategic-level elites in successive governments to maintain control of public service provision (including the formally more autonomous HE) through neo-Taylorist managerialism, imposing a chronic demand for government investment in regulatory surveillance or assessment exercises. Since the accountability regime is funded through taxation, it contributes to the perpetuation of austerity measures bounding the UK government spending deficit—recently exacerbated by an unprecedented level of borrowing to cope with the COVID-19 pandemic. The regime has become deeply institutionalized as an enduring means for government elites to contain public service operation and pre-empt concerted resistance through a perennial source of 'background' intimidation, ensuring a high degree of compliance.

Other policy instruments range from inducements to do what government elites want; through capacity-building via leadership development interventions and persuasive communication advocating leaderism linked to regulated marketization reform; to serial system-changing—with each iteration 'failing forward' and perpetuating the churn of ameliorative change. Since these policy levers and any potential meta-levers are the province of strategic-level elites in government, only they are positioned to relinquish any ambition to acculturate senior staff from public service organizations towards perceiving themselves as leaders responsibilized to act as change agents for whichever government is in office at any time. (The one exception here is the UK government civil service, as the only public service sector whose role is both to support the government of the day in developing and implementing its policies and to provide services connected mainly with workfare.) Government alone is also positioned to consider whether and, if so, how far to ease up on the accountability regime so that senior staff are freed from some of the burden that ensuring compliance imposes. Less reliance on labour-intensive surveillance would save considerably on the opportunity costs it incurs, while also alleviating the background intimidation that militates against 'unsafe' engagement in further innovation for service improvement that is sensitive to local contexts.

Predicting the past: limitations of national leadership development interventions for promoting learning

National public service leadership development interventions may be inherently underpowered, not only to overlay extant professional cultures, but also to support much of the contextualized learning necessary for maximizing the effectiveness of group activity to achieve some collective task. These institutionalized interventions may be incapable of yielding a high 'return on investment'. Practical experience and underlying research in training and development intervention design and evaluation are long established. Both suggest that the national leadership development interventions we have examined in England and major interventions in other Anglophone countries could have variably limited potential for promoting the learning, practice, and organizational 'performance' their instigators desire, and often claim. Support is frequently missing for necessary 'learning-by-doing' in the context of use—not just learning-by-practising in the 'safe space' of the training setting or even conducting individual projects in the workplace. Learning-by-doing the job involves all members of the group whose individual contributions are required to achieve a shared work task, where both the process and outcomes matter. Self-evidently, most professional learning through the experience of doing the job remains unsupported, and starkly so if this learning is in preparation for an aspirational future role. Learning is achieved through accumulated individual and collective action, and maybe reflection on it, in the workplace. The risks of failure are lower and the potential for maximizing learning greater where appropriate learning support is provided with planning action, monitoring its intended and unintended consequences, reflecting on the action taken and its impacts (or lack of them), and planning further action. Yet elements of individual and group support with learning through doing the job were rare in the interventions we investigated empirically and their subsequent incarnations in England (and seemingly also in our examples from four other Anglophone countries, but here our evidence was restricted to website and documentary sources).

Multiple studies of leadership development, based on participant self-reporting, were conducted at the Center for Creative Learning in the 1980s. The cumulative results suggested that most learning occurs through the experience of authentic engagement in doing leadership in the workplace, rather than in a classroom-based training session (McCall, 2010). The practical '70:20:10' learning and development model articulated by two of the researchers, Lombardo and Eichinger (1996), claimed that about 70 per cent of development ensues from challenging experiences in the normal job, maybe 20 per cent from feedback, which could include structured feedback provided through coaching and mentoring, and only around 10 per cent from formal classroom-based training interventions.

Advances in academic educational research from the 1980s on supporting the 'transfer' of training into workplace practice (Eraut, 1994; Joyce & Showers, 1988; Kirkpatrick & Kirkpatrick, 2005; Wallace, 1991) and in training evaluation design reaching back to the 1950s (Kirkpatrick, 1998) point to the importance of trying out in the workplace what has been learned in the training room, and how the additional learning *in the context of use* that transfer entails may be enhanced through observation and formative feedback. To the extent that workplace practice involves group interaction, as with leadership, it is salient for development support to be extended to more than one group member, as all involved have to learn how to work together effectively (Wallace, 1996). We have already noted how the leadership development provision mostly targeted individuals as leaders, omitting support for others within their leadership nexus who were expected to accept or even facilitate their leading activity, and maybe take initiatives of their own. Since much provision focused on individual preparation for another role carrying greater management responsibility, even workplace projects could not fully replicate the context of use in an aspirational future job. By design, most provision was located away from the workplace, leaving participants largely unsupported with the additional workplace learning entailed in learning transfer. Even coaching and mentoring, while directly informing individual leadership practice, was confined to learning by talking about leadership, rather than engaging with others at work and being supported in reflecting on what happened, why, and what to do in future.

Evaluation of interventions becomes technically more difficult the further along the putative chain of impact evaluators go in generating evidence: from participant satisfaction with provision; through their learning of knowledge, skills, and attitudes and their application of that learning within their organizational workplace practice; to its effect on the process of pursuing and the achievement of organizational purposes. An academic review of NLDB evaluation practices in our empirical investigation (Chapter 7) found that they rarely extended to the impact of leadership on organizational change (Riley & Stoll, 2007). Even external evaluations of the NCSL (DfES, 2004d) and LFHE (Blue Alumni, 2010; McCracken, McCrory, Farley, & McHugh, 2021; Oakleigh Consulting Ltd, 2006) stopped short of tracking any link between individual participation in leadership development programmes and improving service provision within the organizational jurisdictions of participants. So there is little evaluation evidence of leadership development interventions impacting on the organizational outcomes that matter to government politicians. Modest evidence exists of impact on individual career enhancement, at least for AdvanceHE (2021b), in terms of TMP alumni subsequently gaining a vice-chancellor appointment. Yet it is unclear how causally instrumental the symbolic capital constituted by the record of participation in the TMP programme was in securing them the top job.

Our verdict on the learning support offered by the national leadership development interventions which we studied is, therefore, 'could do better'. Freeing up the interventions to do better might include, first, eschewing leader-centricity and starting at the other end of leadership, as a phenomenon, by focusing on asymmetrical influencing, facilitating influencing by others, mutual dependence, and collaborative working to achieve a collective task—as is common in team development interventions. Second it would be advisable to start at the other end of learning to do leadership by, say, arranging for external or peer observation and formative feedback on learning to work together on collective workplace tasks, perhaps supported by individual coaching and opportunities for informational learning and reflection away from the workplace. A third step is prioritizing the provision of individual support for the entire process of transition embodied in preparing for and then experiencing rapid workplace learning entailed in the early days of occupying a position carrying greater management responsibility. Preparation cannot enable aspirants to pre-learn what they can only learn in the context of use: how to do the new job in a new role, sometimes in a new organization.

Finally, a note of caution: the possibility of even a modest shift in these alternative directions is tempered by the sheer degree of institutionalization characterizing the major leadership development interventions we studied, and likely to be replicated elsewhere. Since institutions or sub-institutions and their operational logics are the outcome of agency, they can be refashioned through agency. Any significant departure from the new normal will rest with corporate agents, who will have to address multiple factors favouring the maintenance of present provision and its administrative arrangements. Alternatives might be more labour-intensive, so more costly to mount, than largely classroom-based training of individuals with, or aspiring towards, responsibility for the work of others. Building and consolidating the present configuration of national or regional interventions may have taken a decade or more. Where strategic-level elites in government are involved, the way things are done serves their material and ideal interests: the interventions are sensitive to the context of the public sector they serve (Chapter 7) and 'owned' by a government department, with ministerial turf to protect. Such interventions may not be very successful in acculturating senior staff as change agents for reforms furthering public service neoliberalization, but sanction-incurring accountability regimes ensure compliance anyway. There is also enough compatibility with the diverse interests of intermediate-level and local-level elites who share a stake in a national or regional leadership development intervention to favour its perpetuation. At the intermediate level, elites may include senior staff from representative bodies either involved in establishing and operating interventions, or otherwise interested in supporting the career development and restricted professionalization of their public service senior staff members; this motivation alone serves the material interest of senior officials in training large numbers of individuals as leaders. At the local level, elites include senior staff with posts carrying management responsibility and aspirant elites seeking individual career enhancement as restrictively professionalized leaders.

In conclusion, the national and regional interventions appear to operate as a 'weapon of mass distraction', directly assisting or indirectly favouring government elites' continuing domination of senior staff in public service organizations through symbolic violence. Diverting the attention of participants towards seeking credentials for advancing their career as individual professionalized leaders, rather than giving priority to expressing public service professional values, prompts their misrecognition of the interventions and unwitting collusion in perpetuating their own subordination. In such circumstances they may become increasingly acculturated towards being professional leaders, perhaps further weakening allegiance to their public service-based ideology of professionalism framing provision. The Organisation for Economic Cooperation and Development (OECD, 2019b) (Chapter 1) has called on member countries to pledge more of the same. It is already clear that extensive sunk investment in leader-centric leadership development interventions with, according to this study, limited acculturative and learning potential has raised expectations amongst senior staff and aspirants towards senior positions in public service organizations. The interventions have become a valued opportunity—even entitlement—to build symbolic capital favouring individual career enhancement through participating in leadership development provision. The perpetuation and expansion of present leader-centric leadership development practice may serve the career-promotion and professionalization interests of intermediate and local-level elites alike. So strategic-level elites in governments bent on acculturating senior staff as leaders of reforms serving further public service neoliberalization by investing in major leadership development interventions may find, ironically, that they can't do much with them, can't do without them.

Implementing NLDBs for schools, healthcare, higher education: context, generative mechanisms, outcomes

Context: Constitutional background of 'British exceptionalism' enabling unilateral action by central government
Variegated neoliberalization of public services through regulated marketization, supported by managerialism
Public service regulated marketization reforms of previous Conservative government
Labour government's public service reform agenda promoting a social democratic variant of neoliberalization
Residual public service professional ideology amongst staff in public service organizations

Leader-centric construal of leadership by central government, shared by representative bodies for groups of staff in public service organizations and by senior staff in these organizations, frames interventions involving an NLDB

+

Remote containment by central government of public service transformation, promoting transmission of reforms into practice

Attempted acculturative formal co-optation by central government of senior staff in public service organizations as change agents leading the implementation of reforms, via the elite policy meta-lever of leadership development interventions involving an NLDB, implemented by NLDB senior officials

Specification by central government of NLDB remit (or vetting for HE), financial allocation, reporting requirements, review

Mediatory subversion by NLDB senior officials of central government acculturative formal co-optation of senior staff in public service organizations, sharing a leader-centric construal of leadership but diluting the linkage of provision with change agency for reforms, supported by representative bodies promoting members' professionalization as leaders

Delimitation by central government of NLDB senior official mediatory subversion via NLDBs' remit, financial allocation, reporting, review, cross-NLDB coordination

Mediatory subversion by senior staff of their acculturative formal co-optation, as leaders expressing their service professional or administrative and management values

Leader capital indexation by senior staff of participating in NLDB provision as credentials for their professional and career development

Accreditation by central government for school headship, senior staff participation in NLDB provision viewed by job selectors as an asset

Restricted further professionalization of senior staff as leaders of and within public service organizations, construed by central government as local leaders who influence others to transmit reforms into practice, initiate local changes compatible with reforms, and ensure the government's service performance expectations are met

Immediate outcomes of the leadership development interventions involving an NLDB: limited impact as an elite policy meta-lever, institutionalization of the acculturative formal co-optation of senior public service staff more as professional leaders than as change agents for government-driven reforms, but constrained to operate within bounds set by remote containment, restricting expression of their residual professional public service ideology

Legacy of NLDBs: contribution to the international proliferation and institutionalization of leadership development interventions involving NLDBs, contexts offer varying potential to operate as an elite policy meta-lever, senior staff in England more acculturated as change agents for reforms than middle managers or frontline staff

Indirect outcomes: contribution to further variegated neoliberalization of public services and bounded innovation changing public services as institutions, in which services are provided by neo-bureaucratic organizations where hierarchical relationships contain weaker horizontal relationships, operating within polyarchic governance regimes sustaining central government domination of public service providers and users

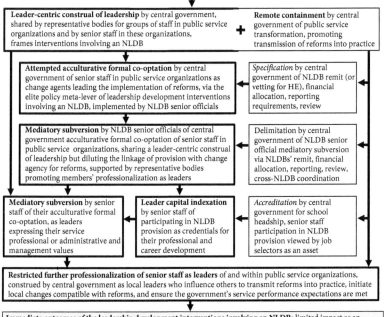

References

Abbott, A. (1988). *The system of professions: an essay on the division of expert labour*. Chicago: University of Chicago Press.

Adams, I. (1998). *Ideology and politics in Britain today*. Manchester: Manchester University Press.

AdvanceHE. (2019). *Helping HE shape its future: statutory report and accounts, year ended 31 July 2019*. https://www.advance-he.ac.uk/sites/default/files/2020-02/AHE%20Statutory%20Accounts%202018-19_0.pdf.

AdvanceHE. (2021a). *Development programmes*. https://www.advance-he.ac.uk/programmes-events/development-programmes

AdvanceHE. (2021b). *Top management programme for higher education*. https://www.advance-he.ac.uk/programmes-events/development-programmes/executive-and-senior-leadership/top-management-programme

Ajemian, R. (1987). Where is the real George Bush? *Time Magazine*, 26 January. http://content.time.com/time/subscriber/article/0,33009,963342,00.html

Alvesson, M., & Spicer, A. (2011). *Metaphors we lead by: understanding leadership in the real world*. London: Routledge.

American Council on Education. (2021). *ACE fellows program*. https://www.acenet.edu/Programs-Services/Pages/Professional-Learning/ACE-Fellows-Program.aspx

Anderson, B., & Minneman, E. (2014). The abuse and misuse of the term 'austerity': implications for OECD countries. *OECD Journal on Budgeting*, 14(1), 109–122.

Appleby, P. H. (1947). Toward better public administration. *Public Administration Review*, 7(2), 93–99.

Archer, M. (1995). *Realist social theory: the morphogenetic approach*. Cambridge: Cambridge University Press.

Archer, M. (2003). *Structure, agency and the internal conversation*. Cambridge: Cambridge University Press.

Archer, M., Decoteau, C., Gorski, P., Little, D., Porpora, D., Rutzou, T., Smith, C., Steinmetz, G., & Vandenberghe, F. (2016). What is critical realism? *Perspectives*, 38(2), 4–9.

ASCL. (2006a). ASCL President's address to annual conference, March 2006: sustaining leadership.

ASCL. (2006b). *Courses: Homerun for headship*. London: ASCL Management and Professional Services.

Ashworth, R., Boyne, G., & Delbridge, R. (2009). Escape from the iron cage? Organizational pressures and isomorphic pressures in the public sector. *Journal of Public Administration Research and Theory*, 19(1), 165–187.

Baker, M. (2008). *Can naming and shaming help schools?* BBC News, 13 June. http://news.bbc.co.uk/1/hi/education/7453301.stm

Barber, M. (2007). *Instruction to deliver*. London: Politico's.

Bass, B. M. (1985). *Leadership and performance beyond expectations*. New York: Free Press.

Bastow Institute of Educational Leadership. (2021). *Leadership initiatives*. https://www.bastow.vic.edu.au/leadership-initiatives

Bennett, N., Wise, C., Woods, P., Philip, A., & Harvey, J. A. (2003). *Distributed leadership: a review of the literature*. Nottingham: National College for School Leadership.

Bennis, W., & Nanus, B. (1985). *Leaders: strategies for taking charge*. New York: Harper Collins.

Berry, J. W. (1997). Immigration, acculturation and adaptation. *Applied Psychology*, 46(1), 5–68.

Bevan, G., & Hood, C. (2006). What's measured is what matters: targets and gaming in the English public healthcare system. *Public Administration*, 84(3), 517–538.

Beveridge, W. (1942). *Social insurance and allied services* (CM6404). London: HMSO.

Bhaskar, R. (1978). *A realist theory of science* (2nd ed.). Leeds: Leeds Books.

Blair, T. (1996a). The agenda for a generation: Ruskin College Oxford, 16 December. In D. Gillard (Ed.), *Education in England: the history of our schools*. http://www.educationengland.org.uk/documents/speeches/1996ruskin.html

Blair, T. (1996b). *Labour Party annual conference speech, 1 October 1996*. http://www.aparchive.com/metadata/youtube/c93efcd34c5321db2a572c12f45003ba

Blair, T. (2010). *A journey*. London: Hutchinson.

Blue Alumni. (2010). *Evaluation of the Leadership Foundation for Higher Education: a report to HEFCE*. London: Blue Alumni.

Blunkett, D. (2000). *National College for School Leadership (remit letter)*. London: DfEE.

Boas, T. C., & Gans-Morse, J. (2009). Neoliberalism: from new liberal philosophy to anti-liberal slogan. *Studies in Comparative International Development, 44*(2), 137–161.

Bolam, R. (Ed.) (1982). *School-focused in-service training*. London: Heinemann.

Bolam, R. (1986). The National Development Centre for School Management Training. In E. Hoyle & A. McMahon (Eds), *The management of schools: world yearbook of education 1986* (pp. 252–271). London: Kogan Page.

Bolam, R. (2004). Reflections on the NCSL from a historical perspective. *Educational Management Administration and Leadership, 32*(3), 251–267.

Bolden, R. (2006). *Leadership development in context: Leadership South West report 3*. Exeter: University of Exeter.

Bolden, R. (2011). Distributed leadership in organizations: a review of theory and research. *International Journal of Management Reviews, 13*(3), 252–269.

Bolden, R., Petrov, G., & Gosling, J. (2009). Distributed leadership in higher education. *Educational Management Administration and Leadership, 37*(2), 257–277.

Bolton, R. (2019). *Higher education funding in England*. (Briefing paper 7393). London: House of Commons Library https://researchbriefings.files.parliament.uk/documents/CBP-7973/CBP-7973.pdf.

Bone, A., & Bourner, T. (1998). Developing university managers. *Higher Education Quarterly, 52*(3), 283–299.

Bourdieu, P. (1984). *Distinction: a social critique of the judgement of taste*. Cambridge, MA: Harvard University Press.

Bourdieu, P. (1986). The forms of capital. In J. G. Richardson (Ed.), *Handbook of theory and research for the sociology of education* (pp. 241–258). New York: Greenwood Press.

Bourdieu, P., & Passeron, J.-C. (1990). *Reproduction in education, society and culture*. London: Sage.

Brenner, N., Peck, J., & Theodore, N. (2010). Variegated neoliberalization: geographies, modalities, pathways. *Global Networks, 10*(2), 182–222.

Bresnen, M., Hyde, P., Hodgson, D., Bailey, S., & Hassard, J. (2015). Leadership talk: from managerialism to leaderism in health care after the crash. *Leadership, 11*(4), 451–470.

Brown, R., & Carasso, H. (2013). *Everything for sale? The marketisation of UK higher education*. Abingdon, Oxon: Routledge.

Brundrett, M. (2001). The development of school leadership preparation programmes in England and the USA: a comparative analysis. *Educational Management Administration and Leadership, 29*(2), 229–245.

Brunetto, Y. (2001). Mediating change for public-sector professionals. *International Journal of Public Sector Management, 14*(6), 465–481.

Buchanan, D. A., Addicot, R., Fitzgerald, L., Ferlie, E., & Baeza, J. (2007). Nobody in charge: distributed change agency in healthcare. *Human Relations, 60*(7), 1065–1090.

Burns, J. M. (1978). *Leadership*. New York: Harper & Row.

Burton, M. (2013). *The politics of public service reform: from Thatcher to the coalition*. Basingstoke: Palgrave Macmillan.

Cabinet Office. (1999). *Modernising government*. London: Cabinet Office.

Cabinet Office. (2006). *Evaluating the impact of leadership development: an evaluation framework*. London: Cabinet Office.

Cabinet Office. (2008). *Excellence and fairness: achieving world class public services*. London: Cabinet Office.

Cabinet Office. (2009). *Cabinet Office review of public service leadership development: summary report*. London: Cabinet Office.

Caldwell, R. (2003). Models of change agency: a fourfold classification. *British Journal of Management, 14*(2), 131–142.

Callaghan, R. (1962). *Education and the cult of efficiency*. Chicago: University of Chicago Press.

Case, P., Case, S., & Catling, S. (2000). Please show you're working: a critical assessment of the impact of OFSTED inspection on primary teachers. *British Journal of the Sociology of Education, 21*(4), 605–621.

Causer, G., & Exworthy, M. (1999). Professionals as managers across the public sector. In M. Exworthy & S. Halford (Eds), *Professionals and the new managerialism in the public sector* (pp. 83–101). Buckingham: Open University Press.

CCHL. (2021a). *LEADS framework.* https://leadscanada.net/site/about/about-us/framework? nav= sidebar

CCHL. (2021b). *Vision, mission and values.* https://www.cchl-ccls.ca/site/about/college/mission vision?nav=sidebar

Centre for Higher Education Research and Development. (2021). *Certificate in university and college administration (CUCA).* https://umextended.ca/cherd-programs/certificate-university-college-administration/

Clark, D. (2002). Neoliberalism and public service reform: Canada in comparative perspective. *Canadian Journal of Political Science, 35*(4), 771–793.

Clarke, J., & Newman, J. (1997). *The managerial state: power, politics and ideology in the remaking of social welfare.* London: Sage.

Clarke, J., Newman, J., Smith, N., Vidler, E., & Westmarland, L. (2007). *Creating citizen-consumers: changing publics and changing public services.* London: Sage.

Clegg, S. R., Courpasson, D., & Phillips, N. (2006). *Power in organizations.* London: Sage.

Conger, J. A., & Kanungo, R. N. (1998). *Charismatic leadership in organizations.* Thousand Oaks, CA: Sage.

Conservative Party. (2015). *Strong leadership, a clear economic plan, a brighter, more secure future.* London: Conservative Party.

Coopers & Lybrand. (1988). *Local management of schools.* London: HMSO.

Cornelissen, J. P. (2005). Beyond compare: metaphor in organization theory. *Academy of Management Review, 30*(4), 751–764.

Courpasson, D. (2011). Part 1 'Roads to resistance': the growing critique from managerial ranks in organization. *Management, 2011/1*(14).

Craig, R., Mernic, J., & Tourish, D. (2014). Perverse audit culture and accountability of the modern public university. *Financial Accountability and Management, 30*(1), 1–24.

Currie, G., & Lockett, A. (2011). Distributing leadership in health and social care: concertive, conjoint or collective? *International Journal of Management Reviews, 13*(3), 286–300.

Dahl, R. A. (1971). *Polyarchy: participation and opposition.* New Haven, CT: Yale University Press.

Danermark, B., Ekstrom, M., Jakobsen, L., & Karlsson, J. C. (2002). *Explaining society: critical realism in the social sciences.* London: Routledge.

Day, D. (2001). Leadership development: a review in context. *Leadership Quarterly, 11*(4), 581–613.

Day, D. (2011). Leadership development. In A. Bryman, D. Collinson, K. Grint, M. Uhl-Bien, & B. Jackson (Eds), *The Sage handbook of leadership* (pp. 37–50). London: Sage.

DBIS. (2016). *Success as a knowledge economy: teaching excellence, social mobility and student choice.* London: DBIS.

Deal, T., & Kennedy, A. (1982). *Corporate cultures.* Reading, MA: Addison Wesley.

Deem, R. (1998). 'New managerialism' and higher education: the management of performances and cultures in universities in the United Kingdom. *International Studies in Sociology of Education, 8*(1), 47–70.

Deem, R. (2017). New managerialism in higher education. In J. C. Shin & P. Texeira (Eds), *Encyclopedia of international higher education systems and institutions.* Dordrecht: Springer. doi:https://doi.org/10. 1007/978-94-017-9553-1_308-1

Deem, R., & Brehony, K. (2005). Management as an ideology: the case of 'new managerialism' in higher education. *Oxford Review of Education, 31*(2), 217–235.

Deem, R., Hillyard, S., & Reed, M. (2007). *Knowledge, higher education and the new managerialism.* Oxford: Oxford University Press.

Denis, J.-L., Langley, A., & Sergi, V. (2012). Leadership in the plural. *Academy of Management Annals, 6*(1), 211–283.

DES. (1983). *Teaching quality* (Cm8836). London: DES.

Devlin, N., Harrison, A., & Derrett, S. (2002). Waiting in the NHS: Part 1—a diagnosis. *Journal of the Royal Society of Medicine, 95*(5), 223–226.

DfE. (2010). *The importance of teaching* (Cm7980). London: DfE.

DfE. (2015). *National standards of excellence for headteachers.* London: DfE.

DfE. (2016). *Educational excellence everywhere* (Cm9230). London: DfE.

DfE. (2020). *National Professional Qualification (NPQ): Headship Framework.* London: DfE.

DfE. (2021a). *National Professional Qualifications (NPQs) reforms.* https://www.gov.uk/government/publications/national-professional-qualifications-npqs-reforms/national-professional-qualifications-npqs-reforms

DfE. (2021b). *Professional development for school leaders.* https://www.gov.uk/government/collections/professional-development-for-school-leaders

DfEE. (1997). *Excellence in Schools* (Cm3681). London: DfEE.

DfEE. (1998). *Teachers meeting the challenge of change.* London: DfEE.

DfEE. (1999). *National College for School Leadership: a prospectus.* London: DfEE.

DfES. (2001). *Schools achieving success* (Cm5230). London: DfES.

DfES. (2003a). *The future of higher education* (Cm5735). London: DfES.

DfES. (2003b). *A new specialist system: transforming secondary education.* London: DfES.

DfES. (2004a). *National standards for headteachers.* Nottingham: DfES.

DfES. (2004b). *Five year strategy for children and learners: putting people at the heart of public services* (Cm 6272). London: The Stationery Office.

DfES. (2004c). *Guidance on the mandatory requirement to hold the National Professional Qualification for Headship (NPQH).* London: DfES.

DfES. (2004d). *School leadership: end to end review of school leadership policy and delivery.* London: DfES.

DfES. (2005). *Higher standards, better schools for all: more choice for parents and pupils* (Cm 6677). London: DfES.

DHSS. (1983). *NHS management enquiry (the Griffiths report).* London: DHSS.

Docherty, T. (2011). *For the university: democracy and the future of the institution.* London: Bloomsbury.

DoH. (1993). *Managing the new NHS.* London: HMSO.

DoH. (1997). *The new NHS: modern, dependable* (Cm3807). London: The Stationery Office.

DoH. (2000). *The NHS plan: a plan for investment, a plan for reform* (Cm4818-I). London: The Stationery Office.

DoH. (2002a). *Delivering the NHS Plan: next steps on investment, next steps on reform* (Cm 5503). London: The Stationery Office.

DoH. (2002b). *Managing for excellence in the NHS.* London: DoH.

DoH. (2004a). *The NHS improvement plan: putting people at the heart of public services* (Cm 6268). London: The Stationery Office.

DoH. (2004b). *Payment by results—preparing for 2005: DoH response to consultation.* London: DoH.

DoH. (2005a). *Health reform in England: update and next steps.* London: DoH.

DoH. (2005b). *The way forward: the NHS Institute for Learning, Skills and Innovation.* London: DoH.

DoH. (2006). *The NHS in England: the operating framework for 2007/08.* London: DoH.

DoH. (2008). *High quality care for all: NHS next stage review final report.* London: The Stationery Office.

DoH. (2009). *NHS takes the lead on leadership.* https://www.wired-gov.net/wg/wg-news-1.nsf/0/67E7AAC9EDD4F6BF80257544003A87F7?OpenDocument

DoH. (2010a). *Equity and excellence: liberating the NHS* (Cm7881). London: DoH.

DoH. (2010b). *Liberating the NHS: report of the arm's-length bodies review.* London: DoH.

DoH. (2016). *Delivering high quality, effective, compassionate care: developing the right people with the right skills and the right values.* London: DoH.

Domhoff, G. W. (2013). *Who rules America? The triumph of the corporate rich.* New York: McGraw Hill.

Drezner, D. W. (2017). *The ideas industry: how pessimists, partisans, and plutocrats are transforming the marketplace of ideas.* New York: Oxford University Press.

Du Gay, P. (2008). Keyser Süze elites: market populism and the politics of institutional change. *Sociological Review, 56*(1), 80–102.

Dunford, R., & Palmer, I. (1996). Metaphors of popular management discourse: the case of corporate re-structuring. In D. Grant & C. Oswick (Eds), *Metaphor and organisations* (pp. 95–109). London: Sage.

Education Council New Zealand. (2018). *Educational leadership capability framework*. Wellington: ECNZ.

Edwards, B. (1993). *The National Health Service: a manager's tale 1946–1992*. London: Nuffield Provincial Hospitals Trust.

Edwards, P., O'Mahoney, J., & Vincent, S. (Eds). (2014). *Studying organizations using critical realism: a practical guide*. Oxford: Oxford University Press.

Efficiency Unit. (1988). *Improving management in government: the next steps. Report to the Prime Minister*. London: Her Majesty's Stationery Office.

Emmerson, C., Farquharson, C., & Johnson, P. (2019). *The IFS Green Budget*. London: Institute for Fiscal Studies https://www.ifs.org.uk/uploads/The-2019-IFS-Green-Budget.pdf.

Emmerson, C., Johnson, P., & Joyce, R. (2015). *The IFS Green Budget*. London: Institute for Fiscal Studies https://ifs.org.uk/uploads/gb/gb2015/gb2015.pdf.

Eraut, M. (1994). *Developing professional knowledge and competence*. London: Falmer Press.

Erickson, M., Hanna, P., & Walker, C. (2020). The UK higher education senior management survey: a statactivist response to managerial governance. *Studies in Higher Education*. doi:10.1080/03075079.2020.1712693

Etzioni, A. (1969). *The semi-professions and their organization: teachers, nurses, social workers*. New York: Free Press.

Evetts, J. (2012). Professionalism: value and ideology. *Sociopedia.isa*, 1–10. DOI: 10.1177/205684601231.

Exworthy, M. (1994). The contest for control in community health services: general managers and professionals dispute decentralisation. *Policy and Politics*, *22*(1), 17–29.

Fairclough, N. (2003). *Analysing discourse: textual analysis for social research*. London: Routledge.

Fairclough, N. (2006). *Language and globalization*. Abingdon: Routledge.

Fairclough, N. (2015). *Language and power* (3rd ed.). Abingdon: Routledge.

Farquharson, C., & Sibieta, L. (2019). *2019 annual report on education spending in England: schools*. London: Institute for Fiscal Studies https://www.ifs.org.uk/uploads/R162-Annual-report-on-education-spending-in-england-schools.pdf.

Farrell, C., & Morris, J. (2003). The 'neo-bureaucratic' state: professionals, managers and professional managers in schools, general practices and social work. *Organization*, *10*(1), 129–156.

Farrell, C., & Morris, J. (2004). Resigned compliance: teacher attitudes towards performance-related pay in schools. *Educational Management Administration and Leadership*, *32*(1), 81–104.

Ferguson, D., & Francis-Devine, B. (2021). *Public sector pay*. (CBP8037). London: House of Commons Library https://researchbriefings.files.parliament.uk/documents/CBP-8037/CBP-8037.pdf.

Ferlie, E., Ashburner, L., Fitzgerald, L., & Pettigrew, A. (1996). *The new public management in action*. Oxford: Oxford University Press.

Ferlie, E., Fitzgerald, L., Wood, M., & Hawkins, C. (2005). The (non) spread of innovations: the mediating role of professionals. *Academy of Management Journal*, *48*(1), 117–134.

Fielden, J. (2009). *Mapping leadership development in higher education*. London: Leadership Foundation for Higher Education.

Firetail Ltd. (2016). *Class of 2030: which universities will rise—and how will they do it?* London: Firetail Ltd. https://www.firetail.co.uk/class-of-2030

Fitzgerald, L., Ferlie, E., McGivern, G., & Buchanan, D. A. (2013). Distributed leadership patterns and service improvement: evidence and argument from English healthcare. *Leadership Quarterly*, *24*(1), 227–239.

Fleetwood, S. (2004). An ontology for organisation and management studies. In S. Fleetwood & S. Ackroyd (Eds), *Critical realist applications in organisation and management studies* (pp. 25–50). London: Routledge.

Fleetwood, S. (2014). Bhaskar and critical realism. In P. Adler, P. Du Gay, G. Morgan, & M. Reed (Eds), *Oxford handbook of sociology, social theory and organisation studies* (pp. 182–219). Oxford: Oxford University Press.

Fletcher, G. (1989). *The Keynesian revolution and its critics: issues of theory and policy for the monetary production economy*. Basingstoke: Palgrave Macmillan.

Flyvbjerg, B. (2001). *Making social science matter: why social enquiry fails and how it can succeed again*. Cambridge: Cambridge University Press.

Foster, C., & Plowden, F. (1996). *The state under stress*. Buckingham: Open University Press.

Freeguard, G., Shepheard, M., Guerin, B., Pope, T., & Zodgekar, K. (2020). *Whitehall monitor 2020*. London: Institute for Government https://www.instituteforgovernment.org.uk/sites/default/files/publications/whitehall-monitor-2020_1.pdf.

Friedman, M. (1962). *Capitalism and freedom*. Chicago: University of Chicago Press.

General Medical Council Intelligence Unit. (2011). *Specialties, sub-specialties and progression through training: the international perspective*. London: General Medical Council.

Gibb, C. A. (1954). Leadership. In G. Lindzey (Ed.), *Handbook of social psychology* (Vol. 2, pp. 877–917). Boston, MA: Addison-Wesley.

Giddens, A. (1993). *New rules of sociological method* (2nd ed.). Cambridge: Polity Press.

Giddens, A. (1998). *The third way: the renewal of social democracy*. Cambridge: Polity Press.

Gill, R. (2014). Academics, cultural workers and critical labour studies. *Journal of Cultural Economy*, 7(1), 12–30.

Gillard, D. (2018). *Education in England: a history*. http://www.educationengland.org.uk/history/index.html

Glatter, R. (1972). *Management development for the education profession*. London: Harrop.

Gore, A. (1993). *From red tape to results: creating a government that works better and costs less. Report of the National Performance Review*. Washington D.C.: U.S. Government Printing Office.

Gorski, P. (2013). Beyond the fact/value distinction: ethical naturalism and the social sciences. *Society*, 50(6), 543–553.

Gosling, J., Bolden, R., & Petrov, G. (2009). Distributed leadership in higher education: what does it accomplish? *Leadership*, 5(3), 299–310.

Gouldner, A. (1971). *The coming crisis of western sociology*. London: Heinemann.

Greany, T. (2018). Balancing the needs of policy and practice, while remaining authentic: an analysis of leadership and governance in three national school leadership colleges. *Welsh Journal of Education*, 20(2). doi:https://doi.org/10.16922/wje.20.2.5

Greany, T., & Higham, R. (2018). *Hierarchy, markets and networks: analysing the 'self-improving school-led system' agenda in England and the implications for schools*. London: UCL Institute of Education Press.

Grint, K. (2011). A history of leadership. In A. Bryman, D. Collinson, K. Grint, B. Jackson, & M. Uhl-Bien (Eds), *Sage handbook of leadership* (pp. 3–14). London: Sage.

Gronn, P. (2000). Distributed properties: a new architecture for leadership. *Educational Management Administration and Leadership*, 28(3), 317–338.

Gronn, P. (2002). Distributed leadership as a unit of analysis. *Leadership Quarterly*, 13(4), 423–451.

Haddon, C. (2012). *The Efficiency Unit in the early 1980s and the 1987 Next Steps Report*. London: Institute for Government.

Hall, P., & Soskice, D. (2001). An introduction to varieties of capitalism. In P. Hall & D. Soskice (Eds), *Varieties of capitalism: the institutional foundations of comparative advantage* (pp. 1–68). Oxford: Oxford University Press.

Hall, S., Critcher, C., Jefferson, T., Clarke, J., & Roberts, B. (1978). *Policing the crisis: mugging, the state, and law and order*. London: Macmillan.

Hall, S., & O'Shea, A. (2013). Common-sense neoliberalism. *Soundings*, 55, 9–25.

Halligan, J. (2010). The fate of administrative tradition in Anglophone countries during the reform era. In M. Painter & B. G. Peters (Eds), *Handbook of public administration* (pp. 129–142). Basingstoke: Palgrave Macmillan.

Hansard. (2010). *Education funding. 5 July 2010: Column 50*. London: House of Commons https://publications.parliament.uk/pa/cm201011/cmhansrd/cm100705/debtext/100705-0002.htm#10070511000002.

Hansard. (2020). *Welcome to Hansard: the official report of all Parliamentary debates*. https://hansard.parliament.uk/

Harker, R. (2019). *NHS funding and expenditure*. (CBP0724). London: House of Commons Library https://researchbriefings.files.parliament.uk/documents/SN00724/SN00724.pdf.

Harris, R. E. (1949). New police college opened in Britain. *Journal of Criminal Law and Criminology*, 40(2), 217–222.

Harvey, D. (2007). *A brief history of neoliberalism*. Oxford: Oxford University Press.

Hassard, J., Hyde, P., Cox, W., Granter, E., & McCann, L. (2017). Exploring health work: a critical-action perspective. *Journal of Health Organization and Management, 31*(5), 567–580.

Hatch, M. J., Kostera, M., & Kozminski, A. K. (2006). The three faces of leadership: manager, artist, priest. *Organizational Dynamics, 35*(1), 49–68.

Hayek, F. A. (1944). *The road to serfdom*. London: Routledge.

Healthcare Commission. (2009). *Investigation into Mid Staffordshire NHS Foundation Trust*. London: Healthcare Commission.

HEFCE. (2002). *HEFCE Good Management Practice programme: progress report on projects*. Bristol: HEFCE.

HEFCE. (2004). *HEFCE Strategic plan 2003–08*. Bristol: HEFCE.

Higley, J., & Burton, M. (2006). *Elite foundations of liberal democracy*. Lanham, MD: Rowman and Littlefield.

HMIC. (2003). *Centrex: Central Police Training and Development Authority 2003 inspection*. London: The Home Office.

Hodgetts, S. (2007). Raising the bar—management competence. *National Association for Primary Care Review: Practice Management Supplement, 7*.

Hood, C. (1991). A public management for all seasons? *Public Administration, 69*(Spring), 3–19.

Horsley, S., Roberts, E., Barwick, D., Barrow, S., & Allen, D. (1996). Recent trends, future needs: management training for consultants. *Journal of Management in Medicine, 10*(2), 47–53.

House, R. J., Hanges, P. J., Javidan, M., Dorfman, P. W., & Gupta, V. (Eds). (2004). *Culture, leadership, and organizations: the GLOBE study of 62 societies*. Thousand Oaks, CA: Sage.

Hoyle, E. (2001). Teaching as a profession. In N. J. Smelser & P. B. Baltes (Eds), *International encyclopedia of the social and behavioral sciences* (pp. 15472–15476). Amsterdam: Elsevier.

Hoyle, E., & Wallace, M. (2005). *Educational leadership: ambiguity, professionals and managerialism*. London: Sage.

Hoyle, E., & Wallace, M. (2007). Beyond metaphors of management: the case for metaphoric re-description in education. *British Journal of Educational Studies, 55*(4), 426–442.

Hoyle, E., & Wallace, M. (2014). Organisational studies in an era of educational reform. *Journal of Educational Admininistration and History, 46*(3), 244–760.

Huberman, M., & Miles, M. (2002). *The qualitative researcher's companion*. Thousand Oaks, CA: Sage.

Hughes, M. G. (1976). The professional-as-administrator: the case of the secondary school head. In R. S. Peters (Ed.), *The role of the head* (pp. 50–62). London: Routledge & Kegan Paul.

Hunt, A. (1997). 'Moral panic' and moral language in the media. *British Journal of Sociology, 48*(4), 629–648.

Hyde, P., Granter, E., Hassard, J., & McCann, L. (2016). *Deconstructing the welfare state: managing healthcare in the age of reform*. Abingdon: Routledge.

Jack, A., & Hale, T. (2019). London higher education provider goes into administration. https://www.ft.com/content/150b7c7a-b476-11e9-8cb2-799a3a8cf37b

Jessop, B. (1994). The transition of post-Fordism and the Schumpterian workfare state. In R. Burrows & B. Loader (Eds), *Towards a post-Fordist welfare state?* (pp. 13–37). London: Routledge.

Jessop, B. (2016). The heartlands of neoliberalism and the rise of the austerity state. In S. Springer, K. Birch, & J. MacLeavy (Eds), *The handbook of neoliberalism* (pp. 410–421). London: Routledge.

Jessop, B. (2019). Authoritarian neoliberalism: periodization and critique. *South Atlantic Quarterly, 118*(2), 243–361.

John, P. (2011). *Making policy work*. Abingdon, Oxon: Routledge.

Jones, D., Visser, M., Stokes, P., Ortenblad, A., Deem, R., Rodgers, P., & Y Tarba, S. (2020). The performative university: 'targets', 'terror' and 'taking back freedom' in academia. *Management Learning, 51*(4), 363–377.

Joseph, K. (1976). *The Stockton Lecture: Monetarism is not enough*. London: Centre for Policy Studies. https://www.margaretthatcher.org/document/110796

Joyce, B., & Showers, B. (1988). *Student achievement through staff development*. New York: Longman.

Judge, K., Solomon, M., Miller, D., & Philo, G. (1992). Public opinion, the NHS, and the media: changing patterns and perspectives. *British Medical Journal, 304*(4 Apr), 892–895.

Kamensky, J. (1999). *National Partnership for Reinventing Government (formerly the National Performance Review): a brief history.* https://govinfo.library.unt.edu/npr/whoweare/history2.html

Kickert, W. (1995). Steering at a distance: a new paradigm of public governance in Dutch higher education. *Governance, 8*(1), 135–157.

Kickert, W. (2012). How the UK government responded to the fiscal crisis: an outsider's view. *Public Money and Management, 32*(3), 169–176.

King's Fund. (1975). *Invitation to initiative: report on the education and training of senior managers in the National Health Service.* London: King's Fund.

King's Fund. (2011). *The future of leadership and management in the NHS: no more heroes.* London: King's Fund.

King's Fund. (2016). *Deficits in the NHS 2016.* London: King's Fund.

Kirkpatrick, D. (1998). *Evaluating training programs: the four levels* (2nd ed.). San Francisco: Berrett-Koehler.

Kirkpatrick, D., & Kirkpatrick, J. (2005). *Transferring learning to behaviour: using the four levels to improve performance.* San Francisco: Berrett-Koehler.

Klijn, E. H., & Koppenjan, J. (2016). *Governance networks in the public sector.* Abingdon, Oxon: Routledge.

Klikauer, T. (2015). What is managerialism? *Critical Sociology, 41*(7–8), 1103–1119.

Kooiman, J. (2003). *Governing as governance.* London: Sage.

Kotter, J. P. (1988). *The leadership factor.* New York: Free Press.

KPMG. (2016). *What works: the trillion dollar quest.* Amstelveen, Netherlands: KPMG.

Kunda, G. (1992). *Engineering culture: control and commitment in a high-tech corporation.* Philadelphia, PA: Temple University Press.

L H Martin Institute. (2021). *Emerging leaders and managers program (eLAMP).* https://melbourne-cshe.unimelb.edu.au/lh-martin-institute/study/all-courses/leadership-programs/elamp#program-structure

Labour Party. (1992). *It's time to get Britain working again (general election manifesto).* London: Labour Party.

Labour Party. (1994). *Opening doors to a learning society: a policy statement on education.* London: Labour Party.

Labour Party. (1996). Renewing the National Health Service: Labour's agenda for a healthier Britain. *International Journal of Health Services, 26*(2), 269–308.

Labour Party. (1997). *New Labour: because Britain deserves better (general election manifesto).* http://www.labour-party.org.uk/manifestos/1997/1997-labour-manifesto.shtml

Labour Party. (2005). *Britain forward, not back (general election manifesto).* London: Labour Party.

Lakoff, G., & Johnson, M. (2003). *Metaphors we live by.* Chicago: University of Chicago Press.

Larson, M. S. (1977). *The rise of professionalism.* Berkeley, CA: University of California Press.

Learmonth, M. (2005). Doing things with words: the case of 'management' and 'administration'. *Public Administration, 83*(3), 617–637.

Leithwood, K., Chapman, J., Corson, D., Hallinger, P., & Hart, A. (Eds). (1996). *The international handbook of educational leadership and administration.* Dordrecht: Kluwer.

Leithwood, K., Mascall, B., Strauss, T., Sacks, R., Memon, N., & Yashkina, A. (2007). Distributing leadership to make schools smarter: taking the ego out of the system. *Leadership and Policy in Schools, 6*(1), 37–67.

Leithwood, K., Tomlinson, D., & Genge, M. (1996). Transformational school leadership. In K. Leithwood, J. Chapman, D. Corson, P. Hallinger, & A. Hart (Eds), *International handbook of educational leadership and administration* (pp. 785–840). Dordrecht: Kluwer.

LFHE. (2004a). *Annual report 2003–04.* London: LFHE.

LFHE. (2004b). *Introducing the Leadership Foundation for Higher Education: engaging with leaders in the higher education sector.* London: LFHE.

LFHE. (2005). *Prospectus 2005: engaging with leaders in higher education.* London: LFHE.

LFHE. (2010). *Annual review 2009–2010.* London: LFHE.

LFHE. (undated). *Top management programme: strategic leadership for effective change.* London: LFHE.

Lippmann, W. (1922). *Public opinion.* New York: Harcourt, Brace and Company.

Loan-Clarke, J. (1996). Health-care professionals and management development. *Journal of Management in Medicine, 10*(6), 24–35.

Locke, J. (1690/1997). *An essay concerning human understanding*. London: Penguin Books.

Lombardo, M. M., & Eichinger, R. W. (1996). *The career architect development planner*. Minneapolis: Lominger.

Lowe, R. (2007). *The death of progressive education: how teachers lost control of the classroom*. Abingdon: Routledge.

Lowe, R. (2011). *The official history of the British Civil Service: reforming the civil service, Volume 1: The Fulton years, 1966–81*. Abingdon: Routledge.

Lukes, S. (2005). *Power: a radical view* (2nd ed.). London: Palgrave Macmillan.

Lynch, K. (2014). New managerialism: the impact on education. *Concept, 5*(3), 1–11.

Malik, S. (2014). *Al-Madinah free school ordered to shut down secondary wing*. https://www.theguardian.com/education/2014/feb/07/al-madinah-free-school-secondary

Mann, R. D. (1959). A review of the relationship between personality and performance in small groups. *Psychological Bulletin, 56*(4), 241–270.

Marx, K. (1852). *The Eighteenth Brumaire of Louis Bonaparte*. https://www.marxists.org/archive/marx/works/1852/18th-brumaire/ch01.htm

McCall, M. W. (2010). Peeling the onion: getting inside experience-based leadership development. *Industrial and Organizational Psychology, 3*(1), 61–68.

McCauley, C. D., Moxley, R. S., & Van Velsor, E. (Eds). (1998). *The Center for Creative Leadership handbook of leadership development*. San Francisco: Jossey-Bass.

McCracken, M., McCrory, Farley, H., & McHugh, M. (2021). *Leadership journeys: tracking the impact and challenge of the Top Management Programme*. London: AdvanceHE.

McDonnell, L. M., & Elmore, R. F. (1987). Getting the job done: alternative policy instruments. *Educational Evaluation and Policy Analysis, 9*(2), 133–152.

McGuigan, J. (2014). The neoliberal self. *Culture Unbound, 6*, 223–240.

McMahon, A., & Bolam, R. (1990). *Management development and educational reform: a handbook for LEAs*. London: Paul Chapman.

Meadows, S., Levenson, R., & Baeza, J. (2000). *The last straw: explaining the NHS nursing shortage*. London: King's Fund.

Middlehurst, R. (1989). *Leadership development in universities, 1986–1988. Final report to the Department of Education and Science*. Guildford: University of Surrey.

Middlehurst, R. (1993). *Leading academics*. Buckingham: SRHE/Open University Press.

Mills, C. W. (1956). *The power elite*. New York: Oxford University Press.

Mirowski, P., & Plehwe, D. (Eds). (2009). *The road from Mont Pelerin: the making of the neoliberal thought collective*. Cambridge, MA: Harvard University Press.

Moran, M. (2007). *The British regulatory state: high modernism and hyper-innovation*. Oxford: Oxford University Press.

Morgan, C., Hall, V., & Mackay, H. (1983). *The selection of secondary school headteachers*. Milton Keynes: Open University Press.

Morris, J., Farrell, C., & Reed, M. (2017). The indeterminacy of 'temporariness': control and power in neo-bureaucratic organizations and work in UK television. *Human Relations, 69*(12), 2274–2297.

Muijs, D., Ainscow, M., Chapman, C., & West, M. (2011). *Collaboration and networking in education*. London: Springer.

Mumford, A. (1989). *Management development: strategies for action*. New York: Hyperion Books.

Mutch, A. (2018). Practice, substance, and history: reframing institutional logics. *Academy of Management Review, 43*(2), 242–258.

NAHT. (2007). *Statement of policy 2007–2008*. Haywards Heath: NAHT.

National Center for Educational Statistics. (2020). *Digest of Educational Statistics: Table 203.20. Enrollment in public elementary and secondary schools, by region, state, and jurisdiction: selected years, fall 1990 through fall 2029*. Washington, DC https://nces.ed.gov/programs/digest/d20/tables/dt20_203.20.asp.

National Committee of Inquiry into Higher Education. (1997). *Higher education in the learning society (the Dearing Report)* London: HMSO.

National Policy Board for Educational Administration. (2015). *National standards for educational leaders*. Reston, VA: NPBEA.

NCHL. (2016). National Center for Healthcare Leadership names new board members (4th May). https://www.prweb.com/pdfdownload/13386619.pdf

NCHL. (2018). *Health leadership competency model 3.0*. Chicago: NCHL.

NCLSCS. (2010). *Annual report and accounts 2009–10*. London: The Stationery Office.

NCSL. (2001). *Leadership development framework*. Nottingham: NCSL.

NCSL. (2003). *NCSL corporate plan*. Nottingham: NCSL.

NCSL. (2005a). *70,000 heads are better than one*. Nottingham: NCSL.

NCSL. (2005b). *Prospectus 2005*. Nottingham: NCSL.

NCSL. (2006a). *Corporate plan 2006–09*. Nottingham: NCSL.

NCSL. (2006b). *National leaders of education (NLE)*. Nottingham: NCSL.

NCSL. (2009). *Annual report and accounts 2008–09*. London: The Stationery Office.

New Zealand Ministry of Education. (2021). *Educational leaders: leadership development*. https://www.educationalleaders.govt.nz/Leadership-development

New Zealand Ministry of Health. (2021). *The public health leadership programme*. Wellington: NZMoH.

Newman, J. (2000). Beyond the NPM? Modernizing public services. In J. Clarke, S. Gewirtz, & E. McLaughlin (Eds), *New managerialism, new welfare?* (pp. 45–61). London: Sage.

Newman, J. (2001). *Modernising governance: New Labour, policy and society*. London: Sage.

Newman, K., & Cowling, A. (1993). Management education for clinical directors: an evaluation. *Journal of Management in Medicine, 7*(5), 27–35.

NHS Confederation. (2007). *Management in the NHS: the facts*. London: NHS Confederation.

NHS Elect. (2021). *Marketing and design support*. https://www.nhselect.nhs.uk/Bespoke-Services/Marketing-support

NHS Information Centre. (2008). *Staff in the NHS 1997–2007 (England)*. Leeds: NHS Information Centre.

NHS Leadership Academy. (2013). *The healthcare leadership model*. Leeds: NHS Leadership Academy.

NHS Leadership Academy. (2014). *NHS Leadership Academy: an overview*. https://www.leadershipacademy.nhs.uk/wp-content/uploads/2014/11/NHS-Leadership-Academy-full-pack.pdf

NHS National Improvement and Development Board. (2016). *Developing people—improving care: a national framework for action on improvement and leadership development in NHS-funded services*. London: DoH.

NHSIII. (2005). *Introducing the NHS Institute for Innovation and Improvement*. Coventry: NHSIII.

NHSIII. (2006a). *Strategic plan overview 2006/07*. Coventry: NHSIII.

NHSIII. (2006b). *NHS Institute for Innovation and Improvement 2006/07 plans*. Coventry: NHSIII.

NHSIII. (2006c). *The blue book: October 2006—September 2007, portfolio of development opportunities for senior leaders in the NHS*. Coventry: NHSIII.

NHSIII. (2009). *Annual report and accounts of the NHS Institute for Innovation and Improvement 2008–09*. London: The Stationery Office.

NHSIII. (2010). *Annual report and accounts of the NHS Institute for Innovation and Improvement 2009–10*. London: The Stationery Office.

NHSLC. (2002). *NHS leadership qualities framework*. London: NHSLC.

NHSLC. (2003). *An introduction to the NHS Leadership Centre*. London: NHSLC.

NHSTA. (1988). *Doctors and management development: policy proposals*. Bristol: NHSTA.

NLC. (2020). *Public service leaders programme brochure 2021/22*. London: Cabinet Office https://www.nationalleadership.gov.uk/wp-content/uploads/2020/12/NLC-Programme-Year-3-Brochure.pdf.

North, D. (1990). *Institutions, institutional change and economic performance*. Cambridge: Cambridge University Press.

Northouse, P. G. (2019). *Leadership: theory and practice* (8th ed.). Thousand Oaks, CA: Sage.

Nuffield Trust. (2019). *NHS reform timeline*. https://www.nuffieldtrust.org.uk/health-and-social-care-explained/nhs-reform-timeline/

NYC Leadership Academy. (2015). *Accomplishments report 2014–15*. New York: NYC Leadership Academy.

Nye, J. (2004). *Soft power: the means to success in world politics*. New York: Public Affairs.

NZWiL. (2015). *New Zealand women in leadership programme: diversity in leadership, promoting better sector performance*. Wellington: Universities New Zealand.

O'Mahoney, J., & Vincent, S. (2014). Critical realism as an empirical project. In P. Edwards, J. O'Mahoney, & S. Vincent (Eds), *Studying organizations using critical realism: a practical guide* (pp. 1–20). Oxford: Oxford University Press.

O'Reilly, D., & Reed, M. (2011). The grit in the oyster: professionalism, managerialism and leaderism as discourses of UK public services modernization. *Organization Studies, 32*(8), 1079–1101.

Oakleigh Consulting Ltd. (2006). *Final report: interim evaluation of the Leadership Foundation for Higher Education.* Manchester: Oakleigh Consulting Ltd.

OECD. (2001). *Public sector leadership for the twenty-first century.* Paris: OECD.

OECD. (2010). *Making reform happen: lessons from OECD countries.* Paris: OECD.

OECD. (2019a). *OECD legal instruments.* https://legalinstruments.oecd.org/en/general-information

OECD. (2019b). *Recommendation of the Council on Public Service Leadership and Capability.* Paris: OECD.

Office for National Statistics. (2018). *The 2008 recession 10 years on.* https://www.ons.gov.uk/economy/grossdomesticproductgdp/articles/the2008recession10yearson/2018-04-30

Ofsted. (1997). *The annual report of Her Majesty's Chief Inspector of Schools: standards and quality in education 1995/96.* London: The Stationery Office.

Ofsted. (2003). *Leadership and management: what inspection tells us.* London: Ofsted.

Ofsted. (2013). *School report: Al-Madinah School.* Manchester: Ofsted.

Ontario College of Teachers. (2017). *Principal's qualification program guideline July 2017.* Toronto: OCT.

Ontario Institute for Educational Leadership. (2013). *The Ontario Leadership Framework: a school and system leader's guide for putting Ontario's Leadership Framework into action.* Toronto: OIEL.

Ontario Ministry of Education. (2021). *Leadership Development: Ontario Leadership Strategy.* http://www.edu.gov.on.ca/eng/policyfunding/leadership/actionplan.html

OPM. (2006). *The market for leadership development in the public sector.* London: Office for Public Management.

OPSR. (2002). *Reforming our public services.* London: OPSR.

OPSR. (2003). *Inspecting for improvement: developing a customer focused approach.* London: OPSR.

OPSR. (2005). *Putting people at the heart of public services.* London: Cabinet Office.

Osborne, D., & Gaebler, T. (1992). *Reinventing government: how the entrepreneurial spirit is transforming the public sector.* Reading, MA: Addison Wesley.

Osborne, S. (Ed.) (2010). *The new public governance?* Abingdon: Routledge.

Oxford English Dictionary. (2021). http://www.oed.com/

Packard, D. (1996). *The HP way: how Bill Hewlitt and I built our company.* New York: Harper Collins.

Page, C. (2008). The origins of policy. In M. Moran, M. Rein, & R. E. Goodin (Eds), *The Oxford handbook of public policy* (pp. 207–227). Oxford: Oxford University Press.

Pahl, R., & Winkler, J. T. (1974). The economic elite: theory and practice. In P. Stanworth & A. Giddens (Eds), *Elites and power in British society* (pp. 102–122). Cambridge: Cambridge University Press.

Peck, J. (2001). *Workfare states.* New York: Guildford Press.

Peck, J. (2010). *Constructions of neoliberal reason.* Oxford: Oxford University Press.

Peck, J., & Theodore, N. (2010). Exporting workfare/importing welfare-to-work: exploring the politics of Third Way policy transfer. *Political Geography, 20*(4), 427–460.

Peck, J., & Theodore, N. (2019). Still neoliberalism? *The South Atlantic Quarterly, 118*(245–265).

Performance and Innovation Unit. (2001). *Strengthening leadership in the public sector: a research study by the PIU.* London: Stationery Office.

Perkin, H. (1969). *Key profession: the history of the Association of University Teachers.* London: Routledge.

Peters, T., & Waterman, R. (1982). *In search of excellence: lessons from America's best run companies.* New York: Harper Collins.

Pierson, P. (1998). Irresistable forces, immovable objects: post-industrial welfare states confront permanent austerity. *Journal of European Public Policy, 5*(4), 539–560.

Plehwe, D. (2009). Introduction. In P. Mirowski & D. Plehwe (Eds), *The road from Mont Pelerin: the making of the neoliberal thought collective* (pp. 1–42). Cambridge, MA: Harvard University Press.

Pollitt, C. (1993). *Managerialism and the social services* (2nd ed.). Oxford: Blackwell.

Pollitt, C. (2007). New Labour's re-disorganization: hyper-modernism and the costs of reform—a cautionary tale. *Public Management Review, 9*(4), 529–543.

Pollitt, C., & Bouckaert, G. (2017). *Public management reform* (4th ed.). Oxford: Oxford University Press.

Pollitt, C., Harrison, S., Hunter, D. J., & Marnoch, G. (1991). General management in the NHS: the initial impact 1983–1988. *Public Administration, 69*(1), 61–83.

Pont, B., Nusche, D., & Moorman, H. (2008). *Improving school leadership volume 1: policy and practice.* Paris: OECD.

Porpora, D. (2013). Morphogenesis and social change. In M. S. Archer (Ed.), *Social morphogenesis* (pp. 25–37). Dordrecht: Springer.

Posner, R. (2003). *Public intellectuals: a study of decline.* Cambridge, MA: Harvard University Press.

PSLC. (2006). *Customer focussed leadership learning resources.* London: Cabinet Office.

Public Services Leadership Taskforce. (2018). *Better public services.* London: Cabinet Office https://assets. publishing.service.gov.uk/government/uploads/system/uploads/attachment_data/file/799567/6.4846_CO_CPSL-Report_A4-P_WEB_NoLogo__002.pdf.

Rafferty, A. M. (1993). *Leading questions: a discussion paper on the issues of nurse leadership.* London: King's Fund.

Rainey, H. (2014). *Understanding and managing public organizations* (5th ed.). San Francisco, CA: Jossey-Bass.

Redden, G., Phelan, S., & Baker, C. (2020). Different routes up the same mountain? Neoliberalism in Australia and New Zealand. In S. Dawes & M. Lenormand (Eds), *Neoliberalism in context* (pp. 61–82). London: Palgrave Macmillan.

Reed, M. (2002). New managerialism, professional power and organizational governance in UK universities: a review and assessment. In A. Amaral, G. Jones, & B. Karseth (Eds), *Governing higher education: national perspectives on institutional governance* (pp. 163–186). Dordrecht: Kluwer.

Reed, M. (2011). The post-bureaucratic organization and the control revolution. In S. Clegg, M. Harris, & H. Hopfl (Eds), *Managing modernity: beyond bureaucracy?* (pp. 230–256). Oxford: Oxford University Press.

Reed, M. (2012a). Masters of the universe: power and elites in organization studies. *Organization Studies, 33*(2), 203–221.

Reed, M. (2012b). Researching organizational elites: a critical realist perspective. In D. Courpasson, D. Golsorkhi, & G. Sallz (Eds), *Research in the Sociology of Organizations 34,* 21–53. New York: Emerald.

Reed, M. (2018). Elites, professions, and the neoliberal state: critical points of intersection and contention. *Journal of Professions and Organization, 5*(3), 297–312.

Reed, M., & Wallace, M. (2015). Elite discourse and institutional innovation: making the hybrid happen in English public services. *Research in the sociology of Organizations, 43,* 269–302.

Rhodes, G. (1981). *Inspectorates in British government: law enforcement and standards of efficiency.* London: Allen and Unwin.

Riley, K., & Stoll, L. (2007). *Evaluation of public sector leadership development: an exploratory review of perspectives and outcomes.* London: London Centre for Leadership in Learning.

Rivett, G. (2019). *National Health Service history.* http://www.nhshistory.net/index.htm

Sabatier, P., & Jenkins-Smith (Eds). (1993). *Policy change and learning: an advocacy coalition approach.* Boulder, CO: Westview Press.

Savage, M., & Williams, K. (2008). Elites: remembered in capitalism and forgotten by social science. *Sociological Review, 56*(1), 1–24.

Sayer, A. (2004). Foreword: why critical realism? In S. Fleetwood & S. Ackroyd (Eds), *Critical realist applications in organisation and management studies* (pp. 6–19). London: Routledge.

Sayer, A. (2010). Reductionism in social science. In R. Lee (Ed.), *Questioning nineteenth-century assumptions about knowledge, II: reductionism* (pp. 5–39). Albany: State University of New York Press.

Sayer, A. (2011). *Why things matter to people: social science, values and ethical life.* Cambridge: Cambridge University Press.

Schein, E. H. (2010). *Organizational culture and leadership.* San Francisco: Jossey-Bass.

Schumpeter, J. A. (1942). *Capitalism, socialism, and democracy* (3rd ed.). New York: Harper and Brothers.

Scott, J. (1996). *Stratification and power: structures of class, status and command.* Cambridge: Cambridge University Press.

Scott, J. (2001). *Power.* Cambridge: Polity Press.

Scott, J. (2008). Modes of power and the re-conceptualization of elites. *Sociological Review, 56*(1), 25–43.

Select Committee on Education and Employment. (1998). *Ninth report: the role of headteachers.* http://www.publications.parliament.uk/pa/cm199798/cmselect/cmeduemp/725/72504.htm#note6

Selznick, P. (1949). *The TVA and the grass roots.* New York: Harper.

Shattock, M. (1970). A changing pattern of university administration. *Universities Quarterly, 24*(3), 310–320.

Shepherd, S. (2018). Managerialism: an ideal type. *Studies in Higher Education, 43*(9), 1668–1678.

Simons, H. (Ed.) (1980). *Towards a science of the singular*. Norwich: Centre for Applied Research in Education, University of East Anglia.

Simons, H. (2009). *Case study research in practice*. London: Sage.

Skowronek, S. (1997). *The politics presidents make: leadership from John Adams to Bill Clinton*. Cambridge, MA: Belknap Press.

Smircich, L. (1983). Concepts of culture in organizational analysis. *Administrative Science Quarterly, 28*(3), 339–358.

Smith, P. (1992). Consultants in management training: learning and doing. *Journal of Management in Medicine, 6*(2), 11–26.

Smyth, J. (1961). *Sandhurst: the history of the Royal Military College, Woolwich, the Royal Military College, Sandhurst, and the Royal Military Academy, Sandhurst*. London: Weidenfeld and Nicolson.

Southworth, G. (1998). *Leading improving primary schools: the work of headteachers and deputy heads*. London: Falmer.

Spillane, J. P., Halverson, R., & Diamond, J. B. (2001). Investigating school leadership practice: a distributed perspective. *Educational Researcher, 30*(3), 23–28.

Spours, K., Coffield, F., & Gregson, M. (2007). Mediation, translation and local ecologies: understanding the impact of policy levers on FE colleges. *Journal of Vocational Education and Training, 59*(2), 193–212.

Springer, S., Birch, K., & MacLeavy, J. (2016). An introduction to neoliberalism. In S. Springer, K. Birch, & J. MacLeavy (Eds), *The handbook of neoliberalism* (pp. 1–14). Abingdon: Routledge.

State of Victoria Department of Education and Training. (2007). *The developmental learning framework for school leaders*. Melbourne: VDET.

State of Victoria Department of Health and Human Services. (2019a). *CEO leadership capability framework*. Melbourne: VDHHS.

State of Victoria Department of Health and Human Services. (2019b). *Leadership and learning action plan*. Melbourne: VDHHS.

Steer, R., Spours, K., Hodgson, A., Finlay, I., Coffield, F., Edward, S., & Gregson, M. (2007). 'Modernisation' and the role of policy levers in the learning and skills sector. *Journal of Vocational Education and Training, 59*(2), 175–192.

Stewart, G. L., Courtright, S. H., & Manz, C. C. (2011). Self-leadership: a multi-level review. *Journal of Management, 37*(1), 185–222.

Stewart, R. (1989). *Leading in the NHS: a practical guide*. London: Macmillan.

Stogdill, R. M. (1948). Personal factors associated with leadership: a survey of the literature. *Journal of Psychology, 25*(1), 35–71.

Strategy Unit. (2006). *The UK's approach to public service reform—a discussion paper*. London: Cabinet Office.

Strategy Unit. (2007). *HM Government policy review—building on progress: public services*. London: Cabinet Office.

Sutton Trust & Social Mobility Commission. (2019). *Elitist Britain 2019: the educational backgrounds of Britain's leading people*. London: Sutton Trust.

Swartz, D. L. (2013). *Symbolic power, politics and intellectuals: the political sociology of Pierre Bourdieu*. Chicago, IL: Chicago University Press.

Swedberg, R. (2005). Can there be a sociological concept of interest? *Theory and Society, 34*(4), 359–390.

Swedberg, R. (2018). How to use Max Weber's ideal type in sociological analysis. *Journal of Classical Sociology, 18*(3), 181–196.

Taylor, C. (2004). *Modern social imaginaries*. Durham, NC: Duke University Press.

Taylor, F. W. (1911). *The principles of scientific management*. New York: Harper & Brothers.

Thomas, G., Martin, R., & Riggio, R. E. (2013). Leading groups: leadership as a group process. *Group Processes and Intergroup Relations, 16*(1), 3–16.

Thornton, P., Ocasio, W., & Lounsbury, M. (2012). *The institutional logics perspective: a new approach to culture, structure, and process*. Oxford: Oxford University Press.

Tourish, D., & Pennington, A. (2002). Transformational leadership, corporate cultism and the spirituality paradigm: an unholy trinity in the workplace? *Human Relations, 55*(2), 147–172.

Treasury. (1998a). *Modern services for Britain: investing in reform*. London: HM Treasury.

Treasury. (1998b). *Public services for the future: modernisation, reform, accountability*. London: HM Treasury.

Treasury. (2000). *Public services productivity: meeting the challenge. A joint report by the Public Services Productivity Panel.* London: HM Treasury.

TTA. (1998). *National standards for headteachers.* London: TTA.

US Department of Education. (2016). *Investing in innovation (i3).* Washington, DC https://www.ed.gov/open/plan/investing-innovation-i3.

UCoSDA. (1994). *Higher education management and leadership: towards a national framework for preparation and development.* Sheffield: UCoSDA.

Universities New Zealand. (2021). *New Zealand universities women in leadership programme (NZUWiL).* https://www.universitiesnz.ac.nz/about-universities-new-zealand/expert-and-working-groups/new-zealand-universities-women-leadership

Useem, M. (1984). *The inner circle: large corporations and the rise of business political activity in the US and UK.* New York: Oxford University Press.

UUK. (2017). *Report of the review group on UK higher education sector agencies.* London: UUK.

UUK. (undated). *A guide to Universities UK.* London: UUK.

UUK/SCOP. (2003). *Business case for the Leadership Foundation for Higher Education.* London: UUK/SCOP.

Van Wart, M., Hondegham, A., & Schwella, E. (Eds). (2015). *Leadership and culture: Comparative models of top civil servant training.* Basingstoke: Palgrave Macmillan.

Vernon, J. (2018). The making of the neoliberal university in Britain. *Critical Historical Studies, 5*(2), 267–280.

Vizard, P., & Obolenskaya, P. (2013). *Labour's record on health (1997–2010).* London: London School of Economics https://sticerd.lse.ac.uk/dps/case/spcc/wp02.pdf.

Wallace, M. (1991). *School-centred management training.* London: Paul Chapman.

Wallace, M. (1996). When is experiential learning not experiential learning? In G. Claxton, T. Atkinson, M. Osborn, & M. Wallace (Eds), *Liberating the learner: lessons for professional development in education* (pp. 16–31). London: Routledge.

Wallace, M. (1998). A counter-policy to subvert education reform? Collaboration among schools and colleges in a competitive climate. *British Educational Research Journal, 24*(2), 195–215.

Wallace, M. (2007). Coping with complex and programmatic public service change. In M. Wallace, M. Fertig, & E. Schneller (Eds), *Managing change in the public services* (pp. 13–35). Oxford: Blackwell.

Wallace, M., Fertig, M., & Schneller, E. (Eds). (2007). *Managing change in the public services.* Oxford: Blackwell.

Wallace, M., & Huckman, L. (1999). *Senior management teams in primary schools: the quest for synergy.* London: Routledge.

Wallace, M., O'Reilly, D., Morris, J., & Deem, R. (2011). Public service leaders as change agents—for whom? Mediatory responses to leadership development in England. *Public Management Review, 13*(1), 65–93.

Wallace, M., & Pocklington, K. (2002). *Managing complex educational change: large-scale reorganisation of schools.* London: RoutledgeFalmer.

Warde, E., & Bennett, T. (2008). A culture in common: the cultural consumption of the UK managerial elite. *Sociological Review, 56*(1), 240–259.

Weber, M. (1947). *The theory of social and economic organization.* London: Collier Macmillan.

Weber, M. (1978). *Economy and society, volume II.* Berkeley, CA: University of California Press.

Wedel, J. (2009). *Shadow elite: how the world's new power brokers undermine government, democracy, and the free market.* New York: Basic Books.

Weinrich, P. (2009). 'Enculturation' not 'acculturation': conceptualising and assessing identity processes in migrant communities. *International Journal of Intercultural Relations, 33*(2), 124–139.

Whitchurch, C. (2013). *Reconstructing identities in higher education: the rise of third space professionals.* London: Routledge.

Whitty, G. (2012). Policy tourism and policy borrowing in education: a transatlantic case. In G. Steiner-Khamsi & F. Waldow (Eds), *World yearbook of education 2012: policy borrowing and lending in education* (pp. 354–370). Abingdon: Routledge.

Willmott, H. (1995). Managing the academics: commodification and control in the development of university education in the UK. *Human Relations, 48*(9), 993–1027.

Wilson, W. (1887). The study of administration. *Political Science Quarterly, 2*(2), 197–222.

Wolf, A., & Jenkins, A. (2021). *Managers and academics in a centralising sector: the new staffing patterns of UK higher education*. London: Policy Institute, King's College London.

Xypolia, I. (2016). Divide et impera: vertical and horizontal dimensions of British imperialism. *Critique: Journal of Socialist Theory, 44*(3), 221–231.

Yin, R. K. (2003). *Case study research: design and methods* (3rd ed.). Thousand Oaks: Sage.

Yukl, G. (2013). *Leadership in organizations* (8th ed.). Harlow, Essex: Pearson.

Zaleznik, A. (1977). Managers and leaders: are they different? *Harvard Business Review* (May–June), 67–78.

Index

Figures and tables are indicated by an *f* and *t* respectively, following the page number.

Note that indexing is done to paragraph, figure, or table level. Therefore, terms indexed with a two-page reference span (e.g., 19–20) will appear on one of the pages only in some instances. Indexed citations of authors are restricted to locations where their work is quoted or specifically discussed.